Reader's Digest

OUR ISLAND HERITAGE

OUR ISLAND HERITAGE
was edited and designed by
The Reader's Digest Association Limited
London

First Edition

ISBN 0 276 48942 X
Printed in Great Britain

Reader's Digest

OUR ISLAND HERITAGE

VOLUME ONE

From Early Times to the Elizabethans

Published by The Reader's Digest Association Limited
London • New York • Montreal • Sydney • Cape Town

CONTRIBUTORS

The publishers wish to express their gratitude to the following for their major contributions to OUR ISLAND HERITAGE

CONSULTANT EDITOR
The Lord Briggs FBA, MA, BSc (Econ)

PROJECT EDITOR
Harriet Jillings BA, PGCE

EDITORIAL CONTRIBUTORS
David Blomfield MA
Shirley Wilson

TIME CHART IN VOLUME THREE
Peter S. Leuner BSc, MSc

PROJECT DESIGNER
Julie Busby

PICTURE RESEARCH by *IKON*
Wendy Brown
Diana Phillips
Christine Vincent

CARTOGRAPHER
Malcolm Porter

INDEXER
Michèle Clarke BA

COPY EDITORS
Carol Compton
Anne Jenkins

In addition, Reader's Digest is grateful to the authors and publishers of the many books that have been consulted in the preparation of this work.

A full list of acknowledgments appears at the back of Volume Three, as does information regarding ownership of copyright in all the material.

OUR ISLAND HERITAGE
comprises condensations of:

A HISTORY OF THE
ENGLISH-SPEAKING PEOPLES

by Winston S. Churchill

and

FAREWELL THE TRUMPETS

by James Morris

together with much extra
material prepared by The Reader's Digest
under the direction of

The Lord Briggs

All four volumes of *A History of the English-Speaking Peoples*
(The Birth of Britain, The New World, The Age of Revolution
and *The Great Democracies)* are published by Cassell Limited.
Farewell The Trumpets is published by Faber.

VOLUME ONE

Contents

INTRODUCTION

CHAPTERS

SOCIAL HISTORY SECTIONS

COLOUR SECTIONS

INTRODUCTION

The Mists of Time

by Asa Briggs

Our story centres in an island, not widely sundered from the Continent, and so tilted that its mountains lie all to the west and north, while south and east is a gently undulating landscape of wooded valleys, open downs, and slow rivers. It is very accessible to the invader, whether he comes in peace or war, as pirate or merchant, conqueror or missionary. Those who dwell there are not insensitive to any shift of power, any change of faith, or even fashion, on the mainland, but they give to every practice, every doctrine that comes to it from abroad, its own peculiar turn and imprint. . . . As we gaze back into the mists of time we can very faintly discern the men of the Old Stone Age, and the New Stone Age; the builders of the great megalithic monuments; the newcomers from the Rhineland, with their beakers and tools of bronze . . . .

Thus Winston Churchill introduced the first volume of his monumental work, *A History of the English-Speaking Peoples*, on which the main narrative of these three volumes is substantially based. Today, Churchill is rightly remembered and revered more for the fact that he made history than that he wrote it. Deeds counted for more than words. Yet he loved reading history and writing it. While he was young and while Queen Victoria was still on the throne he published among other books his still pre-eminently readable *The River War*, a lengthy study in which the Mahdi of the Sudan figures in retrospect as a kind of proto-Hitler. Churchill's style was already formed. It was richly distinctive, as distinctive as his voice, which millions were to get to know.

A History of the English-Speaking Peoples was conceived before the Second World War during which Churchill emerged as one of a handful of great historical figures. It was not completed, however, until Hitler had been disposed of. I was very fortunate myself as a young historian to be asked after the war to send Churchill comments on the last of his volumes. Some of them he actually took account of: I can trace them in the text. As for the rest, he doubtless had good reasons for ignoring them. I greatly treasure the signed copies he sent me, including his magnificent first volume, and I actually hesitated, although I was short of money at the time, whether or not to accept his cheque. I wish now that I had kept it.

Churchill's history, like all histories which dare to span the centuries, is *a* history of the English-speaking peoples and not *the* history. There can be no one single definitive account of what has happened in these islands since 55 BC. Moreover, Churchill was interested not only in these islands, but in Europe and in what he called the Commonwealth and Empire: the phrase rolled off his tongue. There are certainly many other versions of what happened there. Churchill himself was at pains to explain that he was not "gazing back into the mists of time" as a professional historian. He was gazing back, he claimed, because there were many things in the past which seemed significant to him in the light of his own experience. His, he insisted, was a personal view.

Nevertheless, it was because his experience was unique that what he has bequeathed to us is a very special personal view indeed. Because the present lived for him, he could make the past live too. Because his own contribution to history was so substantial, he could judge other people's contributions. He had knowledge as well as insight. He seldom hesitated in his judgments, and since he loved controversy he never hesitated to be controversial. But he would not always have claimed to be right, and that is why he turned to professional historians.

All historians write from a particular vantage point in time as well as in space. Churchill's *History* appeared in 1956, nearly twenty years after he had begun it. The perspectives of 1956 were very different from those of 1936, when Hitler was already disturbing the world but when few people, to Churchill's disgust, seemed willing to stop him in his tracks. The perspectives of the late 1980s are as different from those of 1956 as those of 1956 were from those of 1936. A whole generation has passed. The Second World War has retracted into history. More history has been made, much of it uninspiring, much of it disturbing, even alarming. Historical figures have come and gone, problems have multiplied.

Nevertheless, there have been continuities since 1956 as well as breaks in the sequence, and there is much in Churchill that is as relevant to our time as it was to his own. All that is relevant has been retained in this condensed edition of his work. What he said has sometimes to be supplemented and in places qualified, even contradicted, but this edition sticks to his words. There is no doubt that they were worth writing and that they were written in a way that has enriched the language that he treasured.

In these volumes the story has been brought nearer the present by adding a condensation of James Morris's *Farewell the Trumpets*. Morris,like Churchill, believes that history should be colourful, should have a broad sweep and should be written in order to be read and enjoyed by large numbers of people. Morris, now better known as Jan Morris, deals with events that Churchill did not foresee and that he would have regretted—no *Farewell the Trumpets* for Churchill! Morris's viewpoint is very different from Churchill's, but in my opinion it is complementary. The two together make a unique whole.

I have tried to complement Churchill in a different manner. First I have updated this country's domestic history, what Churchill would have called "home affairs". Second, I have strengthened throughout what I would call the social history dimension, not least in relation to the earlier periods of our history, including the earliest, where some of the most exciting new research has been concentrated since Churchill's time. My own book, *A Social History of England*, also quite deliberately called *a* history, explored history from below as well as history from above, and some of its themes, economic as well as social, figure in these pages. There are edited eyewitness accounts and illustrations throughout the main text, and colour sections showing examples of buildings, artefacts and paintings from our past. I believe that Churchill would have appreciated this approach. He knew the importance of firing the popular imagination. That is why his title included the word "peoples". That is why, when he took office as Prime Minister in 1940, offering his countrymen only "blood, toil, tears and sweat", he said simply, in conclusion, "Come then, let us go forward together with our united strength."

History for Churchill was more than an escape or a consolation. It was a key to understanding, and it was, above all, a source of strength. Humbly but confidently I agree with him.

WORCESTER COLLEGE, OXFORD

CHAPTER 1
BRITANNIA

A contemporary Roman coin shows the likeness of Julius Caesar, who invaded Britain in 55 BC. His invasion failed to make a lasting conquest, and Britain was not to become part of the Roman Empire for another hundred years.

In the summer of the Roman year 699, now described as the year 55 before the birth of Christ, the Proconsul of Gaul, Gaius Julius Caesar, turned his gaze upon Britain. In the midst of his wars in Germany and in Gaul he became conscious of this heavy island which stirred his ambitions and already obstructed his designs. He knew that it was inhabited by tribesmen of the same Celtic stock that confronted the Roman arms in Germany, Gaul, and Spain. Refugees from Gaul were welcomed and sheltered in Britannia. The islanders had helped the local tribes in campaigns along the coasts of Brittany in the previous year. To Caesar the island now presented itself as an integral part of his task of subjugating the northern barbarians to the rule and system of Rome. The land not covered by forest or marsh was verdant and fertile. The climate, though far from genial, was equable and healthy. The natives, though uncouth, had a certain value as slaves for rougher work on the land, in mines, and even about the house. There was talk of a pearl fishery, of tin and also of gold.

Other reasons added their weight. In Rome, at the centre and summit, only vague ideas prevailed about Britannia. Herodotus about 445 BC had heard of the tin of mysterious islands in the far west, which he called the Cassiterides, and in the middle of the fourth century BC Pytheas of Marseilles — surely one of the greatest explorers in history — made two voyages in which he actually circumnavigated the British Isles. But for the Romans these were the ultimate fringes of the world. The idea of Roman legions landing in the remote, unknown, fabulous island of the vast ocean of the north would create a novel thrill and topic in all ranks of Roman society.

Moreover, Britannia was the prime centre of the Druidical religion, and the unnatural principle of human sacrifice was carried by the British Druids to a ruthless pitch. The mysterious priesthoods of the forests bound themselves and their votaries together by the most deadly sacrament that men can take. Here, perhaps, upon these wooden altars of a sullen island, there lay one of the secrets, awful, inflaming, unifying, of the tribes of Gaul. Here then was the largest issue. Caesar's vision pierced the centuries, and where he conquered civilisation dwelt.

Thus, in this summer fifty-five years before the birth of Christ, he withdrew his army from Germany, and throughout July marched westward by long strides towards the Gallic shore somewhere about the modern Calais.

Caesar saw the Britons as a tougher and coarser branch of the Celtic tribes whom he was subduing in Gaul. With an army of ten legions, less than fifty

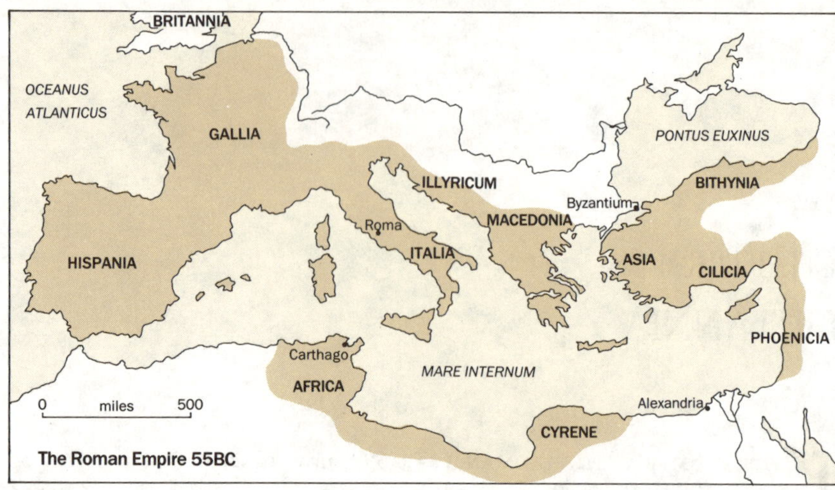

The Roman Empire in 55 BC. Britain was to be one of the last Roman conquests, and perhaps the most troublesome of them all to govern.

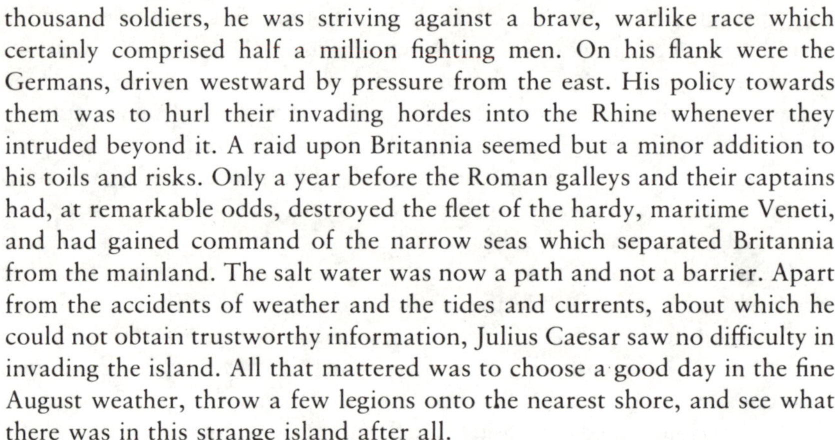

thousand soldiers, he was striving against a brave, warlike race which certainly comprised half a million fighting men. On his flank were the Germans, driven westward by pressure from the east. His policy towards them was to hurl their invading hordes into the Rhine whenever they intruded beyond it. A raid upon Britannia seemed but a minor addition to his toils and risks. Only a year before the Roman galleys and their captains had, at remarkable odds, destroyed the fleet of the hardy, maritime Veneti, and had gained command of the narrow seas which separated Britannia from the mainland. The salt water was now a path and not a barrier. Apart from the accidents of weather and the tides and currents, about which he could not obtain trustworthy information, Julius Caesar saw no difficulty in invading the island. All that mattered was to choose a good day in the fine August weather, throw a few legions onto the nearest shore, and see what there was in this strange island after all.

What was, in fact, this island which now for the first time in coherent history was to be linked with the great world? We have dug up in the present age from the gravel of Swanscombe a human skull which is certainly a quarter of a million years old. Biologists perceive important differences from the heads that hold our brains today, but there is no reason to suppose that this remote Paleolithic ancestor was not capable of all the crimes, follies, and infirmities definitely associated with mankind. Evidently for prolonged, almost motionless, periods, such men and women, naked or wrapped in the skins of animals, prowled about the primaeval forests and plashed through wide marshes, hunting each other and other wild beasts. Already man had found out that a flint was better than a fist, but so far he had only learnt to chip his flints into rough tools.

The stone circle of Castlerigg, near Keswick in Cumbria, is thought to be four thousand years old. The outer circle of thirty-eight stones has a diameter of one hundred feet, while ten further stones form a second circle inside.

At the close of the Ice Age changes in climate brought about the collapse of the hunting civilisations of this Old Stone Age Man, and after a very long period of time the tides of invasion brought Neolithic culture into the western forests. The newcomers had a primitive agriculture. They scratched the soil and sowed the seeds of edible grasses. Presently they constructed earthwork enclosures on the hilltops, such as Windmill Hill, near Avebury, into which they drove their cattle at nighttime. Moreover, Neolithic man had developed a means of polishing his flints into perfect shape for killing. This betokened a great advance, but others were in prospect.

In these early days, Britain was part of the Continent. A wide plain joined England and Holland, in which the Thames and the Rhine met together and poured their waters northward. In some slight movement of the earth's surface this plain sank a few hundred feet and admitted the ocean to the North Sea and the Baltic. Then another tremor, important for our story, sundered the cliffs of Dover from those of Cape Gris Nez, and the scour of the ocean tides made the Straits of Dover and the English Channel.

Bronze Age axeheads were made by the lost wax process, a technique of casting bronze in which a wax model is used to form a mould made of clay, and is then melted and drained off. They were a sign of wealth and would have been much prized by their owners.

While what is now our island was still joined to the Continent, another great improvement was made in human methods of destruction. Copper and tin were discovered and worried out of the earth; the one too soft and the other too brittle for the main purpose, but, blended by human genius, they opened the Age of Bronze. Other things being equal, the men with bronze could beat the men with flints.

The infiltration of bronze weapons and tools from the Continent was spread over many centuries. Professor R G Collingwood has drawn us a picture of what is called the Late Bronze Age. "Britain," he says, "as a whole was a backward country by comparison with the Continent; primitive in its civilisation, stagnant and passive in its life . . . . Its people lived either in isolated farms or in hut-villages, situated for the most part on the gravel of riverbanks, or the light upland soils such as the chalk downs or oolite plateaus, which by that time had been to a great extent cleared of their native scrub; each settlement was surrounded by small fields, tilled either with a foot-plough of the type still used not long ago by Hebridean crofters, or else at best with a light ox-drawn plough which scratched the soil without turning the sod; the dead were burnt and their ashes, preserved in urns, buried in regular cemeteries. Thus the land was inhabited by a stable and industrious peasant population, living by agriculture and the keeping of livestock, augmented no doubt by hunting and fishing. They made rude pottery without a wheel, and still used flint for such things as arrowheads; but they were visited by itinerant bronze-founders able to make swords, spears, socketed axes, and many other types of implement and utensil, such as sickles, carpenter's tools, metal parts of wheeled vehicles, buckets and cauldrons . . . . There was certainly a distinction between rich and poor, since many kinds of metal objects belonging to the period imply a considerable degree of wealth and luxury."

About 400 BC the march of invention brought a new factor upon the scene. Iron was dug and forged. Men armed with iron entered Britain from the Continent and killed the men of bronze. At this point we can plainly recognise across the vanished millennia a fellow being. A biped capable of slaying another with iron is evidently to modern eyes a man and a brother. It cannot be doubted that for smashing skulls iron is best.

The Iron Age brought with it a revival of the hilltop camps, which had ceased to be constructed since the Neolithic Age. During the third and fourth centuries before Christ, a large number of these were built in the inhabited parts of our island. They consisted of a single rampart sometimes of stone, but usually an earthwork revetted with timber and protected by a single ditch.

These camps were not mere places of refuge. They appear to have come into existence gradually as the Iron Age newcomers multiplied and developed a tribal system from which tribal wars presently arose.

The last of the successive waves of Celtic inroad and supersession which

THE EARLY BRITONS

THE EARLIEST EVIDENCE of human occupation in Britain—handaxes—relates to a time when Britain was not an offshore island, but part of a bigger European land mass. The first Britons were hunters who followed their game from the main continent to the grasslands of what is now England. Farmers came later: the clearing of land, the growing of crops and the development of stock-breeding marked a major transformation in human history. Flints and stone had already been used before this so-called neolithic revolution, which can be studied from tombs and from surviving pottery.

The exploitation of metals began with copper and bronze and ended with iron. When Julius Caesar landed in Britain in 55 BC iron had been in use for six hundred years. It was used for implements and for weapons. The nearer we get in time to the Roman invasion the more archaeological evidence we have at our disposal. Horses figure on Iron-Age buckets and on the first coins. They drew chariots as well as ploughs.

Since there is no written evidence for the life of these distant times, we have to rely on the judgments not of historians, but of archaeologists. And for earlier periods, before Man appeared, we turn to the geologists. It was less than nine thousand years ago that the separation of the island from the continent took place.

Our dating of objects, including cereals and bones, has become scientific since an American, Willard Libby, developed radiocarbon techniques during the late 1940s, and won a Nobel Prize for his invention of carbon-14 (C-14) dating. The latest and most comprehensive Oxford laboratory technique is accelerator mass spectrometry (AMS) which harnesses nuclear physics. As a result of using these techniques it is now believed that the first neolithic farmers arrived as early as 6,000 years ago. The date of the first Stonehenge has been revised too: work on it began not less than 1,800 years before Julius Caesar came.

AN IRON-AGE FARM SETTLEMENT (above) has been reconstructed at Butser, near Petersfield in Hampshire. The centrepiece is a huge roundhouse, based on evidence from a ground plan of 300 BC found at Pimperne, Dorset. The original took two hundred trees and five tonnes of wheat thatch to rebuild, is thought to have had an upper storey, and housed a number of families. Possibly the aisle between the two rings of wooden posts which supported the rafters was used for livestock in the winter months. The animals kept at Butser are direct descendants of ancient breeds, and the cereals under cultivation are high-protein Iron-Age strains.

EARLY MAN WAS A SUPERB ARTIST CRAFTSMAN, and could also be vain. This torc, or neck ring (above) found at Snettisham in Norfolk, is made of an alloy of gold and silver and has a diameter of nearly eight inches.

THIS BEAKER FROM THE WEST KENNETT LONG BARROW (right) in Wiltshire is typical of the finely decorated pottery which gave its name to the "Beaker Folk" who invaded Britain from the Rhineland and Brittany in the second millennium BC. Pottery was made as early as 3,500 BC and the first firings were probably carried out on an open bonfire.

A PREHISTORIC MAN *(below) found preserved in a bog at Lindow Moss, Cheshire in 1984, has been christened Pete Marsh by archaeologists. Carbon-14 dating suggests that he lived about 500* BC. *He was twenty-five years old and was probably a nobleman chosen for ritual sacrifice: his stomach contained remnants of porridge or bread, and he was garrotted by the rope, which is still round his neck, before his body was thrown into the marsh.*

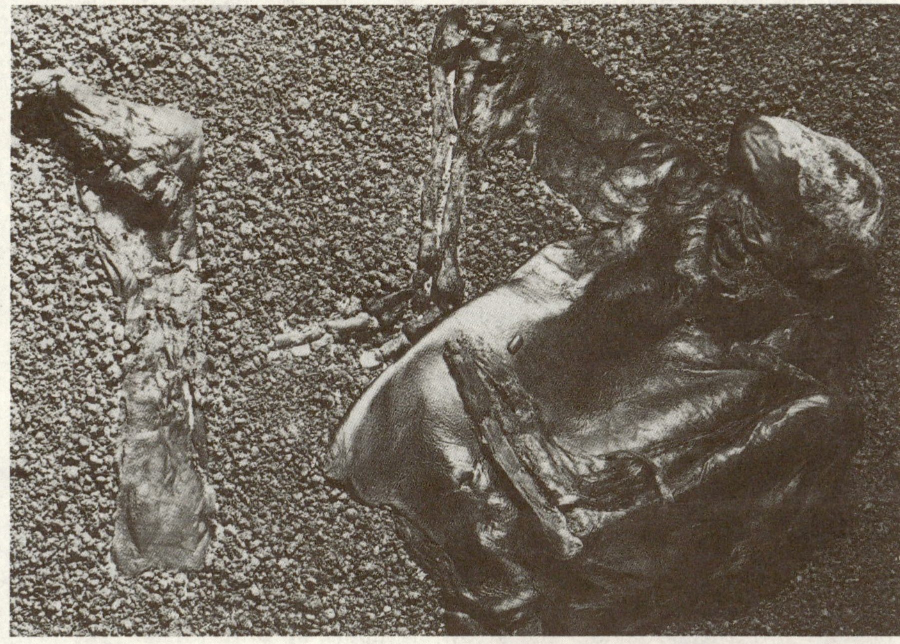

LARGE STONE OR MEGALITHIC MONUMENTS *were common in neolithic times. Pentre Ifan burial chamber (above) in Pembrokeshire, South Wales, is built of "blue" stones like those at Stonehenge. The evidence from burial chambers has puzzled archaeologists: many have contained a succession of occupants.*

MANY EARLY SETTLEMENTS *have been found on chalk hills in the southwest. Maiden Castle, or Mai Dun (right) in Dorset, is the largest surviving Iron-Age hill-fort in Britain, with a perimeter of two miles. The earthworks are a recent development in Mai Dun's history: the triple ramparts were constructed shortly after Caesar's first invasion in 55* BC, *and piles of sling stones attest to there having been serious warfare there.*

FLINT HANDAXES *(above) were copiously faceted, and were highly-prized possessions of Early Man. Grime's Graves, a prehistoric flintmine, can be visited near Thetford in Norfolk.*

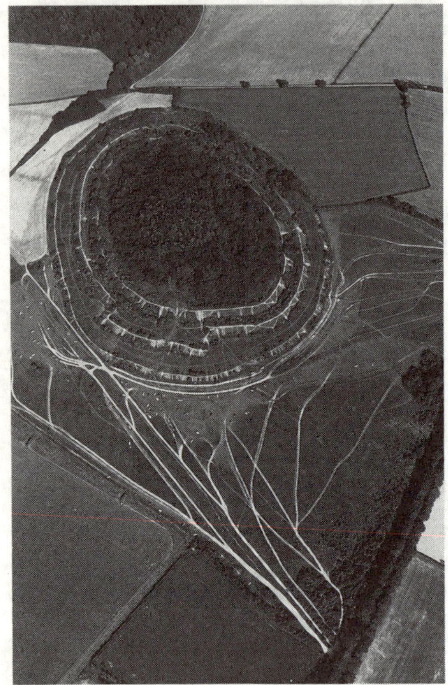

Aerial view of the extensive triple ramparts of Badbury Rings, in Dorset. This hill-fort was a minor settlement, with strong palisade fences built on top of the formidable banks, which deterred enemies and wild animals. Wolves and bears inhabited Britain in Iron Age times, which lasted roughly for the seven hundred years preceding the birth of Christ.

marked the Iron Age came in the early part of the first century BC bringing in by far the most enlightened invaders who had penetrated the recesses of the island. They were a people of chariots and horsemen, less addicted to the hill-forts in which the existing inhabitants put their trust. They built new towns in the valleys, sometimes even below the hilltop on which the old fort had stood. They introduced for the first time a coinage of silver and copper. This active, alert, conquering, and ruling race established themselves wherever they went with ease and celerity, and might have looked forward to a long dominion. But the tramp of the legions had followed hard behind them, and they must now defend the prize they had won against still better men and higher systems of government and war.

Late in August 55 BC Caesar sailed from Boulogne with eighty transports and two legions at midnight, and with the morning light saw the white cliffs of Dover crowned with armed men. He judged the place "quite unsuitable for landing", since it was possible to throw missiles from the cliffs onto the shore. He therefore sailed seven miles farther, and descended upon Albion on the low, shelving beach between Deal and Walmer. But the Britons, observing these movements, kept pace along the coast and were found ready to meet him. There followed a scene upon which the eye of history has rested. The islanders, with their chariots and horsemen, advanced into the surf to meet the invader. Caesar's transports and warships grounded in deeper water. The legionaries, uncertain of the depth, hesitated in face of the shower of javelins and stones, but the Eagle-bearer of the Tenth Legion plunged into the waves with the sacred emblem, and Caesar brought his warships with their catapults and arrow-fire upon the British flank. The Romans, thus encouraged and sustained, leapt from their ships, and, forming as best they could, waded towards the enemy. There was a short ferocious fight amid the waves, but the Romans reached the shore, and, once arrayed, forced the Britons to flight.

Caesar's landing however was only the first of his troubles. His cavalry, in eighteen transports, caught by a sudden gale, drifted far down the Channel, and were thankful to regain the Continent. Then the high tide of the full

THE ROMAN INVASION OF 55 BC

Julius Caesar's own account, written in the third person, is taken from his Commentaries on the Gallic War.

The build of the warships apparently sprung a surprise on the natives and, as their greater manoeuvrability was obvious, Caesar ordered them to draw away from the transports. He had them rowed up to a station on the enemy's exposed flank from which our barrage of slings, artillery and arrows might force their withdrawal. Our men reaped considerable benefit from these tactics. The build of the ships, the dash of the oars and the novel type of barrage demoralised the natives. They halted and actually beat a slight retreat. Our men had come to a standstill mainly because of the depth of water; but the standard-bearer of the Tenth Legion prayed to the gods for a blessing on the legion. "You must jump for it, fellows," he shouted, "unless you mean to let them get the Eagle. I for one shall do my duty to my country and my captain." He roared this out and plunged overboard to carry his Eagle towards the other side. At this, our men encouraged one another not to let a thing like that happen and leapt overboard to a man. Those on the ships within sight followed suit in a general advance.

Their oars made Roman galleys easy to manoeuvre. This stone relief from the first century BC is in the Vatican Museum, Rome.

moon which Caesar had not understood wrought grievous damage to his fleet at anchor. "A number of ships," he says, "were shattered, and the rest, having lost their cables, anchors, and the remainder of their tackle, were unusable, which naturally threw the whole army into great disorder and consternation. For they had no other vessels in which they could return, nor any materials for repairing the fleet; and, since it had been generally understood that they were to return to Gaul for the winter, they had not provided themselves with a stock of grain for wintering in Britain."

The Britons had sued for peace after the battle on the beach, but now that they saw the plight of their assailants their hopes revived and they broke off the negotiations. In great numbers they attacked the Roman foragers. But discipline and armour once again told their tale and the British submitted. Their conqueror imposed only nominal terms. Breaking up many of his ships to repair the rest, he was glad to return with some hostages and captives to the mainland.

Caesar never even pretended that his expedition had been a success. To supersede the record of it he came again the next year, this time with five legions and some cavalry conveyed in eight hundred ships. The islanders were overawed by the size of the armada. The landing was unimpeded and, after easily destroying the forest stockades in which the British sheltered, Caesar crossed the Thames near Brentford. But the British had found a leader in the chief Cassivellaunus, who kept pace with the invaders march by march with his chariots and horsemen. Caesar gives a detailed description of the chariot fighting:

"In chariot fighting the Britons begin by driving all over the field hurling javelins, and generally the terror inspired by the horses and the noise of the wheels are sufficient to throw their opponents' ranks into disorder. Then, after making their way between the squadrons of their own cavalry, they jump down from the chariots and engage on foot. In the meantime their charioteers retire a short distance from the battle and place the chariots in such a position that their masters, if hard pressed by numbers, have an easy means of retreat to their own lines. Thus they combine the mobility of cavalry with the staying-power of infantry; and by daily training and practise they attain such proficiency that even on a very steep incline they are able to control the horses at full gallop, and to check and turn them in a moment. The charioteers can then run along the chariot pole, stand on the yoke, and get back into the chariot as quick as lightning."

Cassivellaunus, using these mobile forces and avoiding a pitched battle with the Roman legions, escorted them on their inroad and cut off their foraging parties.

Nonetheless Caesar captured his first stronghold and the tribes began to make terms for themselves; a well-conceived plan for destroying Caesar's base on the Kentish shore was defeated however. At this juncture Cassivellaunus, by a prudence of policy equal to that of his tactics, negotiated a surrender of hostages and a promise of tribute and submission, in return for which Caesar was again content to quit the island. In a dead calm "he set sail late in the evening and brought all the fleet safely to land at dawn". This time he proclaimed a conquest.

Caesar had his triumph, and British captives trod their dreary path at his tail through the streets of Rome, but thanks to Cassivellaunus, for nearly a hundred years no invading army landed upon the island coasts.

CHAPTER 2

SUBJUGATION

Bronze head of the Emperor Claudius (AD 41–45). It was found in the River Alde, Suffolk, in 1902, and is thought to be part of a complete figure which stood in a public square in Roman Colchester.

Head of the tribal chief Cunobelinus, after whom Shakespeare named his play, Cymbeline. His territory in the southeast, with its capital at Colchester, occupied an area roughly corresponding to modern Hertfordshire.

DURING THE HUNDRED YEARS WHICH followed Julius Caesar's invasion the British developed a life of their own, enjoying amid their internecine feuds the comforting illusion that no one was likely to attack them again. However, their contacts with the mainland and with the civilisation of the Roman Empire grew, and trade flourished in a wide range of commodities. Roman traders carried back to Rome tales of the wealth and possibilities of Britannia, if only a stable government were set up.

In the year AD 41 the murder of the Emperor Caligula brought his uncle, the clownish scholar Claudius, to the throne of the world. No one can suppose that any coherent will to conquest resided in the new ruler, but in this triumphant period there were always available for a new emperor a number of desirable projects, well thought out beforehand, any one of which might catch the fancy of the latest wielder of supreme power.

The advantages of conquering the recalcitrant island Britannia were thus paraded before the new monarch, and his interest was excited by the idea of gaining a military reputation. He gave orders that this dramatic and possibly lucrative enterprise should proceed. So in the year 43, almost one hundred years after Julius Caesar's evacuation, a powerful, well-organised Roman army of some twenty thousand men was prepared for the invasion and subjugation of Britain.

The internal situation favoured the invaders. Cunobelinus (Shakespeare's Cymbeline) had established an overlordship over the southeast of the island, with his capital at Colchester. But in his old age dissensions had begun to impair his authority, and on his death his sons Caractacus and Togodumnus had no time to form a union of the tribal kingdom before the Roman commander, Plautius, and his legions arrived. The people of Kent fell back on the tactics of Cassivellaunus, and Plautius had much trouble in searching them out; but when he did find them he first defeated Caractacus, and then his brother, somewhere in east Kent. Then, advancing along Caesar's old line of march, he came on the River Medway. A Roman historian, writing over a century later, said, "The barbarians thought that the Romans would not be able to cross without a bridge, and consequently bivouacked in rather careless fashion on the opposite bank . . ." But the Roman general sent across "a detachment of Germans, who were accustomed to swim easily in full armour across the most turbulent streams. These fell unexpectedly upon the enemy, but instead of shooting at the men they disabled the horses that drew the chariots, and in the ensuing confusion not even the enemy's mounted men could save themselves." Nevertheless the Britons faced them on the second day, and were only broken by a flank attack, Vespasian — one day to be Emperor himself — having discovered a ford higher up. This victory marred the stage-management of the campaign. Plautius had won his battle too soon. Something had to be done to show that the Emperor's presence was necessary to victory. So Claudius, who had been waiting on events in Gaul, crossed the seas, bringing substantial reinforcements, including a number of elephants. A battle was procured, and the Romans won. Claudius returned to Rome to receive from the Senate the title of "Britannicus" and permission to celebrate a triumph.

But the British war continued. The Britons would not come to close quarters with the Romans, but took refuge in the swamps and the forests, hoping to wear out the invaders so that, as in the days of Julius Caesar, they should sail back with nothing accomplished. Caractacus escaped to the Welsh border, and, rousing its tribes, maintained an indomitable resistance for more than six years. It was not till AD 50 that he was finally defeated by a new general, Ostorius, the successor of Plautius, who reduced to submission the whole of the more settled regions from the Wash to the Severn. Escaping from the ruin of his forces in the west Caractacus sought to raise the Brigantes in the north. Their queen, however, handed him over to the Romans. "The fame of the British prince," wrote Suetonius, "had by this time spread over the provinces of Gaul and Italy; and upon his arrival in the Roman capital the people flocked from all quarters to behold him. With a manly gait and an undaunted countenance he marched up to the tribunal where the Emperor was seated, and addressed him in the following terms:

"'If to my high birth and distinguished rank I had added the virtues of moderation Rome had beheld me rather as a friend than a captive, and you would not have rejected an alliance with a prince descended from illustrious ancestors and governing many nations. The reverse of my fortune to you is glorious, and to me humiliating. I had arms, and men, and horses; I possessed extraordinary riches; and can it be any wonder that I was unwilling to lose them? Because Rome aspires to universal dominion must men therefore implicitly resign themselves to subjection? I opposed for a long time the progress of your arms, and had I acted otherwise would either you have had the glory of conquest or I of a brave resistance? I am now in your power. If you are determined to take revenge my fate will soon be forgotten, and you will derive no honour from the transaction. Preserve my life, and I shall remain to the latest ages a monument of your clemency.'

"Immediately upon this speech Claudius granted him his liberty, as he did likewise to the other royal captives."

The conquest was not achieved without one frightful convulsion of revolt. In AD 61, Suetonius, the new governor, had engaged himself deeply in the west. "Because it was the centre of Druid resistance," wrote Tacitus, he prepared to attack "the populous island of Mona [Anglesey], which had become a refuge for fugitives, and he built a fleet of flat-bottomed vessels suitable for those shallow and shifting seas. The infantry crossed in the boats, the cavalry went over by fords; where the water was too deep the men swam alongside their horses. The enemy lined the shore, a dense host of armed men, interspersed with women clad in black like the Furies, with their hair hanging down and holding torches in their hands. Round these were Druids uttering dire curses and stretching their hands towards heaven. These strange sights terrified the soldiers. They stayed motionless, as if paralysed, offering their bodies to the blows. At last, encouraged by the general, and exhorting each other not to quail before the rabble of female fanatics, they advanced their standards, bore down all resistance, and enveloped the enemy in their own flames . . ."

This dramatic scene on the frontiers of modern Wales was the prelude to a tragedy. The king of the East Anglian Iceni had died. Hoping to save his kingdom and family from molestation, he had appointed the Emperor as

The Romans brought unity and wealth to Britain by their communication networks and level of economic development. Lead, tin, jet, textiles and grain paid for imports of wine, glass and silver used in the new Roman towns and villas.

heir jointly with his two daughters. "But," wrote Tacitus, "things turned out differently. His kingdom was plundered by centurions, and his private property by slaves, as if they had been captured in war; his widow Boadicea [relished by the learned as Boudicca] was flogged, and his daughters outraged; the chiefs of the Iceni were robbed of their ancestral properties as if the Romans had received the whole country as a gift, and the king's own relatives were reduced to slavery."

Boadicea's tribe, at once the most powerful and hitherto the most submissive, was moved to frenzy. Boadicea found herself at the head of an army, and nearly all the Britons within reach rallied to her standard. It was a scream of rage against invincible oppression and the superior culture which seemed to lend it power. Boadicea's monument on the Thames Embankment opposite Big Ben reminds us of the harsh cry of "Liberty or Death" which has echoed down the ages.

Boadicea's monument on the Thames Embankment shows the sort of battle chariot which daunted the Roman legionaries. The monument was built by Thomas Thornycroft in 1902.

In all Britain there were only four Roman legions, at most twenty thousand men. The Fourteenth and Twentieth were with Suetonius on his Welsh campaign. The Ninth was at Lincoln, and the Second at Gloucester.

The first target of the revolt was Camulodunum (Colchester), the centre of Roman authority and Roman religion, where recently settled veterans had been ejecting the inhabitants and driving them away from their lands. The Britons were encouraged by omens. The statue of Victory fell face foremost, as if flying from the enemy. The sea turned red. The Roman officials, businessmen, bankers, usurers, and the Britons who had participated in their authority and profits, found themselves with a handful of old soldiers in the midst of a "multitude of barbarians". Suetonius was a month distant. The Ninth Legion was a hundred and twenty miles away. There was neither mercy nor hope. The town was burnt to ashes. Everyone, Roman or Romanised, was massacred and everything destroyed. Meanwhile the Ninth Legion was marching to the rescue. The victorious Britons advanced from the sack of Colchester to meet it. By sheer force of numbers they overcame the Roman infantry and slaughtered them to a man, and the commander, Petilius Cerialis, was content to escape with his cavalry. Such were the tidings which reached Suetonius in Anglesey. He realised at once that his army could not make the distance in time to prevent even greater disaster, "but," wrote Tacitus, "undaunted, he made his way through a hostile country to Londinium, a town which, though not dignified by the title of colony, was a busy emporium for traders." This is the first mention of London in literature. Though fragments of Gallic or Italian pottery which antedate the Roman conquest have been found there, it is certain that the place attained no prominence until the Claudian invaders brought a mass of army contractors and officials to the most convenient bridgehead on the Thames.

Suetonius reached London with only a small mounted escort. He had sent orders to the Second Legion to meet him there from Gloucester, but the commander, appalled by the defeat of the Ninth, had not complied. The citizens of London implored Suetonius to protect them, but when he heard that Boadicea was marching south he took the hard but right decision to leave them to their fate. His only course was to rejoin the Fourteenth and Twentieth Legions, who were marching from Wales to London along the line of the Roman road now known as Watling Street. Unmoved by the entreaties of the inhabitants, he gave the signal to march, receiving within his lines all who wished to go with him.

The slaughter which fell upon London was universal. No one was spared, neither man, woman, nor child. The wrath of the revolt concentrated itself upon all of those of British blood who had lent themselves to the wiles and seductions of the invader. In recent times, with London buildings growing taller and needing deeper foundations, the power-driven excavating machines have encountered at many points the layer of ashes which marks the effacement of London at the hands of the natives of Britain.

Boadicea then turned upon Verulamium (St Albans), another trading centre to which high civic rank had been accorded. A like total slaughter and obliteration was inflicted. No less than seventy thousand citizens and allies were slain in these three cities according to Tacitus. "For the barbarians would have no capturing, no selling, nor any kind of traffic usual in war; they would have nothing but killing, by sword, cross, gibbet, or fire."

This is probably the most horrible episode which our island has known. We see the crude and corrupt beginnings of a higher civilisation blotted out by the ferocious uprising of the native tribes. Still, it is the primary right of men to die and kill for the land they live in, and to punish with exceptional severity all members of their own race who have warmed their hands at the invader's hearth.

"And now Suetonius, having with him the Fourteenth Legion, with the veterans of the Twentieth, and the auxiliaries nearest at hand, making up a force of about ten thousand fully armed men . . . selected a position in a defile closed in behind by a wood, where there was an open flat unsuited for ambuscades, drew up his Legions in close order, with the light-armed troops on the flanks, while the cavalry was massed at the extremities of the wings." The day was bloody and decisive. On both sides it was all for all. At heavy adverse odds Roman discipline and tactical skill triumphed. No quarter was given, even to the women. "Some say that little less than eighty thousand Britons fell, our own killed being about four hundred, with a somewhat larger number wounded." These are the tales of the victors. Boadicea poisoned herself. On hearing of the success of the Fourteenth and Twentieth the commander of the Second Legion, who had both disobeyed his general and deprived his men of their share in the victory, fell upon his sword.

This tombstone of a Roman standard-bearer is now in the Yorkshire Museum. Crack troops such as those known as the Praetorian Guard were often needed to quell the fierce uprisings of the British tribes.

A legionary soldier shown in effigy on a tomb in the London Museum wears civilian dress. He was probably attached in a clerical capacity to his legion headquarters staff.

Suetonius now thought only of vengeance, and indeed there was much to repay. All hostile or suspect tribes were harried with fire and sword. Worst of all was the want of food, and the extermination of the entire ancient British race might have followed but for the remonstrances of a new procurator, supported by his treasury seniors at Rome, who saw themselves about to be possessed of a desert instead of a province.

The Procurator, Julius Classicianus, whose tombstone is now in the British Museum, pleaded vehemently for the pacification of the warrior bands, who still fought on without seeking truce or mercy, starving and perishing in the forests and the fens.

In the end it was resolved to make the best of the Britons. The loss in a storm of some of Suetonius's warships was made the pretext and occasion of his supersession, and a peace was made with the desperate tribesmen which enabled their blood to be perpetuated in the island race.

In AD 78 a governor was sent to Britannia, in whom military ability was united with a statesmanlike humanity: Agricola. According to Tacitus (who had married his daughter), he proclaimed that "little is gained by conquest if followed by oppression." He mitigated the severity of the corn tribute, encouraged and aided the building of temples, courts of justice, and dwelling-houses. He provided a liberal education for the sons of the chiefs, and the well-to-do classes were conciliated and became willing to adopt the toga and other Roman fashions.

"Step by step they were led to practices which disposed to vice — the lounge, the bath, the eloquent banquet. All this in their ignorance they called civilisation, when it was but part of their servitude."

Although in the Senate and governing circles in Rome it was constantly explained that the Imperial policy adhered to the principle of the great Augustus, that the frontiers should be maintained but not extended, Agricola was permitted to conduct six campaigns of expansion in Britannia. In the third he reached the Tyne, in the fifth the line of the Forth and Clyde and here on this wasp-waist of Britain he might well have dug himself in. But there was no safety or permanent peace for the British province unless he could subdue the powerful tribes and bands of desperate warriors who had been driven northward by his advance. Therefore in his sixth campaign he marched northward again with all his forces.

The decisive battle was fought in AD 83 at Mons Graupius, a place unidentified, though some suggest the Pass of Killiecrankie. The whole of Caledonia, all that was left of Britannia, a vast host of broken, hunted men, resolved on death or freedom, confronted in their superiority of four or five to one the skilfully handled Roman legions and auxiliaries, among whom no doubt many British renegades were serving. Apparently, as in so many ancient battles, the beaten side were the victims of misunderstanding, and the fate of the day was decided against them before the bulk of the forces realised that a serious engagement had begun. Reserves descended from the hills too late to achieve victory, but in good time to be massacred in the rout. The last organised resistance of Britain to the Roman power ended at Mons Graupius. Here, according to the Roman account, "ten thousand of the enemy were slain, and on our side there were about three hundred and sixty men." Clive's victory at Plassey, which secured for the British Empire a long spell of authority in India was gained against greater odds with smaller forces and with smaller losses.

A stone carving found near the remains of the Antonine Wall in Scotland shows the victory of a Roman legionary over British tribesmen.

The way to the entire subjugation of the island was now open, and had Agricola been encouraged or at least supported by the Imperial Government the course of history might have been altered. But Caledonia was to Rome only a sensation: the real strain was between the Rhine and the Danube. Counsels of prudence prevailed, and the remnants of the British fighting men were left to moulder in the northern mists.

So in the wild north and west freedom found refuge among the mountains, but elsewhere the conquest and pacification were at length complete and Britannia became one of the forty-five provinces of the Roman Empire. The great Augustus had proclaimed as the Imperial ideal the creation of a commonwealth of self-governing cantons. Each province was organised as a separate unit, and within it municipalities received their charters and rights, and in all provinces the principle was followed of adapting the form of government to local conditions. No prejudice of race, language, or religion obstructed the universal character of the Roman system. The only divisions were those of class, and these ran unchallenged throughout the ordered world. There were Roman citizens, and there were slaves. On this basis therefore the life of Britain now developed.

CHAPTER 3

THE ROMAN PROVINCE

FOR NEARLY THREE HUNDRED YEARS Britain, reconciled to the Roman system, enjoyed in many respects the happiest, most comfortable, and most enlightened times its inhabitants have had. In this period, almost equal to that which separates us from the reign of Queen Elizabeth I, well-to-do persons in Britain lived better than they ever did until late Victorian times. A wealthy British-Roman citizen building a country house regarded the baths and the hypocaust which warmed it as indispensable. Yet for the next fifteen hundred years his descendants lived in the cold of unheated dwellings, mitigated by occasional roastings at gigantic wasteful fires. As for baths, they were completely lost till the middle of the nineteenth century. In all this long, bleak intervening gap cold and dirt clung to the most fortunate and highest in the land.

In culture and learning Britain was a pale reflection of the Roman scene, but there was law; there was order; there was peace; there was warmth; there was food, and a long-established custom of life. The population was free from barbarism without being sunk in sloth or luxury. Some culture spread even to the villages. Roman habits percolated; the use of Roman utensils and even of Roman speech steadily grew. The British thought themselves as good Romans as any. Indeed, it may be said that of all the provinces few assimilated the Roman system with more aptitude than the islanders. In all, the army of occupation numbered less than forty thousand men, and after a few generations was locally recruited and almost of purely British birth. The British legionaries and auxiliaries were rated equal or second only to the Illyrians as the finest troops in the Empire. There was a sense of pride in sharing in so noble and widespread a system. To be a citizen of Rome was to be a citizen of the world, raised upon a pedestal of unquestioned superiority above barbarians or slaves. Movement across the

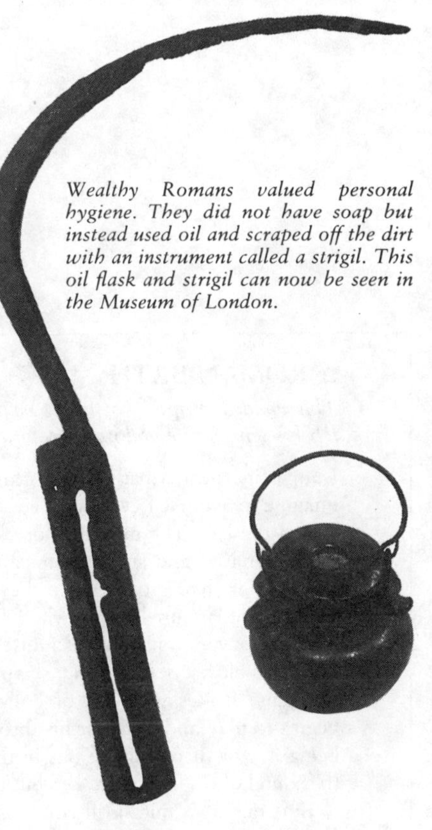

Wealthy Romans valued personal hygiene. They did not have soap but instead used oil and scraped off the dirt with an instrument called a strigil. This oil flask and strigil can now be seen in the Museum of London.

Bacchus, the Roman god of wine, rides on a tiger in the centre of a mosaic pavement found in Leadenhall Street, London.

great Empire was as rapid as when Queen Victoria came to the throne, and no obstruction of frontiers, laws, currency, or nationalism hindered it. There is a monument at Norwich erected to his wife by a Syrian resident in Britain. British sentinels watched along the Rhine, the Danube, and the Euphrates. Troops from Asia Minor, peering through the mists at the Scottish raiders, preserved the worship of Mithras along the Roman Wall. During the third century this Persian sun-god was a powerful rival to Christianity and, as was revealed by the impressive temple discovered at Walbrook in 1954, it could count many believers in Roman London.

Here and there were wars and risings. Rival emperors suppressed each other. Legions mutinied. Usurpers established themselves in the provinces affected on these occasions. In Britain too many thrusting spirits shot forward to play a part in the deadly game of Imperial politics, with its unparalleled prizes and fatal forfeits. Yet the violent changes at the summit of the Empire did not affect so much as might be supposed the ordinary life of its population. They had their law; they had their life, which flowed on, if momentarily disturbed, in the main unaltered. A poll in the fourth century would have declared for an indefinite continuance of the Roman regime.

In our own fevered, changing and precarious age, where all is in flux and nothing is accepted, we must survey with respect a period when, with only three hundred thousand soldiers, widespread peace in the entire known world was maintained from generation to generation, and when the first pristine impulse of Christianity lifted men's souls to the contemplation of new and larger harmonies beyond the ordered world around them.

The gift which Roman civilisation had to bestow was civic and political. Towns were planned in chessboard squares for communities dwelling under orderly government. The buildings rose in accordance with the pattern standardised throughout the Roman world. Each was complete with its forum, temples, courts of justice, gaols, baths, markets, and main drains. During the first century the builders evidently took a sanguine view of the resources and future of Britannia, and all their towns were projected to meet an increasing population. It was a period of hope.

The experts dispute the population of Roman Britain. The army, the civil

A ROMAN BATH

This vivid description of living near a Roman bath has been left by Seneca, the philosopher, writing about AD 57.

I am living near a bath: sounds are heard on all sides. Just imagine for yourself every conceivable kind of noise that can offend the ear. The men of more sturdy muscle go through their exercises, and swing their hands heavily weighted with lead: I hear their groans when they strain themselves, or the whistling of laboured breath when they breathe out. . . . If one is rather lazy, and merely has himself rubbed with unguents, I hear the blows of the hand slapping his shoulders, as the massagist strikes with flat or hollow palm. If a ball-player begins to play and to count his throws it's all up for the time being . . . or there is some one in the bath who loves to hear the sound of his own voice . . . but the hair-plucker from time to time raises his thin shrill voice in order to attract attention, and is only still himself when he is forcing cries of pain from some one, from whose armpits he plucks the hairs.

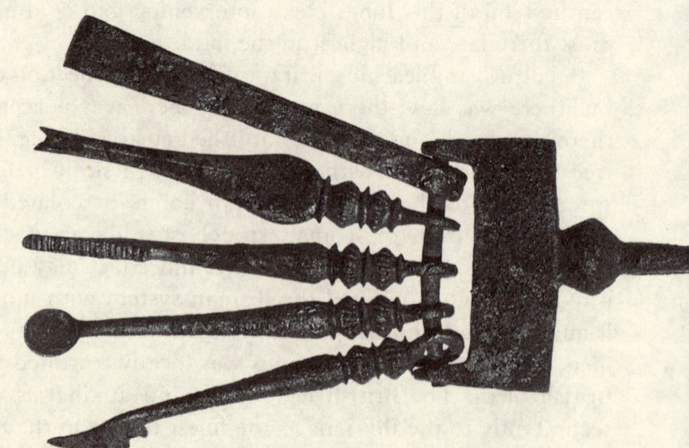

This Roman toilet set includes, besides nail file and cuticle remover, a pair of tweezers for removing unwanted body hair and an instrument for scooping wax from the ears.

services, the townsfolk, the well-to-do, and their dependants amounted to three or four hundred thousand. To grow food for these, under the agricultural methods of the age, would have required on the land perhaps double their number. We may therefore assume a population of at least a million in the Romanised area. There may well have been more. But there are no signs that any large increase of population accompanied the Roman system. In more than two centuries of peace and order the inhabitants remained at about the same number as in the days of Cassivellaunus. The conquerors, who so easily subdued and rallied the Britons to their method of social life, brought with them no means, apart from stopping tribal war, of increasing the productivity of the soil. The cultivated ground was still for the most part confined to the lighter and more easily cultivated upland soils, which had for thousands of years been worked in a primitive fashion. The powerful Gallic plough on wheels was known in Britain, but it did not supplant the native implement, which could only nose along in shallow furrows. With a few exceptions, there was no large-scale attempt to clear the forests, drain the marshes, and cultivate the heavy clay soil of the valleys, in which so much fertility had been deposited. Such mining of lead and tin, such smelting, as had existed from times immemorial may have gained something from orderly administration; but there was no new science, no new thrust of power and knowledge in the material sphere. Thus the economic basis remained constant, and Britain became more genteel rather than more wealthy. The new edifice, so stately and admirable, was light and frail.

This marble head of Mithras, the god of light and guardian against evil, was found at Walbrook, London, in 1954.

These conditions soon cast their shadows upon the boldly planned towns. There are several excavations which show that the original boundaries were never occupied, or that, having been at first occupied, portions of the town fell gradually into decay. There was not enough material wellbeing to make things go. Nevertheless men dwelt safely, and what property they had was secured by iron laws. Urban life in Britannia was a failure, not of existence, but of expansion. It ran on like the life of some cathedral city, some fading provincial town, sedate, restricted, but not without grace and dignity.

We owe London to Rome. An extensive and well-planned city with mighty walls took the place of the wooden trading settlement of AD 61, and soon achieved a leading place in the life of the Roman province of Britain, superseding the old capital, Colchester, as the commercial centre. At the end of the third century money was coined in the London mint, and the city was the headquarters of the financial administration.

The efflorescence of Rome in Britain was found in its villa population all over the settled area. The villas of country gentlemen of modest station were built in the most delightful spots of a virgin countryside, amid primaeval forests and the gushing of untamed streams. A very large number of comfortable dwellings, each with its lands around it, rose and thrived. None is found farther north than Yorkshire or farther west than the Glamorgan sea-plain. The villas still flourished in the fourth century, and in some cases lingered on into the darkening days of the fifth.

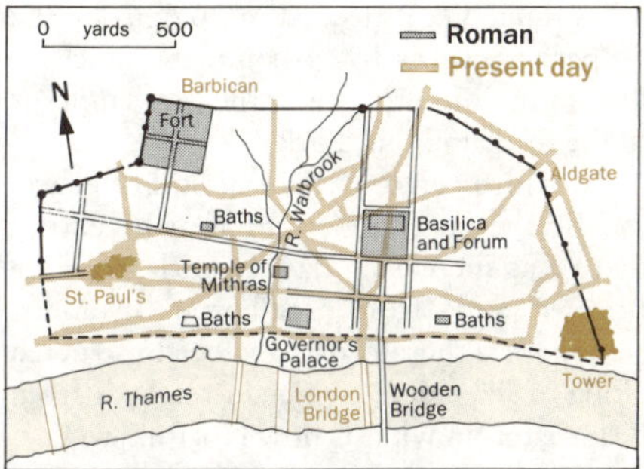

Londinium, the earliest known settlement on the site of present-day London, was constructed by the Romans at the lowest crossing-point of the River Thames. It began as a military establishment, but soon developed as a port.

The need for strong defences at the time when the expansion of the Empire had practically reached its limits was met by the frontier policy of the Emperors Hadrian and Antoninus Pius. The work of Agricola in northern Britain had been left unfinished. No satisfactory line of defence had been erected, and the position which he had won in Scotland had to be gradually abandoned. The Legions fell back on the line of the Stanegate, a road

THE ROMAN ORDER

THE ROMANS RULED BRITAIN FOR four centuries, and there were many changes, economic, social and political, during this long period. Cultivation of the land continued much as before, but there were new straight Roman roads, and without these there could have been no order of any kind. Roman walled towns were built on a grid pattern with a forum or market in the middle and standard Roman institutions, including public baths, amphitheatres, courts of justice and temples. The Emperor was considered a god and people worshipped him at public shrines.

Latin was the imperial language: it offered the key to the civilised Roman way of life. It was the language of the law, of inscriptions, and of coins which bore the Emperor's head. The Christian Constantine became Emperor of all the West in 312, and after that Latin was to remain the language of the Church.

At first Britain was one Roman province, but in the third century it was divided into two, and in the fourth into four, then five. How orderly the province or provinces were at any given time depended on forces both inside the country and outside it. Hadrian's Wall in the north was begun in 122 in an effort to secure the difficult northern frontier against "the barbarians". It took six years to build and was seventy-three miles long. Yet it needed campaigns by the Emperor Severus to "reconquer" much of Britain in 208–11; he was the first emperor to die in Britain, at York.

The third century was a period of peace, but by the last half of the fourth century there was increasing danger both from the Britons and from sea-borne invaders. Strong forts therefore had to be constructed along a coastline which stretched from Brancaster, in what is now Norfolk, to Porchester in Hampshire. But there was now an even greater threat to Rome itself, and so in 407 the Roman army was withdrawn. In 410 the Emperor Honorius instructed the British cities to fend for themselves.

HADRIAN'S WALL, THE BEST-KNOWN MONUMENT of Roman Britain, spans seventy-three miles from the Tyne to the Irish Sea. The section shown above, near Cawfields, runs along precipitous crags. Persistent attacks from Picts and barbarians made it necessary to strengthen the Wall and the troops that guarded it: garrison forts were added in the second century, and a great earthwork rampart was thrown up on the north side. Visitors today can inspect reconstructions of the milecastles which defended the gates, and the observation towers positioned between them. The well-preserved wall forts at Chesters, Housesteads, Carrawburgh and the Stonegate fort at Chesterholm evoke past frontier struggles.

CHILDREN IN ROMAN TIMES were seen as mini-adults. This tombstone (left) in the Guildhall Museum, London, shows a child dressed in a toga identical to his father's, and adopting an identical pose.

ROMAN TOOLS often look surprisingly modern. This carpenter's plane dates from about the fourth century AD, and belonged to an inhabitant of Silchester.

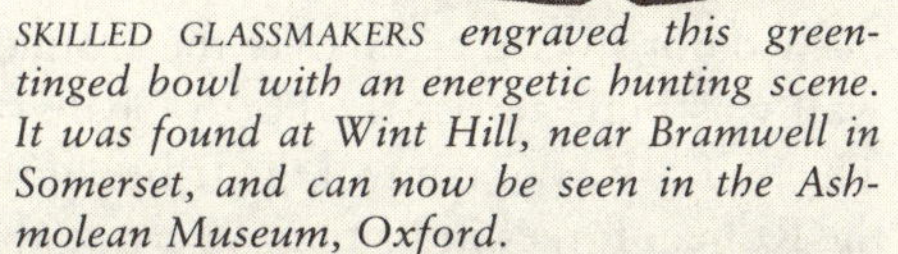

SKILLED GLASSMAKERS *engraved this green-tinged bowl with an energetic hunting scene. It was found at Wint Hill, near Bramwell in Somerset, and can now be seen in the Ashmolean Museum, Oxford.*

THE ROMAN GOD, LAR, *(above) was the deity of home and family. This bronze figure dates from the first century* AD *and is now in the Ashmolean Museum, Oxford. It was customary for Roman families living in villas to have shrines dedicated to their own personal gods. In towns, however, the State religion of Rome was imposed on Britons in the form of temples built in classical style, and worship took place in the open air round an altar placed at the front. There were also mystery religions of eastern origin, including the Cult of Mithras.*

UNDERFLOOR CENTRAL HEATING *was part of the sauna bath suite at Chedworth Villa in Gloucestershire (above). The mosaic floor has collapsed, revealing the hypocaust pillars which supported it. On the right of the picture is a semi-circular room that once contained a hot plunge bath. Like most country residences, this Roman villa also boasts a fine mosaic pavement and, originally, an inner courtyard garden laid out with formal flowerbeds, fountains, statues and herbs.*

IRON KEYS OR "LATCHLIFTERS" *worked by raising pins which secured bolts when they were thrust home. The holes in the handles meant that the keys could be hooked to a nail on the wall or worn on a belt round the waist.*

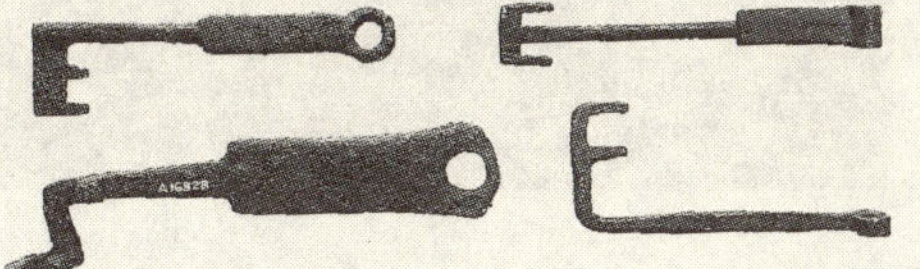

AN EARLY PICTURE OF CHRIST *(above) survives on a mosaic floor found in a villa at Hinton St Mary, Dorset. Christianity threatened the Romans' established ideas about religion because it denied the existence of a multiplicity of gods, and challenged the divinity of the "holy" Roman Emperor.*

running eastward from Carlisle. The years which followed revealed the weakness of the British frontier. The Ninth Legion disappears from history in combating an obscure rising of the tribes in northern Britain. The defences were disorganised and the province was in danger. Hadrian came himself to Britain in 122, and the reorganisation of the frontier began.

During the next five years a military barrier was built between the Tyne and the Solway seventy-three miles long. It consisted of a stone rampart eight to ten feet thick, sustained by seventeen forts, each garrisoned by an auxiliary cohort, about eight castles, and double that number of signal towers. In front of the wall was a thirty-foot ditch, and behind it another ditch which seems to have been designed as a customs frontier and was probably controlled and staffed by the financial administration. The works needed a supporting garrison of about fourteen thousand men, not including some five thousand who, independent of the fighting units in the forts, were engaged in patrol work along the wall. The troops were provisioned by the local population, whose taxes were paid in wheat, and each fort contained granaries capable of holding a year's supply of food.

Twenty years later, in the reign of Antoninus Pius, the Roman troops pushed northward again over the ground of Agricola's conquests, and a new wall was built across the Forth-Clyde isthmus thirty-seven miles in length. The object was to control the tribes of the eastern and central lowlands, but the Roman forces in Britain were not able to man the new defences without weakening their position on Hadrian's Wall and in the west. Somewhere about the year 186 this Antonine Wall was abandoned and the troops were concentrated on the original line of defence. Tribal revolts and Scottish raids continually assailed the northern frontier system, and in places the Wall and its supporting camps were utterly wrecked.

It was not until the Emperor Severus came to Britain in 208 and flung his energies into the task of reorganisation that stability was achieved. So great had been the destruction, so massive were his repairs, that in later times he was thought to have built the Wall, which in fact he only reconstructed. He died at York in 211; but for a hundred years there was peace along the Roman Wall.

We can measure the Roman activity in roadbuilding by the milestones which are discovered from time to time, recording the name of the emperor under whose decree the work was done. These long, unswerving causeways stretched in bold lines across the island. Ordinarily the road was made with

This bronze head of the Emperor Hadrian comes from a gigantic statue found in the Thames at London Bridge and is thought to be an authentic likeness of the man who ordered the construction of the Wall which bears his name. Forts, such as this one called Housesteads, were added after the Wall was officially completed in AD 128, in order to house the extra troops needed to defend the frontier against the Picts.

a bottoming of large stones, often embedded in sand, covered with a surface of rammed gravel, the whole on an average eighteen inches thick. In special cases, or after much repairing, the formation extended to a three-foot thickness. Over Blackstone Edge, where the road was laid upon peat, a sixteen-foot roadspan was made of squared blocks of millstone grit, with a kerb on either side and a line of large square stones down the middle. Upon these the wheels of ancient carts going down the steep hill, brake skidpans have made their grooves.

The first half-century after the Claudian invasion was very active in road-building. In the second century we find most of the work concentrated upon the frontiers of the military districts. By the third century the road system was almost complete and needed only to be kept in repair. It is true that for the period of Constantine the Great no fewer than four milestones have been unearthed, which point to some fresh extension, but by 340 all new work was ended.

A section of Watling Street, at Stony Stratford in Buckinghamshire. The Romans constructed six thousand miles of roads in Britain. Before the motorways were built in this century, most of the main roads in use were of Roman origin.

Carefully conserved, the resources of the Empire in men and material were probably sufficient to maintain the frontiers intact. But they were often wasted in war between rival emperors. By the end of the third century Rome seemed as powerful and stable as ever, but below the surface the foundations were cracking. The cities were everywhere in decline; trade, industry, and agriculture bent under the weight of taxation. Communications were less safe, and some provinces were infected with marauders, peasants who could no longer earn a living on the land.

The Roman world, like an aged man, wished to dwell in peace and tranquillity and to enjoy in philosophic detachment the good gifts which life has to bestow upon the more fortunate classes. But new ideas disturbed the internal conservatism, and outside the carefully guarded frontiers vast masses of hungry, savage men surged and schemed. The essence of the Roman peace was toleration of all religions and the acceptance of a universal system of government. Yet every generation after the middle of the second century saw an increasing weakening of the system and a gathering movement towards a uniform religion. Christianity asked again all the questions which the Roman world deemed answered forever, and some that it had never thought of. Although the varieties of status, with all their grievous consequences, were accepted during these centuries, even by those who suffered from them most as part of the law of nature, the institution of slavery, by which a third of Roman society was bound, could not withstand indefinitely the new dynamic thoughts which Christianity brought with it. The alternations between fanatic profligacy and avenging puritanism which marked the succession of the emperors, the contrast between the morals at the centre of power and those practised by wide communities in many subject lands, presented problems of ever-growing unrest. At the moment when mankind seemed to have solved a very large proportion of its secular difficulties and when a supreme government offered unlimited freedom to spiritual experiment, inexorable forces both within and without drove on the forward march. No rest, no stay. "For here we have no continuing city, but we seek one to come." Strange standards of destiny were unfurled, destructive of peace and order, but thrilling the hearts of men.

From outside, the uncouth barbarians smote upon the barriers. Here on the mainland were savage, fighting animals, joined together in a comradeship of arms, with the best fighting men and their progeny as leaders. In the rough and tumble of these communities, with all their crimes and bestialities, there was a more active principle of life than in the majestic achievements of the Roman Empire. We see these forces swelling like a flood against all the threatened dykes of the Roman world, not only brimming up at the lip of the dam, but percolating insidiously, now by a breach, now in a mere ooze, while all the time men become conscious of the frailty of the structure itself. Floods of new untamed life burst ceaselessly from Asia, driving westward in a succession of waves. Against these there was no easy superiority of weapons. Cold steel and discipline and the slight capital surplus necessary to move and organise armies constituted the sole defences. If the superior virtue of the legion failed all fell. Certainly from the middle of the second century all these disruptive forces were plainly manifest. However, in Roman Britain men thought for many generations that they had answered the riddle of the Sphinx.

They misconceived the meaning of her smile.

CHAPTER 4

THE LOST ISLAND

A fragment of a helmet found in the Sutton Hoo excavations of 1939, shows a victorious Saxon cavalry soldier. The treasure was found inside a Saxon longboat which formed a tomb for a Saxon warrior's burial chamber. Information gained from the excavation has added immeasurably to our knowledge of Saxon Britain.

IN BRITAIN IT WAS FROM THE END of the third century, when Roman civilisation in Britain and the challenge to the supreme structure were equally at their height, that the inroads of barbarian people began. From this time forth the British countryside dwelt under the same kind of menace from the sea — cruel, bloody, and sudden — as do modern nations from the air. The spade of the archaeologist, correcting and enlarging the study of historians, the discovery of stones, inscriptions, coins, and skeletons, the new yields of aerial photography, all point to the same conclusion. The villa life of Britain, upon which the edifice of Roman occupation was built, was in jeopardy. We see the signs of fear spreading through the whole country. The walls of London were furnished with bastion towers, the stones for which were taken from dwelling-houses, now no longer required by a dwindling town population. Here and there the broad Roman gateways of townships were narrowed to half their size with masonry, a lasting proof of the increasing insecurity of the times. Under the Duke of the Northern Marches, Hadrian's Wall, with its garrisons, barred out the northern savages, but now at his side there must stand the Count of the Saxon Shore. All around the four hundred miles of coastline from the Wash to Southampton Water, a line of large fortresses was laboriously built, the chief of which was Richborough. They were bases for a British-Roman fleet, struggling against the sea raids of the Saxon longboats.

Such a fleet, the Classis Britannica, had been maintained from the first century. Tiles with an Admiralty mark show that it had permanent stations at Dover and Lympne. But the whole coast was organised for defence, and for long periods these measures proved effective. Vegetius, writing in the fourth century on the art of war, mentioned a special kind of light galley attached to the British fleet. These vessels, the hulls, sails, the men's clothes, and even faces, were painted sea-green, to make them invisible, and Vegetius wrote that in naval parlance they were called "the Painted Ones". Yet flotilla defence by oared galleys working from bases that were fifty to a hundred miles apart could not contend indefinitely with frequent raiding thrusts.

The Roman Britons were lively and audacious members of the Empire. They took a particularist view, yet wished to have a hand in the game themselves. While glorying in the name of citizens and Romans, and having no desire for independence, both province and army adopted a highly critical attitude towards the Imperial Government. Emperors who disregarded British opinion, or could be accused of neglecting the defences of the province, were the objects of active resentment. A series of mutinies and revolts aggravated the growing dangers of the times. Yet the pages of history reveal the repeated efforts made by the Imperial Government to protect Britannia. Again and again, in spite of revolts and ingratitude, officers and troops were sent to restore order or drive back the barbarians. In 285 the co-Emperor Maximian, deeply concerned by the raiding of the Saxon pirates, strengthened the Channel fleet, and put at its head a naval officer from Belgium named Carausius. This man was tough, resolute, ambitious, and without a scruple; from his base at Boulogne he encouraged the raiders to come and pillage, and then when they were laden with plunder he fell upon them with Roman-British flotillas, and destroyed them without mercy. His success did not satisfy the British community; they accused him of having been in league with those he had destroyed. He explained that this was all part of his ambush; but the fact that he had retained all the spoil in his own hands told heavily against him. Maximian sought to bring him to execution, but Carausius, landing in Britain, declared himself Emperor, gained the island garrison to his cause, and defeated Maximian in a sea battle. On this it was thought expedient to come to terms with the stubborn rebel and in the year 287 Carausius was tacitly recognised as in command of Britain and of Northern Gaul.

For six years this adventurer, possessing sea power, reigned in our island. He seems to have served its interests passably well. However, the Emperor and his colleagues were only biding their time, and in the year 293 they cast away all pretence of friendship. Constantius Chlorus besieged and took Boulogne, the principal continental base of Carausius, who was soon assassinated by one of his officers. The British nation now fell into confusion. The Picts from Scotland were not slow to seize their advantage. The Wall was pierced, and fire and sword wasted the northern district. Chlorus crossed the Channel as a deliverer, and was received by London with gratitude and submission. He restored order.

For two or three generations there were counterstrokes by flotillas of galleys, and hurried marchings of British auxiliaries towards the various thrusts of invasion. But although the process of wearing down was spread over many years, and misery deepened by inches, we must recognise in the year 367 circumstances of supreme and murderous horror. In that fatal year the Picts, the Scots (from Ireland), and the Saxons seemed to work in combination. All fell together upon Britannia. The Duke of the Northern Marches and the Count of the Saxon Shore were killed. A wide-open breach was made in the defences, and murderous hordes poured in upon the fine world of country houses and homesteads. The ruins tell the tale. The Mildenhall silver dinner service, now in the British Museum, is thought to have been buried at this time by its owners, when their villa was surprised by raiders. Evidently they did not live to dig it up again. The villa life of Britain only feebly recovered from the disaster. The towns were already declining.

These plates are part of a magnificent silver Roman dinner service known as the Mildenhall Treasure. Buried in the fourth century by its wealthy Romano-British owners to save it from the Saxon invaders, it was discovered during the Second World War by a farm worker. It consists of thirty-four pieces of highly ornamented silverware and is almost perfectly preserved. It can now be seen in the British Museum.

Now large numbers of people took refuge in them. At least they had walls.

After the disasters of 367 the Emperor Valentinian sent a general, Theodosius, with a considerable force to relieve the province and he achieved his task. In 383, however, the garrison and inhabitants of Britain yielded themselves willingly to a Spaniard, Magnus Maximus, who held the command in Britain and now declared himself Emperor. Scraping together all the troops he could find, and stripping the Wall and fortresses of their already scanty defenders, Maximus hastened to Gaul, and became Master of Gaul and Spain as well as Britain. For five years he struggled to defend his claim to these great dominions, but Theodosius, who was now Emperor himself, at length defeated and slew him. Meanwhile the Wall was pierced again, and Britain lay open to the raiders both from the north and from the sea. Seven years more were to pass before Theodosius could send his general, Stilicho, to the island. This great soldier drove out the intruders and repaired the defences.

Saint Alban, an early Christian martyr, gives a cross to one of his followers. Alban was a soldier in the Roman army who was executed in AD *303 for sheltering a Christian priest. Today the town of St Albans,* Roman Verulamium, *commemorates the saint.*

Stilicho returned to Rome, and was in chief command when in the same year Alaric and the Visigoths invaded Italy. He was forced to recall a further part of the British garrison to defend the heart of the Empire. In 402 he defeated Alaric and in 405 completely destroyed a second vast host. Italy was scarcely clear when a confederacy of Suevi, Vandals, Burgundians and Avars broke through the Rhine frontiers and overran Northern Gaul. The indomitable Stilicho was preparing to meet this onslaught when the British army, complaining that the province was being neglected, mutinied and set up a rival emperor, the third bearing the famous name of Constantine. Instead of protecting the island, he found himself compelled to drain Britain of troops and defend upon the Continent the titles he had usurped. In the supreme theatre for three years, with varying success, he contended with Stilicho, but was finally captured and executed.

By the beginning of the fifth century all the Legions had gone on one errand or another, and to frantic appeals for aid the helpless Emperor Honorious could only send his valedictory message in 410, that "the cantons should take steps to defend themselves".

The first glimpse we have of the British after the Roman Government had withdrawn its protection is afforded by the visit of St Germanus in 429. The Bishop came from Auxerre in order to uproot the Pelagian heresy, which in spite of other preoccupations our Christian island had been able to evolve. This doctrine consisted in assigning an undue importance to free will, and cast a consequential slur upon the doctrine of original sin. It thus threatened to deprive mankind, from its very birth, of an essential part of our inheritance. The Bishop we are assured soon convinced the doubters and eradicated the evil opinions to which they had incautiously hearkened. What kind of Britain did he find? He speaks of it as a land of wealth. There is treasure; there are flocks and herds; food is abundant; institutions, civil and religious, function; the country is prosperous, but at war. An invading army from the north or the east is approaching. It was an army said to be composed of Saxons, Picts, and Scots in ill-assorted and unholy alliance.

Another twelve years passed, and a Gaulish chronicler recorded this sombre note: "The Britons in these days by all kinds of calamities and disasters are falling into the power of the Saxons." What had happened? Something more than the forays of the fourth century: the mass migration from north Germany had begun. Thereafter the darkness closes in.

FROM EARLY TIMES

The earliest inhabitants of our islands left behind them their own, often mysterious, monuments. The Romans, Saxons and Vikings also made their marks upon the landscape: tangible evidence of how they lived and of what they achieved.

STONEHENGE, WILTSHIRE

CHEDDAR GORGE, SOMERSET, *(above)* *slices through the Mendips for more than a mile. Carved out by a river that now runs underground, its vast caverns provided shelter for some of the earliest hunters of the paleolithic age, and there is evidence that they were intermittently occupied from then to Romano-British times. Gough's Cave Museum has a collection of Old Stone Age weapons and tools made from flint, antler and bone, and the skeleton of a man who lived in the Gorge some twelve thousand years ago. At his time the Gorge evidently housed several families of hunters who possessed artistic skill.*

SKARA BRAE, ORKNEY, *(below right)* *a neolithic settlement of some seven houses, has been preserved by the sand that engulfed it in 2500* BC. *The villagers evidently fled in haste, abandoning their treasures. One woman broke her necklace, leaving a trail of beads along an alley. There were some thirty inhabitants, living on seafood and venison, clothed in skins, and adorned with animal-tooth beads, like those (below) now in the Tankerness House Museum, Kirkwall, Orkney.*

SILBURY HILL, WILTSHIRE, *(left) is the largest neolithic construction in Europe. It is one hundred and thirty feet high and covers five and a half acres. It contains over twelve million cubic feet of soil, and it has been estimated that its construction would have required some twenty million man-hours. Folklore says that the enormous mound hides the burial of a mounted warrior in gold armour, but excavations have failed to find any evidence that it was a burial mound. It was built in four stages between 2145* BC *and 95* BC, *perhaps as a great communal work to celebrate life and regeneration, or as a plinth for a stone circle. Its flat top could comfortably accommodate Stonehenge itself.*

AVEBURY, WILTSHIRE, *(above) is the site of the largest stone circle in Europe. The megaliths, which surround the village, were raised about 2300* BC. *The site was perhaps an open temple used in sun worship or fertility rites. Only twenty-seven of the original stones now remain. These stones, called sarsens (meaning "saracen" or foreign to the indigenous chalk), were hauled from Marlborough Downs.*

THE UFFINGTON HORSE, OXFORDSHIRE, *(below) was possibly cut into the chalk downs in the first century* BC. *Over three hundred and fifty feet long and one hundred and thirty feet high, it is similar to galloping horses on late Iron Age coins.*

HAMBLEDON HILL, DORSET, *(left) is one of the most impressive of Iron Age hill-forts, its triple defences festooning the hillside in spectacular fashion. Once it had grown to its present size of twenty-five acres, it was probably packed with small circular huts, now indicated by depressions in the ground. It was one of the great strongholds of the Celtic Durotriges, at the time of the Roman Conquest in* AD *43, at which date its population would have run to many thousands of people.*

BATH, AVON, *(right) was founded by the Romans, under the name of Aquae Sulis. It was dedicated to Sulis-Minerva, a characteristic combination of a Roman and a British deity, both identified with healing. It became a prosperous spa which attracted visitors from all over the Roman Empire. Its great swimming bath was fed by hot springs, and the waters were reputed to cure back troubles. Many of the vertebrae of Roman skeletons discovered at Bath show signs of spinal disorders.*

HADRIAN'S WALL, CUMBRIA AND NORTHUMBERLAND, *(right) stretches for seventy-three miles from the Tyne to the Solway. It was built between* AD *122 and 128, on the personal orders of Emperor Hadrian. The western section was initially built of turf, but later replaced with stone to match the eastern section. It was fifteen feet high, with a sentry walk along the top, and at every mile a small fort manned by thirty soldiers. Carrawburgh Fort was one of the sixteen military camps spaced along Hadrian's Wall, where the garrison was stationed. Its little temple, (above) built in the third century, was dedicated to Mithras, the Persian god popular with the legionaries.*

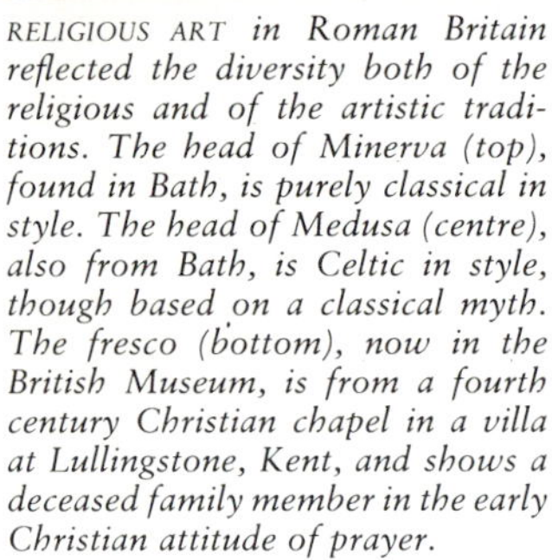

RELIGIOUS ART in Roman Britain reflected the diversity both of the religious and of the artistic traditions. The head of Minerva (top), found in Bath, is purely classical in style. The head of Medusa (centre), also from Bath, is Celtic in style, though based on a classical myth. The fresco (bottom), now in the British Museum, is from a fourth century Christian chapel in a villa at Lullingstone, Kent, and shows a deceased family member in the early Christian attitude of prayer.

TINTAGEL CASTLE, CORNWALL, (right) is famous chiefly for the legend that it was at Tintagel that King Arthur's mother and father met, though there is no real evidence to connect the legendary British leader with this wild and romantic scenery. The castle was built on the site of a Celtic monastery, probably founded by St Juliot in the sixth century.

HOLY ISLAND, NORTHUMBERLAND, *(left) was the site of Lindisfarne Priory, founded by St Aidan in 635. After repeated Viking raids, the monks left in 875.* The Lindisfarne Gospels, *(above) now in the British Museum, are among the finest examples of the Saxons' "Insular" style, which adapted the motifs of secular treasure to those of religious art.*

THE ALFRED JEWEL, *(above) now at the Ashmolean Museum, Oxford, was found four miles away from King Alfred's refuge at Athelney, Somerset. It bears the inscription "Alfred had me made," and may have been one of the bookmarkers the King circulated with his translation of* Pastoral Rule.

THE BOOK OF KELLS, *(right) now at Trinity College, Dublin, is the greatest surviving masterpiece of early Irish art. An illuminated copy of the Gospels, it takes its name from the vanished monastery of Kells, Co. Meath, founded by St Columba in the sixth century.*

ANGLO-SAXON ART *is displayed to wonderful effect in the British Museum, London: the sword pommel (left) found beneath Fetter Lane, London; the silver gilt pins, ornamented with fighting dogs (detail above), found at the River Witham, Lincolnshire; and the helmet, purse and hinged gold clasp from the treasures of the Sutton Hoo burial mound, Suffolk.*

VIKING CRAFTSMANSHIP *is most vividly demonstrated in this Danish memorial stone (far left) now at the Museum of London.*

Upon this darkness we have four windows, each obstructed by dim or coloured glass. First we have the tract of Gildas, later known as "the Wise", written in approximately AD 545. Nearly two hundred years later the Venerable Bede, whose main theme was the history of the English Church, lets fall some precious scraps of information, outside his subject, about the settlement itself. A compilation known as the Historia Britonum contains some documents earlier than Bede. Finally, in the ninth century, and very likely at the direction of King Alfred, various annals preserved in different monasteries were put together as *The Anglo-Saxon Chronicle*. Checking these by each other, and by such certainties as archaeology allows us to entertain, we have the following picture.

Imitating a common Roman practice, the dominant British chief sought about AD 450 to strengthen himself by bringing in a band of mercenaries from over the seas. They proved a trap. Once the road was open fresh fleet-loads made their way across and up the rivers, from the Humber perhaps as far round as Portsmouth. But the British resistance stiffened as the invaders got away from the coast, and their advance was brought to a standstill for nearly fifty years by a great battle won at Mount Badon.

The story of King Arthur and the Round Table owes everything to a twelfth-century historian, Geoffrey of Monmouth, who wrote long after the event. Few references to Arthur's existence were made in his own time, but later poets, among them Tennyson, have woven marvellous legends around his name and Court. This version of the Round Table, made in the Middle Ages, hangs in the hall of Winchester Castle.

So far this tale is confirmed, historically and geographically. Gildas could have heard the story of the mercenaries from old men whom he had known in his youth, and there is no real ground for doubting the statements of Nennius, a compiler probably of the ninth century, and Bede, who agree that the name of the deceived chief who invited these deadly foes was Vortigern. Hengist was the mercenary ready to sell his sword and his ships to anyone who would give him land on which to support his men; and the land he took was the future kingdom of Kent.

Nennius tells us, what Gildas omits, the name of the British soldier who won the crowning mercy of Mount Badon, and that name takes us out of the mist of dimly remembered history into the daylight of romance. It was Arthur. There looms, large, uncertain, dim but glittering, the legend of the Knights of the Round Table. Somewhere in the island a great captain gathered the forces of Roman Britain and fought the barbarian invaders to the death. Around him, around his name and his deeds, shine all that romance and poetry can bestow. Twelve battles, all located in scenes untraceable, with foes unknown, except that they were heathen, are punctiliously set forth in the Latin of Nennius. Later these tales would be retold and embellished by the genius of Mallory, Spenser, and Tennyson. True or false, they have gained an immortal hold upon the thoughts of men.

Certainly the latest and best informed writers unite to proclaim Arthur's reality. They cannot tell where he held sway and fought his battles. They are ready to believe however that there was a great British warrior who kept the light of civilisation burning against all the storms that beat, and that behind his sword there sheltered a faithful following of which the memory did not fail. All four groups of the Celtic tribes which dwelt in the tilted uplands of Britain cheered themselves with the Arthurian legend, and each claimed their own region as the scene of his exploits. From Cornwall to Cumberland a search for Arthur's realm or sphere has been pursued. Yet once Arthur is recognised as the commander of a mobile field army, moving from one part of the country to another and uniting with local forces in each district, the disputes about the scenes of his actions explain themselves. The fourth century witnessed the rise of the cavalry to the dominant position in the

Pair of silver spoons bearing the names Saul and Paul in Greek, found in the Sutton Hoo ship-burial. They date from the seventh century and are now in the British Museum.

battlefield. The Saxon invaders were infantry, fighting with sword and spear, and having little armour. Against such an enemy a small force of ordinary Roman cavalry might well prove invincible. If a chief like Arthur had gathered a band of mail-clad cavalry he could have moved freely about Britain, everywhere heading the local resistance to the invader and gaining repeated victories.

Arthur's twelfth battle, wrote Nennius, ". . . was on Mount Badon, in which there fell in one day nine hundred and sixty men from the onslaught of Arthur only, and no one laid them low save he alone. And in all his battles he was victor. But they, when in all these battles they had been overthrown, sought help from Germany and increased without intermission . . ."

All efforts to fix the battlefield of Mount Badon have failed. A hundred learned investigations have brought no results, but the best claimant to the title is Liddington Camp, which looks down on Badbury, near Swindon. On the other hand, we are able to fix the date with some accuracy, as betweeen 490 and 503. If we could see exactly what happened then we should surely find ourselves in the presence of a theme as well-founded, as inspired, and as inalienable from the inheritance of mankind as the *Odyssey* or the Old Testament. It is all true, or it ought to be. And wherever men are fighting against barbarism, tyranny, and massacre, for freedom, law, and honour, let them remember that the fame of their deeds, even though they themselves be exterminated, may be celebrated as long as the world rolls round. Let us then declare that King Arthur and his noble knights, guarding the sacred flame of Christianity and the theme of a world order, sustained by valour, physical strength, and good horses and armour, slaughtered innumerable hosts of foul barbarians and set decent folk an example for all time.

The invaders themselves, however, were not without their yearnings for order and settled security. Their forays, the rigours they endured, were but the results of the immense pressures behind them as the hordes of avid humanity spread westward from central Asia. In the fifth century, as the pressure from the east grew harder and as the annual raiding parties returned from Britain with plunder and tales of wealth, there was created in the ruling minds a sense of the difficulty of getting to the island, and consequently of the security which would attend its occupation by a hardy and valiant race. Here, perhaps, men might settle down and enjoy the good things of life without the haunting fear of subjugation by a stronger hand. To these savage swords Britain seemed a refuge. Thus, in the wake of the raiders there grew steadily the plan and system of settlement. With despair behind and hope before, the migration to Britain and its occupation grew from year to year.

No uniformity of practice prevailed in the island. There is good reason to think that the newcomers in Kent settled down beside the old inhabitants, whose name, Cantiaci, they adopted. In Northumbria there are strong traces of Celtic law. In Hampshire and Wiltshire a broad belt of British names, from Liss to Deverill, seems to show the natives still cultivating their old friends on the downs.

Yet the evidence of place names suggests that in Sussex extermination was the rule. Farther west there are grounds for thinking that a substantial British population survived, and the old West Saxon code of AD 694 makes careful provision for the rights of "Welshmen" of various degrees. Thus serious writers contend that the Anglo-Saxon conquest was for the bulk of the British community mainly a change of masters. The rich were slaughtered; the brave and proud fell back in large numbers upon the western mountains. Other numerous bands escaped betimes to Brittany, whence their remote posterity were one day to return.

The Saxon was, moreover, a valley settler. His notion of an economic holding was a meadow for hay near the stream, the lower slopes under the plough, the upper slopes kept for pasture. But in many places a long time must have passed before these lower grounds could be cleared and drained, and while this work was in progress what did he live on but the produce of the upland British farms? It is more natural to suppose that he would keep his natives working as serfs on the land with which they were familiar until the valley was ready for sowing. But the language of the valley-settlers, living in compact groups, would be dominant over that of the hill-cultivators, scattered in small and isolated holdings. The study of modern English place names has shown that hill, wood, and stream names are often Celtic in origin, even in regions where the village names are Anglo-Saxon. In this way, without assuming any wholesale extermination, the disappearance of the British language can be explained even in areas where we know a British population to have survived. Thus it came about that both Latin and British yielded to the speech of the newcomers so completely that hardly a trace of either is to be found in our earliest records.

The tiny church of St Lawrence at Bradford on Avon, in Wiltshire, is a near-perfect survival of Saxon architecture.

The history books of our childhood attempted courageously to prescribe exact dates for the main settlements. In 449 Hengist and Horsa, invited by Vortigern, founded the Jutish kingdom of Kent upon the corpses of its former inhabitants. In 477 Ella and his three sons arrived to continue the inroad. In 495 Cerdic and Cynric appeared. In 501 Port, the pirate, founded Portsmouth. In 514 the West Saxons, Stuf and Wihtgar, descended in their turn and put the Britons to flight. In 544 Wihtgar was killed. In 547 came Ida, founder of the kingdom of Northumberland. All that can be said about these dates is that they correspond broadly to the facts, and that these successive waves of invaders, bringing behind them settlers, descended on our unhappy shores.

Certainly of all the tribes of the Germanic race none was more cruel than the Saxons. Their very name, which spread to the whole confederacy of northern tribes, was supposed to be derived from the use of a weapon, the seax, a short one-handed sword.

The society they introduced was based on two principles: the power of money and the power of lordship. If there were rights they were primarily the rights of property. There was no crime committed which could not be compounded by a money payment and there was no offence more heinous than that of theft. An elaborate tariff prescribed in shillings the "wergild" or exact value or worth of every man. An atheling, or prince, was worth 1500 shillings, a shilling being the value of a cow in Kent, or of a sheep elsewhere; an eorl, or nobleman, 300 shillings. A ceorl, now degraded to the word "churl", who was a yeoman farmer, was worth 100 shillings, a laet, or agricultural serf, forty to eighty shillings, and a slave nothing. The life of a slaughtered man could thus be compounded for cash. With money all was possible. Yet wergild at least, as Alfred said long afterwards, was better than the blood feud.

The foundation of the Germanic system was blood and kin. The family was the unit, the tribe was the whole. The great transition which we witness

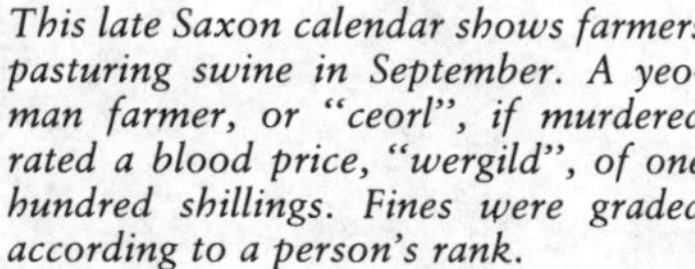

This late Saxon calendar shows farmers pasturing swine in September. A yeoman farmer, or "ceorl", if murdered rated a blood price, "wergild", of one hundred shillings. Fines were graded according to a person's rank.

among the emigrants is the abandonment of blood and kin as the theme of their society and its replacement by local societies and lordship based on the ownership of land. This change arose, like so many of the lessons learnt by men, from the grim needs of war. Fighting for life and foothold against men as hard-pressed as themselves, each pioneering band fell inevitably into the hands of the bravest, most commanding, most fortunate war leader. This was no longer a foray of a few months, or at the outside a year. Here were settlements to be founded. These must be guarded, and who could guard them except the bold chieftains who had gained them over the corpses of their former owners?

Thus the settlement in England was to modify the imported structure of Germanic life. The armed farmer-colonists found themselves forced to accept a stronger state authority owing to the stresses of continued military action. In Germany they had no kings. They developed them in Britain from leaders who claimed descent from the ancient gods. The position of the king continually increased in importance, and his supporters or companions gradually formed a new class in society, which carried with it the germ of feudalism, and was in the end to dominate all other conventions. Insensibly, at first, but with growing speed from the seventh century onwards, a landed aristocracy was created owing all it had to the king. While the resistance of the Britons was vigorously maintained, and the fortunes of the struggle swung this way and that way for nearly two hundred years, this new institution of personal leadership established in the war chief sank deeply into the fibre of the Anglo-Saxon invaders.

CHAPTER 5
ENGLAND

A RED SUNSET; A LONG NIGHT; a pale, misty dawn! But as the light grows it becomes apparent to remote posterity that everything has changed. Night has fallen on Britannia. Dawn rose on England, humble, poor, barbarous, degraded and divided, but alive. Britannia had been an active part of a world state; England was once again a barbarian island. It had been Christian, it was now heathen. Its inhabitants had rejoiced in well-planned cities, with temples, markets, academies. They had nourished craftsmen and merchants, professors of literature and rhetoric. For four hundred years there had been order and law, respect for property, and a widening culture. All had vanished. The buildings, such as they were, were now of wood, not stone. The people had lost entirely the art of writing. Nor did the seeds of recovery spring from the savage hordes who had wrecked the Roman culture. They would certainly have continued to welter indefinitely in squalor, but for the fact that a new force was stirring beyond the seas which, moving slowly, fitfully, painfully, among the ruins of civilisation, reached at length by various paths the unhappy island.

Christianity had not been established as the official religion of the Empire during the first two centuries of the Roman occupation of Britain. It grew with many other cults in the large and easy tolerance of the Imperial system. There arose however a British Christian Church which sent its bishops to the early councils, and had, as we have seen, sufficient vitality to develop the Pelagian heresy of free will from its own unaided heart-searchings. When the evil days overtook the land and the long struggle with the Saxons was fought out the British Church fell back with other survivors upon the western parts of the island. Such was the gulf between the warring races that no attempt was made at any time by the British bishops to Christianise the invaders. Perhaps they were not given any chance of converting them. After an interval one of their leading luminaries, afterwards known as St David, accomplished the general conversion of what is now Wales. But apart from this, British Christianity languished within its refuges, and might well have become moribund but for the appearance of a most remarkable and charming personality.

Celtic Cross from Tipperary, Ireland. This fine example, with its interlaced pattern on the face and carved figures round the base, dates from the eighth century. Many such crosses can still be seen in Ireland, the Isle of Man and the north of England.

St Patrick was a Roman Briton of good family dwelling probably in the Severn valley. His father was a Christian deacon, a Roman citizen, and a member of the municipal council. One day in the early fifth century there descended upon the district a band of Irish raiders, burning and slaying. The young Patrick was carried off and sold into slavery in Ireland. For six years, he tended swine, and loneliness led him to seek comfort in religion. He was led by miraculous promptings to attempt escape. He made his way to a port, found a ship, and persuaded the captain to take him on board. After many wanderings he sailed back in 432 to the wild regions which he had quitted and brought Ireland into touch with the Church of western Europe and made it indissolubly part of universal Christendom. On a somewhat lower plane, although also held in perpetual memory, was the banishing of snakes and reptiles of all kinds from the Irish soil.

It was therefore from Ireland that the Gospel was carried to the north of Britain and for the first time cast its redeeming spell upon the Pictish invaders. Columba, born half a century after St Patrick's death, but an offspring of his Church, and imbued with his grace and fire, proved a new champion of the Faith. From the monastery which he established in the island of Iona his disciples went forth to the British kingdom of Strathclyde, to the Pictish tribes of the north, and to the Anglian kingdom of Northumbria. He is the founder of the Scottish Christian Church. There was however a distinction in the form of Christianity which reached England through the mission of St Columba and that which was more generally accepted throughout the Christianised countries of Europe. It was monastic in its form, and it travelled from the east through northern Ireland to its new home without touching at any moment the Roman centre. The Celtic churches therefore received a form of ecclesiastical government which was supported by the loosely knit communities of monks and preachers, and was not in these early decisive periods associated with the universal organisation of the Papacy.

The first church of St Martin in Canterbury, used by Augustine during the conversion of Kent. Parts of the Roman walls can still be seen, but the church has been largely rebuilt.

In spite of the slow means of travel and scanty news, the Papacy had from an early stage followed with deep attention the results of St Columba's labours. It saw with thankfulness an ardent Christian movement afoot in these remote northern islands, and with concern that it was from the outset independent of the Papal throne. It was therefore decided in the closing decade of the sixth century that a guide and teacher should be sent to England to diffuse and stimulate the Faith, to convert the heathen, and also to bring about an effective working union between British Christians and the main body of the Church. For this high task Pope Gregory selected a cultured monk. St Augustine, as he is known to history, began his mission in 596 under hopeful auspices. Kent had always been the part of the British island most closely in contact with Europe, and the most advanced in culture. The King of Kent had married a Christian, Bertha, daughter of the Frankish king and with her aid Augustine converted King Ethelbert. Upon the ruins of the ancient British church of St Martin he refounded the Christian life of Canterbury, which was destined to become the centre and summit of religious England.

Ethelbert, as overlord of England, exercised an effective authority over the kingdoms of the south and west. His policy was at once skilful and ambitious; his conversion to Christianity, however sincere, was also in consonance with his secular aims. He was himself now, as the only English Christian ruler, in a position where he might hold out the hand to the British princes, and, by using the Christian faith as a bond of union, establish his supremacy over the whole country. This, no doubt, was also in accordance with the ideas which Augustine had carried from Rome. Thus at the opening of the seventh century Ethelbert and Augustine summoned a conference of the British Christian bishops. The place chosen in the Severn valley was on the frontier between the English and British domains. Here, then, would be a chance of a general and lasting peace for both races, reconciled in the name of Jesus Christ.

The discussions were ostensibly confined to interesting but uncontroversial questions. There was the date of Easter, which is still debated, and also the form of the tonsure. Augustine urged the Roman custom of shaving only the top of the head. The British bishops had perhaps imitated the Druidical method of shaving from the centre to the ears, leaving a fringe on the forehead. It was a choice of the grotesque. These matters conveniently offered ample pasture upon which the conferences could browse in public, while the vital issues were settling themselves behind the scenes.

But the British bishops were in no mood to throw themselves into the strong embraces of Rome. Why should they, who had so long defended the Faith against horrible cruelties and oppressions, now receive their guidance from a Saxon Kentish king whose conversion was brand-new, and whose political designs were obvious? When Augustine found himself in the presence of what he deemed to be unreasonable prejudice and deep-seated hostility, he fell back upon threats. If British Christianity would not accept the fair offers now made, the whole influence and prestige of Rome would be thrown against them upon the English side. The Saxon armies would be blessed and upheld by Rome and no sympathy would be felt for these long-faithful British Christians when they had their throats cut by the new English convert states. "If," Augustine exclaimed, "you will not have peace from your friends you shall have war from your foes." But this was no more than the British had faced for the past two hundred years. It was the sort of language they understood. The bishops' conference separated in enmity; the breach was irreparable.

Augustine's mission therefore drew to a dignified but curtailed end. Except for the consecration of Mellitus as Bishop of the East Saxons in a church on the site of St Paul's, he had made little attempt to proselytise outside Kent, though from the title loosely accorded him of "Apostle of the English" he enjoyed for many centuries the credit of having reconverted the once-famous Roman province of Britannia to the Christian faith.

Almost a generation passed before envoys from Rome began to penetrate into northern England and rally its peoples to Christianity, and then it came about in the wake of political and dynastic developments. By a series of victories Redwald, King of the East Angles, had established a wide dominion over the lands of central England from the Dee to the Humber. With Redwald's aid the crown of Northumbria was gained by an exiled prince, Edwin, who by his abilities won his way, step by step, to the foremost position in England. Even before the death of his ally Redwald, Edwin was recognised as overlord of all the English kingdoms except Kent, and later became converted to Christianity by marrying a Christian princess of Kent. Consequently, in her train from Canterbury to Edwin's capital at York there rode in 625 the first Roman missionary to northern England, Paulinus, an envoy who had first come to Britain in the days of Augustine, twenty-four years before.

The ample kingdom of Northumbria, shaped like England itself in miniature, now became Christian. But this blessed event brought with it swift and dire consequences. The overlordship of Northumbria was fiercely resented by King Penda of Mercia, or, as we should now say, of the Midlands. The drama unfolded with staggering changes of fortune. In 633 Penda, the heathen, made an unnatural alliance with the Christian British King of North Wales, Cadwallon, with the object of breaking the Northumbrian power. Here for the first time noticed in history British and English

Augustine preached Christianity in a land that was rich with legends such as that of Wayland the Smith, a mythical maker of armour, shown here in this detail from the Franks Casket. Made from whalebone in the early eighth century, the casket also depicts scenes from legends of many different lands and can be seen in the British Museum.

MEDIEVAL FARMING

In his book English Social History *G. M. Trevelyan describes how the early farming system of the Saxons was eventually developed into the feudal system of the Normans.*

The most characteristic method of cultivation in medieval England was the "open field". It implied a village community, working huge unenclosed fields on a principle of strip allotments. Each farmer had a certain number of arable strips, of half an acre or one acre each. His long narrow strips did not lie next to one another but were scattered over the "open field" between those of his neighbours. The outline of many of these strips can still clearly be seen. The ridge and furrow of pasture fields is one of the commonest features of the English landscape today.

The whole vast open field was surrounded, when necessary, not by permanent hedges but by movable hurdles. There might be two, three or more of these great arable fields belonging to the village and subdivided among the farmers; one of the fields lay fallow while the others were under crop. The meadowlands for hay were cultivated on a similar principle. Both meadowland and arable, after hay and corn had been cut, were thrown open for common pasture.

This system of cultivation, originated by the first Anglo-Saxon settlers, was economically sound as long as the object of each farmer was to raise food for his family rather than for the market. It combined the advantages of individual labour and public control; it saved the expense of fencing; it bound the villagers together as a community and gave to the humblest his own land and a voice in the agricultural policy of the village.

On this democracy of peasant cultivators was [eventually] superimposed the feudal power and legal rights of the lord of the manor. The peasant cultivators, in relation to each other, were a self-governing community, but in relation to the lord of the manor they were serfs. They had not the legal right to leave their holdings: they were "bound to the soil". They must grind their corn at the lord's mill. They could not give their children in marriage without his consent. Above all, they owed him field service on certain days of the year, when they must labour not on their own land but on his.

St Hilda portrayed in stained glass in Oxford cathedral. Hilda, one of many remarkable Saxon women, was related to the royal lines of both Northumbria and East Anglia, and was the foundress of the monastery at Whitby in AD *657, which offered separate accommodation for both men and women.*

The ruins of Whitby Abbey, North Yorkshire. The Synod, or Council of Whitby, was held here in AD *663. At this historic meeting King Oswy of Northumbria decreed that the date of Easter and other Church festivals should be calculated according to Rome. This decision brought Britain into the mainstream of European Christianity; previously the Northumbrian monks had contested Roman authority.*

fought side by side. Politics for once proved stronger than religion or race and in a savage battle near Doncaster Edwin was defeated and slain, and his head — not the last — was exhibited on the ramparts of captured York. This sudden destruction of the greatest king who had hitherto ruled in the island by British Cadwallon was the paying off of very old but very heavy debts. We might almost be seeing again the spirit of Boadicea. But the inherent power of Northumbria was great. Edwin's successor, Oswald, had but to appear to find himself at the head of the newly Christianised and also infuriated Saxon warriors. Within a year of the death of Edwin, Oswald destroyed Cadwallon and his British forces in the last pitched battle between the Britons and the Saxons. The Britons were overthrown and cast aside. The long story of their struggle with the invaders ended thus in no fine way; but what is important to our tale is that it had ended at last.

The destruction of Cadwallon and the clearance from Northumbria of the wild western Britons, whose atrocities had united all the Saxon forces in the north, was the prelude to the struggle with King Penda. He was regarded by the Saxon tribes as one who had brought boundless suffering and slaughter upon them through a shameful pact with the hereditary foe. Nevertheless he prospered for a while. He upheld the claims of Thor and Woden with all the strength of Mercia for seven years. He defeated, decapitated, and dismembered King Oswald, as he had destroyed his predecessor before him. But a younger brother of Oswald, Oswy by name, after a few years settled the family account, and Penda fell by the sword he had drawn too often. Thus the power of Northumbria rose the stronger from the ordeal and eclipse through which its people had passed.

The failure of Ethelbert's attempt to make a Christian reunion of England and Britain left the direction of the immediate future with the Northumbrian Court. It was to York and not to Canterbury that Rome looked, and upon English, not British, armies that the hopes of organised Christendom were placed. When the disasters had overtaken Northumbria, Paulinus had hastened back by sea to Canterbury. Carefully trained as they were in the doctrines, interests, and policy of the Papacy, neither he nor Augustine was the stuff of which martyrs or evangelists are made. This British incursion was too rough. But the lieutenant of Paulinus, one James the Deacon, stuck to his post through the whole struggle, and preached and baptised continually in the midst of rapine and carnage.

Still more important than his work was that of a Celtic mission to Northumbria under St Aidan. Much of Mercia and East Anglia, as well as Northumbria, was recovered to Christianity by the Celtic missionaries. Thus two streams of the Christian faith once more met in England, and the immediate future was to witness a struggle for supremacy between them.

The celebrated and largely successful attempt to solve this struggle took place at the Synod, or Council of Whitby in 663. There the hinging issue was whether British Christianity should conform to the general life plan of Christendom or whether it should be expressed by the monastic orders which had founded the Celtic churches of the north. The issues hung in the balance, but in the end after much pious dissertation the decision was taken that the Church of Northumbria should be a definite part of the Church of Rome and of the Catholic system. Mercia soon afterwards conformed. Though the Celtic leader and his following retired in disgust to Iona, and the Irish clergy refused to submit, the importance of this event cannot be overrated. Instead of a religion controlled by the narrow views of abbots pursuing their strict rule of life in their various towns or remote resorts, there was opened to every member of the English Church the broad vista of a world-state and universal communion. These events brought Northumbria to her zenith. In Britain for the first time there was achieved a unity of faith, morals, and Church government covering five-sixths of the island, with by far the greater and more powerful part becoming directly associated with the Papacy.

There followed a long and intricate rivalry for leadership between the various Anglo-Saxon kings which occupied the seventh and eighth centuries. It was highly important to those whose span of life was cast in that period, but it left small marks on the subsequent course of history. Let a few words suffice. The primacy of Northumbria was menaced and finally ended by the inherent geographical and physical weakness of its position. It was beset from the north by the Picts, on the west by the British kingdom of Strathclyde, in the south by Mercia. Its collapse as the leading community in the island was inevitable.

Northumbria was fortunate however in having in this twilight scene a chronicler whose words have descended to us out of the long silence of the past. Bede, a monk of high ability, working unknown in the recesses of the Church, now comes forward as almost the only audible voice from the British islands in these dim times. The name of "the Venerable Bede" still carries with it a proud renown. He alone attempts to paint for us, and, so far as he can, explain the spectacle of Anglo-Saxon England in its first phase: a Christian England, divided by tribal, territorial, dynastic, and personal feuds into what an Elizabethan antiquary called the Heptarchy, seven kingdoms all professing the Gospel of Christ, and striving over each other for mastery by force and fraud.

For nearly eighty years two Mercian kings asserted or maintained their ascendancy over all England south of the Humber: Ethelbald and Offa. The chronicles of Ethelbald are scanty. He showed charity to the poor; he preserved law and order; in 733 he raided Wessex; and in 740 he laid parts of Northumbria waste while its harassed chief was struggling with the Picts. After this last victory he took to styling himself "King of the Southern English" and "King of Britain". South of the Humber these claims were made good.

Ethelbald, having been at length murdered by his guards, was succeeded by a greater man. Little is known of Offa, a contemporary of Charlemagne, but the imprint of his power is visible not only throughout England but upon the Continent. His policy interlaced with that of Europe; he was reputed to be the first "King of the English", and he had the first quarrel since Roman times with the mainland.

Charlemagne wished one of his sons to marry one of Offa's daughters. Here we have an important proof of the esteem in which the Englishman was held. Offa stipulated that his son must simultaneously marry a daughter of Charlemagne. The founder of the Holy Roman Empire appeared at first incensed at this assumption of equality, but after a while he found it expedient to renew his friendship with Offa. It seems that "the King of the English" had placed an embargo upon continental merchandise, and the inconvenience of this retaliation speedily overcame all points of pride and sentiment. Very soon Offa was again the Emperor's "dearest brother", and

The Venerable Bede, a monk of Jarrow, is seen writing his Ecclesiastical History *which he completed in* AD *731. Bede was the first historian to date historical events from the birth of Christ.*

This coin commemorates the great King Offa of Mercia.

Charlemagne is seen agreeing to arrange that there should be reciprocity of royal protection in both countries for merchants, "according to the ancient custom of trading". Apparently the commodities in question were "black stones", presumably coal from France, in return for English cloaks. Thus we see Offa admitted to equal rank with the greatest figure in Europe. Monarchs of mighty empires do not make marriage contracts for their children and beat out the details of commercial treaties with persons of little or no consequence.

We learn about Offa almost entirely through his impact on his neighbours. It is clear from their records that he suppressed the under-kings of the Severn valley, that he defeated the West Saxons in Oxfordshire and subjugated Berkshire, that he decapitated the King of East Anglia, that he was master of London, that he extirpated the monarchy which Hengist had founded in Kent. He captured its mint and inscribed his name upon the coins issued by the Archbishop of Canterbury. One of these coins tells its own quaint tale. It is a gold dinar, nicely copied from an Arabic die, and is stamped with the superscription *Rex Offa*. The Canterbury mint evidently regarded the Arabic as mere ornamentation, and would have been shocked had they known that it declared "There is no God but one, and Mahomet is his Prophet". Offa established a good understanding with the Pope, and paid a small annual tribute to the Papacy, part of it unwittingly in these same infidel coins which proclaimed an opposite creed.

We have a tangible monument of Offa in the immense dyke which he caused to be built between Saxon England and the still unconquered British. This dyke, which runs over the hills and dales, leaving gaps for the impenetrable forests, from the mouth of the Severn to the neighbourhood of the Mersey, attests to our day the immense authority of the state over which Offa presided. Such works are not constructed except upon a foundation of effective political power. But Offa's Dyke shows policy as well as manpower. In many sections it follows lines favourable to the British, and historians have concluded that it was a boundary rather than a fortification, and resulted from an agreement reached for common advantage. It was not a Roman wall, like those of Antoninus and Hadrian, between savagery and civilisation, but rather the expression of a solemn treaty which for a long spell removed from Offa the menace of a British incursion, and thus set him free with his back secure to parley and dispute with Europe.

Art and culture grew in the track of order. The English had brought with them from their continental home a vigorous barbaric art and a primitive poetry. Once established in the island, this art was profoundly affected by the Celtic genius for curve and colour, a genius suppressed by Roman provincialism, but breaking out again as soon as the Roman hand was removed. Christianity gave them a new range of subjects to adorn. The results are seen in such masterpieces as the Lindisfarne Gospels and the sculptured crosses of northern England. A whole world of refinement and civilisation of which the monasteries were the home, and of which only fragments have come down to us, had come into being. Bede was universally honoured as the greatest scholar of his day. It is to his influence that the world owes the practice, adopted later, of reckoning the years from the birth of Christ. Aldhelm of Malmesbury was the most popular writer in Europe; of no author were more copies made in the monasteries of the Continent. Vernacular poetry flourished; in Wessex the first steps had been taken in the

Lindisfarne
NORTHUMBERLAND
Land ruled by Offa
York
MERCIA
EAST ANGLIA
Offa's Dyke
ESSEX
London
KENT
WESSEX
SUSSEX
0 miles 100

Offa's Dyke, the earthwork boundary close to the Welsh border, bears lasting testimony to the Mercian king's energy and authority in the eighth century. Today the rampart is a favourite place for hiking.

art of prose writing. In the eighth century, indeed, England had claims to stand in the van of western culture.

After the shapeless confusion of darker centuries, obscure to history and meaningless to almost all who lived through them, we now see a purpose steadily forming. England, with an independent character and personality, might scarcely yet be a part of a world civilisation as in Roman times, but there was a new England, closer than ever before to national unity, and with a native genius of her own.

CHAPTER 6

THE VIKINGS

AFTER THE FALL OF IMPERIAL ROME the victorious barbarians were in their turn enthralled by the Gospel of Christ. Though no more successful in laying aside their sinful promptings than religious men and women are today, they had a common theme and inspiration. There was a bond which linked all the races of Europe, and an international organisation at the head of which the Bishop of Rome revived in an ecclesiastical form the vanished authority of the Caesars. Everywhere, from the Euphrates to the Boyne, old gods were forsworn, and a priest of Christ could travel far and wide, finding in every town an understanding brotherhood and a universal if sometimes austere hospitality. The virtual monopoly of learning and the art of writing made the churchmen indispensable to the proud and violent chieftains of the day. The clerics became the civil servants, and often the statesmen, of every Court. They fell naturally, inevitably, into the place of the Roman magistrates whose garb they wore, and wear today. Triumphant barbarism yielded itself insensibly to a structure, reliance upon which was proved on numberless occasions to give success in the unending struggle for power.

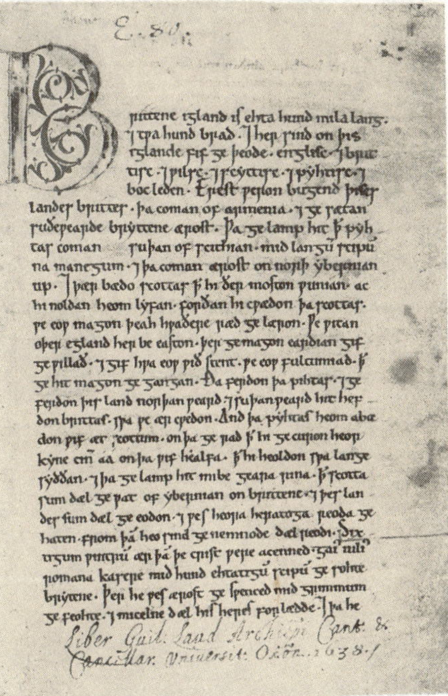

The Anglo-Saxon Chronicle *presents an invaluable source for English history from the invasion of Caesar, which it dates as 60* BC, *to the death of Henry II in 1154. It is now thought that the original chronicler was not King Alfred himself, but a nobleman of his court.*

Upon this revived, convalescent, loosely knit society there now fell two blasting external assaults. The first came from the east, where from 622 Mahomet and his successors, the Caliphs, made themselves masters of all Arabia, Persia, much of the Byzantine Empire, and the whole North African shore. At the beginning of the next century Islam crossed the Straits of Gibraltar and prevailed in Spain, whence it was not finally to be dislodged for nearly eight hundred years. For Britain however was reserved the second invading wave. It came from the north.

One summer day, probably in 789, while, according to *The Anglo-Saxon Chronicle*, "the innocent English people, spread through their plains, were enjoying themselves in tranquillity and yoking their oxen to the plough", news was carried to King Offa's officer, the Reeve of Dorchester, that three ships had arrived on the coast. The Reeve "leapt on his horse and rode with a few men to the harbour [probably Portland], thinking that they were merchants and not enemies. Giving his commands as one who had authority, he ordered them to be sent to the King's town; but they slew him on the spot and all who were with him."

This was a foretaste of the murderous struggle which, with many changes of fortune, was to harry and devastate England for two hundred and fifty years. It was the beginning of the Viking Age.

An eighth-century picture stone from Gotland in Sweden, showing a Viking hero entering the Norse heaven of Valhalla. Underneath the departing warrior is a ship with an embroidered sail spread to catch the wind.

Measure for measure, what the Saxon pirates had given to the Britons was now meted out to the English after the lapse of four hundred years. In the eighth century a vehement manifestation of conquering energy appeared in Scandinavia. Norway, Sweden, and Denmark threw up bands of formidable fighting men, who, in addition to all their other martial qualities, were the hardy rovers of the sea. Their prowess was amazing. One current of marauding vigour struck southward from Sweden, and reached Constantinople. Another contingent sailed in their longboats from Norway to the Mediterranean, and harried all the shores of the inland sea. The third far-ranging impulse carried the Scandinavian buccaneers to the British Isles, to Normandy, to Iceland, and presently across the Atlantic Ocean to the American continent.

The relations between the Danes and the Norwegians were tangled and varying. Sometimes they raided in collusion; sometimes they fought each other; but to Saxon England they presented themselves in the common guise of a merciless scourge and they were incredibly cruel.

The soul of the Vikings lay in the longship. They had evolved, and now, in the eighth and ninth centuries, carried to perfection, a vessel which by its shallow draught could sail far up rivers, and which by its beautiful lines and suppleness of construction could ride out the fiercest storms. Its picture rises before us vivid and bright: the finely carved, dragon-shaped prow; the high, curving stern; the long row of shields, black and yellow alternately, ranged along the sides; the gleam of steel; the scent of murder.

Yet this superb instrument of sea power would have been useless without the men who handled it. In the sagas we read of crews of "champions, or merry men": a ship's company picked no doubt from many applicants, "as good at the helm or oar as they were with the sword". There were strict regulations, or early "Articles of War", governing these crews once they had joined. Men were taken between the ages of sixteen and sixty, but none without a trial of his strength and activity. No feud or old quarrel must be taken up while afloat or on service. No woman was allowed on board. All taken in war was to be brought to the pile or stake, and there sold and divided according to rule. This war booty was personal; that is to say, it was not part of the property which passed by Scandinavian law to a man's kindred. He was entitled to have it buried with him.

In 793, on a January morning, the wealthy monastic settlement of Lindisfarne (or Holy Island), off the Northumbrian coast, was suddenly attacked by a powerful fleet from Denmark. They sacked the place, devoured the cattle, killed many of the monks, and sailed away with a rich booty in gold, jewels, and sacred emblems, and all the monks who were likely to fetch a good price in the European slavemarket. This raid had been planned with care and knowledge. It was executed by complete surprise in the dead of winter before any aid from the shore could reach the island. The news of the atrocity travelled far and wide, not only in England but throughout Europe, and the loud cry of the Church sounded a general alarm.

It was not till 835 that the storm broke in fury, and fleets, sometimes of three or four hundred vessels, rowed up the rivers of England, France, and Russia in predatory enterprises on the greatest scale. For thirty years southern England was constantly attacked. Paris was more than once besieged. In many cases now the raiders settled upon the conquered territory. The Norwegian Vikings, coming from a still more severe climate, found the Scottish islands good for settlement. They colonised the Shetlands, the Faroes, and Ireland. Dublin was founded by the Vikings under Olaf. They reached Greenland and Labrador. They sailed up the St Lawrence. They discovered America; but set little store by the achievement.

For a long time no permanent foothold was gained in England or France. It was not until 865, when resistance on the Continent had temporarily stiffened, that the great Danish invasion of Northumbria and eastern England began.

Saxon England was at this time ripe for the sickle. The invaders broke in upon the whole eastern seaboard, once guarded by the Count of the Saxon Shore, with its Imperial fortresses in ruins, buried already under the soil of centuries. No Roman slaves now plied their oars upon the patrol courses. There was no Imperial Government to send a great commander or a Legion to the rescue. But on all sides were abbeys and monasteries, churches, and even cathedrals, possessed in that starveling age of treasures of gold and silver, of jewels, and also large stores of food, wine, and such luxuries as were known. The pious English had accepted far too literally the idea of the absolution of sins as the consequence of monetary payment to the Church. Their sins were many, their repentances frequent, and the Church had thrived. Here were easy prizes for sharp swords to win.

To an undue subservience to the Church the English at this time added military mismanagement. Their system of defence was adapted to keeping the survivors of the ancient Britons in their barren mountain lands or guarding the frontier against an incursion by a Saxon neighbour. The local noble, upon the summons of his chief or king, could call upon the able-bodied cultivators of the soil to serve in their own district for about forty days. This service, in the "fyrd", was grudgingly given, and when it was over the army dispersed without paying regard to the enemies who might be afoot or the purposes for which the campaign had been undertaken. Now the English were confronted with a different type of enemy. The Danes and Norsemen had not only the advantages of surprise which sea power so long imparted, but they showed both mobility and skill on land. They adopted the habit of fortifying their camps with almost Roman thoroughness. Their stratagems also have been highly praised. Among these "feigned flight" was foremost. Again and again we read that the English put the heathen army to rout, but at the end of the day the Danes held the field. On one occasion their leader, who was besieging a town, declared himself to be dying and begged the bishop of the place to give him Christian burial. The worthy churchman rejoiced in the conversion and acceded to the request, but when the body of

Viking raiders brandishing axes. The carving on this ninth-century stone slab from the monastery of Lindisfarne records the savage attack on this unprotected treasure house in 793.

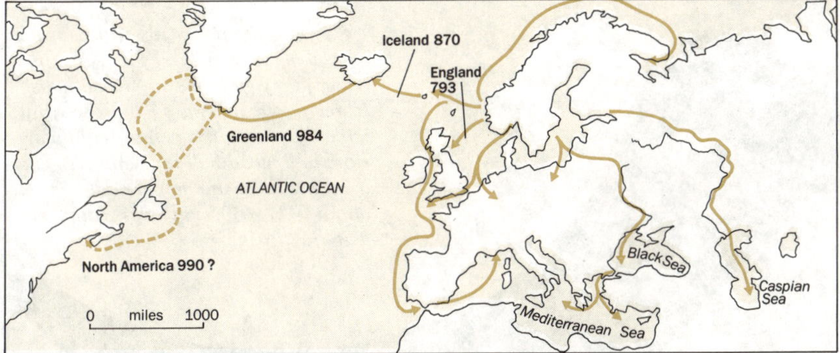

The voyages of the Vikings. The fiords of the Scandinavian coast provided a perfect environment for training seamen, and the barren ridges separating the long harbours encouraged generations of them to seek fertile land elsewhere. The Vikings' determination and skill actually took them to America five centuries before Columbus.

SAXON WAYS OF LIFE

WE KNOW LITTLE ABOUT the first Saxon settlements. For long the Saxons had been regarded as pirates, but after a time they began to clear forest and marsh and soon set up kingdoms. It is still possible to trace these Saxon settlements by modern place-names—such as those ending in *ham* or *worth*, while the later Scandinavian settlements commonly end in *by*, as in Whitby or Derby.

We have learnt a great deal about the lives of the Saxons from the manner of their burial, and certainly spectacular discoveries like that at Sutton Hoo in 1939 of a great ship-burial of the mid-seventh century have revealed much of hitherto unappreciated early Saxon wealth and culture. There is also a considerable body of Saxon literature which adds to our knowledge: in the early eighth century Bede wrote his *Ecclesiastical History*, while *The Anglo-Saxon Chronicle* was put together in the ninth century, and the epic poem *Beowulf*, telling the story of a great warrior, may also date from this era.

Life was hard for most Saxons as they toiled on the land to grow crops and rear animals. They had to face invasion by the Vikings, who were, as they had once been, pirates—that is what the word meant—but who later became traders and settlers. To the Saxons, recent converts to Christianity, they appeared to be "heathen men" interested only in plunder and slaughter; and even after the greatest Saxon king, Alfred of Wessex, defeated them and pushed them back into a separately administered "Danelaw", they came back again and again. Indeed, a second Viking age began in 980, and forty years later a Danish king, Canute, ruled the whole country. His laws were said to be the most advanced in Europe, and for all the Vikings' reputation as adventurers, the word "law" was theirs.

The last years before the Norman Conquest were years of high culture. The Saxons bequeathed a unique artistic contribution to our heritage—from jewels to illuminated manuscripts and churches.

SHORE FORTS WERE BUILT FOR DEFENCE *against invaders from the sea. Many, like the one at Reculver in Kent, shown in this aerial photograph, originated in Roman times to keep out the Saxons, and later were used by the Saxons to deter the Vikings. The photograph shows the remaining outline of the fort, now badly eroded by the sea. The foundations for the pillars of the ruined seventh-century church can also be seen.*

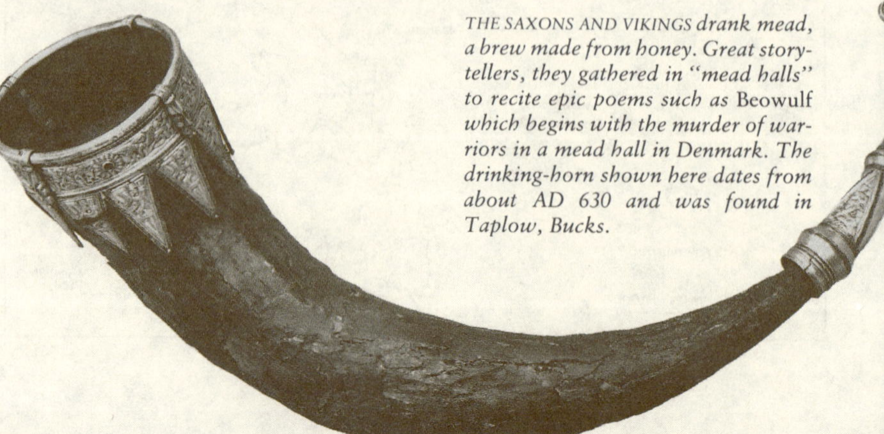

THE SAXONS AND VIKINGS *drank mead, a brew made from honey. Great storytellers, they gathered in "mead halls" to recite epic poems such as* Beowulf *which begins with the murder of warriors in a mead hall in Denmark. The drinking-horn shown here dates from about AD 630 and was found in Taplow, Bucks.*

DAILY LIFE REVOLVED AROUND FARMING *and the church. Very few Saxons lived in towns, though there were settlements of between five and ten thousand inhabitants at London, York, Winchester, Lincoln, Canterbury and Oxford. Their houses were thatched and small, often sunken to roof level for added shelter, with walls made of hurdles plastered with clay and animal hair. The picture (left) shows Saxon youths, the poorer of them barefoot, while the picture (above) depicts workers clearing the land, breaking up the soil and raking in the seed. The rituals of the Church were closely related to farming patterns. Christmas conveniently followed the slaughtering of beasts that were too numerous to be fed during the winter, while the Lenten fast preceded the first crops of spring. Eastertime brought eggs, the symbols of new life.*

THE GERMANIC INFLUENCE OF THE INVADERS *can be seen in Sompting Church, Sussex. The design of the tower is Rhenish, reflecting the origins of Saxon builders about AD 1000.*

THE LINDISFARNE GOSPELS *were made by the monks on Holy Island in honour of St Cuthbert during the first century after Christianity was introduced there in approximately AD 635. The Gospels, a masterpiece of Saxon art, are illustrated in soft bright colours. The St Matthew portrait (above) shows the face of Christ peeping from behind a curtain to inspire his apostle. The richly decorated initial letters elsewhere in the Gospels are interlaced with elaborate curving designs. These have a marked Celtic influence, often featuring animals and elongated birds.*

THE HIGH QUALITY OF SAXON CRAFTSMANSHIP *is evident in the Fuller Brooch shown above. The five senses are depicted: Sight is shown in the centre, then Taste (upper left) and, clockwise, Smell, Touch and Hearing. It is made of silver, dates from about AD 860 and can be seen in the British Museum.*

THE EXCAVATION AT SUTTON HOO, *near Woodbridge, Suffolk revealed a unique ship-burial containing not human bones, but the treasure belonging to a Saxon king. Items from Europe and Byzantium were included. The boat itself shows the narrow streamlined keel which enabled the Saxon invaders not only to trade abroad, but to sail far up rivers inland.*

It was the wealth of the Church that most attracted Viking greed. The Ardagh Chalice was found in Co. Limerick, in Ireland. Caskets from Britain containing sacred relics have been found in Norway.

the deceased Viking was brought into the town for Christian burial it suddenly appeared that the attendants were armed warriors disguised in mourning, who without more ado set to work on sack and slaughter. There are many informing sidelights of this kind upon the manners and customs of the Vikings. They were, in fact, the most audacious and treacherous type of pirate and shark that had ever yet appeared, and, owing to the very defective organisation of the Saxons and the conditions of the period, they achieved a fuller realisation of their desires than any of those who have emulated their proficiency — and there have been many.

In Viking legend at this period none was more famous than Ragnar Lodbrok, or "Hairy-breeches". His prow had ranged from the Orkneys to the White Sea. In 845 he led a Viking fleet up the Seine and attacked Paris. The onslaught was repulsed, and plague took an unforeseeable revenge upon the buccaneers. He then turned his mobile arms against Northumbria. Here again fate was adverse. According to Scandinavian story, he was captured by King Ella of Northumbria, and cast into a snakepit to die. Among the coiling mass of loathsome adders he sang to the end his death-song. Ragnar had four sons, and as he lay among the venomous reptiles he uttered a potent threat: "The little pigs would grunt now if they knew how it fares with the old boar." The skalds, the Scandanavian bards, tell us how his sons received the news. Bjorn "Ironside" gripped his spear shaft so hard that the print of his fingers remained stamped upon it. Hvitserk was playing chess, but he clenched his fingers so tightly upon a pawn that the blood started from under his nails. Sigurd "Snake-eye" was trimming his nails with a knife, and kept on paring until he cut into the bone. But the fourth son was the one who counted. Ivar, the Boneless, demanded the precise details of his father's execution, and his face "became red, blue, and pale by turns, and his skin was swollen with anger."

A form of vengeance was prescribed by which sons should requite the killer of their fathers. It was known as the "Blood-red Eagle". The flesh and ribs of the killer must be cut and sawn out in an aquiline pattern, and then the dutiful son with his own hands would tear out the palpitating lungs. This was the doom which in legend overtook King Ella. But the actual consequences to England were far more serious. Ivar the Boneless was a warrior of command and guile. He was the mastermind behind the Scandinavian invasion of England in the last quarter of the ninth century. He first appeared in 865 in East Anglia. In the spring of 866 his powerful army, organised on the basis of ships' companies, but now all mounted not for fighting but for locomotion, rode north along the old Roman road and was ferried across the Humber.

He laid siege to York. And now — too late — the Northumbrians, who had been divided in their loyalties between two rival kings, forgot their feuds and united in one final effort. They attacked the Danish army before York. At first they were successful; the heathens were driven back upon the city walls. The defenders sallied out, and in the confusion the Vikings defeated them all with grievous slaughter, killing both their kings and destroying completely their power of resistance.

Simeon of Durham, writing a hundred and fifty years after this disastrous battle at York, underlines these lamentations:

"The army raided and there filled every place with bloodshed and sorrow. Far and wide it destroyed the churches and monasteries with fire and sword. When it departed from a place it left nothing standing but roofless walls. So great was the destruction that one can scarcely see anything left of those places, nor any sign of their former greatness."

But Ivar's object was nothing less than the conquest of Mercia, which, as all men knew, had for nearly a hundred years represented the strength of England. Ivar lay before Nottingham. The King of Mercia called for help from Wessex. The old King of Wessex was dead, but his two sons, Ethelred and Alfred, answered the appeal. They marched to his aid, and offered to join him in his attack upon the besiegers' lines; but the Mercians flinched, and preferred a parley. Ivar warred with policy as well as arms. He had not harmed churches at York and Ripon. He was content to set up a vassal king, one Egbert, in Northumbria, and after ending the campaign of 868 by a treaty which left him master of Nottingham he spent the winter fortifying himself in York.

Dragon's-head prow of a Viking ship found in the River Scheldt in Belgium.

While the Danes in their formidable attempt at conquest spread out from East Anglia, subdued Mercia, and ravaged Northumbria, the King of Wessex and his brother Alfred quietly built up their strength. Their fortunes turned on balances so delicate and precarious that even the slightest addition to their burdens must have been fatal. It was therefore a deliverance when Ivar, after breaking the Treaty of Nottingham and subjecting King Edmund of East Anglia to martydom, suddenly quitted England forever. He had conquered Mercia and East Anglia. He had captured the major stronghold of the kingdom of Strathclyde, Dunbarton. Laden with loot and seemingly invincible, he settled in Dublin, and died there peacefully two years later.

The Danish raiders now stayed longer every year. In the summer the fleets came over to plunder and destroy, but each year the tendency was to dally in a more genial and more verdant land. At last the warrior's absence on the raids became long enough for him to bring over his wife and family. Thus again behind piracy and rapine there grew the process of settlement. Behind their frontier lines the soldiers of one decade were to become the colonists and landowners of the next. They cut their way with their swords, and then planted themselves deeply in the soil. The warrior-type of farmer asserted from the first a status different from the ordinary agriculturist.

Without any coherent national organisation to repel from the land on which they had settled the ever-unknowable descents from the seas, the Saxons, now for four centuries entitled to be deemed the owners of the soil, very nearly succumbed completely to the Danish inroads. That they did not was due to the sudden apparition in an era of confusion and decay of one of the great figures of history.

CHAPTER 7

ALFRED THE GREAT

THE STORY OF ALFRED is made known to us in some detail in the pages of Asser, a monk of St David's, who became Bishop of Sherborne. Alfred began as second-in-command to his elder brother, King Ethelred. There were no jealousies between them, but a marked difference of temperament. Ethelred inclined to the religious view that faith and prayer were the prime agencies by which the heathen would be overcome.

Alfred, the best-known and greatest Saxon king, still dominates Winchester from the Buttercross, in the town centre.

Alfred, although also devout, placed the emphasis upon policy and arms.

In earlier years the overlordship of Mercia had never been popular, and her kings had made the serious mistake of quarrelling with the See of Canterbury. When, in 825, the Mercian army, invading Wessex, was overthrown by Alfred's grandfather, King Egbert, at Ellandun, near Swindon, all the south and east made haste to come to terms with the victor, and the union of Kent, the seat of the Primate, with Wessex, now the leading English kingdom, created a solid southern bloc. Now, all eyes turned to Wessex, where there was a royal house going back without a break to the first years of the Saxon settlement.

The Danes had occupied London, not then the English capital, but a town in the kingdom of Mercia, and their army had fortified itself at Reading. Moving forward, they met the forces of the West Saxons, led by Alfred and Ethelred on the Berkshire downs, and here, in January 871, was fought the battle of Ashdown. The Vikings, with their brightly painted shields and banners, their finery and golden bracelets, made the West Saxons seem modest by contrast. The fight was long and hard. "The heathens," said Asser, "had seized the higher ground, and the Christians had to advance uphill. There was in that place a single stunted thorn tree which we have seen with our own eyes. Round about this tree, then, the opposing ranks met in conflict, with a great shouting from all men — one side bent on evil, the other side fighting for life and their loved ones and their native land." At last the Danes gave way, and, hotly pursued, fled back to Reading. The whole breadth of Ashdown — meaning the Berkshire hills — was strewn with their corpses, among which were found the body of one of the Viking kings and five of his earls.

The results of this victory did not break the power of the Danish army; in a fortnight they were again in the field. But the Battle of Ashdown justly takes its place among historic encounters because of the greatness of the issue. This was the first time the invaders had been beaten in the field. Since the West Saxons were victorious the hope still burnt for a civilised Christian existence in this island. Alfred had made the Saxons feel confidence in themselves again. They could hold their own in open fight. The story of this conflict at Ashdown was for generations a treasured memory of the Saxon writers. It was Alfred's first battle.

All through the year 871 the two armies waged deadly war. King Ethelred soon fell sick and died. At twenty-four Alfred became King, and entered upon a desperate inheritance. To and fro the fighting swayed, with varying fortunes. The Danes were strongly reinforced from overseas; "the summer army", as it was called, innumerable, eager to fight against the army of the West Saxons, arrived to join them. Seven or eight battles were fought, and we are told the Danes usually held the field. At Wilton, in the summer, about a month after Alfred had assumed the Crown, he sustained a definite defeat in the heart of his own country. His numbers had been worn down by death and desertion, and once again in the field the Vikings' ruse of a feigned retreat was successful.

On the morrow of this misfortune Alfred thought it best to come to terms while he still had an army. We do not know the conditions, but there is no doubt that a heavy payment was among them. Alfred and his Saxons had in all this fighting convinced the Vikings of their redoubtable force, and by this inglorious treaty and stubborn campaign Alfred secured five years in which

The White Horse on Westbury Down, one of several "white horses", was carved to commemorate Alfred's victory over the Danes at Ashdown in 871.

to consolidate his power. He had always counted upon the invaders dividing, and the stresses that were at work within the heathen army justified his policy.

Still maintaining their grip on London, the Danes moved back to the Midlands, which were now in complete submission. They set up a local puppet, in a fashion which has often been imitated since, after he had given hostages and taken an oath "that he would not obstruct their wishes, and would be obedient in everything".

But now in the last quarter of the century a subtle, profound change came over the "Great Heathen Army". Some of the Danes wished to settle on the lands they already held; the rest were for continuing the war at a suitable moment till the whole country was conquered. Perhaps these two bodies acted in concert, the former providing a sure and solid base, the latter becoming an expeditionary force. Thus, after mauling the kingdom of Strathclyde and carrying off the stock and implements of agriculture, nearly half of the sea-pirates settled themselves in Northumbria and East Anglia. Henceforward they began to till the ground for a livelihood. Here was a great change. The ships' companies, acting together, had hitherto fought ashore as soldiers. All their organisation of settlements was military. The sailors had turned soldiers, and the soldiers had turned yeomen. They preserved that spirit of independence, regulated only by comradeship and discipline for vital purposes, which was the life of the longship.

The whole of the east of England thus received a class of cultivators who, except for purposes of common defence, owed allegiance to none; who had won land with the sword, and was loyal only to the army which enabled them to keep it. From Yorkshire to Norfolk this sturdy, upstanding stock took root. As time passed they forgot the sea; they forgot the army; they thought only of the land — their own land. They liked the life.

They were not dependent wholly upon their own labour. They must have exploited the former possessors and their serfs. The distribution of the land was made around a unit which could support a family. What eight oxen could plough in a certain time under prescribed conditions, became the measure of the holding. They worked hard themselves, but obviously they used the local people too.

Thus the Danish differs in many ways from the Saxon settlement four hundred years earlier. There was no idea of exterminating the old population. The two languages were not very different; the way of life, the methods of cultivation, very much the same. The colonists — for such they had now

The remains of the wooden coffin of St Cuthbert (above) are now in Durham Cathedral. The bones of the revered saint were taken from the ruined monastery of Lindisfarne to Chester-le-Street and then finally to a shrine at Durham which was built by the Normans in 1104. The intricately-wrought gold cross (top) was found inside the coffin.

become — brought their families from Scandinavia, but also it is certain that they established human and natural relations with the expropriated English. The bloodstream of these vigorous individualists, proud and successful men of the sword, mingled henceforward in the island race. A vivifying, potent, lasting, and resurgent quality was added to the breed. As modern steel is hardened by the alloy of special metals in comparatively small quantities, this strong strain of individualism, based upon land ownership, was afterwards to play a persistent part, not only in the blood but in the politics of England.

The reformed and placated pirate-mariners brought with them many Danish customs. They had a different notation, which they would have been alarmed to hear described as the "duodecimal system". They thought in twelves instead of tens, and in our own day in certain parts of East Anglia the expression "the long hundred" (*i.e.* 120) is heard on market days.

These considerations may aptly fill the five years' breathing-space which Alfred had gained by courageous fighting and politic Danegeld. In this interval Halfdene, the Viking leader, departed like Ivar from the scene. The tortured, plundered Church requited his atrocities by declaring that God punished him in the long run by madness and a smell which made his presence unendurable to his fellows.

At Lindisfarne, in Dane-ravaged Northumbria, a pathetic tale is told. The ruined monks quitted their devastated, polluted sanctuary and carried on their shoulders the body of St Cuthbert and the bones of St Aidan. After seven years of pilgrimage by land and sea they established themselves in a new patrimony of St Cuthbert at Chester-le-Street. The veneration felt throughout the north for St Cuthbert brought such wealth to his See that in 995 its bishops began to build a new cathedral on the rock at Durham. Thither St Cuthbert's bones were taken, and so great was his prestige that until the nineteenth century the Bishops of Durham were Prince-Bishops, exercising immense power in north eastern England.

Alfred's dear-bought truce was over. Guthrum, the new leader of the mobile and martial part of the heathen army, had formed a large design for the subjugation of Wessex. He operated by sea and land. The land army marched to Wareham, close to Portland Bill, where the sea army joined him in Poole harbour. In this region they fortified themselves, and proceeded to attack Alfred's kingdom by raid and storm from every quarter. The prudent King sought peace and offered an indemnity. At the same time it seems probable that he had hemmed in the land army very closely at Wareham. The Danes took the gold, and "swore upon the Holy Ring" they would depart and keep a faithful peace. With a treachery to which all adjectives are unequal they suddenly darted away and seized Exeter. Alfred, mounting his infantry, followed after, but arrived too late. They were in the fortress. But let all heathen beware of breaking oaths! A frightful tempest smote the sea army, who sought to join their comrades by sea. They were smitten in the neighbourhood of Swanage by the elements, which in those days were believed to be personally directed by the Almighty. A hundred and twenty ships were sunk, and upward of five thousand of these perjured marauders perished. Thus the whole careful plan fell to pieces, and Alfred, watching and besetting Exeter, found his enemies in the summer of 877 in the mood for a new peace. The Danes swore it with oaths of still more compliant solemnity, and they kept it for about five months.

Then in January 878 occurred the most surprising reversal of Alfred's fortunes. His headquarters and Court lay at Chippenham, in Wiltshire. It was Twelfth Night, and the Saxons, who in these days of torment refreshed themselves by celebrating the feasts of the Church, were off their guard. Down swept the ravaging foe. The whole army of Wessex, sole guarantee of England south of the Thames, was dashed into confusion. Many were killed. The most part stole away to their houses. A strong contingent fled overseas. Refugees arrived with futile appeals at the Court of France. Only a handful of officers and personal attendants hid themselves with Alfred in the marshes and forests of Somerset and the Isle of Athelney which rose from the quags. This was the darkest hour of Alfred's fortunes. It was some months before he could even start a guerrilla. He led "with thanes and vassals an unquiet life in great tribulation. . . For he had nothing wherewith to supply his wants except what in frequent sallies he could seize either stealthily or openly, both from the heathen and from the Christians who had submitted to their rule." He lived as Robin Hood did in Sherwood Forest long afterwards.

This is the moment when those gleaming toys of history were fashioned for the children of every age. We see the warrior-king disguised as a minstrel harping in the Danish camps. We see him acting as kitchen-boy to a Saxon housewife. The celebrated story of Alfred and the cakes first appears in a late edition of Bishop Asser's life. It runs: "It happened one day that the countrywoman who was the wife of the cowherd with whom King Alfred was staying was going to bake bread, and the King was sitting by the fireside making ready his bow and arrows and other weapons. A moment came when the woman saw that her bread was burning; she rushed up and removed it from the fire, upbraiding the undaunted King with these words [recorded, strangely, in the original in Latin hexameters]: 'Alack, man, why have you not turned over the bread when you see that it is burning, especially as you so much like eating it hot.' The misguided woman little thought that she was talking to King Alfred, who had fought so vigorously against the heathen and won so many victories over them."

The leaders of the Danish army felt sure at this time that mastery was in their hands. To the people of Wessex it seemed that all was over. Their forces were dispersed, the country overrun; their King, if alive, was a fugitive in hiding. It is the supreme proof of Alfred's personal quality that he was able in such a plight to exercise his full authority and keep contact with his subjects.

Towards the end of Lent the Danes suffered an unexpected misfortune. The crews of twenty-three ships, after committing many atrocities in Wales, sailed to Devon and marched to the attack of one of Alfred's strongholds on Exmoor. The place was difficult to assail, but "in besetting it they thought that the King's thanes would soon give way to hunger and thirst. . .since the fortress had no supply of water. The Christians, before they endured any such distress, by the inspiration of heaven judged it to be better either to suffer death or to gain the victory. Accordingly at daybreak they suddenly rushed forth against the heathen, and at the first attack they laid low most of the enemy, including their king. A few escaped to their ships."

Eight hundred Danes were killed, and the spoils of the victory included an enchanted banner called the Raven, of which it was said that the three daughters of Ragnar Lodbrok had woven it in a single day, and that "in every battle in which that banner went before them the raven in the middle

The story of Alfred burning the cakes is surely one of Britain's best-loved tales. Alfred probably failed to prevent the cakes or, more likely, unleavened bread rolls, from burning on a hot greased stone placed next to the fire. This method of cooking was commonly practised, and it would have produced appetising results with a crisp and delicious crust.

of the design seemed to flutter as though it were alive if they were going to have the victory". On this occasion it did not flutter, but hung listlessly in its silken folds. The event proved that it was impossible for the Danes to win under these conditions.

Alfred, cheered by this news and striving to take the field again, continued a brigand warfare against the enemy while sending his messengers to summon the local militia, for the end of May. There was a general response; the King was loved and admired. The news that he was alive and active caused widespread joy. All the fighting men came back. The troops of Somerset, Wiltshire and Hampshire concentrated near Selwood. A point was chosen near where the three shires met, and we can see from this the burden which lay upon Alfred's tactics. Nevertheless here again was an army; "and when they saw the King they received him like one risen from the dead, after so great tribulations, and they were filled with great joy".

Battle must be sought before they lost interest. The Danes still lay upon their plunder at Chippenham. Alfred advanced to Ethandun — now called Edington — and on the downs was fought the largest and culminating battle of Alfred's wars. All was staked. All hung in the scales of fate. On both sides the warriors dismounted; the horses were sent to the rear. The shield-walls were formed, the masses clashed against each other, and for hours they fought with sword and axe. But the heathen lost, and fled from the cruel and clanging field. Terrified by hunger, cold, and fear, and at the last full of despair, they begged for peace. They offered to give without return as many hostages as Alfred should care to pick and to depart forthwith.

But Alfred had had longer ends in view. It is strange that he should have wished to convert these savage foes. Baptism as a penalty of defeat might lose its spiritual quality. The workings of the spirit are mysterious, but we must still wonder how the hearts of these hardbitten swordsmen and pirates could be changed in a single day. Indeed these mass conversions had become almost a matter of form for defeated Viking armies. It is reported that one old veteran declared he had been through this washing twenty times, and complained that the alb with which he was supplied was by no means up to the average standard. But Alfred meant to make a lasting peace with Guthrum and his army. He could have starved them into surrender and slaughtered them to a man. He wished instead to divide the land with them, and that the two races, in spite of fearful injuries given and received, should dwell together in amity. He stood godfather to Guthrum, King of the Viking army; he raised him from the font; he entertained him for twelve days; he presented him and his warriors with costly gifts; he called him his son.

This sublime power to rise above the whole force of circumstances, to remain unbiased by the extremes of victory or defeat, to persevere in the teeth of disaster, to greet returning fortune with a cool eye, to have faith in men after repeated betrayals, raises Alfred far above the turmoil of barbaric wars to his pinnacle of deathless glory.

Fourteen years intervened between the victory of Ethandun and any serious Danish attack. In spite of much uneasiness and disturbance, by the standards of those days there was peace. Alfred worked ceaselessly to strengthen his realm. He had been content that the Danes should settle in East Anglia, but he cultivated the best relations with the harassed kingdom of Mercia, which had become tributary to the Danes, though still largely unoccupied by them. In 886 the King married his eldest daughter to the regent, Ethelred.

This act set the seal upon the cooperation of the South and the Midlands.

The first result of this new unity was the recovery of London in 886. London had long been the emporium of Christian England. Now the city was set on the road to becoming the national capital. We read in *The Anglo-Saxon Chronicle*: "King Alfred restored London, and all the English — those of them who were free from Danish bondage — turned to him, and he then entrusted the borough to the keeping of the ealdorman Ethelred." It would seem that heavy fighting and much slaughter attended the regaining of London, but of this nothing has been recorded. We know little more than the bare fact, and that Alfred after the victory made the citizens organise an effective defence force and put their walls in the highest order.

King Alfred's main effort was to restore the defences and raise the efficiency of the West Saxon force. He reorganised the local militia, dividing it into two classes which practised a rotation of service. Though his armies might be smaller, Alfred's peasant soldiers were encouraged not to desert on a long campaign, because they knew that their land was being looked after by the half of the militia that had stayed at home. The modesty of his reforms shows us the enormous difficulties which he had to overcome, and proves that even in that time of mortal peril it was almost impossible to keep the English under arms. The King fortified the whole country by boroughs, running down the Channel and then across to the Severn estuary and so back by the Thames valley, assigning to each a contributory district to man the walls and keep the fortifications in repair. Alfred saw too the vision of English sea power, that to be safe in an island it was necessary to command the sea. He made great departures in ship design, and hoped to beat the Viking numbers by fewer ships of much larger size.

But the big ships were beyond the skill of their inexperienced seamen to handle. In an action when nine of them fought six pirate vessels several were run ashore "most awkwardly", says the *Chronicle*, and only two of the enemy fell into Alfred's hands, to afford him the limited satisfaction of hanging their crews at Winchester. Still, the beginning of the English navy must always be linked with King Alfred.

In spite of the disorders a treaty was achieved after the reconquest of London in 886. Significance attaches to the terms in which the contracting parties are described. On Alfred's side there are "the counsellors of the English nation", on Guthrum's "the people who dwell in East Anglia". The organisation of the Danelaw, based entirely upon the army and the subjugated inhabitants, had not yet assumed the form of a State. The English, on the other hand, had already reached the position of "King and Witan" [council]; and none did more to enforce the idea than Alfred himself. The

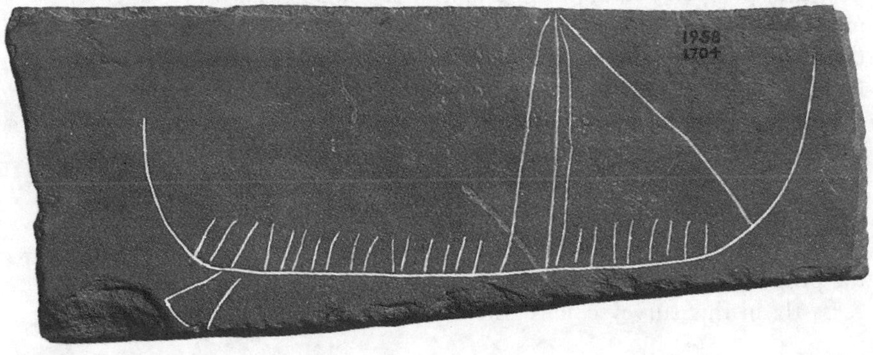

This Viking drawing on stone, found in Shetland, shows the single mast and the high carved prow of their longships, which ranged the seas.

This wooden carving of a warrior's head, found at Sigtuna, Sweden, shows the characteristic nose- and eye-guard of the Vikings' helmets.

treaty defined a political boundary running up the Thames, up and along the Lea to its source, then to Bedford, and after by the Ouse to Watling Street, beyond which no agreement was made. This line followed no natural frontiers. It recognised a war front. It was drawn in No Man's Land.

The second part of the treaty is curious and instructive. Both sides were familiar with the idea of a "wergild". In order to deal with the ceaseless murders and physical injuries which the anarchic conditions had produced, a scale for compensation or revenge must at all cost be agreed. Nothing would stop the Danes from killing and robbing the English, and vice versa; but if there was to be any cessation of war a tariff must be agreed. Both Danish and English peasant tenants were accordingly valued at two hundred silver shillings each, and men of higher rank were assigned a wergild of eight and a half marks of pure gold. In accepting this clause of the treaty Guthrum was in fact undertaking not to discriminate in wergilds between his English and Danish subjects. Alfred had gained an important point, which is evidence of the reality of his power.

King Alfred's Book of Laws, or Dooms, as set out in the existing laws of Kent, Wessex, and Mercia, attempted to blend the Mosaic code with Christian principles and old Germanic customs. He inverted the Golden Rule. Instead of "Do unto others as you would that they should do unto you", he adopted the less ambitious principle, "What ye will that other men should *not* do to you, that do ye not to other men", with the comment, "By bearing this precept in mind a judge can do justice to all men; he needs no other law books. Let him think of himself as the plaintiff, and consider what judgment would satisfy him." The King, in his preamble, explained modestly that "I have not dared to presume to set down in writing many laws of my own, for I cannot tell what will meet with the approval of our successors." Yet the Laws of Alfred, continually amplified by his successors, grew into that body of customary law administered by the shire and hundred courts out of which, with much manipulation by feudal lawyers, the Common Law was founded.

The King encouraged by all his means religion and learning. Above all he sought the spread of education. His advice to the Bishop of Worcester has been preserved: "I would have you informed that it has often come into my remembrance what wise men there formerly were among the English race, both of the sacred orders and the secular; and what happy times those were throughout the English race, and how the kings who had the government of the folk in those days obeyed God and His ministers; and they on the one hand maintained their peace and morality and their authority within their borders, while at the same time they enlarged their territory abroad; and how they prospered both in war and in wisdom. So clean was it fallen away in the English race that there were very few on this side Humber who could understand their Mass-books in English, or translate a letter from Latin into English; and I ween that there were not many beyond the Humber."

He sought to reform the monastic life, which in the general confusion had grossly degenerated. "If anyone takes a nun from a convent without the King's or the bishop's leave he shall pay 120 shillings, half to the King and half to the bishop. . . . If she lives longer than he who abducted her she shall inherit nothing of his property. If she bears a child it shall inherit no more of the property than its mother."

Lastly in this survey comes Alfred's study of history. He it was, Asser

Part of the Cuerdale Hoard of Viking silver, found in a chest near the river Ribble, in Lancashire. This is the largest Viking hoard ever discovered in northern Europe, and dates from 903. It can now be seen in the British Museum.

wrote, who set on foot the compiling of *The Anglo-Saxon Chronicle*. The fact that the early entries are fragmentary gives confidence that the compilers did not draw on their imagination. From King Alfred's time they are exact, and sometimes written with historic grasp and eloquence.

We discern across the centuries a commanding and versatile intelligence, wielding with equal force the sword of war and of justice; cherishing religion, learning, and art in the midst of adversity and danger; welding together a nation, and seeking always across the feuds and hatreds of the age a peace which would smile upon the land.

One final war awaited Alfred. It was a crisis in the Viking story. Guthrum died in 891, and the pact which he had sworn with Alfred, and loosely kept, ended. Suddenly in the autumn of 892 a Viking armada of two hundred and fifty ships appeared off Lympne, carrying to the invasion of England "the Great Heathen Army" that recently had ravaged France. They disembarked and fortified themselves at Appledore, on the edge of the forest. They were followed by eighty ships conveying a second force of raiders who sailed up the Thames and established themselves on its southern bank at Milton, near Sittingbourne. Thus Kent was to be attacked from both sides. This immense concerted assault confronted Alfred with his third struggle for life. The English, as we may call them — for the Mercians and West Saxons stood together — had secured fourteen years of unquiet peace in which to develop their defences. Many of the southern towns were fortified, and the militia had been improved in organisation, though its essential weaknesses had not been removed. There had been a regathering of wealth and food; there was a settled administration, and the allegiance of all was given to King Alfred. Also he had a valiant son. At twenty-two Edward could lead his father's armies to the field. The Mercians also had produced in Ethelred a fit companion to the West Saxon prince. The King, in ill-health, is not often seen in this phase at the head of armies; we have glimpses of him, but the great episodes of the war were centred upon the young leaders.

The Danes, under Haesten, fortified themselves at Benfleet, on the Thames below London, and their earthworks can be traced to this day. Thence they

An idealised portrait of King Alfred appears in Matthew Paris's history, Chronica Majora, *written in the thirteenth century.*

sallied forth to plunder, leaving a moderate garrison in their stronghold. This the princes now assaulted. It had very rarely been possible in these wars to storm a well fortified place; but Alfred's son and son-in-law with a strong army from London fell upon Benfleet and "put the army to flight, stormed the fort, and took all that there was within, goods as well as women and children, and brought all to London. And all the ships they either broke in pieces or burnt or brought to London or Rochester." Such are the words of *The Anglo-Saxon Chronicle*. When in the nineteenth century a railway was being made across this ground the charred fragments of the ships and numbers of skeletons were unearthed upon the site of Benfleet. In the captured stronghold the victors found Haesten's wife and his two sons. These were precious hostages, and King Alfred was much criticised at the time, and also later, because he restored them to Haesten. The ninth century found it very hard to understand this behaviour when the kingdom was fighting desperately against brutal marauders, but that is one of the reasons why in the aftertime the King is called "Alfred the Great". The war went on, but so far as the records show Haesten never fought again. It may be that mercy and chivalry were not in vain.

In 896 the war petered out, and the Vikings, whose strength seemed at this time to be in decline, dispersed, some returning to the Danelaw (as the districts settled by the Danes were called), some going back to France. "By God's mercy," exclaims the *Chronicle*, in summing up the war, "the [Danish] army had not too much afflicted the English people." Alfred had well defended the island home.

Alfred died in 899, and his son Edward was immediately acclaimed King. Alfred's blood gave the English a series of great rulers, and while his inspiration held, victory did not quit the Christian ranks. In 910 war was renewed in Mercia. The main forces of Wessex and Kent were sent by Edward, who was with the fleet, to the aid of the Mercians, and in heavy fighting at Tettenhall, in Staffordshire, the Danes were decisively defeated. This English victory was a milestone in the long conflict. The Danish armies in Northumbria never recovered from the battle, and the Danish Midlands and East Anglia thus lay open to English conquest. Up to this point Mercia and Wessex had been the defenders, often reduced to the most grievous straits. But now the tide had turned. Fear camped with the Danes.

CHAPTER 8

THE SAXON DUSK

Athelstan, the third of the great West Saxon kings, grandson of Alfred, sought at first, in accordance with the traditions of his house, peaceful relations with the unconquered parts of the Danelaw; but upon disputes arising, marched into Yorkshire in 926, and there established himself. Northumbria submitted; the kings of the Scots and of Strathclyde acknowledged him as their "father and lord", and the Welsh princes agreed to pay tribute. There was an uneasy interlude; then in 933 came a campaign against the Scots, and in 937 a general rebellion and renewed war, organised by all the hitherto defeated characters in the drama. The whole of north Britain — Celtic, Danish, and Norwegian, pagan and Christian — together presented a hostile front under Constantine, King of the Scots, and Olaf of Dublin, with Viking reinforcements from Norway. On this occasion neither life nor time was wasted in manoeuvres. The fight that followed is recorded for us in an Icelandic saga and an English poem. According to the saga, Athelstan challenged his foes to meet him in a pitched battle, and to this they blithely agreed. The English King even suggested the place where all should be put to the test. The armies, very large for those impoverished times, took up their stations. Tempers rose high as these masses of manhood flaunted their shields and blades at one another and flung their gibes across a narrow space; and there was presently a fierce clash between the Northumbrian and the Icelandic Vikings on the one hand and a part of the English army on the other. In this, although the Northumbrian commander fled, the English were worsted. But on the following day the real trial of strength was staged. The rival hosts paraded in all the pomp of war. All day long the battle raged.

The original victory song on Brunanburh opens to us a view of the Anglo-Saxon mind, with its primitive imagery and war-delight. "Here Athelstan King, of earls the lord, the giver of the bracelets of the nobles, and his brother also, Edmund the Aetheling, an age-long glory won by slaughter in battle, with the edges of swords, at Brunanburh. The wall of shields they cleaved, they hewed the battle shafts with hammered weapons, the foe flinched. . . .The field was coloured with the warriors' blood! After that the sun on high. . . . glided over the earth, God's candle bright! till the noble creature hastened to her setting. There lay soldiers, many with darts stuck down, northern men over their shields shot. So were the Scotch; weary of battle, they had had their fill! They left behind them, to feast on carrion, the dusty-coated raven with horned beak, the black-coated eagle with white tail, the greedy battle-hawk, and the grey beast, the wolf in the wood."

The victory of the English was overwhelming. Constantine fled back to the north, and Olaf retired with his remnants to Dublin. Thus did King Alfred's grandson, the valiant Athelstan, become one of the first sovereigns of Western Europe. He styled himself on coin and charter *Rex totius Britanniae*. These claims were accepted on the Continent. His three sisters were wedded respectively to the Carolingian king, Charles the Simple, to the Capetian, Hugh the Great, and to Otto the Saxon, a future Holy Roman Emperor. He even installed a Norwegian prince, who swore allegiance and was baptised as his vassal, at York. Here again one might hope that a decision in the long quarrel had been reached; yet it persisted; and when Athelstan died, two years after Brunanburh, and was succeeded by his half-brother, Edmund, a youth of eighteen, the beaten forces welled up once more against him. Edmund was succeeded by his brother Edred, the youngest son of Alfred's son Edward the Elder. He too maintained the realm against all comers, and, beating them down by force of arms, seemed to have quenched forever the rebellious fires of Northumbria.

Historians select the year 954 as the end of the first great episode in the Viking history of England. A hundred and twenty years had passed since the impact of the Vikings had smitten the island. For forty years English Christian society had struggled for life. For eighty years five warrior kings — Alfred, Edward, Athelstan, Edmund, and Edred — defeated the invaders. The English rule was now restored, though in a form changed by the passage of time, over the whole country. Yet underneath it there had grown up, deeply rooted in the soil, a Danish settlement covering the great

King Athelstan, Alfred's grandson, presents a copy of Bede's works to St Cuthbert, the seventh-century English saint. The works of Bede are now in the Bodleian Library in Oxford.

eastern plain, in which Danish blood and Danish customs survived under the authority of the English king.

In the brilliant and peaceful reign of Edgar, son of Edmund, all this long building had reached its culmination. The reconquest of England was accompanied step by step by a conscious administrative reconstruction which has governed the development of English institutions from that day to this. The shires were reorganised, each with its sheriff or reeve, a royal officer directly responsible to the Crown. The hundreds, subdivisions of the shire, were created, and the towns prepared for defence. An elaborate system of shire, hundred, and borough courts maintained law and order and pursued criminals. Taxation was reassessed. Finally, with this military and political revival marched a great rebirth of monastic life and learning together with the beginning of our native literature. The movement was slow and English in origin, but advanced with great strides in mid-century as it came into contact with the religious revival on the Continent. The work of Dunstan, Archbishop of Canterbury, and his younger contemporaries, Oswald, Bishop of Worcester, and Ethelwold, Bishop of Winchester, was to revive the strict observance of religion within the monasteries, and thereby indirectly to reform the Episcopate as more and more monks were elected to bishoprics. Another and happy, if incidental, result was to promote learning and the production of splendid illuminated manuscripts, which were much in demand in contemporary Europe. Many of these, designed for the religious instruction of the laity, were written in English. The Catholic Homilies of Elfric, Abbot of Eynsham, mark, we are told, the first achievement of English as a literary language — the earliest vernacular to reach this eminence in the whole of Europe. From whatever point of view we regard it, the tenth century is a decisive step forward in the destinies of England. Despite the catastrophic decline of the monarchy which followed the death of Edgar, this organisation and English culture were so firmly rooted as to survive two foreign conquests in less than a century.

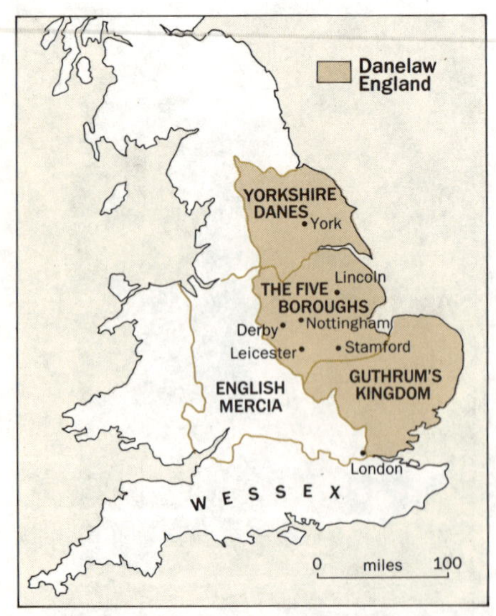

This map of the Danelaw shows the areas of Viking settlement. The Saxon kings enriched the English language and culture by allowing the Danes to settle, but they were constantly harassed by demands for more land and money.

It must have seemed to contemporaries that with Edgar's magnificent coronation at Bath in 973, on which all coronation orders since have been based, the seal was set on the unity of the realm. Everywhere the courts are sitting regularly, in shire and borough and hundred; there is one coinage, and one system of weights and measures. The arts of building and decoration are reviving; learning begins to flourish again in the Church; there is a literary language, a King's English, which all educated men write. Civilisation has been restored to the island. But now the political fabric which nurtured it was about to be overthrown. Twenty-five years of peace had lapped the land, and the English, so magnificent in stress and danger, so invincible under valiant leadership, relaxed under its softening influences. Hitherto strong men armed had kept the house. Now a child, a weakling, a vacillator, succeeded to the warrior throne. We have reached the days of Ethelred the Unready. But this expression, which conveys a truth, means literally Ethelred the Ill-counselled, or Ethelred the "Redeless".

In 980 serious raids began again. Chester was ravaged from Ireland. The people of Southampton were massacred by marauders from Scandinavia or Denmark. Thanet, Cornwall, and Devon all suffered butchery and pillage. At the Battle of Maldon, fought in 991 the English were worsted. Then followed the most shameful period of Danegeld.

We have seen that Alfred in his day had never hesitated to use money as well as arms. Ethelred used money instead of arms. He used it in ever-increasing quantities, with ever-diminishing returns. He paid as a bribe in 991 twenty-two thousand pounds of gold and silver, with rations for the invaders. In 994, with sixteen thousand pounds, he gained not only a brief respite, but the baptism of the raider, Olaf, thrown in as a compliment. In 1002 he bought a further truce for twenty-four thousand pounds of silver, but on this occasion he was himself to break it. In their ruin and decay the English had taken large numbers of Danish mercenaries into their service.

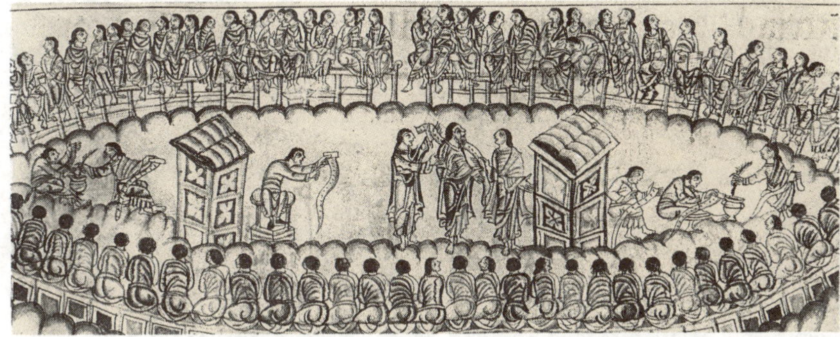

A monastic school at Christ Church, Canterbury. Scholars surround their teachers for lessons in Latin and English conversation. The teaching was mainly oral, but "textbooks" were used. One of the most famous of them was a series of dialogues in question and answer form, written by Elfric, Abbot of Eynsham, in 1005.

Ethelred suspected these dangerous helpers of a plot against his life. Panic-stricken, he planned the slaughter of all Danes in the south of England, whether in his pay or living peaceably on the land. This atrocious design was executed in 1002 on St Brice's Day. Among the victims was Gunnhild, the wife of one of the principal Vikings, and sister of Sweyn, King of Denmark. Sweyn swore implacable revenge, and for two years executed it upon the wretched islanders. Exeter, Wilton, Norwich, and Thetford all record massacres, which shows how widely the retaliation was applied. The fury of the avenger was not slaked by blood. It was baffled, but only for a space, by famine. The Danish army could no longer subsist in the ruined land, and departed in 1005 to Denmark. But the annals of 1006 show that Sweyn was back again, ravaging Kent, sacking Reading and Wallingford. At last Ethelred, for thirty-six thousand pounds of silver, the equivalent of three or four years' national income, bought another short-lived truce.

A desperate effort was now made to build a fleet. In the energy of despair an immense number of vessels were constructed by the poor, broken people, starving and pillaged to the bone. The new fleet was assembled at Sandwich in 1009. "But," says the *Chronicle*, "we had not the good fortune nor the worthiness that the shipforce could be of any use to this land." Its leaders quarrelled. Some ships were sunk in the fighting; others were lost in a storm and the rest were abandoned by the naval commanders.

There is the record of a final payment to the Vikings in 1012. This time forty-eight thousand pounds' weight of silver was exacted, and the oppressors enforced the collection by the sack of Canterbury, holding Archbishop Alphege to ransom, and finally killing him at Greenwich because he refused to coerce his flock to raise the money.

It is vain to recount further the catalogue of miseries. In earlier ages such horrors remain unknown because unrecorded. Just enough flickering light plays upon this infernal scene to give us the sense of its utter desolation and hopeless wretchedness and cruelty. It suffices to note that in 1013 Sweyn, accompanied by his younger son, Canute, came again to England, subdued

The Battle of Maldon in 991 was a defeat for the English. It is commemorated in a rousing Anglo-Saxon poem, and by a statue to the English hero, Byrhtnoth, which stands outside All Saints Church, Maldon in Essex.

the Yorkshire Danes and the five boroughs in the Danelaw, was accepted as overlord of Northumbria and Danish Mercia, sacked Oxford and Winchester in a punitive foray, and, though repulsed from London, was proclaimed King of England, while Ethelred fled for refuge to the Duke of Normandy, whose sister he had married. On these triumphs Sweyn died at the beginning of 1014. There was another respite. The English turned again to Ethelred, "declaring that no lord was dearer to them than their natural lord, if he would but rule them better than he had done before."

But soon the young Danish prince, Canute, set forth to claim the English Crown. At this moment the flame of Alfred's line rose again in Ethelred's son, Edmund — Edmund Ironside, as he soon was called. At twenty he was famous. Although declared a rebel by his father, and acting in complete disobedience to him, he gathered forces, and in a brilliant campaign struck a succession of heavy blows. He gained battles, he relieved London, he contended with every form of treachery; the hearts of all men went out to him. New forces sprang from the ruined land. Ethelred died, and Edmund, last hope of the English, was acclaimed King. In spite of all odds and a heavy defeat he was strong enough to make a partition of the realm, and then set himself to rally his forces for the renewal of the struggle; but in 1016, at twenty-two years of age, Edmund Ironside died, and the whole realm abandoned itself to despair.

At Southampton, even while Edmund lived, the lay and spiritual chiefs of England agreed to abandon the descendants of Ethelred forever and recognise Canute as King. All resistance, moral and military, collapsed before the Dane, and the last sons of the house of Wessex fled into exile. The young Danish prince received this general and abject submission in a good spirit, although a number of bloody acts were required to secure his position. He made good his promise to fulfil the duties of a king both in spiritual and temporal affairs to the whole country. The English magnates agreed to buy off the Danish army with a huge indemnity, and the new King, in "an oath of his soul", endorsed by his chiefs, bound himself to rule for all.

There were three principles upon which sovereignty could be erected: conquest, which none could dispute; hereditary right, which was greatly respected; and election, which was a kind of compromise between the two. It was upon this last basis that Canute began his reign. He made a point of submitting himself to the laws whereby he ruled. Everyone knows the lesson Canute administered to his flatterers when he sat on the seashore and forbade the tide to come in. He even in his military capacity subjected himself to the regulations of his own Household troops. At the earliest moment he disbanded his great Danish army and trusted himself broadly to the loyalty of the humbled English. He married Emma of Normandy, the widow of Ethelred, and so forestalled any action by the Duke of Normandy on behalf of her descendants by Ethelred.

Canute became the ruling sovereign of the north. He was already King of Denmark when he conquered England, and he made good his claim to be King of Norway. Scotland offered him its homage. The Viking power, although already undermined, still stretched across the world, ranging from Norway to North America, and through the Baltic to the East. But of all his realms Canute chose England for his home and capital. He liked, we are told, the Anglo-Saxon way of life. He wished to be considered the "successor of Edgar", whose seventeen years of peace still shone brightly by contrast with succeeding times. He ruled according to the laws, and he made it known that these were to be administered in austere detachment from his executive authority.

He built churches, he professed high devotion to the Christian faith and to the Papal diadem. He honoured the memory of St Edmund and St Alphege, whom his fellow-countrymen had murdered, and brought their relics with pious pomp to Canterbury. From Rome, as a pilgrim, in 1027, he wrote a letter to his subjects couched in exalted and generous terms, promising to administer equal justice, and laying particular emphasis upon the payment of Church dues. His daughter was married to the Emperor Conrad's eldest son, who ultimately carried his empire across Schleswig to the banks of the Eider. These remarkable achievements, under the blessing of God and the smiles of fortune, were in large measure due to King Canute's own personal qualities. Here again we see the power of a great man to bring order out of ceaseless broils, and to command harmony and unity to be his servants, and how the lack of such men has to be paid for by the inestimable suffering of the many.

Meanwhile across the waters of the English Channel a new military power was growing up. The Viking settlement founded in Normandy in the early years of the tenth century had become the most vigorous military state in France. In less than a hundred years the sea-rovers had transformed themselves into a feudal society. Such records as exist are overlaid by legend. We do not even know whether Rollo, the traditional founder of the Norman state, was a Norwegian, a Dane, or a Swede. Norman history begins with the Treaty of Saint-Clair-sur-Epte, made by Rollo with Charles the Simple, King of the West Franks, which affirmed the suzerainty of the King of France and defined the boundaries of the Duchy of Normandy.

In Normandy a class of knights and nobles arose who held their lands in return for military service, and sublet to inferior tenants upon the same basis. The Normans, with their craving for legality and logic, framed a

CANUTE AND THE WAVES

This account of the King's confrontation with the tide was written a century after his death in 1035 and appears in Henry of Huntingdon's History of the English. *The story was probably handed down orally.*

At the very summit of his power, Canute ordered his throne to be set on the seaside when the tide was rising. He addressed the mounting waters, "You are under my sway and there has never been anyone who has resisted my rule without being punished. I therefore command you not to rise on to my land and you are not to dare to wet the clothes or limbs of your master." The sea rose in the usual way and wetted the feet and legs of the monarch without showing any respect. The King accordingly leapt up and said: "Know all inhabitants of earth, that vain and trivial is the power of kings nor is anyone worthy of the name of king save Him whose nod heaven and earth and sea obey under laws eternal." King Canute, therefore, never again set the golden crown upon his neck but set it forever above an image of the Lord which is nailed to a cross, in honour of God the great king. By His mercy may the soul of King Canute rest in peace.

Bosham, near Chichester, is reputed to be the place where Canute vainly commanded the retreat of the waves. It was also the home of the future King Harold and Bosham Church appears on the Bayeux Tapestry.

general scheme of society, from which there soon emerged an excellent army. Order was strenuously enforced. No one but the Duke might build castles or fortify himself. The Court or "Curia" of the Duke consisted of his household officials, of dignitaries of the Church, and of the more important tenants, who owed him not only military service but also personal attendance. Here the administration was centred. The Dukes of Normandy created relations with the Church which became a model for medieval Europe. They were the protectors and patrons of the monasteries in their domains. They welcomed the religious revival of the tenth century, and secured the favour and support of its leaders. But they made sure that bishops and abbots were ducal appointments.

It was from this virile and well-organised land that the future rulers of England were to come. Between the years 1028 and 1035 the Viking instincts of Duke Robert of Normandy turned him seriously to plans of invasion. His death and his failure to leave a legitimate heir suspended the project, but only for a while.

The figure of Emma, sister of Robert of Normandy, looms large in English history at this time. Ethelred had originally married her from a reasonable desire to supplement his failing armaments by a blood tie with the most vigorous military state in Europe. Canute married her to give him a united England. Of her qualities and conduct little is known. Nevertheless few women have stood at the centre of such remarkable converging forces. In fact Emma had two husbands and two sons who were Kings of England.

In 1035 Canute died, and his empire with him. He left three sons, two by a former wife and one, Hardicanute, by Emma. These sons were ignorant and boorish Vikings, and many thoughts were turned to the representatives of the old West Saxon line, Alfred and Edward, sons of Ethelred and Emma, then living in exile in Normandy. The elder, Alfred, "the innocent Prince" as the chronicler calls him, hastened to England in 1036, ostensibly to visit his again-widowed mother, the ex-Queen Emma. A Wessex earl, Godwin, was the leader of the Danish party in England. He possessed great abilities and exercised the highest political influence. The venturesome Alfred was arrested and his personal attendants slaughtered. The unfortunate prince himself was blinded, and in this condition soon ended his days in the monastery at Ely. The guilt of this crime was generally ascribed to Godwin. The succession being thus simplified, Canute's sons divided the paternal inheritance. One, Sweyn, reigned in Norway for a spell, but his two brothers who ruled England were short-lived, and within seven years the throne of England was again vacant.

Godwin continued to be the leading figure in the land, and was now master of its affairs. There was still living in exile in Normandy Edward, the remaining son of Ethelred and Emma, younger brother of the ill-starred Alfred. In these days of reviving anarchy all men's minds turned to the search for some stable institution. This could only be found in monarchy, and the illustrious line of Alfred the Great possessed unequalled claims and titles. A sense of sanctity and awe still attached to any who could claim descent from the great king, and beyond him to Egbert and immemorial antiquity. Godwin saw that he could consolidate his power and combine both English and Danish support by making Edward king, bargaining, however, for the restriction of Norman influence in England. Edward made no difficulty; he was welcomed home and crowned; and for the following

Canute and his wife Emma present a charter to the Church. The King and the Church were closely connected in the eyes of the people. Emma was originally the queen of Ethelred, whom Canute conquered.

twenty-four years, with one brief interval, England was mainly governed by Godwin and his sons.

Edward was a quiet, pious person, without liking for war or much aptitude for administration. His Norman upbringing made him the willing though gentle agent of Norman influence, so far as Earl Godwin would allow. Norman prelates appeared in the English Church, Norman clerks in the royal household, and Norman landowners in the English shires. To make all smooth Edward was obliged to marry Godwin's young and handsome daughter, but we are assured by contemporary writers that this union was no more than formal. According to tradition the King was a kindly, weak, chubby albino. His saintliness brought him as the years passed a reward in the veneration of his people, who forgave him his weakness for the sake of his virtues. He is known to us as Edward the Confessor.

Coin of Edward the Confessor, the last Anglo-Saxon king. The disease of scrofula, a tubercular disorder of the glands of the neck, was reputedly cured by Edward's touch. He was canonised a century after his death by Pope Alexander III for his supposed gifts of healing.

Meanwhile the Godwin family maintained their dictatorship under the Crown. Nepotism in those days was not merely the favouring of a man's own family; it was almost the only way in which a ruler could procure trustworthy lieutenants. The family tie, though frequently failing, gave at least the assurance of a certain identity of interest. We must not therefore hasten to condemn Earl Godwin because he parcelled out the English realm among his relations; neither must we marvel that other ambitious magnates found a deep cause of complaint in this distribution of power, and that for some years a bitter intrigue was carried on between Norman and Anglo-Danish influences at the English Court.

A crisis came in the year 1051, when the Norman party at Court succeeded in driving Earl Godwin into exile. During Godwin's absence William of Normandy is said to have paid an official visit to Edward in England in quest of the succession to the Crown. Very likely King Edward promised that William should be his heir. But in the following year Godwin returned, backed by a force raised in Flanders, and with the active help of his son Harold. Together father and son obliged King Edward to take them back into power. Many of the principal Norman agents were expelled, and the authority of the Godwin family was felt again throughout the land.

Seven months after his restoration Godwin died, in 1053. Since Canute first raised him to eminence he had been thirty-five years in public life. Harold, his eldest surviving son, succeeded to his father's great estates. He now filled his part to the full, and for the next thirteen adventurous years was the virtual ruler of England. In spite of the antagonism of rival Anglo-Danish earls, and the opposition of the Norman elements still attached to the Confessor's Court, the Godwins, father and son, maintained their rule under what we should now call a constitutional monarchy. A brother of Harold's became Earl of East Anglia, and a third son of Godwin, Tostig, who courted the Normans and was high in the favour of King Edward, received the Earldom of Northumbria, dispossessing the earls of those regions. But there was now no unity within the house of Godwin. Harold and Tostig soon became bitter foes. All Harold's competence, vigour, and shrewdness were needed to preserve the unity of the realm. Even so, as we shall see, the rift between the brothers left the land a prey to foreign ambitions.

The political condition of England at the close of the reign of Edward the Confessor was thus one of widespread weakness. Illuminated manuscripts, sculpture, metalwork and architecture of much artistic merit were still produced, religious life flourished, and a basis of sound administration and law remained, but the virtues and vigour of Alfred's posterity were exhausted and the Saxon monarchy itself was in decline. The descendants of the prolific Ethelred the Unready died out with strange rapidity, and at this moment only a sickly boy and his sister and the aged sovereign represented the warrior dynasty which had beaten the Vikings and reconquered the Danelaw. The great earls were becoming independent in the provinces.

Though England was still the only state in Europe with a royal treasury to which sheriffs all over the country had to account, royal control over the sheriffs had grown lax. The King lived largely upon his private estates and governed as best he could through his household. The remaining powers of the monarchy were in practice severely restricted by a little group of Anglo-Danish notables. The main basis of support for the English kings had always been this select Council, never more than sixty, who in a vague manner regarded themselves as the representatives of the whole country. It was in fact a committee of courtiers, the greatest thanes, and ecclesiastics. But at this time this assembly of "wise men" in no way embodied the life of the nation. It weakened the royal executive without adding any strength of its own. Its character and quality suffered in the general decay. It tended to fall into the hands of the great families. As the central power declined a host of local chieftains disputed and intrigued in every county, pursuing private and family aims and knowing no interest but their own. Feuds and disturbances were rife. The people, too, were hampered not only by the many conflicting petty authorities, but by the deep division of custom between the Saxon and the Danish districts. Absurd anomalies and contradictions obstructed the administration of justice. The system of land tenure varied from complete manorial conditions in Wessex to the free communities of the Danelaw in the north and east. There was no defined relation between lordship and land. A thane owed service to the King as a personal duty, and not in respect of lands he held. The island had come to count for little on the Continent, and had lost the thread of its own progress. The defences, both of the coast and of the towns, were neglected. To the coming conquerors the whole system, social, moral, political, and military, seemed effete.

The figure of Edward the Confessor comes down to us faint, misty, frail. The medieval legend, carefully fostered by the Church, whose devoted servant he was, surpassed the man. The lights of Saxon England were going out, and in the gathering darkness a gentle, grey-beard prophet foretold the end. When on his deathbed Edward spoke of a time of evil that was coming upon the land his inspired mutterings struck terror into the hearers. Only Archbishop Stigand, who had been Godwin's stalwart, remained unmoved, and whispered in Harold's ear that age and sickness had robbed the monarch of his wits. Thus on January 5, 1066, ended the line of the Saxon kings. The national sentiment of the English, soon to be conquered, combined in the bitter period that lay before them with the gratitude of the Church to circle the royal memory with a halo. As the years rolled by his spirit became the object of popular worship. The Normans also had an interest in his fame. For them he was the King by whose wisdom the Crown had been left, or so they claimed, to their Duke. Hence both sides blessed his memory, and until England appropriated St George during the Hundred Years' War, St Edward the Confessor, canonised in 1161, was the kingdom's patron saint. St George proved undoubtedly more suitable to the islanders' needs, moods and character.

CHAPTER 9

THE NORMAN INVASION

ENGLAND, DISTRACTED BY FACTION and rivalry at home, had for a long time lain under rapacious glare from overseas. The Scandinavians sought to revive the empire of Canute. The Normans claimed that their Duke held his cousin Edward's promise of the throne. The prize was large enough for the separate ambitions of both the hungry powers.

One morning Duke Robert of Normandy, the fourth descendant of Rollo, was riding towards his capital town, Falaise, when he saw Arlette, daughter of a tanner, washing linen in a stream. His love was instantly fired. He carried her to his castle and, although already married to a lady of quality, lived with her for the rest of his days. To this romantic but irregular union there was born in 1027 a son, William, afterwards famous.

Duke Robert died when William was only seven, and in those harsh times a minor's hold upon his inheritance was precarious. Rival ambitions stirred throughout Normandy. Were they to be ruled by a bastard? Was the grandson of a tanner to be the liege lord of the many warrior families? The taint of bastardy clung, and sank deep into William's nature. It embittered and hardened him. When, many years afterwards, he besieged the town of Alençon the citizens imprudently hung out hides upon the walls, shouting, "Hides for the tanner!" William repaid this taunt by devastating the town.

It was, however, the declared policy of King Henry of France to recognise and preserve the minor upon the ducal throne. He became his feudal overlord. But for this the boy could hardly have survived. In 1047, when he was twenty, a formidable conspiracy was organised against him, and at the outset of the revolt he narrowly missed destruction. William was hunting in the heart of the disaffected country. His seizure was planned, but his fool broke in upon him with a timely warning to fly for his life. By daybreak he had ridden forty miles and was for the moment safe in loyal Falaise. Knowing that his own strength could not suffice, he rode on ceaselessly to appeal for help to his overlord. This was not denied. King Henry took the field. William gathered together his loyal barons and retainers. At the Battle

The Bayeux Tapestry tells the story of the Norman invasion through Norman eyes. It justifies William's actions by emphasising Harold's treachery in having himself crowned in Westminster Abbey after having sworn fealty to the Norman duke.

The Bayeux Tapestry: the Normans chop down trees, saw them into planks, and construct ships to transport the Norman cavalry to England. The ships resembled Viking longboats: the Normans were by origin Vikings from north Europe.

of Val-ès-Dunes, fought entirely on both sides by cavalry, the rebels were routed, and thenceforward, for the first time, William's position as Duke of Normandy was secure.

Within the existing social system the sense of affinity to a liege lord, and the acceptance of the Papal authority in spiritual matters, united the steel-clad knights and nobles over an ever-widening area of Europe. To this was added the conception of a warrior aristocracy, animated by ideas of chivalry, and knit together in a system of military service based upon the holding of land. This institution was accompanied by the rise of mail-clad cavalry to a dominant position in war, and new forces were created which could not only conquer but rule.

In no part of the feudal world was the fighting quality of a new organisation carried to a higher pitch than among the Normans. William was a master of war, and thereby gave his small duchy some of the prestige which England had enjoyed thirty years before under Canute. He and his knights now looked out upon the world with fearless and adventurous eyes. Good reasons for gazing across the Channel were added to the natural ambitions of warlike men. William, like his father, was in close touch with the Saxon Court, and had watched every move on the part of the supporters of the Anglo-Danish party, headed by Godwin and his son Harold.

Fate played startlingly into the hands of the Norman Duke. On some visit of inspection, probably in 1064, Harold was driven by the winds onto the French coast. The Count of Ponthieu, who held sway there, looked upon all shipwrecked mariners and their gear as treasure-trove, Duke William asked for the release of King Edward's thane, acting at first by civil request, and later by armed commands. The Count of Ponthieu reluctantly relinquished his windfall and conducted Harold to the Norman Court. A friendship sprang up between William and Harold. We see them, falcon on wrist, in sport; Harold taking the field with William against the Bretons, or rendering skilful service in hazardous broils. But the Duke looked forward to his future succession to the English Crown. He saw the power which Harold wielded under Edward the Confessor, and how easily he might convert it into sovereignty. He therefore invited Harold to make a pact with him whereby he himself should become King of England, and Harold the earl of Wessex, being assured thereof by marriage with William's daughter.

All this story is told with irresistible charm in the tapestry chronicle of the reign commonly attributed to William's wife, Queen Matilda, but actually designed by English artists under the guidance of his half-brother, Odo, Bishop of Bayeux. It is of course the Norman version, and was for generations proclaimed by their historians as a full justification — and already even in those days aggressors needed justifications — of William's invasion of England. The Saxons contended that this was mere propaganda. It is probable however that Harold swore a solemn oath to renounce all rights or designs upon the English Crown, and it is likely that if he had not done so he might never have seen either Crown or England again. The feudal significance of this oath making Harold William's man was enhanced by a trick novel to those times, yet adapted to their mentality. Under the altar or table upon which Harold swore there was concealed a sacred relic. An oath thus reinforced had a triple sanctity, well recognised throughout Christendom.

By this time William had consolidated his position at home. He had destroyed the armies of his rivals and ambitious relations, he had stabilised his western frontier against Brittany, and in the southwest he had conquered Maine from the most powerful of the ruling houses of northern France, the Angevins. He had forced the powers in Paris who had protected his youth to respect his manhood; and by his marriage with Matilda, daughter of the Count of Flanders, he had acquired a useful ally on his eastern flank. Meanwhile Harold, liberated, was conducting the government of England with genuine acceptance and increasing success.

At length, in January 1066, Edward the Confessor died, absolved, we trust, from such worldly sins as he had been tempted to commit. With his dying breath, in spite of his alleged promise to William, he is supposed to have commended Harold, his young, valiant counsellor and guide, as the best choice for the Crown which the Witan, or Council, could make. At any rate, Harold, at the beginning of the fateful year 1066, was blithely accepted by London, the Midlands, and the south, and crowned King with all solemnity in Westminster Abbey.

This event opened again the gates of war. The elevation of a non-royal personage was strongly resented by the nobility. Moreover, the entire structure of the feudal world rested upon the sanctity of oaths. Against the breakers of oaths the censures both of chivalry and the Church were combined with blasting force. At this very moment the Almighty, reaching down from His heavenly sphere, made an ambiguous gesture. The tailed comet or "hairy star" which appeared at the time of Harold's coronation is now identified by astronomers as Halley's comet; and it is evident that this example of divine economy in the movements for mundane purposes of celestial bodies might have been turned by deft interpretation to Harold's advantage. But the conquerors have told the tale, and in their eyes this portent conveyed the approaching downfall of a sacrilegious upstart.

Two rival projects of invasion were speedily prepared. The first was from Scandinavia. The successors of Canute in Norway determined to revive their traditions of English sovereignty. An expedition was already being organised when Tostig, Harold's revengeful half-brother, now ousted from his Earldom of Northumbria, arrived with full accounts of the crisis in the island and of the weak state of its defences. Norway's King Harold Hardrada set forth to conquer the English Crown.

In September 1066 Harold of England heard that a Norwegian fleet, with Hardrada and Tostig on board, had sailed up the Humber, beaten the local

The Bayeux Tapestry: the Norman fleet of longships, with brightly patterned sails, crosses the Channel. The ships carry warriors, warhorses, weapons, shields and stores of food and wine.

The Bayeux Tapestry: the Normans, having landed at Pevensey, drag their longships ashore. They have removed some of their clothes to avoid getting wet. The borders of the Bayeux Tapestry are a useful source for social historians.

levies under Earls Edwin and Morcar, and encamped near York at Stamford Bridge. He now showed the fighting qualities he possessed. The news reached him in London, where he was waiting to see which invasion would strike him first, and where. At the head of his troops he hastened northward to York, calling out the local levies as he went. His rapidity of movement took the northern invaders completely by surprise. Within five days of the defeat of Edwin and Morcar, Harold reached Stamford Bridge.

The battle began. The Englishmen charged, but at first the Norsemen, though without their armour, kept their battle array. After a while, deceived by what proved to be a feint, the common ruse of those days, they opened up their shield rampart and advanced from all sides. This was the moment for which Harold had waited. The greatest crash of weapons arose. Hardrada was hit by an arrow in the throat, and Harold's valiant house-carls, themselves of Viking blood, charged home. The victorious Harold buried Hardrada in the seven feet of English earth he had scornfully promised him, but he let his son Olaf go in peace with his surviving adherents. Tostig paid for his restless malice with his life. Though the Battle of Stamford Bridge has been overshadowed by Hastings it has a claim to be regarded as one of the decisive contests of English history. Never again was a Scandinavian army able seriously to threaten the power of an English king.

At the moment of victory news reached the King from the south that "William the Bastard" had landed at Pevensey. William's invasion had been planned like a business enterprise. The resources of Normandy were obviously unequal to the task; but the Duke's name was famous throughout the feudal world, and the idea of seizing and dividing England commended itself to the martial nobility of many lands. The shares in this enterprise were represented by knights or ships, and it was plainly engaged that the lands of the slaughtered English would be divided in proportion to contributions, subject of course to a bonus for good work in the field. France was deeply interested. Mercenaries came from Flanders. Normans from South Italy and Spain, nobles and knights answered the advertisement.

During the summer of 1066 this great gathering of audacious buccaneers assembled in a merry company around St Valery, at the mouth of the Somme. Ships had been built in all the French ports from the spring onward, and by the beginning of August a considerable fleet, carrying about seven thousand fighting men, of whom the majority were persons of rank and quality, was ready to follow the Duke and share the wealth of England.

But the winds were contrary. For six whole weeks there was no day when the south wind blew. The heterogeneous army, bound by no ties of feudal allegiance, patriotism, or moral theme, began to bicker. Only William's repute as a managing director and the rich pillage to be expected held them together. At length extreme measures had to be taken with the weather. The bones of St Edmund were brought from the Church of St Valery and carried with military and religious pomp along the seashore. This proved effective, for the very next day the wind changed. William gave the signal. The whole fleet put to sea, with all their stores, weapons, coats of mail, and great numbers of horses.

On September 28 the fleet came safely to anchor in Pevensey Bay. There was no opposition to the landing. The local militia had been called out this year four times already to watch the coast, and having, in true English style, come to the conclusion that the danger was past because it had not yet

The sites of the Norman landing at Pevensey and the battleground near Hastings. William's army did not immediately engage with Harold's which was three hundred miles north at the time of William's landing, conquering the Norwegian leader Harold Hardrada at Stamford Bridge in east Yorkshire.

arrived had gone back to their homes. As the tale goes, William landed flat on his face as he stepped out of the boat. "See," he said, turning the omen, "I have taken England with both my hands." He occupied himself with organising his army, raiding for supplies, and building some defensive works for the protection of his fleet and base. Thus a fortnight passed.

Meanwhile Harold and his house-carls, sadly depleted by the slaughter of Stamford Bridge, marched night and day to London. They covered the two hundred miles in seven days. In London most of the principal persons in Wessex and Kent hastened to join, bringing their retainers and local militia with them. Remaining only five days in London, Harold marched out towards Pevensey, and in the evening of October 13 took up his position upon the slope of a hill which barred the direct march upon the capital.

The military opinion of those as of these days has criticised his staking all upon an immediate battle. Some have suggested that he should have used the tactics Cassivellaunus had employed against Caesar. But these critics overlook the fact that whereas the Roman army consisted only of infantry, and the British of charioteers and horsemen, Duke William's was essentially a cavalry force assisted by archers, while Harold had nothing but foot-soldiers who used horses only as transport. It is one thing for mounted forces to harry an infantry army, and the opposite for bands of foot-soldiers to use these tactics against cavalry. Besides, King Harold had great confidence in his redoubtable axe-men, and it was in good heart that he formed his shield-wall on the morning of October 14. Some modern authorities suppose the battle was fought by five or six thousand Norman knights and men-at-arms, with a few thousand archers, against eight to ten thousand axe-and-spear-men, but the numbers may have been fewer. However it may be, at the first streak of dawn William set out from his camp at Pevensey, and Harold, eight miles away, awaited him in resolute array.

As the battle began Ivo Taillefer, a minstrel knight who had claimed the right to make the first attack, advanced up the hill on horseback, throwing his lance and sword into the air and catching them before the English army. He charged deep into the English ranks, and was slain. Then the cavalry charges of William's mail-clad knights, cumbersome in manoeuvre, beat in vain upon the dense, ordered masses of the English. Neither the arrow hail nor the assaults of the horsemen could prevail against them. Never, it was said, had the Norman knights met foot-soldiers of this stubbornness. They

The Bayeux Tapestry: during the Battle of Hastings the Norman cavalry attack the English infantry, who stand in close formation protected by lozenge-shaped shields. While they remained packed closely the English had a good chance of success, but the Normans pretended to flee and the English broke ranks. This part of the battle is not shown on the Bayeux Tapestry as it represents the Normans in a less valiant light than the traditional view.

The Bayeux Tapestry: Harold, with a decorated shield and a heavy handlebar moustache, is shot in the eye by a Norman archer. The English army despair, and William is left victorious. The scenes on the border of the tapestry reflect the savagery of the battle: corpses are stripped of their armour.

were utterly unable to break through the shield-walls, and they suffered serious losses from deft blows of the axe-men, or from the javelins or clubs hurled from the ranks behind. But the arrow showers took a cruel toll. So closely, it was said, were the English wedged that the wounded could not be removed, and the dead scarcely found room to sink upon the ground.

The autumn afternoon was far spent before any result had been achieved, and it was then that William adopted the time-honoured ruse of a feigned retreat, while keeping a powerful force in his own hands. The house-carls around Harold preserved their discipline and kept their ranks, but the sense of relief to the less trained forces after these hours of combat was such that seeing their enemy in flight proved irresistible. They surged forward on the impulse of victory, and when halfway down the hill were savagely slaughtered by William's horsemen. There remained, as the dusk grew, only the valiant bodyguard who fought around the King and his standard. William now directed his archers to shoot high into the air, so that the arrows would fall behind the shield-wall, and one of these pierced Harold in the right eye, inflicting a mortal wound. He fell at the foot of the royal standard, unconquerable except by death. The hard-fought battle was now decided. William, who had fought in the foremost ranks and had three horses killed under him, could claim the victory.

The dead King's naked body, wrapped only in a robe of purple, was hidden among the rocks of the bay, and later transferred to Waltham Abbey, which he had founded. Although here the English once again accepted conquest and bowed to a new destiny, yet ever must the name of Harold Godwin be honoured in the island for which he and his famous house-carls fought indomitably to the end.

CHAPTER 10

WILLIAM THE CONQUEROR

The head of William, Duke of Normandy and King of England shown on a coin. The Norman kings' territories in France posed problems of defence and government while their rulers were in England. The situation was to be the cause of numerous wars for the next four hundred years.

FOR MORE THAN A YEAR William had been directly planning to invade England and claim the English throne. Now he had, within a month of landing, annihilated the only organised Saxon army and killed his rival. Yet his work was but begun. The very disunity which had made assault successful made subjugation lengthy. Saxon lords in the north and in the west might carry on endless local struggles. Cautiously the advance began upon London.

William was a prime exponent of the doctrine of mass terrorism through the spectacle of bloody and merciless examples. When he arrived near London he marched round the city by a circuitous route, isolating it by a belt of cruel desolation. From Southwark he moved to Wallingford, and thence through the Chilterns to Berkhamsted, where the leading Saxon notables and clergy came meekly to his tent to offer him the Crown.

On Christmas Day, Aldred, Archbishop of York, crowned William King of England at Westminster.

He rapidly established his power over all England south of the Humber, but the north still remained under its Saxon lords, Edwin and Morcar, unsubdued and defiant. The King gathered an army and marched towards them. The track of William in the north was marked for generations upon the countryside and in the memories of the survivors and their descendants. From coast to coast the whole region was laid desolate, and for long years after tales were told of the rotting bodies of the famine-stricken by the roadside. England north of the Humber was also in Norman control, and it was now clear that Normandy had the force and spirit to absorb all Saxon England. But whether William would retain the whole of his conquests unchallenged was not settled till his closing years. The Saxon resistance died hard. Chroniclers have painted for us the last stand of Hereward the Wake in the broad wastes of the fens round Ely. Not until five years after Hastings, in 1071, was Hereward put down. In his cause had fallen many of the Saxon thanage, the only class from whose ranks new leaders could spring. The building of Ely Castle symbolised the end of their order.

Other internal oppositions arose. In 1075 a serious revolt of disaffected Norman knights broke out in the Midlands, East Anglia, and on the Welsh border, and one surviving Saxon leader, Waltheof, joined them. The King in Normandy must hasten back to crush the rebels. The Saxon population supported the Conqueror against chaos. The militia took the field. Vengeance was reserved for Waltheof alone, and his execution upon a hill outside Winchester is told in moving scenes by the Saxon-hearted monkish chroniclers of the time. Medieval legend ascribed the fate of William in his later years to the guilt of this execution. It marked also the final submission of England. Norman castles guarded the towns, Norman lords held the land, and Norman churches protected men's souls. All England had a master, the conquest was complete, and the work of reconstruction began.

Woe to the conquered! Here were the Normans entrenched on English soil, masters of the land and the fullness thereof. An armed warrior from Anjou or Maine or Brittany, or even from beyond the Alps and the Pyrenees, took possession of manor and county, according to his rank and prowess, and set to work to make himself secure. Everywhere castles arose. These were not at first the massive stone structures of a later century; they were simply fortified military posts consisting of an earthen rampart and a stockade, and a central keep made of logs. From these strongpoints horsemen sallied forth to rule and exploit the neighbourhood; above them all, at the summit, sat William, active and ruthless, delighting in his work, requiring punctual service from his adherents, and paying good spoil to all who did their duty.

In their early days the Normans borrowed no manners and few customs from the islanders. The only culture was French. So surviving Saxon notables repeated the experience of the Ancient Britons; all who could learnt French, as formerly the contemporaries of Boadicea had learnt Latin. At first the conquerors, who despised the uncouth English as louts and boors, ruled

The Normans dominated the land from the motte and bailey castles which they built at strategic points overlooking rivers and towns. The soil which was dug to produce the moat was piled in the middle to form a high mound or motte on which the castle was built. The first castles were made of wood, and only later replaced by stone constructions. This fine Norman castle is at Restormel, in Cornwall.

One of the greatest Norman legacies is their architecture. The round-headed arch with its dogtooth pattern is typical of their decorative stone carving, and can be clearly seen in this picture of the Norman church at Iffley on the outskirts of Oxford.

by the force of sharpened steel. But very soon in true Norman fashion they intermarried with the free population and identified themselves with their English past.

William's work in England is the more remarkable from the fact that all the time as Duke of Normandy he was involved in endless intrigues and conflicts with the King of France. Though England was a more valuable possession than Normandy, William and his sons were always more closely interested in their continental lands. The French kings, for their part, placed in the forefront of their policy the weakening of these Dukes of Normandy, now grown so powerful, and whose frontiers were little more than twenty miles from Paris. Queen Matilda was a capable regent at Rouen, but plagued by the turbulence of her sons. The eldest, Robert, reckless and spendthrift, with his father's love of fighting and adventure but without his ruthless genius or solid practical aims, resented William's persistent hold on life. Many a time the father was called across the Channel to chastise rebellious towns and forestall the conspiracies of his son with the French Court. Robert, driven from his father's lands, found refuge in King Philip's castle of Gerberoi. William marched implacably upon him. Beneath the walls two men, visors down, met in single combat, father and son. Robert wounded his father in the hand and unhorsed him, and would indeed have killed him but for a timely rescue by an Englishman, Tokig of Wallingford, who remounted the overthrown Conqueror. Both were sobered by this chance encounter, and for a time there was reconciliation.

Matilda died, and with increasing years William became fiercer in mood. Stung to fury by the forays of the French, he crossed the frontier to sack the town of Mantes. As William rode through the streets his horse stumbled among the burning ashes and he was thrown against the pommel of the saddle. He was carried in agony to the priory of St Gervase at Rouen. There, high above the town, he lay, through the summer heat of 1087, fighting his grievous injury. When death drew near his sons came to him. William, whose one virtue had been filial fidelity, was named to succeed the Conqueror in England. The graceless Robert would rule in Normandy at last. For the youngest, Henry, there was nothing but five thousand pounds of silver, and the prophecy that he would one day reign over a united Anglo-Norman nation. This proved no empty blessing.

Fear fell upon the Conqueror's subjects when it was known that he was dying. What troubles would follow the end of a strong ruler? On September 9, 1087, as the early bells of Rouen Cathedral echoed over the hills, William and his authority died. The caitiff attendants stripped the body and plundered the chamber where he lay, but the clergy of Rouen bore him to the Church of St Stephen at Caen, which he had founded. The Conqueror came thus humbly to his grave. But his work lived.

The Norman achievement in England was not merely military in character. Although knight-service governed the holding of property and produced a new aristocracy, much was preserved of Saxon England. The Normans were administrators and lawyers rather than legislators. Their centre of government was the royal Curia, or Council, the final court of appeal and the instrument of supervision; here were preserved and developed the financial and secretarial methods of the Anglo-Saxon kingdom. The whole system of Saxon local government, also of immense usefulness for the future — the counties, the sheriffs, and the courts — survived, and through this the King maintained his widespread contacts with the country. In fact the Conqueror himself by these means collected the information for his great Domesday inquest in 1086. When it became necessary that all feudal controversies arising out of the Conquest should be speedily settled, a vast sworn inquiry was made into the whole wealth of the King's feudal vassals, from whom he derived a large part of his own income. The inquest or description, as it was called, was carried through with a degree of minuteness and regularity unique in that age and unequalled for centuries after. The result of this famous survey showed that the underlying structure of England and its peasant life were little changed by the invasion. Not only the courts, but also the dues and taxes such as Danegeld, were preserved, and the local militia raised by the counties survived, and proved serviceable to William and his successors. Thus in the future government of England both Norman and Saxon institutions were unconsciously but profoundly blended.

This carving from the crook of a bishop's crosier, now in the Victoria and Albert Museum, South Kensington, demonstrates a high standard of Norman design and craftsmanship.

In some respects all this was a sudden acceleration of the drift towards the manorial system, a process which had already gone a long way in Anglo-Saxon England, and certainly in Wessex. But even in Wessex the idea still persisted that the tie of lord and man was primarily personal, so that a free man could go from one lord to another and transfer his land with him. The essence of Norman feudalism, on the other hand, was that the land remained under the lord, whatever the man might do. Thus the landed pyramid rose up tier by tier to the King, until every acre in the country could be registered as held of somebody by some form of service. But besides the services which the man owed to the lord-in-arms there was the service of attending the courts of the hundred and the county, which were, apart from various exemptions, courts of the King, administering old customary law. This survival of the hundred, the county court, and the sheriff makes the great difference between English and continental feudalism. In England the King is everywhere — if he wants to know anything he tells his officer, the sheriff, to impanel a jury and find out, or in later days, to send some respectable persons to Westminster and tell him.

The little provinces of England, with the King's officers at the head of each, gave him exactly the balance of power he needed for all purposes of law and finance, but were at the same time incapable of rebelling as units. The old English nobility disappeared after the Battle of Hastings. But all over Domesday Book the opinion of what we should later call the gentry of the shire is quoted as decisive. This is the class — people of some consideration in the neighbourhood, with leisure to go to the sheriff's court and thereafter to Westminster. Out of this process in time the Pyms and Hampdens arose. The Conquest was the supreme achievement of the Norman race. It linked the history of England anew to Europe, and prevented forever a drift into the narrower orbit of a Scandinavian empire. Henceforward, English history marched with that of races and lands south of the Channel.

The patterned columns in the nave of Durham Cathedral are as famous as its dominating position. The massive stone walls suggest that it was built not only for spiritual purposes but also as a symbol of power.

The effect of the Conquest on the Church was no less broad and enlivening when William turned to the religious sphere. The key appointment was the Archbishopric of Canterbury. In 1070 the Saxon Stigand was deposed and succeeded by Lanfranc. A Lombard of high administrative ability, Lanfranc rapidly infused new life into the English Church. Organisation and discipline were reformed. Older sees were transplanted from villages to towns — Crediton to Exeter, and Selsey to Chichester. New episcopal seats were established, and by 1087 the masons were at work on seven new cathedrals.

DOMESDAY BOOK

DOMESDAY BOOK is an invaluable, though incomplete, survey of England's land and people, commissioned by the first Norman king, William I, at Christmas 1085. It was a testimony to his power that he could order it to be carried out meticulously, hundred by hundred—the land units into which the Saxons had divided their counties—and that the conquered Saxons recognised its authority. It was they, not the king, who called the final version Domesday, because it reminded them of the Last Judgment, described in the book of *Revelation* and depicted in church wall paintings.

There are two Domesday volumes, and they cover most parts of England, though London was omitted.

One major object of the exercise was financial—to protect and increase the king's revenue; and as one chronicler complained "there was not even an ox or a cow or a pig that was not set down in writing". It was completed with remarkable speed and was almost ready when William died in 1087. Yet the making of it was not the conclusion but the beginning of its history; it was a working record throughout the Middle Ages and it has been well used by historians as a source of information.

In the England of Domesday nine people out of ten lived in rural settlements. Only one in twenty-five lived in a town of over two thousand inhabitants—there were ten such towns, including York, Norwich and Leicester—and nearly half of those were Londoners. A number of craftsmen such as masons, smiths and weavers, and a few officials, lived in the farming communities.

The population was densest in the east of the country, and particularly thin in the north, and there were heavily wooded areas where few people lived at all. The survey gave no details of landscapes, crop yields nor communications, and some of its statistics are clearly inadequate. For example, in a country noted for its eating of fish, very few fishermen were counted.

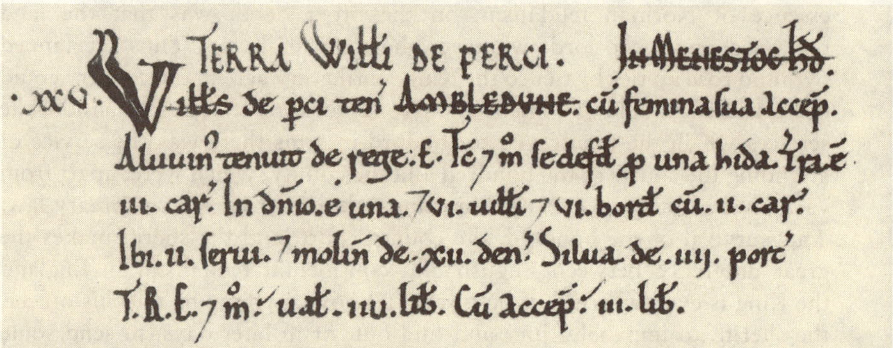

THE "GREAT DOMESDAY" BOOK *(top) contains a digest of information about most of England, prepared for the Treasury at Winchester. The closed book beside it is the more detailed "Little Domesday", which covers East Anglia. The books stand on the iron-studded Domesday Chest in which they were kept. The survey was made by requiring juries, under oath, to answer questions such as "What is the manor (village) called? Who holds it? How much ploughing, woodland and pasture is there? How many oxen, sheep and swine?" An extract (above) about Hampshire, from the "Great Domesday", is written in Latin by one of the two main scribes, on parchment made from sheepskin. The sheets of vellum were pricked and ruled with a sharp pointed tool on the hair side. The marks showed through to form a writing guide on the flesh side. Writing was a laborious business and scribes managed only about three hundred lines a day. Quills needed sharpening and a monk (left) holds a knife with which to perform this task. The illustration is from a twelfth-century manuscript in Trinity College, Cambridge.*

AUTHORITY AND POWER lay in the hands of the lords of the manor. They received labour and services from their tenants, who thus paid for the use of their holdings in land. When armies were needed, the tenants had to provide military service too; it was illegal for serfs (labourers) to move away from their native manor. The scenes (right) from a medieval book of psalms show Sir Geoffrey Luttrell at dinner with his family, while his servants chop meat into portions.

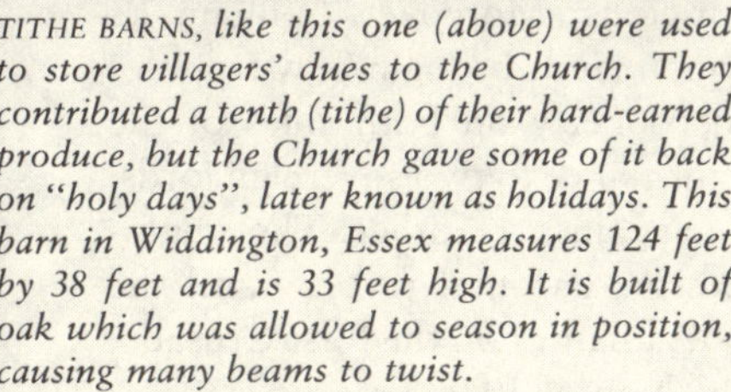

TITHE BARNS, like this one (above) were used to store villagers' dues to the Church. They contributed a tenth (tithe) of their hard-earned produce, but the Church gave some of it back on "holy days", later known as holidays. This barn in Widdington, Essex measures 124 feet by 38 feet and is 33 feet high. It is built of oak which was allowed to season in position, causing many beams to twist.

THE RIDGES AND FURROWS of ancient ploughlands (right) are seen in this aerial view of the deserted village of Lower Ditchford, Gloucester. In Domesday times, the land would have been organised in the Open Field or Three Field system. Tenants farmed strips in each field, one of which lay fallow every year.

THE GRUELLING WORK OF PEASANTS is commemorated in this detail from the Bayeux Tapestry (left), which depicts Norman and English life just before Domesday was compiled.

New abbeys sprang up all over the country which attested the piety of the conquerors, though few of the new houses attained to the wealth or standing of the older foundations. These monasteries and bishoprics were the chief centres of religion and learning, until after a century they were gradually eclipsed by the rise of the universities. But the new Churchmen were even less disposed than the nobles to draw any deep line across history at the Norman conquest. Slowly but surely the Frenchmen came to venerate the old English saints and English shrines, and the continuity of religious life was maintained.

The spirit of the long-vanished Roman Empire, revived by the Catholic Church, thus returned once more to the island, bringing with it three dominant ideas. First, a Europe in which nationalism or even the conception of nationality had no place, but where one general theme of conduct and law united the triumphant martial classes upon a plane far above race. Secondly, the idea of monarchy, in the sense that kings were the expression of the class hierarchy over which they presided and the arbiters of its frequently conflicting interests. Thirdly, there stood triumphant the Catholic Church, combining Roman imperialism and Christian ethics, pervaded by the social and military system of the age, jealous for its own interests and authority, but still preserving all that was left of learning and art.

CHAPTER 11

GROWTH AMID TURMOIL

This late medieval manuscript picture creates an idealised impression of Jerusalem bathed in light.

The first generation after the Norman Conquest formed a period when the victorious army and caste were settling themselves upon the lands they had gained. Under William the Conqueror this process had been harsh and thorough. Under his son William, dubbed Rufus, the Red, it was not less harsh, but also capricious. Moreover, William I's decision to divide his English from his Norman lands brought new troubles in its train. The greater barons possessed property on both sides of the Channel. They therefore now owed feudal allegiance to two sovereign lords, and not unnaturally they sought to play one against the other. The Anglo-Norman realms were thus vexed by successive baronial revolts until the feckless Robert eventually departed in a fit of gallantry on the First Crusade, leaving Normandy pawned to Rufus for the loan of 10,000 marks.

The crusading spirit had for some time stirred the minds of men all over Western Europe. The Seljuk Turks were pressing hard upon the Byzantine Empire in Asia Minor, and harassing devout pilgrims from Europe through Syria to the Holy Land. The Byzantine Emperor appealed to the West for help, and in 1095 Pope Urban II, who had long dreamt of recovering Jerusalem for Christendom, called on the chivalry of Europe to take the Cross. The response was immediate, overwhelming, and at first disastrous. An itinerant monk named Peter the Hermit took up the cry to arms. So powerful was his preaching that in 1096 an enthusiastic but undisciplined train of twenty thousand men, most of them peasants unskilled in war, set off from Cologne under his leadership. Few of them ever reached the Holy Land. After marching through the Balkans the majority perished by Turkish arrows amid the mountains of Asia Minor.

The so-called "People's Crusade" thus collapsed. But by now the magnates of Europe had rallied to the Cause. Four armies, each numbering perhaps ten thousand men, and led by some of the greatest nobles of the age, converged on Constantinople from France, Germany, Italy, and the Low Countries. The Byzantine Emperor was embarrassed. He had hoped for manageable mercenaries as reinforcements. Instead, he found camped around his capital four powerful and ambitious hosts.

The march of the Crusaders through his dominions into the Turkish-held lands was marred by intrigue and by grievous disputes. But there was hard fighting too. A way was hacked through Asia Minor; and Antioch, once a great bastion of the Christian faith, which the Turks had taken, was recaptured in 1098. The Crusaders were cheered and succoured by the arrival off the Syrian coast of a fleet commanded by an English prince, Edgar the Atheling, great-nephew of Edward the Confessor. Thus by a strange turn of fortune the displaced heir of the Saxon royal line joined hands with Robert of Normandy, the displaced heir of William the Conqueror.

Aided by jealousy between the Turks and the Sultans of Egypt, the Crusaders pressed forward. On June 7, 1099, they reached their long-sought goal and encamped about Jerusalem, then in Egyptian hands. On July 14 the city fell to their assault. Many of the principal Crusaders thereupon went home, but for nearly a century a mixed international body of knights, all commonly called Franks, ruled over a string of Christian principalities in Palestine and along the coast of Syria. Western Christendom, so long the victim of invaders, had at last struck back and won its first great footing in the Eastern world.

Meanwhile in England, Rufus's extortions and violent methods had provoked the baronage throughout his reign. In August 1100 he was mysteriously shot through the head by an arrow while hunting in the New Forest, leaving a memory of shameless exactions and infamous morals, but also a submissive realm to his successors. The main progress in his reign was financial; but the new feudal monarchy was also more firmly established, and in territory its sway was wider than at Rufus's accession. The Norman lords whom the Conqueror had settled upon the Welsh Marches (Borders) had fastened a lasting grip upon southern Wales. The northern counties had been finally brought under Norman control, and a military frontier drawn against the Scots.

Prince Henry, the youngest of the royal brothers, had been a member of the fatal hunting party in the New Forest. There is no proof that he was implicated in the death of his brother, but he certainly wasted no time in mourning. He made straight for Winchester, and gained possession of the royal treasury. Evidently he represented a strong movement of opinion among the leading classes, and he had a policy of his own. His scholarship deserved the title of *Beauclerc* which the custom of his day accorded him. He set the precedent of proclaiming a charter upon his accession, by which he guaranteed that the rights of the baronage and the Church should be respected. At the same time, having seen the value of Saxon loyalty in the reigns of his father and his brother, he promised the conquered race good justice and the laws of Edward the Confessor. He knew that the friction caused by the separation of Normandy from England was by no means soothed. Duke Robert was already on his way back from his Crusade and the barons on both sides of the Channel would profit from fraternal strife to

The Temple Church, London, was constructed by the Knights Templar in 1185 on the model of the Church of the Holy Sepulchre in Jerusalem. The Holy City was the Crusaders' destination, but few ever reached it. Many died on the long journey without facing the infidel.

In the summer of 1100, William Rufus was mysteriously killed in a hunting accident in the New Forest. William was a forceful king who had infuriated the Church by postponing clerical appointments so that he could enrich himself from Church revenues while positions remained vacant. Contemporary manuscripts, like this one from the Bodleian Library, Oxford, portray the King's death with some relish.

drive hard bargains in their own interests. Henry's desire to base himself in part at least upon the Saxon population of England led him to make a marriage with Matilda, niece of the last surviving Saxon claimant to the English throne and descendant of the old English line of kings. The barons, mollified by the charter, accepted this decisive step.

Henry was now ready to face Robert whenever he should return. In September 1100 this event occurred. Immediately the familiar incidents of feudal rebellion were renewed in England, and for the next six years the King had to fight to make good his title. But the root evil lay in Normandy, and in 1105, having consolidated his position in England, Henry crossed the Channel. In September 1106 the most important battle since Hastings was fought at Tinchebrai. King Henry's victory was complete. Duke Robert was carried to perpetual prison in England. Normandy acknowledged Henry's authority, and the control of Anglo-Norman policy passed from Rouen to London. The Saxons, who had fought heartily for Henry, regarded this battle as their military revenge for Hastings. By this new comradeship with the Crown, as well as by the royal marriage with Matilda, they felt themselves relieved from some at least of the pangs of being conquered. The shame was gone; the penalties could be endured. Through these two far-reaching factors a certain broad measure of unity was re-established.

Henry was free for the time being to devote himself to internal government and to strengthening the power of the Crown throughout the land. There survived in medieval Europe a tradition of kingship more exalted than that of feudal overlord, the Roman conception of the king as the anointed vicegerent of God upon earth. Henry now set himself to inject his idea of kingship into the Anglo-Norman state; and in so doing he could not help reviving, whether consciously or not, the English conception of the King as the keeper of the peace and guardian of the people.

The centre of government, the King's Council, was an ill-defined body consisting of those tenants-in-chief whose feudal duty it was to attend when summoned, and those personal servants of the monarch who could be used for government service as well as for their household duties. Henry realised that royal servants who were members of the minor baronage, if formed into a permanent nucleus, would act as a brake upon the turbulence of the greater feudatories. Here were the first beginnings, tentative, modest but insinuating, of a civil administrative machinery, which within its limits was more efficient and persistent than anything yet known. These officials soon developed a vested interest of their own. Families like the Clintons and the Bassetts, whom the King, as the chronicler put it, had "raised from the dust to do him service", entrenched themselves in the household offices, and created what was in fact an official class.

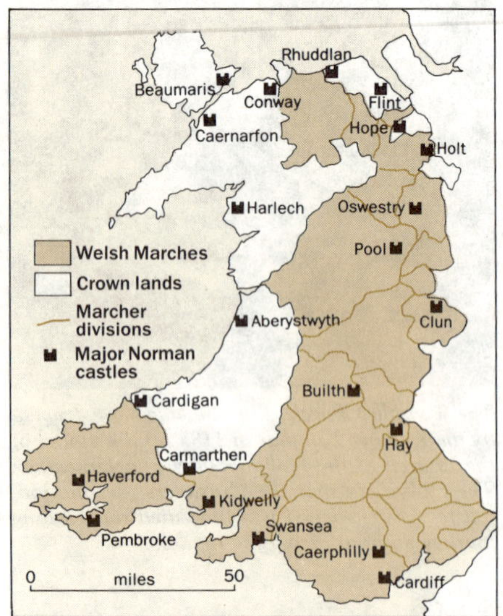

A contemporary chronicler recorded that William the Conqueror subdued Wales by building fortified castles along the borders (marches). "Wales was in his power and he built castles there, and he entirely controlled that race."

The power of any government depends ultimately upon its finances. It was therefore in the business of gathering and administering the revenue that this novel feature first became apparent. The sheriffs of counties collected not only the taxes and fines accruing to the Crown, but also the income from the royal estates, and they were responsible, when they appeared yearly at the royal treasury, for the exact payment of what was due from each of their counties. Henry's officials created a special organ to deal with the sheriffs and the business the sheriffs transacted. This was the Exchequer, still regarded simply as the council meeting for financial purposes, but gradually acquiring a life of its own. It took its name from the chequered boards used for greater ease of calculation in Roman numerals. Thus the earliest specialised department of royal administration was born.

One of the most fertile sources of revenue arose from the fines imposed by the courts upon delinquents. The barons realised this too, and their manorial courts provided them with important incomes, which could at once be turned into armed retainers. Within their domains they enjoyed a jurisdiction over nearly all laymen. But in the county court and in the courts of the hundreds, the Crown had at its disposal the old Saxon system of justice. These time-honoured institutions could well be used to rival the feudal courts of the baronage. Henry therefore revised and regularised the holding of the county courts, and made all men see that throughout the land there was a system of royal justice. King's officers — judges as they became — in their occasional circuits administered this justice, and the very nature of their function brought them often into clash not only with humble suitors and malefactors, but with proud military magnates.

The King thus entered into a nationwide competition with the baronage as to who could best deserve the rich spoils of the law. Through his control of the sheriffs he bound together the monarchy and the old Saxon system of local justice. The Conqueror had set the example when in the Domesday survey he combined the continental system of getting information by means of bodies of men sworn to tell the truth with the English organisation by shire and hundred. His son for other purposes continued and intensified the process, sending officials constantly from his Household through the kingdom, and convening the county courts to inquire into the claims of the royal

A TWELFTH-CENTURY MANSION

Gerald of Wales, the son of a powerful Norman baron and a Welsh princess, describes the fortified house in Manorbier, Pembrokeshire, where he was born in about 1146. Gerald described himself in his thirties as "a young man, with Nature's bounty of delicate features — they were not to last — and greatly distinguished by my handsome physique". This extract is taken from Gerald's account of a trip made in 1188, and recorded in his book The Journey Through Wales.

Only about three miles from Pembroke Castle is the fortified mansion know as Manorbier. There the house stands, visible from afar because of its turrets and crenellations, on the top of a hill which is quite near the sea. There is an excellent fishpond, a most attractive orchard and hazel-nut trees which grow to a great height. A stream of water which never fails winds its way along a valley, which is strewn with sand by the strong sea-winds. It runs down from a large lake, and there is a watermill on its bank. To the west it is washed by a winding inlet of the Severn Sea. . . . Boats on their way to Ireland from almost any part of Britain scud by before the east wind, and from this vantage-point you can see them brave the ever-changing violence of the winds.

This is a region rich in wheat, with fish from the sea and plenty of wine for sale. What is more important than all the rest is that, from its nearness to Ireland, heaven's breath smells so wooingly there.

Of all the different parts of Wales, Dyved is at once the most beautiful and the most productive. Of all Dyved, the province of Pembroke is the most attractive; and in all Pembroke, Manorbier is the most pleasant place by far. You will not be surprised to hear me lavish such praise upon it, when I tell you that this is where my own family came from, this is where I myself was born. I can only ask you to forgive me.

In these parts of Pembroke, in our own times, unclean spirits have been in close communication with human beings. They are not visible, but their presence is felt all the same. They have been in the habit of throwing refuse all over the place, more keen perhaps to be a nuisance than to do any real harm. They are a cause of annoyance to both host and guests alike, ripping up their clothes of linen, and their woollen ones, too, and even cutting holes in them.

Manorbier Castle, Dyfed, was the birthplace of Gerald of Wales. Now a picturesque ruin, it is open to visitors in summer.

revenue and to hear cases in which the Crown was interested. From these local inquiries by royal officials there were to spring far-reaching consequences in the reign of Henry II. The chroniclers spoke well of Henry I. "Good man he was," they declared, "and there was great awe of him. In his days no man dared to harm another." They bestowed upon him the title "Lion of Justice", and none has sought to rob him of it.

We must regard his reign as a period when the central government, by adroit and sharp accountancy and clerking, established in a more precise form the structure and resources of the State. In the process the stresses grew between the royal authority and the feudal leaders upon whom the local government of the land depended. The King's hand, though it lay heavy upon all, became increasingly a protection of the people against the injustice and caprice of the local rulers. We see therefore the beginning of an attachment to the King or central government on the part of the people, which invested the Crown with a new source of strength, sometimes forthcoming and sometimes estranged, but always to be gathered, especially after periods of weakness and disorder, by a strong and righteous ruler.

The Anglo-Norman State was now powerful. Henry was lord of England, Normandy, and Maine. In 1109 his daughter Matilda was betrothed to Henry V, Holy Roman Empereror and King of Germany. On the other hand, the reunion of England after Tinchebrai had stirred the hostility of France, and his position in Normandy was continually threatened by the claims of Robert's son, William the Clito, who until his death in 1128 was backed by King Louis, and also by the neighbouring state of Anjou, which disputed King Henry's rights in Maine. Warfare darkened the later years of the reign, though from the military point of view Henry was easily able to hold his own against any army the French could put into the field.

What may be judged malignant fortune now intervened. The King had one son, and on this young man of seventeen many hopes and assurances were founded. In the winter of 1120 he was coming back from a visit to France in the royal yacht, called the *White Ship*. Off the coast of Normandy the vessel struck a rock and he was drowned. None dared tell it to the King. When at last he heard the tidings it is said he never smiled again. This was more than the agony of parental grief for an only son. It portended the breakdown of a system and prospect upon the consolidation of which the whole life's work of Henry stood. The spectre of a disputed succession glared again upon England and the forces of anarchy grew.

A silver penny of Queen Matilda, or Maud. Civil war broke out in 1139 because of a disputed succession between Henry I's nephew, Stephen, and his daughter, Maud.

There were two claimants, each of whom had a fair share of right. The King had a daughter, Matilda, or Maud as the English called her, but although there was no Salic Law in the Norman code, this clanking, jangling aristocracy, mailed and spurred, did not take kindly to the idea of a woman's rule. Against her stood the claim of Stephen, son of the Conqueror's daughter Adela. Stephen, Count of Blois, was leader of the Norman barons, and possessed great estates in England; he was the rightful male heir. The English have never in later ages barred queens, and perhaps queens have served them best. But here at this time was a deep division, and a quarrel in which all parties could take sides. The whole interest of the baronage, supported at this juncture by the balancing weight of the Church, was to limit the power of the Crown and regain their control of their own districts. Now in a division of the royal authority they saw their chance.

King Henry in the grey close of his life spent his remaining years in trying to establish a kind of "pragmatic sanction" for a family succession which would spare his widespread domains from civil war. At the age of thirteen Maud had been married to the Holy Roman Emperor. In 1125, five years after the *White Ship* sank, he died, and at twenty-two she was a widow and an Empress. Fierce, proud, hard, cynical, living for politics above all other passions, however turbulent, she was fitted to bear her part in any war. On two separate occasions Henry called his murmuring barons together and solemnly swore them to stand by Maud. Subsequently, in order to enhance her unifying authority, and to protect Normandy from the claims of Anjou after his death, he married her to Geoffrey the Count of Anjou, thus linking the interests of the most powerful state in northern France with the family and natural succession in England. Henry I expired on December 1, 1135, in the confident hope that his daughter Maud would carry on his work. But she was with her husband in Anjou and Stephen was the first on the scene. Swiftly returning from Blois, he made his way to London and claimed the Crown. The secular forces were divided and the judgment of the Church would be decisive. Here Stephen had the advantage that his brother Henry was Bishop of Winchester. With Henry's help Stephen made terms with the Church, and was crowned and anointed King. It was however part of the tacit compact that he should relax the severe central control which during the two preceding reigns had so much offended the nobility.

Manuscript portraits of the four Norman kings: William I (top left), his younger son, William Rufus (top right), Rufus's younger brother, Henry I (bottom left), and Henry's nephew, Stephen (bottom right). Each king holds a model of a church which he founded.

There was an additional complication. Henry I had a bastard son, Robert of Gloucester, a distinguished soldier and a powerful magnate in the West Country, who is usually regarded as one of the rare examples of a disinterested baron. Robert did not rate his chances sufficiently high to compete with either of the legitimate heirs. Almost from the beginning he loyally supported his half-sister Maud, and became one of Stephen's most determined opponents.

A succession established on such disputable grounds could only be maintained unchallenged by skilful sovereignty. Yet Stephen in the early years of his reign lost the support of the three essential elements of his strength. The baronage, except those favoured by the new monarchy, were sure that this was the long-awaited moment to press their claims. The novel Civil Service, the great officials all linked together by family ties, armed with knowledge, with penmanship, trained to administration, now also began to stand aside from the new King. Many prelates were offended because Stephen violated clerical privilege by imprisoning the great administrative family of Roger, Bishop of Salisbury, whom he suspected of being about to change sides.

"When the traitors perceived," in the words of *The Anglo-Saxon Chronicle,* that King Stephen was "a mild man and soft and good and *did no justice,* then did they all manner of horrors. They had done homage to him and sworn oaths, but they held no faith."

Persuaded of the English decay, King David of Scotland, who was Maud's uncle, crossed the border and laid claim to Northumbria. The Archbishop of York advanced against him, with the support of the mass of the northern counties. He displayed the standards of the Yorkshire saints, and in a murderous battle at Northallerton, henceforward known as the Battle of the Standard, repulsed and slaughtered the invaders. This reverse, far from discouraging the malcontents, was the prelude to civil war. In 1139 Maud, freed from entanglements that had kept her in France, entered the kingdom to claim her rights. She found her chief support in the Church and among the men who had governed England under Henry I, antagonised by Stephen's weakness towards the barons. In 1141 a more or less general rebellion broke out against his rule, and he himself was taken prisoner at the Battle of Lincoln. For nearly a year Maud, uncrowned, was in control of England. The Londoners after some trial liked her even less than Stephen. Rising in fury, they drove her out of the capital. She fought on indomitably. But the strain upon the system had been too great. The island dissolved into confused civil war. During the six years that followed there was neither law nor peace in large parts of the country.

The civil war developed into the first successful baronial reaction against the centralising policy of the kings. Stephen, faced with powerful rivals, had failed to preserve the rights of the Crown. The royal revenues decreased, royal control of administration lapsed; much of the machinery itself passed for a time out of use. Baronial jurisdiction reasserted its control; baronial castles overawed the people. It seemed that a divided succession had wrecked the work of the Norman kings.

The sufferings of the Fen Country, where there was a particularly ferocious orgy of destruction during the anarchy, are grimly described in *The Anglo-Saxon Chronicle* by a monk of Peterborough. "Every powerful man made his castles and held them against the King. . . Many thousands they killed with hunger. I neither can nor may tell all the horrors and all the tortures that they did to the wretched men of this land. And it lasted the nineteen winters while Stephen was King; and ever it was worse. Wheresoever men tilled the earth bare no corn, for the land was all ruined by such deeds; and they said that Christ and his saints were asleep."

These horrors may not have been typical of the country as a whole. Over large parts of England fighting was sporadic and local in character. It was the central southern counties that bore the brunt of civil war. But these commotions bit deep into the consciousness of the people. It was realised then how vital an institution a strong monarchy was for the security of life and property. Men looked back with yearning to the efficient government of Henry I. But a greater than he was at hand.

In 1147 Robert of Gloucester died and the leadership of Maud's party devolved upon her son, Henry. Geoffrey's marriage with Maud had united the Norman and Angevin lands, and the child of this marriage was from his birth in 1133 recognised as the "master of many people", and he carried into English history the emblem of his house, the broom, the *Planta Genesta*, which later generations were to make the name of this great dynasty, the Plantagenets. He embodied all the ability, all the energy, and not a little of that passionate, ruthless ferocity which, it was whispered, came to the house of Anjou from no mortal source, but from a union with Satan himself.

When scarcely fifteen, in 1147, Henry actively championed his claim to the English throne on English soil. His band of followers was then defeated by Stephen's forces and he took refuge in Normandy. The Empress Maud gave up her hopes of succession the following year and joined her son in the duchy. She never set foot in England again. Works of piety, natural to the times, filled many of her days. But in the years that followed Henry's triumph she played an important political part as regent in Normandy and in his hereditary Angevin dominions. During her interventions in England in quest of the Crown the charge of arrogance was often levelled against her; but in her older age she proved a sagacious counsellor to her son.

For a few years of comparative peace King Stephen was left in uneasy possession. In the meantime Henry was invested by his parents in 1150 as Duke of Normandy. The next year his father's death made him also Count of Anjou, Touraine, and Maine. In his high feudal capacity Henry repaired to Paris to render homage to his lord the King of France, of which country he already possessed, by the accepted law of the age, a large part.

Louis VII was a French Edward the Confessor; he practised with faithful simplicity the law of Christ. All his days were spent in devotion, and his nights in vigil or penance. These pious and exemplary habits did not endear him to his queen. Eleanor of Aquitaine was in her own right a reigning princess, with the warmth of the south in her veins. She had already complained that she had "married a monk and not a king" when this square-shouldered, ruddy youth, with his "countenance of fire", sprightly talk, and overflowing energy, suddenly presented himself before her husband as his most splendid vassal. Eleanor did not waste words in coming to a decision. The Papacy bowed to strong will in the high feudal chiefs, and Eleanor obtained a divorce from Louis VII in 1152 on the nominal grounds of consanguinity. But what staggered the French Court and opened the eyes of its prayerful King was the sudden marriage of Eleanor to Henry two months later. Thus half of France passed out of royal control into the hands of Henry. Rarely have passion and policy flowed so buoyantly together. The marriage was one of the most brilliant political strokes of the age. Henry afterwards admitted his designs, and accepted the admiration of Europe for

BRITAIN'S MEDIEVAL CATHEDRALS

In his book Makers of the Realm, *Sir Arthur Bryant describes the building of the country's Norman cathedrals.*

Nothing gives a clearer idea of the might of the medieval Church than to stand in one of the cathedrals, still towering above the roofs of our modern towns, that were first raised as monastic churches. They express the universal sense of the importance of religion and the soaring imagination and practical genius of men who had mastered the lost Roman art of vaulting great spaces in stone. Most of them were originally built on the site of smaller Saxon churches by English masons in the massive Norman style under the prelates whom the Conqueror imported from Normandy, and rebuilt in a still more ambitious style under the successors in the latter twelfth and early thirteenth centuries.

These vast edifices were miracles of construction. They were built without any but the most elementary mechanism for moving and lifting large weights, by men whose wealth consisted almost entirely of crops, flocks and herds and whose sole means of transport were wheeled carts drawn by oxen. To realise the magnitude of their achievement one has only to reckon what it would cost, even with modern machinery and power, to rebuild in stone every cathedral and parish church in England. Yet this is what the men of the twelfth and thirteenth centuries did at a time when the population was only a small fraction of its present size. Faith alone could have caused men to sacrifice and accomplish so much.

The architecture of these cathedrals expressed the unity of existence in which their builders believed: the ordered vaulting; the pillars rising out of the earth like trees; the stone walls and arches carved with flowers and leaves, animals and men; the light of heaven flooding in through windows, at first plain but later painted, like the ceilings, in brilliant colours; the arches soaring into the sky, and the whole made one by the idea, implicit in every image and symbol, of God over all and judging all, and Christ and his Mother, the Virgin, pitying and loving all.

Stone ribs fan out like a palm tree from the central pier of the Chapter House at Wells Cathedral.

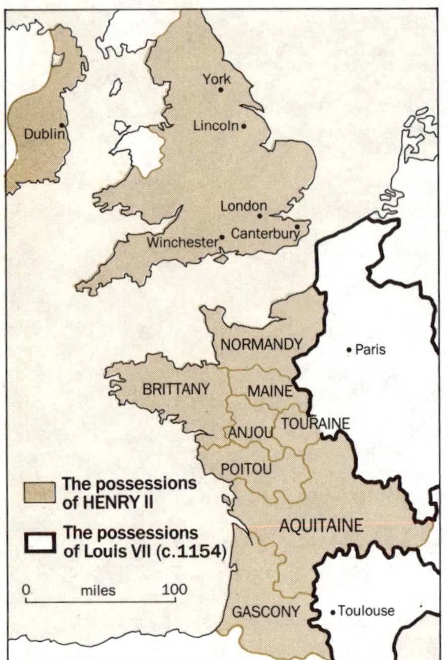

Henry II's marriage to Eleanor of Aquitaine vastly increased his empire. Her duchy in the southwest of France, combined with Henry's lands in the north, seriously threatened the possessions of King Louis VII.

their audacity. He was nineteen and she was probably thirty; and, uniting their immense domains, they made common cause against all comers.

War in all quarters lay before the royal pair. The joining to Normandy and Anjou of Poitou, Saintonge, Périgord, the Limousin, the Angoumois, and Gascony, with claims of suzerainty over Auvergne and Toulouse, fascinated and convulsed the feudal Christian world. Everywhere men shook their heads over this concentration of power, this spectacle of so many races and states, sundered from each other by long feuds or divergent interests, now suddenly flung together by the hot blood of a love intrigue. From all sides the potentates confronted the upstart. The King of France, who certainly had every conceivable cause of complaint; King Stephen of England, who disputed Henry's title to the Norman duchy, though without force to intervene across the Channel; the Count of Champagne; the Count of Perche; and Henry's own brother, Geoffrey — all spontaneously, and with good reason, fell upon him.

A month after the marriage these foes converged upon Normandy. But the youthful Duke Henry beat them back, ruptured and broken. The Norman army proved once again its fighting quality. He turned forthwith to England. It was a valiant figure that landed in January 1152, and from all over England, distracted by civil wars, hearts and eyes turned towards him. Merlin had prophesied a deliverer; had he not in his veins blood that ran back to William the Conqueror, and beyond him, through his grandmother Matilda, the long-vanished Anglo-Saxon line? A wild surge of hope greeted him from the tormented islanders, and when he knelt after his landing in the first church he found "to pray for a space, in the manner of soldiers", the priest pronounced the wish of the nation in the words, "Behold there cometh the Lord, the Ruler, and the kingdom is in his hand".

There followed battles: Malmesbury, where the sleet, especially directed by Almighty God, beat upon the faces of his foes; Wallingford, where King Stephen by divine interposition fell three times from his horse before going into action. Glamour, terror, success, attended this youthful, puissant warrior, who had not only his sword, but his title deeds. The baronage, on the other hand, saw their interest favoured by a stalemate; they wanted neither a victorious Stephen nor a triumphant Henry. The weaker the King the stronger the nobles. A treaty was concluded at Winchester in 1153 whereby Stephen made Henry his adopted son and his appointed heir. On this Henry did homage, and when a year later Stephen died he was acclaimed and crowned King of England with more general hope and rejoicing than had uplifted any monarch in England since the days of Alfred the Great.

CHAPTER 12

HENRY PLANTAGENET

THE ACCESSION OF HENRY II began one of the most pregnant and decisive reigns in English history. The new sovereign ruled an empire, and, as his subjects boasted, his warrant ran "from the Arctic Ocean to the Pyrenees". England to him was but one — the most solid though perhaps the least attractive — of his provinces. But he gave to England that effectual element of external control which was indispensable to the growth of national unity. He was accepted by English and Norman as ruler of both races and of the whole country. After the hideous anarchy of civil war between robber barons all due attention was paid to his commands. Thus, though a Frenchman, with foreign speech and foreign modes, he shaped our country in a fashion of which the outline remains to the present day.

After a hundred years of being the encampment of an invading army and the battleground of its quarrelsome descendants, England became finally and for all time a coherent kingdom, based upon Christianity and upon that Latin civilisation which recalled the message of ancient Rome. Henry Plantagenet first brought England, Scotland, and Ireland into a certain common relationship; he re-established the system of royal government which his grandfather, Henry I, had prematurely erected. He relaid the foundations of a central power, based upon the Exchequer and the judiciary, which was ultimately to supersede the feudal system of William the Conqueror. The King gathered up and cherished the Anglo-Saxon tradition of self-government under royal command in shire and borough; he developed and made permanent assizes as they survive today. It is to him we owe the enduring fact that the English-speaking race all over the world is governed by the English Common Law rather than by the Roman. By his Constitutions of Clarendon he sought to fix the relationship of Church and State and to force the Church in its temporal character to submit itself to the life and law of the nation. In this endeavour he had, after a deadly struggle, to retreat, and it was left to Henry VIII, though centuries later, to avenge his predecessor by destroying the shrine of St Thomas at Canterbury.

The Plantagenets took their name from a sprig of broom (Latin planta *meaning "broom" and* genista *meaning "sprig") which was an insignia in the crest of the Counts of Anjou. A later emblem was the sinister boar, or "hogge", which was to be mocked by enemies of the family.*

A vivid picture is painted of this gifted man: square, thick set, bull-necked, with powerful arms and coarse, rough hands; his legs bandy from endless riding; a large, round head and closely cropped red hair; a freckled face; a voice harsh and cracked. Intense love of the chase; other loves, which the Church deplored and Queen Eleanor resented; frugality in food and dress; days entirely concerned with public business; travel unceasing; moods various. It was said that he was always gentle and calm in times of urgent peril, but became bad-tempered and capricious when the pressure relaxed. "He was more tender to dead soldiers than to the living, and found far more sorrow in the loss of those who were slain than comfort in the love of those who remained." He journeyed hotfoot around his many dominions, arriving unexpectedly in England when he was thought to be in the South of France. He carried with him in his tours of each province wains loaded with ponderous rolls which represented the office files of his day. His Court and train gasped and panted behind him.

But this twelfth-century monarch, with his lusts and sports, his hates and his schemes, was no materialist; he was the Lord's Anointed. The offices of religion, the fear of eternal damnation, the hope of even greater realms beyond the grave, accompanied him from hour to hour. He drew all possible delights and satisfactions from this world and the next. At times he was smitten with remorse and engulfed in repentance. He is portrayed to us in convulsions both of spiritual exaltation and abasement.

This was no secluded monarch: people broke in upon him at all hours with business, with tidings, with gossip, with visions, with complaints. Talk rang high in the King's presence and to His Majesty's face among the nobles and courtiers, and the jester, invaluable monitor, castigated all impartially and with unstinted licence.

Such was the man who succeeded to the troubled and divided inheritance of Stephen. Already before his accession to the English throne Henry had fought the first of his many wars to defend his continental inheritance. Ever since the emergence of the strong Norman power a hundred years before, the French monarch had struggled ceaselessly against the encroachments of great dukedoms and countships upon the central government, but Henry II's accession to the island throne in 1154 threatened France with far graver dangers. Hitherto there had always been political relief in playing off over-mighty subjects one against another. The struggle between Anjou and Normandy in the eleventh century had rejoiced the French king. But when in one hour Henry II was King of England, Duke of Normandy, Lord of Aquitaine, Brittany, Poitou, Anjou, Maine, and Guienne, ruler from the Somme to the Pyrenees of more than half France, all balance of power among the feudal lords was destroyed.

Louis VII found instead of a dozen principalities, divided and jealous, one single imperial power, whose resources far surpassed his own. He was scarcely the man to face such a combination. Still, some advantages remained to the French king. The Angevin Empire was more impressive on the map than in reality. It was a motley, ill-knit collection of states, flung together by the chance of a single marriage, and lacking unity both of purpose and strength. There was no pretence of a single, central government; no uniformity of administration or customs; no common interests or feelings of loyalty. Weak as Louis VII appeared in his struggle with the enterprising and active Henry, the tide of events flowed with the French monarchy, and even Louis left it more firmly established than he found it.

The main method of the French was simple. Louis could no longer set the Count of Anjou against the Duke of Normandy, but he could still encourage both in Anjou and in Normandy those local feuds and petty wards which sapped the strength of the feudal potentates. Nor was the exploiting of family quarrels an unfruitful device. In the later years of his reign the sons of Henry II, eager, turbulent, and proud, allowed themselves to be used by Louis VII and by his successor, the wily and gifted Philip Augustus, against the King their father.

How, we may ask, did all this affect the daily life of England and her history? A series of personal feudal struggles fought in distant lands, the quarrels of an alien ruling class, were little understood and less liked by the common folk. Yet these things long burdened their pilgrimage. For many generations their bravest and best were to fight and die by the marshes of the Loire or under the sunbaked hills of southern France in pursuit of the dream of English dominion over French soil. For this two centuries later Englishmen triumphed at Crécy, Poitiers, and Agincourt, or starved in the terrible Limoges march of the Black Prince. For this they turned fertile France into a desert. Throughout the medieval history of England war with France is the interminable and often the dominant theme. It groped and scraped into every reach of English life, moulding and fretting the shape of English society and institutions.

No episode opens to us a wider window upon the politics of the twelfth century in England than the quarrel of Henry II with his great subject and former friend, Thomas Becket, Archbishop of Canterbury. We have to realise the gravity of this conflict. The military State in feudal Christendom bowed to the Church in things spiritual; it never accepted the idea of the transference of secular power to priestly authority. But the Church, enriched continually by the bequests of hardy barons, anxious in the death agony about their life beyond the grave, became the greatest landlord and capitalist in the community. Rome used its ghostly arts upon the superstitions of almost all the actors in the drama. The power of the State was held in constant challenge by this potent interest. Questions of doctrine might well have been resolved, but how was the government of the country to be carried on under two conflicting powers, each possessed of immense claims

The crowning of Henry II's son, Henry, by Archbishop Roger of York in 1170 was the immediate cause of the famous quarrel between the King and Thomas Becket, his Archbishop of Canterbury.

upon limited national resources? This conflict was not confined to England. It was the root question of the European world, as it then existed.

Under William the Conqueror schism had been avoided in England by tact and compromise. Under Lanfranc the Church worked with the Crown, and each power reinforced the other against the turbulent barons or the oppressed commonalty. But now a great personality stood at the summit of the religious hierarchy, Thomas Becket, who had been the King's friend. As his Chancellor, he had in both home and foreign affairs loyally served his master. He had reorganised the imposition of scutage, a tax that allowed money to commute personal service in arms, and thus eventually pierced the feudal system to its core. He had played his part in the acquisition of Brittany. The King felt sure that in Becket he had his own man — no mere servant, but a faithful comrade and colleague in the common endeavour. It was by the King's direct influence and personal effort that Becket was elected Archbishop of Canterbury.

From that moment all his gifts and impulses ran in another channel. Whereas hitherto as a courtier and a prince he had rivalled all in magnificence and pomp, he now sought by extreme austerities to gather around himself the fame and honour of a saint. Becket pursued the same methods and ambitions in the ecclesiastical as previously he had done in the political sphere; and in both he excelled. He now championed the Church against the Crown in every aspect of their innumerable interleaving functions. He clothed this aggressive process with those universal ideas of the Catholic Church and the Papal authority which far transcended the bounds of our island. After a tour upon the Continent and a conclave with the religious dignitaries of France and Italy he returned to England imbued with the resolve to establish the independence of the Church hierarchy of the

THE CHRISTIAN HERITAGE

THE CHURCH EXERCISED a powerful influence on all aspects of daily life. Christian events studded the calendar, which was otherwise dictated by the seasons. Birth, marriage and death all had their Christian rituals, the church being at the centre of village life. And if the boundaries between the religious and the secular were often blurred, so too were those between the religious and the magical: it was necessary to declare in the year 1236 that "fonts are to be kept closed by locks because of witchcraft."

Religion and art went closely together. Norman architecture was at its most impressive in the great cathedrals, which can still be seen today. Unfortunately, the past glory of many medieval monasteries can only be guessed at from their ruins. Fountains Abbey, in Yorkshire, which was established in 1132, was destroyed in the sixteenth century when Henry VIII broke with the Church of Rome. It was only one of hundreds destroyed by the King.

The monasteries and abbeys provided many social services: they gave food and shelter to the poor and needy, and their guesthouses lodged richer travellers.

Architecture changed significantly during the Middle Ages, with many of the finest parish churches being built in the fifteenth century. Some of the music which was sung in them has survived. So, too, have chronicles compiled and illuminated by monks, and other religious prose and poetry. The first schools were monastic, and the old universities have buildings which are part of the Christian heritage. The Church was at the centre of learning and it also provided kings with a supply of bishops and other clergy who were willing to devote a large part of their time to public affairs and to the governing of the country. There were many disputes and quarrels, but there was a long record of indispensable service.

MEDIEVAL RELIGION RELIED on strong visual appeal. The way to God's presence was indicated in churches and cathedrals by lofty arches pointing up to heaven. Stained glass windows vividly presented the stories of the Bible. Most cathedrals took generations to build. Salisbury (above) was an exception: started in 1220, it was completed, except for the fine fourteenth-century steeple, within fifty years. On the left is a rare picture of some cathedral builders at work. The measurements they took were extremely accurate and they had enough knowledge to design and use simple mechanical building aids. Here a pulley system hoists heavy materials to the men constructing the walls. The cathedral builders were craftsmen in stone who worked with amazing sensitivity and skill.

THE FIRST MONKS FROM CONTINENTAL EUROPE *were Benedictines. This illustration from a book of psalms shows Saint Benedict and his monks who came from the great abbeys in Normandy. The emphasis of the Order lay on work and prayer. Later the Cistercians founded monasteries in the countryside, where they chose fertile sites, like those of Rievaulx and Fountains Abbeys, and became proficient farmers.*

ARCHITECTURAL WONDERS *such as these strong yet delicate ribs of stone supporting the heavy roof of the lantern at Ely Cathedral are a hallmark of medieval Christian architects. The picture is taken looking up into the Octagon, from the north transept. Many stages of medieval architecture are in evidence at Ely, which was the work of generations of builders.*

SCENES FROM EVERYDAY LIFE *were depicted by craftsmen in wood and stone. The man above is playing a musical instrument by putting his right hand on the finger stops while adjusting the tension of the strings with a handle operated by his left hand. The carving comes from Beverley Minster, in Yorkshire. Such realistic insights into everyday life can be seen in many medieval cathedrals.*

SINGING WAS A PART OF WORSHIP. *Plainsong, or the singing of notes without strict metre, and chanting, or singing on the same note, connected the Catholic Church with eastern religions. By the thirteenth century monks were able to write music and make beautiful musical scores like this missal (above) which is to be found in Durham Cathedral Priory.*

HERBAL MEDICINE *was one of the benefits brought by the monks to the surrounding community. They had knowledge of the medicinal values of many kinds of herbs, and grew them in herb gardens attached to their monasteries. Infirmaries and almshouses were added to most monasteries.*

A contemporary manuscript shows Henry II quarrelling with Becket in the presence of soldiers who, seeking to gain favour with the King, later murdered the Archbishop. But Henry II was deeply repentant after Becket's death, and underwent frequent penance throughout the remainder of his life.

State as represented by the King. Thus he opened the conflict which the wise Lanfranc had throughout his life striven to avoid.

In a loose and undefined way Saxon England had foreshadowed the theory to which the Elizabethan reformers long afterwards returned. Both thought of the monarch as appointed by God, not only to rule the State, but to protect and guide the Church. In the eleventh century however, under Pope Gregory VII and his successors, Rome now began to make claims which were hardly compatible with the notions of the sovereignty of the King in all matters temporal and spiritual. The Gregorian movement held that the government of the Church ought to be in the hands of the clergy, under the supervision of the Pope. According to this view, the King was a mere layman whose one religious function was obedience to the hierarchy. The Church was a body apart, with its own allegiance and its own laws. Who, then, was to appoint the bishops? And, when once appointed, to whom, if the Pope commanded one thing and the King another, did they owe duty?

The struggle between Henry II and Becket is confused by the technical details over which it was fought. There was however good reason why the quarrel should have been engaged upon incidents of administration rather than upon the main principles which were at stake. The Crown resented the claim of the Church to interfere in the State; but in the Middle Ages no king dared to challenge the Church outright. It was not till the sixteenth century that an English king in conflict with the Papacy dared to repudiate the authority of Rome and nakedly declare the State supreme, even in spiritual matters. In the twelfth century the only practicable course was compromise. The Church at this time was in no mood for a bargain. In England it had gained greatly in power since the days of William the Conqueror. Stephen in his straits had made sweeping concessions to the Church, whose political influence then reached its zenith. These concessions, Henry felt, compromised his royal rights. He schemed to regain what had been lost, and as the first step in 1162 appointed his trusted servant Becket to be Archbishop of Canterbury. Missing the ominous signs of the change in Becket's attitude, he proceeded to his second step, the publication in 1164 of the Constitutions of Clarendon. In these Henry claimed, not without considerable truth, to be restating the customs of the kingdom as they had been before the anarchy of Stephen's reign. But Becket resisted. He regarded Stephen's yieldings as irrevocable gains by the Church. When, in October 1164, he was summoned to appear before the Great Council and explain his conduct he haughtily denied the King's authority and placed himself under the protection of the Pope and of God.

Thus he ruptured that unity which had hitherto been deemed vital in the English realm. Stiff in defiance, Becket took refuge on the Continent. The whole thought of the ruling classes in England was shaken by this grievous dispute. It endured for six years, during which time the Archbishop of Canterbury remained in his French exile. Only in 1170 was an apparent reconciliation brought about between him and the King at Fréteval, in Touraine. Each side appeared to waive its claims in principle. The Archbishop was promised a safe return and full possession of his see. King and Primate met for the last time in the summer of 1170. "My lord," said Thomas at the end, "my heart tells me that I part from you as one whom you shall see no more in this life." He returned to Canterbury resolved to seek from the Pope unlimited powers of excommunication. "The more potent and fierce the prince is," he wrote, "the stronger stick and harder chain is needed to bind him and keep him in order." And, "I go to England, to peace or to destruction I know not; but God has decreed what fate awaits me."

Meanwhile, in Becket's absence, Henry had resolved to secure the peaceful accession of his son, the young Henry, by having him crowned in his own lifetime. The ceremony had been performed by the Archbishop of York, assisted by six other bishops. This action was bitterly resented by Becket as an infringement of a cherished right of his see. After the Fréteval agreement Henry supposed that bygones were bygones. But Becket had other views.

His welcome home after the years of exile was astonishing. At Canterbury the monks received him as an angel of God. "I am come to die among you," he said in his sermon, and again, "In this Church there are martyrs, and God will soon increase their number." He made a triumphal progress through London, scattering alms to the beseeching and exalted people. Then hotfoot he proceeded to renew his excommunication of the clergy who had taken part in the crowning of young Henry. These unfortunate priests and prelates travelled in a bunch to the King who was in Normandy. They said that the Archbishop was ready "to tear the crown from the young King's head."

Henry Plantagenet was transported with passion. "What a pack of fools and cowards," he cried, "I have nourished in my house, that not one of them will avenge me of this turbulent priest!" A council was immediately summoned to devise measures for reasserting the royal authority. In the main it shared the old King's anger. Second thoughts prevailed. With all the stresses that existed in that fierce and ardent society, it was not possible that the realm could support a fearful conflict between Church and State.

But meanwhile another train of action was in process. Four knights had

THE MURDER OF THOMAS BECKET

This account of the Archbishop's murder in 1170 is by Edward Grim, the only man present who tried to prevent it. He was badly wounded, but he heard Becket's last words and wrote his story between five and seven years later.

Straightway the four knights entered the house of prayer and reconciliation with swords sacrilegiously drawn, causing horror to the beholders by their very looks and the clanging of their arms. Inspired by fury the knights called out, "Where is Thomas Becket, traitor to the King and realm?"

At this, intrepid and fearless, he descended from the stair where he had been dragged by the monks in fear of the knights, and in a clear voice answered, "I am here, no traitor to the king, but a priest. Why do ye seek me?". . . .

The murderers cried, "Absolve and restore to communion those whom you have excommunicated, and restore their powers to those whom you have suspended." He answered, "There has been no satisfaction, and I will not absolve them." "Then you shall die," they cried, "and receive what you deserve." "I am ready," he replied, "to die for my Lord."

Scarce had he said the words than the wicked knight leapt upon him suddenly and wounded him on the head, cutting off the top of the crown; and by the same blow he wounded the arm of him who tells this. For he, when the others fled, stuck close to the sainted archbishop and held him in his arms till the one he interposed was almost severed.

Then the archbishop received a second blow on the head but still stood firm. At the third blow he fell on his knees and elbows, saying in a low voice, "For the Name of Jesus and the protection of the Church I am ready to embrace death." Then the third knight inflicted a terrible wound as he lay, by which the sword was broken against the pavement, and the crown was separated from the head; so that the blood white with the brain and the brain red with blood, dyed the surface of the virgin mother Church with the life and death of the confessor and martyr in the colours of the lily and the rose.

The site of Thomas Becket's martyrdom in Canterbury Cathedral, on December 29, 1170.

heard the King's bitter words. They travelled fast to the coast. They crossed the Channel. They called for horses and rode to Canterbury. There on December 29, 1170 they found the Archbishop in the cathedral. He confronted them with Cross and mitre, fearless and resolute. After haggard parleys they fell upon him, cut him down with their swords, and left him bleeding like Julius Caesar, with a score of wounds to cry for vengeance.

This tragedy was fatal to the King. The murder of one of the foremost of God's servants, like the breaking of a feudal oath, struck at the heart of the age. All England was filled with terror. They acclaimed the dead Archbishop as a martyr; and immediately it appeared that his relics healed incurable diseases. Here indeed was a crime, vast and inexpiable. When Henry heard the appalling news he was prostrated with grief and fear. All the elaborate process of law which he had sought to set on foot against this rival power was brushed aside by a brutal, bloody act; and though he had never dreamt that such a deed would be done there were his own hot words to fasten on him the guilt of murder, and, still worse, sacrilege.

The immediately following years were spent in trying to recover what he had lost by a great parade of atonement for his guilt. He made pilgrimages to the shrine of the murdered Archbishop. He subjected himself to public penances. On several anniversaries, stripped to the waist and kneeling humbly, he submitted to be scourged by the triumphant monks. We may however suppose that the corporal chastisement, which apparently from the contemporary pictures was administered with birch rods, was mainly symbolic. Under this display of contrition and submission the King laboured perseveringly to regain the rights of State. By the Compromise of Avrances in 1172 he made his peace with the Papacy on comparatively easy terms. To many deep-delving historians it seems that in fact, though not in form, he had by the end of his life re-established the main principles of the Constitutions of Clarendon, which are after all in harmony with what the English nation or any virile and rational race would mean to have as their law. Certainly the Papacy supported him in his troubles with his sons. But Becket's sombre sacrifice had not been in vain. Until the Reformation the Church retained the system of ecclesiastical courts independent of the royal authority, and the right of appeal to Rome, two of the major points upon which Becket had defied the King.

The earliest surviving picture of the martyrdom of Thomas Becket, forming a full-page miniature in a Latin psalter made in England in about 1200.

Eighteen years of life lay before the King after Becket's death. In a sense, they were years of glory. All Europe marvelled at the extent of Henry's domains, to which in 1171 he had added the lordship of Ireland. Through the marriages of his daughters he was linked with the Norman King of Sicily, the King of Castile, and Henry the Lion of Saxony, who was a most powerful prince in Germany. Diplomatic agents spread his influence in the Lombard cities of northern Italy.

Yet Henry knew well that his splendour was tenuous and transient; he had also deep-clouding family sorrows. During these years he was confronted with no fewer than four rebellions by his sons. For the three eldest he had provided glittering titles: Henry held Normandy, Maine, and Anjou, Richard was given Aquitaine, and to Geoffrey went Brittany. These boys were typical sprigs of the Angevin stock. They wanted power as well as titles, and they bore their father no respect. Urged on by their mother, Queen Eleanor, who now lived in Poitiers apart from her husband, between 1173 and 1186 they rose in revolt in various combinations. On each occasion they could count on the active support of the watchful King of France. Henry treated his ungrateful children with generosity, but he had no illusions. The royal chamber at Westminster at this time was adorned with paintings done at the King's command. One represented four eaglets preying upon the parent bird, the fourth one poised at the parent's neck, ready to pick out the eyes. "The four eaglets," the King is reported to have said, "are my four sons, who cease not to persecute me even unto death. The youngest of them, whom I now embrace with so much affection, will some time in the end insult me more grievously . . . than any of the others."

So it was to be. John, whom he had striven to provide with an inheritance equal to that of his brothers, joined the final plot against him. In 1188 Richard, his eldest surviving son, after the death of young Henry, was making war upon him in conjunction with King Philip of France. Already desperately ill, Henry was defeated at Le Mans and recoiled into Touraine. When he saw in the list of conspirators against him the name of his son John, upon whom his affection had strangely rested, he abandoned the struggle with life. "Let things go as they will," he gasped. "Shame, shame on a conquered King." So saying, this hard, violent, brilliant, and lonely man expired at Chinon on July 6, 1189. The pious were taught to regard this melancholy end as the further chastisement of God upon the murderer of Thomas Becket. Such is the bitter taste of worldly power. Such are the correctives of glory.

A pilgrim's badge representing St Thomas, who in medieval times was revered as a healer. The steps leading to his tomb in Canterbury Cathedral have been worn hollow by the tread of millions of pilgrims.

CHAPTER 13

THE ENGLISH COMMON LAW

ENGLAND HAS HAD GREATER SOLDIER-KINGS and subtler diplomatists than Henry II, but no man has left a deeper mark upon our laws and institutions. Like his Norman predecessors and his sons, Henry II possessed an instinct for the problems of government and law. The names of his battles have vanished with their dust, but his fame will live with the English Constitution and the English Common Law.

This great King was fortunate in his moment. William I and Henry I had brought to England or preserved there all those instruments through which their successor was to work. They themselves could move but slowly and with caution. The land must settle itself to its new rules and rulers. In 1154 however Henry of Anjou had come to a country which nearly twenty years of anarchy had prepared for the acceptance of a strong hand at the centre. Raised a Frenchman, the ruler of more than half France, he brought to his task the qualities of vision, wide experience, and a strength that did not scruple to stoop to cunning. The disasters of Stephen's reign determined Henry not only to curb baronial independence and regain the ground lost by his predecessor, but to go much further. In place of a multitude of manorial courts where local magnates dispensed justice whose quality and character varied with the customs and temper of the neighbourhood, he planned a system of royal courts which would administer a law common to all men and to all England.

The policy was not without peril. The King was wise enough to avoid a direct assault, for he knew that to lay a finger upon the sanctity of customary

The formality of a modern court of law is evident in this fifteenth-century picture of the Court of Common Pleas, Westminster. The Royal Judges presided over cases brought before them by all sections of society.

rights would provoke disaster. Faced with this barrier, Henry shrewdly opposed custom to custom and cloaked innovation in the respected garb of conservatism. His plan was to stretch old principles to take on new meanings. In an unwritten Constitution the limits of the King's traditional rights were vaguely defined. This opened a shrewd line of advance. Fastening upon the elastic Saxon concept of the King's Peace, Henry used it to draw all criminal cases into his courts. Those who broke the King's Peace could be tried in the King's court, but the King's Peace was limited, and often embraced only offences committed in the King's presence or on the King's highway or land. Cautiously and quietly Henry began to claim that the King's Peace extended over all England, and that no matter where it was broken offenders should be tried in the King's courts. Civil cases he attracted by straining a different principle, the old right of the King's court to hear appeals in cases where justice had been refused and to protect men in possession of their lands. The changes were introduced gradually and without legislation. Rarely is it possible to state the date at which any innovation was made; yet at the King's death a clever man might have looked back and seen how much had been altered in the thirty-five years that Henry II had sat on the English throne.

But if Henry was to pose as a conservative in the legal sphere he must be consistent. Compulsion could play little part in his programme; it had to be the first principle of his policy to attract cases to his courts rather than to compel them. A bait was needed with which to draw litigants to the royal courts; the King must offer them better justice than they could have at the hands of their lords. Henry accordingly threw open to litigants in the royal courts a new procedure for them – trial by jury. *Regale quoddam beneficium* a contemporary called it – a royal boon; and the description illuminates both the origin of the jury and the part it played in the triumph of the Common Law. Henry did not invent the jury; he put it to a new purpose. Unknown in this country before the Conquest, in origin the jury was an administrative instrument: the King had the right to summon a body of men to bear witness under oath about the truth of any question concerning the royal interest. It was through this early form of jury that William the Conqueror had determined the Crown rights in the great Domesday survey. The genius of Henry II, perceiving its possibilities, turned to regular use in the courts an instrument which so far had only been used for administrative purposes.

Only the King had the right to summon a jury. Henry accordingly restricted it to those who sought justice before the royal judges. It was an astute move. Until this time both civil and criminal cases had been decided through the oath, the ordeal, or the duel. The court would order one of the litigants to muster a body of men who would swear to the justice of his cause and whom it was hoped God would punish if they swore falsely. Or the court would condemn him, under the supervision of a priest, to carry a red-hot iron, or eat a morsel of bread, or be plunged in a pool of water. If the iron did not burn or the bread choke or the water reject him, so that he could not sink, then Divine Providence was adjudged to have granted a visible sign that the victim was innocent. The duel, or trial by battle, was a Norman innovation based on the theory that the God of Battles will strengthen the arm of the righteous, and was at one time much favoured for deciding disputes about land. Monasteries and other substantial landowners took the precaution however of assisting the Almighty by retaining professional

THE NORMAN INHERITANCE

Imposing castles, great cathedrals and wealthy abbeys rose as citadels of Norman Christianity in the heart of a hostile land. These bastions of stone serve as memorials to that rugged age.

CASTLE HEDINGHAM, ESSEX

CASTLE RISING, NORFOLK, *(left) stands on some of the most spectacular earthworks in England. Built in the twelfth century, it was later acquired by the Dukes of Norfolk to whom it still belongs. The origin of the main earthworks is uncertain, but some of the site may date back to the Roman occupation. The castle was apparently never subjected to major siege, and at one time was the residence of Queen Isabella, mother of Edward III.*

CASTLE HEDINGHAM, ESSEX, *was once one of the strongest castles in England. Built in the twelfth century to dominate the Colne Valley, its imposing stone keep is among the best preserved examples of Norman military architecture. The magnificent hall (above) was two storeys high and was used principally as a banqueting hall where king, court and friends were entertained by the lord and his family.*

TELHAM HILL, EAST SUSSEX, *(above) is one of the two hills over which the Battle of Hastings was fought. The battle took its name from the neighbouring town of Hastings, where the Norman troops were quartered. Battle Abbey, (left) was built to commemorate the Norman victory on nearby Senlac Hill, where the Saxons made their last stand, the high altar being placed over the spot where Harold was fatally wounded.*

WINDSOR CASTLE, BERKSHIRE, *(above) was founded by William the Conqueror, on a site once used by both the Celts and the Romans. The stone fortifications, together with the Round Tower, date from the twelfth century. It has since been the most regal of royal residences, with additions being made by successive monarchs. St George's Chapel, built in 1475, is the Chapel of the Order of the Garter.*

THE TOWER OF LONDON, *which began as a simple earthwork thrown up by the Normans in 1066, later became the most important symbol of the Conquest. The two outer rings of walls of the completed fortress were added in the thirteenth century. The White Tower, (left) so called because once it was whitewashed, was begun in 1080, and was completed by William II before 1100. The Chapel of St John, (above) probably the oldest of the Tower's four chapels, is a superb example of the stern severity of Norman architecture. From the fourteenth century, Knights of the Bath spent all-night vigils there before being dubbed.*

CLONFERT CATHEDRAL, CO. GALWAY, *(right) was originally part of one of the monasteries founded by St Brendan the Navigator, who was reputed to have travelled to America. This portal, with its vigorous decorations, dates from the twelfth century. There are similarities with Norman architecture, as both stem from the Romanesque tradition but this is emphatically Irish in character.*

THE JEW'S HOUSE, LINCOLN, *(left) one of the oldest houses in Britain, is a reminder that Jews were essential to the prosperity of medieval towns, as Christians could not act as moneylenders. The house may have belonged to the famous merchant, Aaron the Jew, whose clients included kings and bishops, and whose operations extended from Kent to Cumberland. Such stone houses were symbols of power and wealth. They were also strongholds, vital to moneylenders, who were often threatened by anti-Jewish riots. The house was built in the middle of the twelfth century.*

MELROSE ABBEY, BORDERS, (above) was founded by Cistercian monks in the valley of the Tweed in 1136. Nearby Berwick provided a convenient market for the monks to sell their wool. It was close to the main road from England to Edinburgh, and donations from many eminent visitors turned it into one of the wealthiest abbeys in Scotland. Its situation also made it vulnerable in any dispute between the kings of England and Scotland. It was sacked by Edward II and Richard II. The heart of Robert Bruce is buried beneath a window in the Abbey.

LINCOLN CATHEDRAL, LINCOLNSHIRE, (above) was built on the site of a Saxon minster, at first in the Norman style in the eleventh century, and then partly rebuilt in 1185 as a magnificent example of early Gothic. Its Treasury contains one of the originals of Magna Carta.

YORK MINSTER, YORKSHIRE, contains much medieval stained glass (left). This panel in a nave window resembles those seen in the cathedral at Chartres, indicating that it was glazed in the mid-twelfth century.

DURHAM CATHEDRAL, DURHAM, *(above) the finest example of Norman architecture in Europe, was built by the monks of Lindisfarne, after they were driven from Holy Island by the Vikings. With them they brought the body of St Cuthbert, which the Normans reburied behind the high altar. Fugitives from justice could claim sanctuary by grasping this door-knocker (right) on the north door.*

ELY CATHEDRAL, CAMBRIDGESHIRE, *(left) with its majestic nave, was built by the Normans on the site of a Saxon abbey. Although it had been the refuge of Hereward the Wake, the shrine of the Saxon saint, Queen Ethelburga, was preserved by the Normans and given a place of honour in the choir.*

FOUNTAINS ABBEY, YORKSHIRE, was founded in 1132 on a site that was "fit more for the dens of wild beasts than for the uses of man". At first the monks suffered considerable hardship, but the Abbey became the richest Cistercian house in England. The Cellarium (below) was used to store wool from the Abbey's sheep. The ruins comprise one of the most complete sets of Cistercian buildings to survive the Dissolution of the Monasteries.

champions to protect their property and their rights. All this left small room for debate on points of law. In a more rational age men were beginning to distrust such antics. Thus trial by jury quickly gained favour. But the old processes were long in dying. So late as 1818 a litigant nonplussed the judges by an appeal to trial by battle and compelled Parliament to abolish this ancient procedure.

The jury of Henry II was not the jury that we know. There were various forms of it; but in all there was this essential difference: the jurymen were witnesses as well as judges of the facts. Good men and true were picked, not yet for their impartiality, but because they were the men most likely to know the truth. The modern jury, which knows nothing about the case till it is proved in court, was slow in coming. The process is obscure. A jury summoned to Westminster from distant parts might be reluctant to come. The way was long, the roads unsafe, and perhaps only three or four would arrive. The court could not wait. An adjournment would be costly. To avoid delay and expense the parties might agree to rely on a jury *de circumstantibus*, a jury of bystanders. The few jurors who knew the truth of the matter would tell their tale to the bystanders, and then the whole body would deliver their verdict. In time the jurors with local knowledge would cease to be jurors at all and become witnesses, giving their evidence in open court to a jury entirely composed of bystanders. Such, we may guess, or something like it, was what happened. Very gradually, as the laws of evidence developed, the change came.

These methods gave good justice. Trial by jury became popular. Professional judges removed from local prejudice, whose outlook ranged above the interested or ignorant lord or his steward, armed with the King's power to summon juries, secured swifter decisions, and a strong authority to enforce them. Henry accordingly had to build up almost from nothing a system of royal courts, capable of absorbing a great rush of new work. The instrument to which he turned was the King's Council, the organ through which all manner of governmental business was regularly carried out. At the outset of Henry II's reign it dealt almost indiscriminately with every kind of administrative business. On the judicial side however it was scarcely more than the King's feudal court, where he did justice, among his vassals. Under Henry II all this was changed. The functions of the King's justices became more and more specialised. During the reigns of his sons the Council began to divide into two great courts, the King's Bench and the Common Pleas. They did not become fully separate till a century later. Thereafter, with the

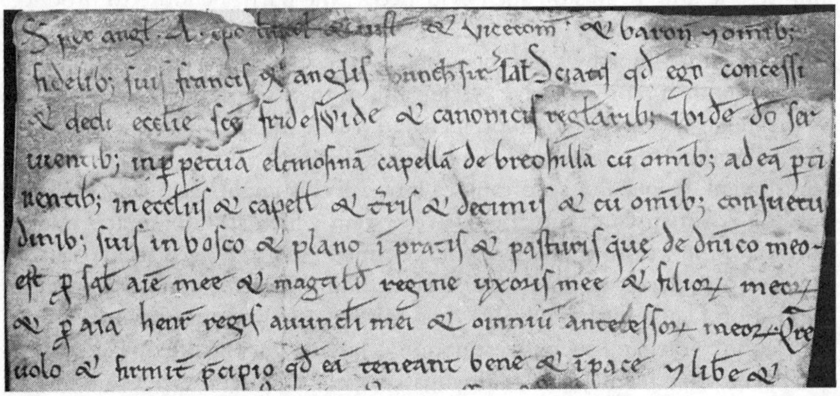
S. rex angl. A. epo ... et vicecom et baron et omib;
fidelib; suis francis et anglis ... sal. Sciatis qd ego concessi
et dedi ecclie sce Frideswide et canonicis regularib; ibide do ser
uientib; in ppetua elemosina capella de breohilla cu omib; ad ea pti
nentib; in ecclesiis et capell et terris et decimis et cu omib; consuetu
dinib; suis in bosco et plano i pratis et pasturis que de dnico meo
est p sal aie mee et Mathild regine uxoris mee et filior meor
et p aia henr regis auunculi mei et omniu antecessor meor. Et re
uolo et firmit pcipio qd ea teneant bene et i pace et libe

The legal system developed rapidly during the reign of Henry II, whose law courts relied on legal documents and writs to a greater extent than before. On the left is a twelfth century writ which gave confirmation to St Frideswide, Oxford, of the chapel of Breohilla.

This manuscript picture shows a medieval law court in session at Middle Temple Hall, one of the three Inns of Court in London. The practice of law was later taught there by lectures, learning and debate.

Court of the Exchequer, they formed the backbone of the Common Law system down to the nineteenth century. In addition, travelling justices were from time to time appointed to hear all manner of business in the shires, whose courts were thus drawn into the orbit of royal justice.

But all this was only a first step. Henry also had to provide means whereby the litigant, eager for royal justice, could remove his case out of the court of his lord into the King's court. The device which Henry used was the royal writ. Baronial rights must be formally respected; but by straining the traditional rights of the Crown it was possible to claim that particular types of case fell within the King's province. Upon this principle Henry evolved a number of set formulae, or writs, each fitted to a certain type of case; any man who could fit his own case to the wording of one of the royal writs might claim the King's justice. The wording of writs was rigid, but for about eighty years new forms of writ might still be given. With each new form a fresh blow was struck at the feudal courts. It was not until the thirteenth century that the number was fixed at something under two hundred. This system then endured for six hundred years. Society had to adapt itself to that unbending framework and inevitably English law became weighted with archaisms and legal fictions. The whole course of a case might depend on the writ with which it was begun, for every writ had its special procedure, mode of trial, and eventual remedy. Yet, cumbersome though it was, the system gave to English law a conservative spirit which guarded and preserved its continuity from that time on in an unbroken line.

It is a maxim of English law that legal memory begins with the accession of Richard I in 1189. The date was set for a technical reason by a statute of Edward I. It could scarcely have been more appropriately chosen however, for with the close of the reign of Henry II we are on the threshold of a new epoch in the history of English law. With the establishment of a system of royal courts, giving the same justice all over the country, the old diversity of local law was rapidly broken down. A modern lawyer, transported to the England of Henry's predecessor, would find himself in strange surroundings; with the system that Henry bequeathed to his son he would feel almost at home. The King had laid the foundations of the English Common Law, upon which succeeding generations would build.

It was in these fateful and formative years that the English-speaking peoples began to devise methods of determining legal disputes which survive in substance to this day. A man can only be accused of a civil or criminal offence which is clearly defined and known to the law. The judge is an umpire. He adjudicates on such evidence as the parties choose to produce. Witnesses must testify in public and on oath. They are examined and cross-examined, not by the judge, but by the litigants themselves or their legally qualified representatives. The truth of their testimony is weighed not by the judge but by twelve "good men and true", and it is only when this jury has determined the facts that the judge is empowered to impose sentence, punishment, or penalty according to law. All this might seem very obvious, until one contemplates the alternative system which still dominates a large portion of the world. Under Roman law, and systems derived from it, a trial in those turbulent centuries, and in some countries even today, is often an inquisition. The judge makes his own investigation into the civil wrong or the public crime, and such investigation is largely uncontrolled. The suspect can be interrogated in private. He must answer all questions put to him. His right to be represented by a legal adviser is restricted. The witnesses against him can testify in secret and in his absence. And only when these processes have been accomplished is the accusation or charge against him formulated and published. Thus often arise secret intimidation, enforced confessions, torture, and blackmailed pleas of guilty. These sinister dangers were extinguished from the Common Law of England.

Most of the Common Law was then unwritten, and in England much still remains so. The English statutes, for example, still contain no definition of the crime of murder, for this, like much other law, rested on the unwritten custom of the land as declared by the inhabitants and interpreted by the judges. Lawyers could only ascertain it by studying reports and records of ancient decisions. A century after Henry's death they began to group themselves into professional communities in London, the Inns of Court, half colleges, half law-schools, but predominantly secular, for the presence of clerics learned in the laws of Rome and the Canon Law of the Roman Church was not encouraged. Here they produced annual law reports, whose authority was recognised by the judges, and which continued in almost unbroken succession for nearly three centuries. The law was already there, in the customs of the land, and it was only a matter of discovering it by diligent study and comparison of recorded decisions in earlier cases and applying it to the particular dispute before the courts. In the course of time the Common Law changed. Lawyers of the reign of Henry II read into the statements of their predecessors meanings and principles which their authors never intended, and applied them to the conditions and problems of their own day. No matter. Here was a precedent. If a judge could be shown that a custom or something like it had been recognised and acted upon in an earlier and similar case he would be more ready to follow it in the dispute before him. This slow but continuous growth of what is popularly known as "case law" ultimately achieved much the same freedoms and rights for the individual as are enshrined in other countries by written instruments such as the French Declarations of the Rights of Man. But English justice advanced very cautiously. Even the framers of Magna Carta did not attempt to lay down new law or proclaim any broad general principles. This was because both sovereign and subject were in practice bound by the Common Law, and the liberties of Englishmen rested not on any enactment of the State, but on immemorial slow-growing custom declared by juries of free men who gave their verdicts case by case in open court.

CHAPTER 14

COEUR DE LION

THE CHRISTIAN KINGDOM FOUNDED at Jerusalem after the First Crusade had stood precariously for a century, guarded by the military orders of the Knights Templars and Hospitallers. Its continued existence was largely due to the disunity that prevailed among the Moslem lands surrounding it. At length the rise of a great national leader of the Turks, or Saracens, united the Moslem power. In 1169 Saladin became Vizier of Egypt. Shortly afterwards he proclaimed himself Sultan. Soon his power was stretching out into Syria, encircling the Crusaders' principalities on the

Richard I, "Coeur de Lion", is shown here with his Crusader's sword and his shield emblazoned with heraldic lions.

Levantine coast. In 1187 Jerusalem surrendered, and thereafter all Palestine and Syria, except Tyre, Antioch, and Tripoli, fell again into Moslem hands.

The shock of these events resounded throughout Europe. The Pope's legates traversed the Courts enjoining peace among Christians and war against the infidel, and an intense movement stirred the chivalry of England, France, and Germany. The magnetism of war and adventure, mingled with a deep counterpart of sacrifice and mysticism, lights the age and its efforts with the charm of true romance. In Germany the Diet of Mainz solemnly "swore the expedition" to the Holy Land. The Kings of France and England agreed upon a joint Crusade, without however ceasing their immediate strife. To the religious appeal was added the spur of the tax-gatherer. The "Saladin tithe" was levied upon all who did not take the Cross. On the other hand, forgiveness of taxes and a stay in the payment of debts were granted to all Crusaders. The strongest armies ever yet sent to the East were raised. Germany marshalled a large array to the standard of Frederick Barbarossa. A Scandinavian fleet bore twelve thousand Norsemen through the Straits of Gibraltar. Thus did armoured Europe precipitate itself upon Asia.

In the midst of these surgings Henry II died in sorrow and disaster. He made no attempt to prescribe the succession, and it passed naturally to Richard. The new King affected little grief at the death of a father against whom he was in arms. He knelt beside his bier no longer than would have been necessary to recite the Lord's Prayer, and turned at once to the duties of his realm. In spite of many harsh qualities, men saw in him a magnanimity which has added lustre to his military renown. At the outset of his reign he confirmed his father's faithful warrior — and Richard's recent adversary — William the Marshal in all his offices and honours, and sent him to England to act in his name. He gave him in marriage a Crown ward, the rich heiress of Pembroke, and at a stroke the Marshal became one of the most powerful of English barons. Indeed it was noted that the King's favour lighted upon those who had stood loyally by his father against him, even to the detriment of those who had been his own fellow rebels.

Richard, with all his characteristic virtues and faults cast in a heroic mould, is one of the most fascinating medieval figures. He has been described as the embodiment of the age of chivalry. In those days the lion was much admired in heraldry, and when Richard's contemporaries called him "Coeur de Lion" they paid a lasting compliment to the king of beasts. Little did the English people owe him for his service, and heavily did they pay for his adventures. He was in England only twice for a few short months in his ten years' reign; yet his memory has always stirred English hearts, and seems to present throughout the centuries the pattern of the fighting man. He was tall and delicately shaped; strong in nerve and sinew, and rejoiced in personal combat. He loved war, not so much for the sake of glory or political ends, but as other men love science or poetry, for the excitement of the struggle and the glow of victory. By this his whole temperament was toned; and, united with the highest qualities of the military commander, love of war called forth all the powers of his mind and body.

William the Marshal, caretaker of the monarchy during King Richard I's crusading days, is here shown in effigy from his tomb in the Temple Church, London.

Although a man of blood and violence, Richard was too impetuous to be either treacherous or habitually cruel. He was open-handed and munificent to profusion; in war circumspect in design and skilful in execution; in politics a child, lacking in subtlety and experience. His political alliances were formed upon his likes and dislikes; his political schemes had neither unity nor clearness of purpose. The advantages gained for him by military genius were flung away through diplomatic ineptitude. When, on the journey to the East, Messina in Sicily was won by his arms, he was easily persuaded to share with his polished, faithless ally, Philip Augustus, fruits of a victory which more wisely used might have foiled the French king's artful schemes. But then he had promised to marry Philip's sister Alice, only to reject her in favour of Berengaria of Navarre. Philip was little soothed for the affront by a compensation of ten thousand marks.

The King's heart was set upon the new Crusade. This task seemed made for him. It appealed to every need of his nature. To rescue the Holy Land from the pollution of the infidel, to charge as a king at the head of knightly squadrons in a cause at once glorious to man and especially acceptable to God, was a completely satisfying inspiration. The English would greatly have liked their King to look after their affairs, to give them peace and order, to nourish their growing prosperity, and to do justice throughout the land. But they understood that the Crusade was a high and sacred enterprise, and the Church taught them that in unseen ways it would bring a blessing upon them. Richard was crowned with peculiar state, by a ceremonial which, elaborating the most ancient forms and traditions of the island monarchy, is still in all essentials observed today. Thereafter the King, for the sake of Christ's sepulchre, virtually put the realm up for sale. Money he must have at all costs for his campaign in far-off Palestine. He sold and re-sold every office in the State. He made new and revolutionarily heavy demands for taxation. He called for "scutage", the commutation of military service for a money payment, and later reintroduced "carucage", a levy on every hundred acres of land. Thus he filled his chests for the Holy Wars. Then confiding the government to two Justiciars, William Longchamp, Bishop of Ely, and Hugh de Puiset, Bishop of Durham, under the supervision of the one trustworthy member of his family, his mother, the old Queen, Eleanor of Aquitaine, he started for the wars in the winter of 1189.

Commemorative brasses were an innovation of the late thirteenth century and often depicted knights at arms. The brass on the left dates from 1277 and is the earliest English example. It shows Sir John d'Abernon and is in Stoke d'Abernon church in Surrey. On the right is Sir Roger de Trumpington of Trumpington, Cambridge.

The glamours of chivalry illumine the tale of this Third Crusade. All the chief princes of Europe gathered in line around Acre rivalling each other in prowess and jealousy. The sanctity of their cause was no bar to their quarrels and intrigues. King Richard dominated the scene. Fighting always in the most dangerous places, striking down the strongest foes, he negotiated all the time with Saladin. An agreement was in fact almost reached. To save his garrison Saladin offered to surrender his Christian captives, to pay a large indemnity, and to give up the Cross, captured by him in Jerusalem, on which Christ — though after twelve hundred years this was far from certain — had suffered. But the negotiations failed, and Richard in his fury massacred in cold blood the two thousand Saracen hostages who had been delivered as guarantees. Within five weeks of his arrival he brought the two years' siege to a successful conclusion.

By the time Acre fell King Richard's glory as a warrior and also his skill as a general were the talk of all nations. But the quarrels of the allies paralysed the campaign. Guy of Lusignan, the exiled King of Jerusalem, was disputing with Conrad of Montferrat for the Crown. Richard took the one side and Philip of France the other. A compromise was arranged, but immediately the French king returned home to intrigue with Prince John against his absent brother. Duke Leopold of Austria, whom Richard had personally insulted, also took his departure. In these circumstances the Crusading army, ably led

A manuscript picture records a knighting ceremony in which a candidate kneels to be dubbed by the king.

by Richard, in spite of the victory at Arsuf, where many thousand infidels were slain, could do no more than reach an eminence which commanded a distant view of the Holy City. The King veiled his eyes, not bearing to look upon the city he could not enter. In the next year, 1192, he captured Jaffa. Once again the distant prospect of Jerusalem alone rewarded the achievement of the Crusaders, and once again they fell back frustrated.

By now the news from England was so alarming that the King felt it imperative to return home. Bishop Longchamp had antagonised the other members of the Council, and provoked them to side with John, who had in turn agreed with King Philip that Philip should attack Normandy while John raised a revolt in England. Richard renewed his negotiations with Saladin. A peace or truce for three years was at length effected, by which the coastal towns were divided and the Holy Sepulchre opened as a place of pilgrimage to small parties of Crusaders. It was as tourists only that they reached their goal.

Later in 1192 the King set out for home. Wrecked in the Adriatic, he sought to make his way through Germany in disguise, but his enemy the Duke of Austria was soon upon his track. He was arrested, and held prisoner in a castle. So valuable a prize was not suffered to remain in the Duke's hands. The Holy Roman Emperor himself demanded the famous captive. For many months his prison was a secret of the Imperial Court, but, as a pretty legend tells us, Blondel, Richard's faithful minstrel, went from castle to castle striking the chords which the King loved best, and at last was rewarded by an answer from Richard's own harp.

Early in 1193, at a moment already full of peril, the grave news reached England that the King was prisoner somewhere in Germany. There was general and well-founded consternation among the loyal bulk of his subjects. John declared that Richard was dead and claimed the Crown. That England was now held for Richard is a proof of the loyalties of the feudal age. A deep sense of his heroic character and sacred mission commanded the allegiance of a large number of resolute, independent people whose names are unknown to history. The Church never flinched; Walter de Coutances of Rouen, who had displaced Longchamp, stood firm; the Queen Mother with septuagenarian vigour stood by her eldest son; these dominated the Council, and the Council held the country. The coasts were guarded against an impending French invasion. John's force melted. In April the strain was relieved by the arrival of authoritative news that Richard was alive. Prince John put the best face he could upon it and stole away to France.

The Holy Roman Emperor demanded the prodigious ransom of a hundred and fifty thousand marks, twice the annual revenue of the English Crown. One hundred thousand was to be ready in London before the King was liberated. Richard approved and the English Council agreed. Meanwhile Philip and John were active on the other side. They offered the Emperor eighty thousand marks to keep the English king under lock and key till Michaelmas 1194, or a hundred and fifty thousand marks to deliver him into their hands. But the Emperor felt that his blackmailing honour was engaged to Richard, with whom he had, perhaps precipitately, settled the figure. Once Philip knew that the Emperor would not go back upon his bargain he sent John his notorious message: "Have a care — the Devil is unloosed."

It remained to collect the ransom. The charge staggered the kingdom. Yet nothing was more sacred than the feudal obligation to ransom the liege lord,

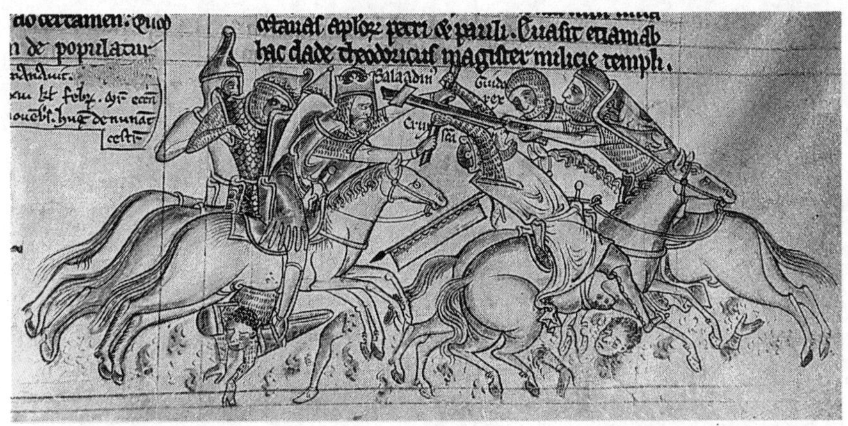

Richard I wrests the True Cross from the infidel leader, Saladin, in this thirteenth-century illustration taken from Matthew Paris's Chronica Majora.

above all when he enjoyed the sanctity of a Crusader. From all the lands a new scutage was taken. All laymen had to give a quarter of their movables. The Church lands bore an equal burden; it was lawful to sacrifice even the most holy ornaments of the cathedrals for the ransom of a Christian lost in the Holy War; they gave their plate and treasure, and three of the monastic orders yielded unresistingly a year's wool crop. Prince John of course set an example in collecting these taxes throughout his shires. The indulgence of Richard had allowed his brother to form a state within a state. John held the shires of Derby, Nottingham, Somerset, Dorset, Devon, and Cornwall; the Earldom of Gloucester, with wide lands in South Wales; the honours of Lancaster, Wallingford, Eye, and Peverel. His agents dwelt upon the sacred duty of all to pay, and he kept the proceeds of their faith and loyalty for himself. Three separate attempts were made to gather the money, and although England and Normandy, taxed to the limit, could not scrape together the whole of the sum required, the Emperor, satisfied that he could get no more, resolved to set his captive at liberty.

At the end of 1193 the stipulated first instalment was paid, and at the beginning of February 1194 Richard Coeur de Lion was released from bondage. He picked his way with care across Europe, avoiding his French domains, and on March 16 arrived again in London among citizens impoverished but still rejoiced to see him and proud of his fame. He found John again in open rebellion, having seized castles and raised forces with French aid. The Council were already acting against the traitor prince, and Richard lent the weight of his strong right arm as well as the majesty of his name to the repression of the revolt. John fled once more to France. The King was recrowned in London with even more elaborate ceremony than before. As he was now plainly at war with Philip Augustus, his first, last, and only measures of government were to raise money and gather knights. These processes well started, he crossed the Channel to defend his French possessions. He never set foot in England again. But the islanders owed him no grudge. All had been done as was right and due.

The mere arrival of the mighty warrior in France was enough to restore the frontiers and to throw King Philip and his forces upon an almost abject defensive. John sought pardon from the brother and liege lord he had so foully wronged. He did not sue in vain. With the full knowledge that if John had had his way he would still be a captive in a German castle, dethroned, or best of all dead — with all the long story of perfidy and unnatural malice in

A Crusader on horseback inspired this water jug which was cast from copper alloy in the late thirteenth century. The water was poured in through the top of the knight's helmet and out through the spout in the horse's head.

his mind, Coeur de Lion pardoned John, embraced him in fraternal love, and restored him to some of his estates, except certain fortresses which the barest prudence obliged him to reserve. This gesture was admired for its grandeur, though not perhaps for its wisdom, by the whole society, lay and spiritual, of Christendom.

The five remaining years of Richard's reign were spent in defending his French domains and raising money for that purpose from England. Once again the country was ruled by a deputy, this time Hubert Walter, a man bred in the traditions of Henry II's official Household: no feudal amateur, but a professional administrator by training and experience. Walter was now Archbishop of Canterbury, and Richard's Justiciar. He was to become King John's Chancellor. Thus for ten years he was the kingdom's chief minister. He had been extremely useful to Richard on the Crusade, on which he had accompanied him, and had been prominent in the organisation of the ransom. Hubert Walter stands out as one of the great medieval administrators. With determination, knowledge, and deft touch he developed the system of strong centralised government devised by Henry II. The royal authority was reasserted in the north; commissions of inquiry dealt with unfinished judicial and financial business; other commissions, with the help of local juries, carried out exhaustive inquiries into royal rights and the administration of justice. A new machinery for keeping the peace was devised, to which the origin of the Justice of the Peace can be traced, and the office of Coroner now emerged clearly for the first time. As head of the Exchequer, Walter de Coutances attempted the revision of taxation and of the existing military system. New assessments of land were begun, weights and measures standardised, and the frauds of cloth workers and dealers purged or curbed. New concessions, involving the precious privilege of local self-government, were granted to London and the principal towns. Throughout the length and breadth of the land the machinery of government was made to work easily and quietly. If there was discontent at the taxes few dared to voice it. One man, a demagogue, "William of the Beard", uttered sentiments which would in similar circumstances readily occur to modern politicians. He was hanged.

Although Richard was an absentee king, whose causes and virtues had proved a drain and disappointment to his subjects, his realm had not suffered so much as it would have seemed. The intrigues of the nobles and the treacheries of Prince John had been restrained by an impersonal government ruling with the force and in the name of high but well-grounded principles. The system of administration — the Civil Service as we may call it — had stood the test, and, undisturbed by royal interventions, consolidated itself, to the general convenience and advantage.

In France, the war with Philip proceeded in a curious fashion. The negotiations were unceasing. Every year there was a truce, which every year was broken as the weather and general convenience permitted. Then in 1197 the skirmishing and parleying were slashed by a fierce event. Something like a battle was fought, and Richard drove the King of France and his army in headlong rout through the streets of Gisors, where the solemn oaths of the Third Crusade had been sworn barely ten years before by the Kings of France and England.

In 1199, when the difficulties of raising revenue for the endless war were at their height, good news was brought to King Richard. It was said that there

Richard I's effigy from the family tomb at Fontevrault, where he lies next to his mother, Eleanor of Aquitaine. He was brought up at her court in Poitiers, where the creed of chivalry was propagated by minstrels and troubadours. Richard was Eleanor's favourite son.

had been dug up near the castle of Chaluz, on the lands of one of his vassals, a treasure of wonderful quality. The King claimed this treasure as lord paramount. The lord of Chaluz resisted the demand, and the King laid siege to his small, weak castle. On the third day, as he rode daringly near the wall, confident in his hard-tried luck, a bolt from a crossbow struck him in the left shoulder by the neck. Gangrene set in, and Coeur de Lion knew that he must pay a soldier's debt. He prepared for death with fortitude and calm. He arranged his affairs; he divided his personal belongings among his friends or bequeathed them to charity. He sent for his mother, the redoubtable Eleanor, who was at hand. He declared John to be his heir, and made all present swear fealty to him. He ordered the archer who had shot the fatal bolt, and who was now a prisoner, to be brought before him. He pardoned him, and made him a gift of money. For seven years he had not confessed for fear of being compelled to be reconciled to Philip, but now he received the offices of the Church with sincere and exemplary piety, and died in the forty-second year of his age on April 6, 1199, worthy, by the consent of all men, to sit with King Arthur and other heroes at some Eternal Round Table, which we trust the Creator of the Universe in his comprehension will not have forgotten to provide. The archer was flayed alive.

CHAPTER 15

MAGNA CARTA

THE CHARACTER OF THE PRINCE who now ascended the throne was already well known. Richard had embodied the virtues which men admire in the lion, but there is no animal in nature that combines the contradictory qualities of John. He united ruthlessness with craft and subtlety. Although from time to time he gave way to furious rages, in which "his eyes darted fire and his countenance became livid", his cruelties were conceived and executed with a cold intelligence. Monkish chronicles have emphasised his violence, greed, malice, treachery, and lust. But other records show that he was often judicious, always extremely capable, and on occasions even generous. He possessed an original and inquiring mind, and to the end of his life treasured his library of books. The difficulties with which he contended, on the whole with remarkable success, deserve cool and attentive study. Moreover, when the long tally is added it will be seen that the British nation owes far more to the vices of John than to the labours of virtuous sovereigns; for it was through the union of many forces against him that the most famous milestone of our rights and freedom was set up.

With the accession of John there emerges plainly in the northern French provinces a sense of unity with one another and with the kingdom of France; at the same time on this side of the Channel the English baronage became ever more inclined to insular and even nationalistic ideas. Ties with the Continent were weakening through the gradual division of honours and appanages (revenues) in England and Normandy between different branches of Anglo-Norman families. Moreover, the growing brilliance of the French Court and royal power in the late twelfth century was a powerful magnet which drew continental loyalties to Paris. King John thus found himself compelled to fight at greater odds than his predecessor for his possessions on the Continent. He was also opposed by an increasing resistance to taxation for that purpose in England.

King John is seen debating with a leader of the Church in this decorative fourteenth-century manuscript picture.

Although Richard had declared John to be King there were two views upon the succession. Geoffrey, his elder brother, who had died in 1186, had left behind him a son, Arthur, Prince of Brittany. It was already possible to hold that this grandson of Henry II of an elder branch had a prior right against John, and that is now the law of primo geniture. William the Marshal put the point before the Archbishop of Canterbury, but they both decided that John had the right. Queen Eleanor stood by her son against the grandson, whose mother she had never liked. John was accepted without demur in England. In the French provinces however the opposite view prevailed. Brittany in particular adopted Arthur. The King of France and all French interests thought themselves well served by a disputed succession. Those who had supported Richard against his father, and John against Richard, found it logical to support Arthur against John.

From the first John feared Arthur. He had been in Brittany and at Arthur's Court when the news of Richard's death reached him. He had made good haste out of so dangerous an area. John's strength lay only in Aquitaine and in Normandy. The war and negotiations continued in the fitful style of the preceding reign, but without the prestige of Coeur de Lion on the side of the English Crown. In 1202 Philip, as John's overlord in respect of certain territories, issued a summons citing John before his Court to answer charges made against him by the barons of Poitou. John declared that the King of England could not submit himself to such a trial. Philip rejoined that the King of France could not lose his rights over a vassal because that vassal happened to acquire another dignity. All legal expedients being exhausted, John, who not even promised safe-conduct for his return, refused to attend the Court, and was accordingly sentenced to be deprived of all the lands which he held in France because of his failure of service to his overlord. Thus armed with a legal right recognised by the jurists of the period, Philip invaded Normandy in the summer of 1202, capturing many towns with practically no resistance. He also knighted Arthur, invested him with all the fiefs of which John had been deprived, except Normandy and Guienne, and betrothed him to his daughter Mary. Arthur was now sixteen.

When we reflect that the French provinces counted just as much with the

Plantagenet kings as the whole realm of England it is obvious that a more virtuous man than John would be incensed at such treatment. His pent-up feelings roused in him an energy unexpected by his foes.

Arthur, hearing that his grandmother Eleanor was at the castle of Mirabeau in Poitou with a scanty escort, surrounded the castle, stormed the outworks, and was about to gain custody of this important and hostile old Queen. Eleanor contrived in the nick of time to send word to John, who was at Le Mans. Her son with ample forces covered the eighty miles between them in forty-eight hours, and surprised Arthur and the besiegers at daybreak. Arthur and all who stood with him fell at a stroke into John's power, and his mother was delivered from her dangerous plight.

Arthur was imprisoned at Falaise and then at Rouen. No one doubted that he lay in mortal peril. All those barons of Brittany who were still loyal to John asked that the prince should be released, and on John's refusal went into immediate rebellion. John felt that he would never be safe so long as Arthur lived. The havoc of disunity that was being wrought throughout the French provinces by the French king using Arthur as a pawn might well have weighed with a better man than John. The horrid crime of murder has often been committed for reasons of State upon lesser temptations than now assailed this exceptionally violent king. No one knows what happened to Arthur. An impenetrable veil descends upon the tragedy of Rouen. The officer commanding the fortress, one Hubert de Burgh, of whom more and better hereafter, gave out that upon the King's orders he had delivered his prisoner at Easter 1203 to the hands of agents sent by John to castrate him, and that Arthur had died of the shock. This explanation by no means allayed the ill-feeling aroused in Brittany and elsewhere. Hubert then declared that Arthur was still alive, and John stated that he was glad his orders had been disobeyed. However it may be, Arthur was never seen again. That he was murdered by John's orders was not disputed.

Arthur had been removed, but John failed to profit by his crime, for his disappearance left unchanged the iron purposes of the French king. Against this persistency Richard had roused men's devotion, but John's nature inspired none. Brittany and the central provinces of the Angevin Empire revolted. Philip had come to terms with each province, and at Easter 1203 he made a voyage down the Loire to Saumur. A deep wedge had been driven between the northern and the southern halves of John's continental possessions. Then, as Philip took fortress after fortress in central Normandy, John's nerve failed, and he quitted Normandy. The Normans, not unwilling to find an excuse for surrender, made English indifference their justification. In June 1204 Rouen itself was taken, and Normandy finally became French.

No English tears need have been shed over this loss. It proved as much in the interest of England as of France. It rid the island of a dangerous, costly distraction and entanglement, turned its thought and energies to its own affairs, and above all left a ruling class of alien origin no interest henceforth that was not English or at least insular. These consolations did not however dawn on John's contemporaries, who saw only disastrous and humiliating defeat, and blamed a king already distrusted by the people and at variance with the nobility.

In England the very success of Henry II in re-establishing order and creating an efficient central administration had left new difficulties for those who came after him. Henry II had created an instrument so powerful that it needed careful handling. He had restored order only at the cost of offending privilege. His fiscal arrangements were original, and drastic in their thoroughness. His work had infringed feudal custom at many points. All this had been accepted because of the King's tactful management and in the reaction from anarchy. Richard I, too, had left England in the hands of able administrators, and the odium of their strict government and financial ingenuity fell on them directly, and stopped short of the King, radiant in the halo of a Crusader. John was at hand to bear the brunt in person.

John, like William Rufus, pressed to logical limits the tendencies of his father's system. There were arrears in the payment of scutage from Richard's reign, and more money was needed to fight the French king. But a division had opened in the baronage. The English barons of John's reign had become distinct from his Norman feudatories. Even King Richard had met with refusals from his English nobles to fight abroad. Disputes about foreign service and payment of scutage lay at the root of the baronial agitation. By systematic abuse of his feudal prerogatives John drove the baronage to violent resistance. English society was steadily developing. Class interests had assumed sharper definition. Many barons regarded attendance or suit at Court as an opportunity for exerting influence rather than for rendering dutiful service. The sense of Church unity grew among the clergy, and corporate feeling in the municipalities. All these classes were needed by the new centralised government; but John preferred to emphasise the more ruthless aspects of the royal power.

The year 1205 brought a crisis. The loss of Normandy was followed by the death of John's mother, to whose influence he had owed much of his position on the mainland. The death of Archbishop Hubert Walter, who for the last ten years had controlled the machinery of administration, deprived him of the only statesman whose advice he respected and whose authority stood between the Crown and the nation. It also re-opened the thorny question of who should elect the Primate of England.

The Papal throne at this time was occupied by Innocent III, one of the greatest of the medieval Popes, renowned for his statecraft and intent on raising to its height the temporal power of the Church. The dispute between John and the monastery of Canterbury over election to the Archbishopric offered Innocent the very chance he sought for asserting Papal authority in England. Setting aside the candidates of the Canterbury clergy and of the Crown, Innocent caused Stephen Langton to be selected with great pomp and solemnity at Rome. King John, confident of sufficient influence in the Papal Court to secure the election of his own candidate, had imprudently acknowledged the validity of the Papal decision beforehand. It was with pardonable anger that he learnt how neatly Innocent had introduced a third candidate whose qualifications were unimpeachable. Stephen Langton was an English cardinal of the highest character, and one of the most famous doctors of the Paris schools. In his wrath, and without measuring the strength of his opponents, the King proceeded to levy a bloodless war upon the Church. Innocent III and Stephen Langton were not men to be browbeaten into surrender, and they possessed in an age of faith more powerful weapons than any secular monarch. When John began to persecute the clergy and seize Church lands, the Pope retaliated by laying all England under an interdict. For more than six years the doors of the churches were thereby closed against the devout; the dead must be buried in unconsecrated ground and without the last Communion. Many of John's subjects were assured of damnation for themselves or their loved ones on this account alone.

When John redoubled the attack upon Church property, the Pope, in 1209, took the supreme step of excommunication. The King's subjects were thereby absolved from their allegiance; his enemies received the blessing of the Church and were sanctified as Crusaders. But John was unabashed. Interdict and excommunication brought no ghostly terrors to his soul. Indeed the interdict, if a menace, was also an opportunity for which John's plans were well matured. The ecclesiastical property of clerics who fled abroad was seized as forfeit by the Crown. Thus the Exchequer overflowed with the spoils. But for the combination of the Church quarrel with stresses of mundane politics, the Crown might have established a position not reached till the days of Henry VIII.

After the loss of Normandy John had embarked upon a series of grandiose schemes for a continental alliance againt Philip Augustus. He found allies in the Emperor Otto IV and the Counts of Toulouse and Flanders; but his breach with the Church hastened a far more formidable league between the King of France and the Papacy, and in 1213 he had to choose between submission and a French invasion, backed by all the military and spiritual resources which Innocent III could set in motion. The King's insecurity at home forced him to bow to the threat, and Innocent rejoiced in victory upon his own terms.

John however was not at the end of his devices, and by a stroke of cunning choice enough to be called political genius he turned defeat into something very like triumph. If he could not prevail he would submit; if he submitted he would repent; if he repented there must be no limits to his contrition. At all costs he must break the closing circle of his foes. He spread before Innocent the lure of temporal sovereignty which he knew the Pontiff could not resist. He offered to make England a fief of the Papacy, and to do homage to the Pope as his feudal lord. Innocent leapt at this addition to his worldy dignities. He forgave the penitent King; he accepted the sovereignty

A PERSONAL VIEW OF KING JOHN

John, who signed Magna Carta in 1215, was probably not as wicked as he is popularly supposed to have been. This vivid account bears the stamp of contemporary propaganda and is taken from Matthew Paris's Chronica Majora.

His mental state underwent a transformation and he tended to welcome the worst suggestions. For it is easy to unbalance an unstable person and to precipitate into crime one already inclined to evil. Then the king heaved deep sighs, began to feel the utmost irritation, started to turn in upon himself and languish. He kept moaning and groaning, "Why did my mother bear me to misery and shame . . . ?" He started to gnash his teeth and roll his staring eyes in fury. Then he would pick up sticks and straws and gnaw them like a lunatic and sometimes he would cast them away half-chewed. His uncontrolled gestures gave indications of the melancholy, or rather madness, that was upon him.

King John riding to hounds. This picture from a fourteenth-century manuscript suggests the energy possessed by this maligned ruler.

Seal of Stephen Langton, who was Pope Innocent III's choice for the Canterbury election in 1207.

of England, and then returned it to John as his vassal with his blessing.

This turned the tables upon John's secular enemies. He was now the darling of the Church. Philip Augustus, who at heavy expense had gathered his armies to invade England as a Crusader for his own purposes, thought himself ill-used by the sudden tergiversation of his spiritual ally. The barons also found meagre comfort in this transformation. Their grievances remained unredressed, their anger unappeased. Even in the English Church there was a keen division. The English Episcopate saw themselves now carried into a subjection to Rome far beyond what their piety or interests required. Stephen Langton himself, the Pope's elect, was as good an Englishman as he was a churchman. He foresaw the unbridled exploitation by Rome of the patronage of the English Church and the wholesale engrossment of its benefices by Italian nominees. He became almost immediately an opposing force to the Pope. King John, who had lain at Dover, may have laughed while he pulled all these strings and threw his enemies into confusion.

Both John and Innocent persevered in their new partnership, and the disaffected barons drew together under the leadership of Stephen Langton. The war with the French king was continued, and John's demands in money and service kept the barons' anger hot. In 1214 an English expedition which John had led to Poitou failed. In northern France the army commanded by his nephew, Otto of Saxony, and by the Earl of Salisbury, was defeated by King Philip at Bouvines. This battle destroyed in a day the whole continental combination on which John's hopes had been based. Here again was the opportunity of the King's domestic enemies. They formed plans to restrain the rule of a despotic and defeated King, and openly threatened revolt unless their terms were accepted.

But John had still one final resource. Encouraged by the Pope, he took the vows of a Crusader and invoked sentence of excommunication upon his opponents. This was not denied him. The conditions of 1213 were not entirely reversed. The barons, who had thought to be Crusaders against an excommunicated King, were now under the ban themselves. But this agile use of the Papal thunders had robbed them of some of their virtues as a deterrent. The barons persisted in their demands in spite of the Papal Bull. A great party in the Church stood with them. In vain did John manoeuvre, by the offer to grant freedom of election to the Church, to separate the clergy from the barons. Although in the final scene of the struggle the Archbishop showed himself unwilling to go to the extreme of civil war, it was he who persuaded the barons to base their demands upon respect for ancient custom and law, and who gave them some principle to fight for besides their own class interests. After forty years' experience of the administrative system established by Henry II the men who now confronted John had advanced beyond the magnates of King Stephen's time. They had learnt to think intelligently and constructively. In place of the King's arbitrary despotism they proposed, not the withering anarchy of feudal separatism, but a system of checks and balances which would accord the monarchy its necessary strength, but would prevent its perversion by a tyrant or a fool. The leaders of the barons in 1215 groped in the dim light towards a fundamental principle. Government must henceforward mean something more than the arbitrary rule of any man, and custom and the law must stand even above the king. It was this idea, perhaps only half understood, that gave unity and force to the barons' opposition and made the Charter which they now demanded imperishable.

On a Monday morning in June, between Staines and Windsor, the barons and churchmen began to collect on the great meadow at Runnymede. An uneasy hush fell on them from time to time. Many had failed to keep their tryst; and the bold few who had come knew that the King would never forgive this humiliation. The handful of resolute men had drawn up, it seems, a short document on parchment. Their retainers and the groups and squadrons of horsemen in sullen steel kept at some distance. For was not armed rebellion against the Crown the supreme feudal crime? Then events followed rapidly. A small cavalcade appeared from the direction of Windsor. Gradually men made out the faces of the King, the Papal Legate, the Archbishop of Canterbury, and several bishops. They dismounted without ceremony. Someone, probably the Archbishop, stated briefly the terms that were suggested. The King declared at once that he agreed. He said the details should be arranged immediately in his chancery. The original "Articles of the Barons" on which Magna Carta is based exist today in the British Museum. They were sealed in a quiet, short scene, which has become one of the most famous in our history, on June 15, 1215. Afterwards the King returned to Windsor. Four days later, probably, the Charter itself was engrossed. In future ages it was to be used as the foundation of principles and systems of government of which neither John nor his nobles dreamt.

At the beginning of the year 1216 indeed there seemed to be every chance that John would still defeat the baronial opposition and wipe out the humiliation of Runnymede. Yet before the summer was out the King was dead, and the Charter survived the denunciation of the Pope and the arbitrament of war. In the next hundred years it was reissued thirty-eight times, at first with a few substantial alterations, but retaining its original characteristics. Little more was heard of it until the seventeenth century, when a Parliamentary Opposition struggling to check the encroachments of the Stuarts upon the liberty of the subject rediscovered it and made of it a rallying cry against oppression. Thus was created the glorious legend of the "Charter of an Englishman's liberties".

If we set aside the rhetorical praise which has been so freely lavished upon the Charter and study the document itself we may find it rather surprising reading. It is not a declaration of constitutional doctrine, but a practical document to remedy current abuses in the feudal system. In the forefront stand the questions of scutage, of feudal reliefs and of wardship. It implies on the King's part a promise of good government for the future, but the terms of the promise are restricted to the observance of the customary privileges and interests of the baronial class. The barons for their part were compelled to make some provision for their tenants, the limits forced on John being vaguely applied to the tenants in chief as well. The villeins, in so far as they were protected, received only such attention as befitted valuable chattels of the manor and not as free citizens of the realm.

Magna Carta must not however be dismissed lightly, in the words of a modern writer, as "a monument of class selfishness". Even in its own day men of all ranks above the status of villeins had an interest in that the tenure of land should be secure from arbitrary encroachment. Moreover, the greatest magnate might hold, and often did hold, besides his estate in chief, parcels of land under the most diverse tenures. Therefore, in securing

THE MAKING OF THE LAW

THE ENGLISH LAW AND the English language have been described by Lord Denning, former head of the Court of Appeal, as the two great glories of English history. Each emerged through gradual development rather than decree.

The origins of English common law, including the jury system, go back far. During the reign of Henry II (1154–1189) great steps forward were taken as the King's courts widened their powers and increased their influence, not only in the London law courts but through travelling justices. Disputes could be resolved which had hitherto been settled only by trial of battle. The first English treatise on law now appeared.

In the reign of Henry's youngest son, John (1199–1216) there was a reaction against royal authority, and the King was forced by his barons to seal Magna Carta, a kind of treaty between king and barons, in 1215. Hastily drafted though it was, Magna Carta became an important long-term document in the history of English freedom, since it defined restraints on the king and baronial privileges which were later to be widened. In particular, it linked taxation with consent.

This link was of crucial importance also in the making of Parliament, which was itself a court. From the reign of Edward I (1272–1307) onwards it included not only lords and Church dignitaries but also a "Commons" of townsfolk and burgesses, together with knights representing the counties. By the reign of Edward III (1327–1377) Parliament refused to vote funds for the King until he promised to remedy disputes and grievances.

By the 1350s the Commons were pressing Edward to allow them to control the principal source of royal revenue, the tax on wool. Eventually the King agreed that this tax should not be levied without the full consent of Parliament.

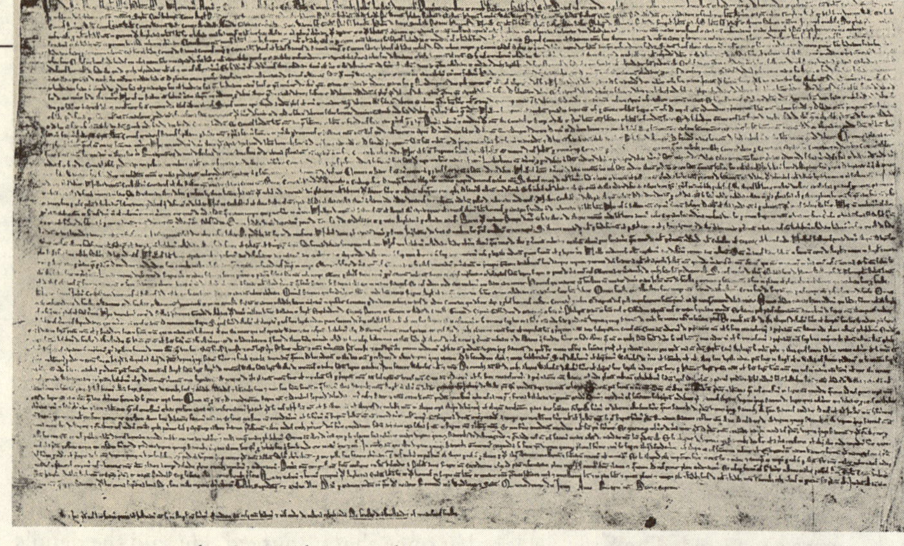

MAGNA CARTA, or the Great Charter, (above) asserted every subject's personal liberty and right to own property. King John had quarrelled with the Church, his barons and the merchants, and they all united against him. Archbishop Stephen Langton drew up the document and he and the other disaffected notables forced John to seal it on June 15, 1215 at Runnymede, near Windsor. The picture above shows the best of the four surviving Charter documents, which contains a detailed clarification of the privileges of the King's subjects. Over the centuries these privileges came to be considered as rights.

THE SEAL OF KING JOHN (above) was the highly visible official ratification of the Magna Carta. In an age when literacy was rare, the King's authorisation had to be easily seen: this seal is nearly four inches in diameter.

THE COURT OF STAR CHAMBER (below) was named after the star pattern on the ceiling of the council chamber at Westminster where it was held. It was formed in 1487 to try, without undue delay, cases brought to the King and his Privy Council. At first the Court was popular, but later it was accused of being arbitrary and was abolished in 1641.

MEDIEVAL GAOLS *were places of imprisonment for felons awaiting trial. Shown above is a surviving lockup, once a chapel, on Bradford on Avon bridge. Often occupied by drunks, it was known as the Blind House.*

THE COURT OF THE KING'S BENCH *(left) shows judges presiding, at the top, while an usher swears in the jury, on the left. Scribes consult scrolls and prepare to record the proceedings. A prisoner with his feet chained together is one of a line of offenders awaiting their turn in the dock. At Westminster the King's judges sat in four main courts: the Common Pleas, the Exchequer, the King's Bench and the Court of Chancery. This picture is an illustration from a book that was produced in about 1450.*

PILLORIES, OR STOCKS, *(above) were for minor criminals, and part of the punishment lay in the public shame attached. Petty offences were investigated by a number of authorities such as the lords of the manor, the Church, the guilds and the travelling justices. No paid local police force existed before the nineteenth century, when in 1829 Robert Peel instigated the metropolitan force.*

themselves, the barons of Runnymede were in fact establishing the rights of the whole landed class, great and small — the simple knight with two hundred acres, the farmer or small yeoman with sixty. And there is evidence that their action was so understood throughout the country.

If the thirteenth-century magnates understood little and cared less for popular liberties or Parliamentary democracy, they had all the same laid hold of a principle which was to be of prime importance for the future development of English society and English institutions. Throughout the document it is implied that here is a law which is above the king and which even he must not break. This reaffirmation of a supreme law and its expression in a general charter is the great work of Magna Carta; and this alone justifies the respect in which men have held it. The reign of Henry II initiated the rule of law. But the work as yet was incomplete: the Crown was still above the law; the legal system which Henry had created could become, as John showed, an instrument of oppression.

Now for the first time the king himself is bound by the law. The root principle was destined to survive across the generations and rise paramount long after the feudal background of 1215 had faded in the past. The Charter became in the process of time an enduring witness that the power of the Crown was not absolute.

The facts embodied in it and the circumstances giving rise to them were buried and misunderstood. The underlying idea of the sovereignty of law, long existent in feudal custom, was raised by it into a doctrine for the national State. And when in subsequent ages the State, swollen with its own authority, has attempted to ride roughshod over the rights or liberties of the subject, it is to this doctrine that appeal has again and again been made, and never, as yet, without success.

CHAPTER 16

KING HENRY III

KING JOHN DIED IN THE TOILS, but he died at bay. The misgovernment of his reign had brought against him what seemed to be an overwhelming combination. He was at war with the English barons who had forced him to grant the Charter. They had invited Louis, son of the implacable Philip, King of France, into the country to be their liege lord, and with him came foreign troops and hardy adventurers. The insurgent barons north of the Humber had the support of Alexander, King of Scots; in the west the rebellion was sustained by Llewellyn, the powerful Prince of North Wales. The towns were mainly against the King; London was vehemently hostile. The Cinque Ports were in enemy hands.

On the other hand, the recreant King had sacrificed the status of the realm to purchase the unswerving aid of the Papacy. A strong body of mercenaries, the only regular troops in the kingdom, were in John's pay. Some of the greatest warrior-nobles, including the venerable William the Marshal, with a strong following of the aristocracy, adhered to his cause. The mass of the people, bewildered by this new quarrel of their masters, on the whole inclined to the King against the barons, and certainly against the invading foreigners. Their part was only to suffer at the hands of both sides. Thus the forces were evenly balanced; everything threatened a long, stubborn civil war. John himself, after a lifetime of subtleties and double-dealing, showed himself possessed, in the last months of his life, of a warlike energy and resource which astonished friend and foe. It was at this moment that he died of dysentery, aggravated by fatigue and too much food and drink. The death of the King in this convulsion of strife changed the conditions of the conflict without ending it. The rival interests and factions that were afoot had many purposes beyond the better government of England. Louis was in the island, and fighting. The rebel lords were deeply involved with their Scottish and Welsh allies; none was in the humour for peace. Yet the sole reason and justification for revolt died with John. His son, Henry, a child of nine, was the undoubted rightful King of England. Upon what ground could the oppressions of the father be visited upon his innocent son? All parties were profoundly sensible of these considerations. William the Marshal acted with honesty and decision. Had he failed in his duty to the Crown the strong centralised monarchy which Henry II had created, and upon which the growing civilisation of the realm depended, might have degenerated into a heptarchy of feudal princes, or even worse. The boy king was crowned at Gloucester, and began his reign of fifty-six years on October 28, 1216. He was anointed by the Papal Legate, and in default of the diadem which John had lost in crossing the Wash a plain gold circlet was placed upon his brow. This was to prove no inadequate symbol of his rule.

William the Marshal, aged seventy, reluctantly undertook what we should now call the Regency. He joined to himself the Earl of Chester, and Hubert de Burgh, John's faithful servant. The wisdom and the weakness of the new Government were alike revealed in the reissue of the Charter.

It was a reign of turmoil and distress, and yet the forces of progress moved doggedly forward. In this period the common people, with their Anglo-Saxon tradition of ancient rights and law running back to remote antiquity, lay suffering under the armoured feet of the nobility and of the royal mercenaries, reinforced in the main by the power of the Church. But the people's masters were disunited. Not only did their jealousies and ambitions and their taste for war keep them at variance, but several rending fissures were opening among them. They were divided into parties; they were cross-cut obliquely by a strong nationalism. It is an age of impulse and experiment, not controlled by any general political theory.

The confusion and monotony of the barons' warfare, against each other, or against the King, sometimes with the Church, more often against the Church, have repelled many readers of history. But the fact is that King Henry III survived all his troubles and left England enjoying a prosperity and peace unknown when he was a child. The cruel war and anarchy lie only upon the surface; underneath, unformulated and largely unrealised by the hard-pressed actors, course all the tides which were to flow in Europe five hundred years later. From out of the conflict there rise the figures of heroes, both warriors and statesmen, from whose tribulations we are separated by long ages, but whose work and outlook unite them to us, as if we read their acts and words in the morning newspaper.

We must examine some of the figures at close quarters. Stephen Langton, the great Archbishop, was the indomitable, unwearying builder of the rights of Englishmen against royal, baronial and even ecclesiastical pretensions. Here is a man who worked for the unity of Christendom through the

The lined face of Henry III in effigy, from Westminster Abbey. The gilt-bronze monument was made in 1291 by William Torel.

Catholic Church; but also for the interests of England against the Papacy: a faithful servant of the Crown, but at the same time a champion of the Charter, and all it meant, and still means. A commanding central figure, practical, resourceful, shifting from side to side as evils forced him, but quite unchanging and unchangeable in his broad, wise, brave, workaday, liberal purpose. Here was, if not an architect of our Constitution, at least a punctual and unfailing Clerk of the Works.

The second personality to emerge from the restless scene is Hubert de Burgh: a soldier and a politician, armed with the practical wisdom which familiarity with courts and camps, with high authorities, ecclesiastical and armoured, may infuse into a man's conduct, and even nature. John's Justiciar, identified with the crimes and the follies of the reign, was yet known to all men as their constant resolute opponent. Under the Marshal, who was himself a star of European chivalry, Hubert was an outstanding leader of resistance to the rebellion against the monarchy. At the same time, he was a solid champion of the rights of England. The island should not be ravaged by greedy nobles, nor pillaged by foreign adventurers, nor mutilated unduly even for the high interests of the Papacy.

The rebellion of the barons was quelled by fights on land and sea. At Lincoln the King's party gained a fantastic but nonetheless decisive victory. In the streets of Lincoln, during a whole day, we are told that four hundred royal knights jostled and belaboured six hundred of the baronial party. Only three were killed in the combat. Contemporary opinion declined to accord the name of battle to this brawl. It was called "the Fair of Lincoln". It is difficult to form a general picture of what was happening. One must suppose that the knights had upon the average at least eight or ten stalwart retainers each, and that the almost invulnerable, chain-mailed monsters waddled about in the throng, chasing away or cutting down the unarmoured folk, and welting each other when they met, hard, but perhaps not too hard. In the upshot the Royalists outwitted and out-walloped the insurgents.

After a year of fighting, Louis of France was compelled to leave the country in 1217, his hopes utterly dashed. The Great Charter was now reissued for the second time in order to show that the Government meant its word. In 1219 the old victorious Marshal died, and Hubert de Burgh ruled the land for twelve years. He was a stern ruler. When Fawkes de Breauté, who had been the chief mercenary of John and William the Marshal during all these recent tumults, grew over-mighty and attempted to disturb the new-found peace of the land, Hubert determined to expel him. On taking Fawkes's stronghold of Bedford Castle in 1224, after two months siege, Hubert

The vitality of the long-lived administrator, William the Marshal, is shown in this manuscript drawing where he successfully unhorses his opponent, Baldwin of Guise.

Hubert de Burgh's White Castle in the Welsh marches. As Justiciar of England, he succeeded William the Marshal in buttressing the monarchy against the over-mighty barons.

hanged in front of its walls the twenty-four surviving knights who had commanded the garrison. In the following year, as a sign of pacification, the Great Charter was again reissued in what was substantially its final form. Thus it became an unchallenged part of English law and tradition.

No long administration is immune from mistakes, and every statesman must from time to time make concessions to wrongheaded superior powers. Hubert throughout his tenure stood for the English point of view, and for the policy of doing the least possible to recover the King's French domains. This he carried out not only by counsel, but by paralysing action.

At last in 1229 he had exhausted his goodwill, and fortune and fate were upon him. The King, now twenty-two years of age, crowned and acting, arrived at Portsmouth with a large army raised by the utmost exercise of his feudal power to defend those estates in France which after the loss of Normandy still pertained to the English Crown. Hubert could not control this, but the transporting of the expedition lay apparently in his department. The King found no ships, or few, awaiting him; no supplies, no money, for his overseas venture. He flew into a rage. Although usually mild, affable, scholarly, and artistic, he drew his sword and rushed upon the Justiciar, reproaching him with having betrayed his trust and being bribed by France. It certainly was a very unpleasant and awkward situation, the army wishing to fight abroad, and the navy and the Treasury unable or unwilling to carry them thither. The quarrel was smoothed down; the King recovered his temper; the expedition sailed in the following year and Hubert retained his place. But not for long. In 1232 he was driven from power by a small palace clique. Threatened in his life, he took sanctuary at Brentwood. He was dragged from this asylum, but the common, humble blacksmith who was ordered to put the fetters on him declared he would die any death rather than do so; and he is said to have used the words which historians have deemed to be the true monument of Hubert de Burgh: "Is he not that most faithful Hubert who so often saved England from the devastation of foreigners and restored England to England?"

De Burgh's conduct had been far from blameless, but his fall had been deliberately engineered by men whose object was not to reform administration but to gain power. The leader of this intrigue was Peter des Roches, the Bishop of Winchester. Des Roches himself kept in the background, but at the Christmas Council of 1232 nearly every post of consequence in the administration was conferred upon his friends, most of them, like him, men of Poitou. More was involved in the defeat of de Burgh than the triumph of des Roches and his party. De Burgh was the last of the great Justiciars who had wielded plenary and at times almost sovereign power. Henceforward the Household offices like the Wardrobe, largely dependent upon the royal will and favour, began to overshadow the great "national" offices, like the Justiciarship, filled by the baronial magnates. As they came to be occupied increasingly by foreign intruders, Poitevins, Savoyards, Provençals, the national feeling of the baronage became violently hostile. Under the leadership of Richard the Marshal, a second son of the faithful William, the barons began to growl against the foreigners. Des Roches retorted that the King had need of foreigners to protect him against the treachery of his natural subjects, and large numbers of Poitevin and Breton mercenaries were brought over to sustain this view. But the struggle was short. In alliance with Prince Llewellyn the young Marshal drove the King among the Welsh Marches, sacked Shrewsbury, and harried des Roches's lands. In the spring of 1234 Henry was forced to accept terms. The Poitevin officials were dismissed, des Roches found it convenient to go on a journey to Italy, and de Burgh was honourably restored to his lands and possessions.

The Poitevins were the first of the long succession of foreign favourites whom Henry III gathered round him in the middle years of his reign. The King's affection was reserved for those who flattered his vanity and ministered to his caprices. He developed a love for extravagant splendour and the culture of medieval Provence, the home of the troubadours and the creed of chivalry, and he naturally preferred to his morose barons the brilliant adventurers of Poitou and Provence. In 1236 he married Eleanor, the daughter of Raymond of Provence. With Eleanor came her numerous and needy kinsmen. A new wave of foreigners descended upon the profitable wardships, marriages, escheats, and benefices, which the disgusted baronage regarded as their own. The King delighted to shower gifts upon his charming relations, and the responsibility for all the evils of his reign was laid upon their shoulders.

An even more copious source of discontent in England was the influence of the Papacy over the grateful and pious King. Pope Gregory IX, at desperate grips with the Holy Roman Emperor Frederick II, made ever greater demands for money, and his Legate, Otto, took an interest in English Church reform. Otto's demand in 1240 for one-fifth of the clergy's rents and movables raised a storm. The rectors of Berkshire published a manifesto denying the right of Rome to tax the English Church, and urging that the Pope, like other bishops, should "live of his own". Nevertheless, early in 1241 Otto returned to Rome with a great treasure; and the Pope rewarded the loyalty of the Italian clergy by granting them the next three hundred vacant English benefices. Robert Grosseteste, scholar, scientist, and saint, and since 1235 Bishop of Lincoln, led the English clergy in evasion or refusal of Papal demands. Although he still believed that the Pope was absolute, he heralded the attacks which Wyclif was more than a century later to make upon the exactions and corruption of the Roman Court.

The Church, writhing under Papal exaction, and the baronage, offended by Court encroachments, were united in hatred of foreigners. A crisis came in 1244, when a baronial commission was appointed to fix the terms of a money grant to the King. The barons insisted that the Justiciar, Chancellor, and Treasurer, besides certain judges, should be elected by the Great Council. Under the influence of the voracious Poitevins Henry adopted a new tone. "Servants do not judge their master," he said. "Vassals do not judge their prince or bind him by conditions." Such language procured no money; and money was the pinch. Henry was forced to sell plate and jewels and give new privileges or new grants of old rights to those who would buy them. Salaries were unpaid, extortion condoned. In 1252 the King, on the pretext of a Crusade, demanded a tithe of ecclesiastical rents and property for three years. On Grosseteste's advice the clergy refused this grant, because the King would not on his part confirm Magna Carta. Next year Grosseteste died, indomitable to the last against both Papal and royal exactions.

Meanwhile Henry had secretly accepted greater continental obligations. The death of the Holy Roman Emperor Frederick in 1250 revived at Rome the old plan of uniting Sicily, over which he had ruled, to the Papal dominions. In 1254 Henry III accepted the Papal offer of the Sicilian Crown for his younger son Edmund. This was a foolish step, and the conditions attached to the gift raised it to the very height of folly. The English King was to provide an army, and he stood surety for Papal debts amounting to the vast sum in those days of about £90,000. When the King's acceptance of the Papal offer became known a storm of indignation broke over his head.

A vigorous portrait of Simon de Montfort on horseback, calling his hounds, which appears on his seal dating from 1258.

The final stroke was the King's complete failure to check the successes of Llewellyn, who in 1256 swept the English out of Wales. Despised, discredited, and frightened, without money or men, the King faced an angered and powerful opposition.

In the last years of Grosseteste's life he had come to hope great things of his friend, Simon de Montfort. French-born Simon had married Henry's sister and had inherited the Earldom of Leicester. He had been governor of the English lands in Gascony for four years. Strong and energetic, he had aroused the jealousy and opposition of the King's favourites; and as a result of their intrigues he had been brought to trial in 1252. The commission acquitted him; but in return for a sum of money from the King he unwillingly agreed to vacate his office. Friendship between Simon and the King was at an end; on the one side was contempt, on the other suspicion. In this way from an unexpected quarter, appeared the leader whom the baronial and national opposition had long lacked.

There were many greater notables in England. Nonetheless there Simon stood with five resolute sons, an alien leader, who was to become the brain and driving force of the English aristocracy. Behind him gradually ranged themselves most of the great feudal chiefs, the whole strength of London as a corporate entity, all the lower clergy, and the goodwill of the nation. A letter of a Court official, written in July 1258, has been preserved. The King, so it says, had yielded to what he felt was overwhelming pressure. A commission for reform of government was set up; it was agreed that "public offices should only be occupied by the English", and that "the emissaries of Rome and the foreign merchants and bankers should be reduced to their proper station". Grants of land to foreigners, the position of the King's Household, the custody of the fortresses, were all called in question.

"The barons," writes our civil servant, "have a great and difficult task which cannot be carried out easily or quickly. They are proceeding . . . *ărociter*. May the results be good!"

CHAPTER 17

THE MOTHER OF PARLIAMENTS

THE LATER YEARS OF HENRY III'S REIGN were momentous in their consequences for the growth of English institutions. This may perhaps be called the seed-time of our Parliamentary system, though few participants in the sowing could have foreseen the results that were eventually to be achieved. The commission for reform set about its work seriously, and in 1258 its proposals were embodied in the Provisions of Oxford, later supplemented and extended in 1259 by the Provisions of Westminster. This baronial movement represented something more than a dislike of alien counsellors. The two sets of Provisions, taken together, represent a considerable shift of interest from the standpoint of Magna Carta. The Great Charter was mainly concerned to define various points of law, whereas the Provisions of Oxford deal with the overriding question of by whose advice and through what officials royal government should be carried on. Many of the clauses of the Provisions of Westminster moreover mark a limitation of baronial rather than of royal jurisdiction. The fruits of Henry II's work were now to be seen; the nation was growing stronger, more self-conscious and self-confident. The more frequent visits of the judges and officials — all of them dependent upon local cooperation — educated the country knights in political responsibility and administration. This process, which shaped the future of English institutions, had its first effects in the thirteenth century.

The staple of the barons' demand was that the King in future should govern by a Council of Fifteen, to be elected by four persons, two from the baronial and two from the royal party. It is significant that the King's proclamation accepting the arrangement is the first public document to be

Westminster Hall, near the present House of Commons, was the scene of a meeting of Parliament in 1265. This was an assembly of barons, the upper clergy, knights of the shires and burgesses (elected representatives) of the cities and boroughs. The word "parliament" had been used earlier to denote assemblies of advisers "parleying" with the king. The 1265 Parliament was more representative, but six centuries were to pass before most people had a voice.

issued in both English and French since the time of William the Conqueror.

For a spell this Council, animated and controlled by Simon de Montfort, governed the land. They held each other in proper check, sharing among themselves the greater executive offices and entrusting the actual administration to "lesser men", as was then widely thought to be desirable. The magnates, once their own class interests were guarded, and their rights — which up to a certain point were the rights of the nation — were secure, did not wish to put the levers of power in the hands of one or two of their number. This idea however of a Cabinet of politicians, chosen from the patriciate, with highly trained functionaries of no political status operating under them, had in it a long vitality.

It is about this time that the word "Parlement" — Parliament — began to be current. In the twelfth century the word generally meant the permanent Council of officials and judges which sat at Westminster to receive petitions, redress grievances, and generally regulate the course of the law, but by the thirteenth "Parliament" establishes itself as the name of two quite different, though united, institutions.

If we translate their functions into modern terms we may say that the first of these assemblies deals with policy, the second with legislation and administration. In the reign of Henry III, and even of Edward I, it was by no means a foregone conclusion that the two assemblies would be amalgamated. Rather did it look as if the English Constitution would develop as did the French Constitution, with a king in Council as the real Government, with the magnates reduced to a mere nobility, and "Parlement" only a clearinghouse for legal business. Our history did not take this course. In the first place the magnates during the century that followed succeeded in mastering the Council and identifying their interests with it. Secondly, the English counties had a life of their own, and their representatives at Westminster were to exercise increasing influence. But without the powerful impulse of Simon de Montfort these forces might not have combined to shape a durable legislative assembly.

It is the merit of Simon de Montfort that he did not rest content with a victory by the barons over the Crown. He turned at once upon the barons themselves. If the King should be curbed, so also must they in their own spheres show respect for the general interest. Upon these issues the claims of the middle classes, who had played a great part in carrying the barons to supremacy, could not be disregarded. The "apprentice" or bachelor knights, who may be taken as voicing the wishes of the country gentry, formed a virile association of their own entitled "the Community of the Bachelors of England". Simon de Montfort became their champion. Very soon he began to rebuke great lords for abuse of their privileges. He wished to extend to the baronial estates the reforms already undertaken in the royal administration. He procured an ordinance from the Council making it plain that the great lords were under the royal authority, which was again — though this he did not stress — under the Council. Here was dictatorship in a new form. It was a dictatorship of the Commonwealth, but, as so often happens to these bold ideas, it expressed itself inevitably through a man and a leader. These developments split the baronial party from end to end; and the King felt he might put the matter to the proof.

The King, the Court party, and the immense foreign interests associated therewith had no intention of submitting indefinitely to the thraldom of the

Knights, in the thirteenth century, acquired their martial skills by training for frequent jousting tournaments.

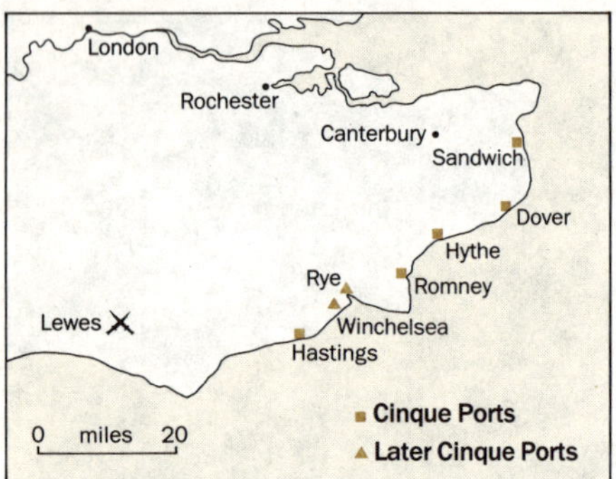

The Cinque Ports were an association of towns dedicated to the defence of the English Channel coast. The original five members were Sandwich, Dover, Hythe, Romney and Hastings. Winchelsea and Rye joined later, in the twelfth century: the sea has now retreated and they are now "stranded" inland. Winchelsea was a planned town laid out between 1282 and 1288 in thirty-nine rectangular lots.

Provisions. His son Edward was already the rising star of all who wished to see a strong monarchy, and supporters of his cause appeared among the poor and turbulent elements in London and the towns. At Easter in 1261 Henry, freed by the Pope from his oath to accept the Provisions of Oxford and Westminster, deposed the officials and ministers appointed by the barons. In July 1262 a civil war broke out, and Simon and his sons, all of whom played vigorous parts, a moiety of barons, the middle class, so far as it had emerged, and powerful allies in Wales together faced in redoubtable array the challenge of the Crown. But by September 1263 a reaction against Simon had become visible: he had succeeded only too well. Edward played upon the discontent among the barons, appealed to their feudal and selfish interest, fomented their jealousy of de Montfort, and so built up a strong royalist party. At the end of the year de Montfort had to agree to arbitration by Louis IX, the French king. The decision went against him. Loyal to his monarchical rank, the King of France defended the prerogative of the King of England and declared the Provisions to be illegal. As Louis was accepted as a saint in his own lifetime this was serious. Already however the rival parties had taken up arms. In the civil war that followed the feudal party more or less supported the King. The people, especially the towns, and the party of ecclesiastical reform, rallied to de Montfort. New controls were improvised in many towns to defeat the royalist sympathies of the municipal oligarchies. In the summer of 1264 de Montfort came south to relieve the pressure which Henry and Edward were exerting on the Cinque Ports.

The King and Prince Edward met him in Sussex with a superior power. At Lewes a fierce battle was fought. In some ways it was a forerunner of Edgehill. Edward, like Rupert four hundred years later, conquered all before him, pursued incontinently, and returned to the battlefield only to find that all was lost. Simon had, with much craft and experience of war, laid a trap to which the peculiar conditions of the ground lent themselves, whereby when his centre had been pierced, his two wings of armoured cavalry fell upon the royal main body from both flanks and crushed all resistance. Owing to a fall from his horse, he was accustomed at this time to be carried with the army in a sumptuous and brightly decorated litter, like the coach of an eighteenth-century general. In this he placed two or three hostages alone and set it among the Welsh in the centre, together with many banners and emblems suggesting his presence. Prince Edward, in his charge, captured this trophy, and killed the unlucky hostages from his own party who were found therein. But meanwhile the King and all his Court and principal supporters were taken prisoners by de Montfort, and the energetic prince returned only to share their plight.

Simon de Montfort was now in every respect master of England, and if he had proceeded by the wholesale slaughter of those who were in his grip he might have long remained so. In those days however, for all their cruelty in individual cases, nothing was pushed to the last extreme. The influences that counted with men in contest for power at the peril of their lives were by no means only brutal. Force, though potent, was not sovereign. Simon made a treaty with the captive King and the beaten party, whereby the rights of the Crown were in theory respected, though in practice the King and his son were to be subjected to strict controls. The general balance of the realm was preserved, and it is clear from Simon's action not only that he felt the power of the opposing forces, but that he aimed at their ultimate unification. He saw himself, with the King in his hands, able to use the authority of the Crown to control the baronage and create the far broader and better political system which, whether he aimed at it or not, must have automatically followed from his success. Thus he ruled the land, with the feeble King and the proud Prince Edward prisoners in his hands. This opens the third and final stage in his career.

All the barons, whatever party they had chosen, saw themselves confronted with an even greater menace than that from which they had used Simon to deliver them. The combination of Simon's genius and energy with the inherent powers of a Plantagenet monarchy and the support of the middle classes, already so truculent, was a menace to their class privileges far more intimate and searching than the misgovernment of John or the foreign encumbrances of Henry III. Throughout these struggles of lasting significance the English barony never deviated from their own self-interest. At Runnymede they had served national freedom when they thought they were defending their own privilege. They had now no doubt that Simon was its enemy. He was certainly a despot, with a king in his wallet and the forces of social revolution at his back. The barons formed a hard confederacy among themselves and with all the forces of the Court not in Simon's hands schemed night and day to overthrow him.

In January 1265 a Parliament met in London to which Simon summoned representatives both from the shires and from the towns. Its purpose was to

REQUIREMENTS OF AN AVERAGE PEASANT

This fascinating insight was originally provided by Alexander Neckam (d. 1217) and edited by U.T. Holmes in his book Daily Living in the 12th Century.

A peasant spending his life in the country, wishing to provide for poverty and old age, should have many kinds of baskets and beehives of willow wands. He should have also a fishing fork shaped like a hook that he may get himself fish. Nor should he be without a willow basket for pressing clabber, in which milk saved from the milking may be transformed into cheese with the whey well extracted. The whey should be kept for the young children to drink.

Afterwards the cheese should be kept in a cheese-box of paper or of marsh reeds, wrapped in leaves and covered against the attacks of flies, mice, stinging flies and such.

Also he should have straw and coarse grains, which are fed to hens, ducks, and geese. He must also have bolting cloth and a strainer, so that he can sift flour with them; he can clarify beer with them too. He must possess a sword, a spade, a threshing sledge, a seed bucket for sowing, a wheelbarrow, a mousetrap, and a wolf trap. He should have also stakes or pales, frequently sharpened and tested in the fire. He should have also a two-headed axe for removing thorns, thistles, brambles, spines, and bad shoots, and holly wood for tying and renewing hedges in order that, taking advantage of carelessness, no thieves may enter into the livestock enclosure and take animals. He should have a large knife also by which he may cut grafts and insert them into trees if there should be need. He may have hoes for removing tares, chicory and

This peasant, drying his boots at his cottage hearth, represents February in a late thirteenth-century calendar. A flitch of bacon hangs over the fire to cure in the smoke.

bennet grass, vetch, darnel, thistles, and avens (herb bennet). Some of these, however, are eradicated better with a curved implement than with a hoe.

He needs a herdsman and a shepherd because of the treachery of wolves, and he must be provided with a fold in order that the sheep placed there may render richer the land with the wealth of their dung. The shepherd must have a hut in which a faithful dog shall pass the night with him. Our peasant should also have a cow barn and mangers: one manger for horses, one for cattle, and if prosperity smiles a bit and Fortune is kind, he should get an ass and a stallion for a stud. He will need also sheep, goats, oxen, cows, heifers, bullocks, bull calves and mules. He must have boxes, nets, and long lines to trap hares, does, kids, stags, hinds and young mules. This is the equipment of the peasant.

give an appearance of legality to the revolutionary settlement, and this, under the guidance of de Montfort, it proceeded to do. Its importance lay however more in its character as a representative assembly than in its work. The constitutional significance which was once attached to it as the first representative Parliament in our history is somewhat discounted by modern opinion. The practical reason for summoning the strong popular element was de Montfort's desire to weight the Parliament with his own supporters: among the magnates only five earls and eighteen barons received writs of summons. Again he fell back upon the support of the country gentry and the burgesses against the hostility or indifference of the magnates. In this lay his message and his tactics.

The Parliament dutifully approved of de Montfort's actions and accepted his settlement embodied in the Provisions. King Henry III abode docilely in Simon's control, and was treated all the time with profound personal respect. Prince Edward enjoyed a liberty which could only have been founded upon his parole not to escape. However, as the baronial storm gathered and many divisions occurred in Simon's party, and all the difficulties of government brought inevitable unpopularity in their train, Edward went out hunting one day with a few friends, and forgot to return as in honour bound. He galloped away through the woodland, first after the stag and then in quest of larger game. He at once became the active organising head of the most powerful elements in English life, to all of which the destruction of Simon de Montfort and his unheard-of innovations had become the supreme object. By promising to uphold the Charters, to remedy grievances and to expel the foreigners, Edward succeeded in uniting the baronial party and in cutting away the ground from under de Montfort's feet. The Earl now appeared as no more that the leader of a personal faction, and his alliance with Llewellyn, grandson of Llewellyn the Great, by which he recognised the claims of the Welsh prince to territory and independence, compromised his reputation. Out-manoeuvred politically by Edward, he had also placed himself at a serious military disadvantage. While Edward and the Marcher barons, as they were called, held the Severn valley, de Montfort was penned in, his retreat to the east cut off, and his forces driven back into South Wales. At the beginning of August, he made an attempt to cross the river and join the forces which his son, Simon, was bringing up from the southeast. He succeeded in passing by a ford near Worcester, but his son's forces were trapped by Edward near Kenilworth and routed. Unaware of this disaster, the Earl was caught in turn at Evesham; and here on August 4 the final battle took place.

It was fought in the rain and half-darkness of a sudden storm. The Welsh broke before Edward's heavy horse, and the small group around de Montfort were left to fight desperately until sheer weight of numbers overwhelmed them. De Montfort died a hero on the field. The old King, a pathetic figure, who had been carried by the Earl in all his wanderings, was wounded by his son's followers, and only escaped death by revealing his identity with the cry, "Slay me not! I am Henry of Winchester, your King."

The great Earl was dead, but his movement lived widespread and deep throughout the nation. The ruthless, haphazard granting away of the confiscated lands after Evesham provoked the bitter opposition of the disinherited. In isolated centres at Kenilworth, Axholme, and Ely the followers of de Montfort held out, and pillaged the countryside in sullen despair. The Government was too weak to reduce them. The whole country suffered from confusion and unrest. The common folk did not conceal their partisanship for de Montfort's cause, and rebels and outlaws beset the roads and forests. A reversion to feudal independence and consequent anarchy appeared imminent. In these troubles Pope Clement IV and his Legate Ottobon enjoined moderation, and after a six-months' unsuccessful siege of Kenilworth Edward realised that this was the only policy. There was strong opposition from those who had benefited from the confiscations. The Earl of Gloucester had been bitterly disillusioned by Edward's repudiation of his promises of reform. Early in 1267 he demanded the expulsion of the aliens and the re-enactment of the Provisions. To enforce his demands he entered London with general acceptance. His action and the influence of the Legate secured pardon and good terms for the disinherited on the compromise principle of "no disinheritance, but repurchase". Late in 1267 the justices were sent out through the country to apply these terms equitably. The records testify to the widespread nature of the disturbances and to the fact that locally the rebellion had been directed against the officials, that it had been supported by the lower clergy, with not a few abbots and priors, and that a considerable number of the country gentry not bound to the baronial side by feudal ties had supported de Montfort.

In the last years of his life, with de Montfort dead and Edward away on Crusade, the feeble King enjoyed comparative peace. More than half a century before he had succeeded to the troubled inheritance of his father in the midst of civil war. At times it had seemed as if he would also die in the midst of civil war. At last however the storms were over; he could turn back to the things of beauty that interested him far more than political struggles. The new Abbey of Westminster, a masterpiece of Gothic architecture, was now dedicated; its consecration had long been the dearest object of Henry III's life. And here in the last weeks of 1272 he was buried.

CHAPTER 18

KING EDWARD I

FEW PRINCES HAD RECEIVED so thorough an education in the art of rulership as Edward I when at the age of thirty-three his father's death brought him to the Crown. He was an experienced leader and a skilful general. He had carried his father on his shoulders; he had grappled with Simon de Montfort, and, while sharing many of his views, had destroyed him. He had learnt the art of war by tasting defeat. When at any time in the closing years of King Henry III he could have taken control he had preferred a filial and constitutional patience, all the more remarkable when his own love of order and reform is contrasted with his father's indolence and the general misgovernment of the realm.

He was of elegant build and lofty stature, a head and shoulders above the height of the ordinary man. His proud brow and regular features were marred only by the drooping left eyelid which had been characteristic of his father. If he stammered he was also eloquent. There is much talk of his limbs. His sinewy, muscular arms were those of a swordsman; his long legs gave him a grip of the saddle, and the nickname of "Longshanks". He

Edward I rides a striking dappled horse into London on his return from the Crusades.

Robert Burnell, Edward I's invaluable chancellor, was rewarded by being made Bishop of Bath and Wells.

presents us with qualities which are a mixture of the administrative capacity of Henry II and the personal prowess and magnanimity of Coeur de Lion. He was animated by a passionate regard for justice and law, as he interpreted them, and for the rights of all groups within the community. Injuries and hostility roused, even to his last breath, a passionate torrent of resistance. But submission, or a generous act, on many occasions earned a swift response and laid the foundation of future friendship

Edward was in Sicily when his father died, but the greatest magnates in the realm, before the tomb had closed upon the corpse of Henry III, acclaimed him King, with the assent of all men. It was two years before he returned to England for his coronation. In his accession the hereditary and elective principles flowed into a common channel, none asking which was the stronger. His conflicts with Simon de Montfort and the baronage had taught him the need for the monarchy to stand on a national footing. If Simon de Montfort in his distresses had called in the middle class to aid him alike against Crown and arrogant nobles, the new king of his own free will would use this force in its proper place from the outset. Proportion is the keynote of his greatest years. He saw in the proud, turbulent baronage and a rapacious Church checks upon the royal authority; but he also recognised them as oppressors of the mass of his subjects; and it was by taking into account to a larger extent than had occurred before the interests of the middle class, and the needs of the people as a whole, that he succeeded in producing a broad, well-ordered foundation upon which an active monarchy could function in the general interest. Thus inspired, he sought a national kingship, an extension of his mastery throughout the British Isles, and a preponderant influence in the councils of Europe.

The first eighteen years of the reign witnessed an outburst of legislative activity for which there was to be no parallel for centuries. Nearly every year was marked by an important statute. Few of these were original, most were conservative in tone, but their cumulative effect was revolutionary. Edward relied upon his Chancellor, Robert Burnell, Bishop of Bath and Wells, a man of humble birth, who had risen through the royal Chancery and Household to his bishopric and until his death in 1292 remained the King's principal adviser. He had not been Chancellor for more than three weeks, after Edward's return to England in 1272, before a searching inquiry into the local administration was begun. Commissioners were sent throughout the land to ask what were the rights and possessions of the King, what encroachments had been made upon them, which officials were negligent or corrupt, which sheriffs "for prayer, price, or favour" concealed felonies, neglected their duties, were harsh or bribed. Similar inquests had been made before; none was so thorough or so fertile.

The First Statute of Westminster in the Parliament of 1275 dealt with the administrative abuses exposed by the commissioners. The Statute of Gloucester in 1278 ordained that the rights of feudal magnates to administer the law within their demesnes should be strictly defined. In 1279 the Statute of Mortmain forbade gifts of lands to be made to the Church, except under royal licence. In 1285 the Statute of Winchester attacked local disorder, and in the same year was issued the Second Statute of Westminster, which strengthened the system of entailed estates. The Third Statute of Westminster dealt with land held, not upon condition, but in fee simple. Land held on these terms might be freely alienated, but it was stipulated for the future that the buyer must hold his purchase not from the seller, but from the seller's lord, and by the same feudal services and customs as were attached to the land before the sale. It thus called a halt to the growth of sub-infeudation, and was greatly to the advantage of the Crown, as overlord, whose direct tenants now increased in number.

The purpose of this famous series of laws was essentially conservative. But economic pressures were wreaking great changes in the propertied life of England. Land gradually ceased to be the moral sanction upon which national society and defence were based. It became by successive steps a commodity, which could in principle, like wool or mutton, be bought or sold, and which under certain restrictions could be either transferred to new owners by gift or testament, or even settled under conditions of entail on future lives which were to be the foundation of a new aristocracy.

Of course only a comparatively small proportion of the land of England came into this active if rude market; but enough of a hitherto solid element was fluid to make a deep stir. In those days, when the greatest princes were pitifully starved in cash, there was already in England one spring of credit bubbling feebly. The Jews had noiselessly lodged themselves in the social fabric of that fierce age. From time to time they could be most helpful to high personages in urgent need of money; and to none more than to a king who did not desire to sue Parliament for it. The spectacle of land which could be acquired on rare but definite occasions by anyone with money led the English Jews into a course of shocking imprudence. Land began to pass into the hand of Israel, either by direct sale or more often by mortgage. In a couple of decades the erstwhile feudal lords were conscious that they had parted permanently for fleeting lucre with a portion of the English soil large enough to be noticed.

For some time past there had been growing a wrathful reaction. Small landowners oppressed by mortgages, spendthrift nobles who had made bad bargains, were united in their complaints. Italian moneylenders were now coming into the country, who could be just as useful in times of need to the King as the Jews. Edward saw himself able to conciliate powerful elements and escape from awkward debts, by the simple and well-trodden path of anti-Semitism. The propaganda of ritual murder and other dark tales, the commonplaces of our enlightened age, were at once invoked with general acclaim. The Jews, held up to universal hatred, were pillaged, maltreated, and finally expelled the realm. Once again the sorrowful, wandering race, stripped to the skin, must seek asylum and begin afresh. To Spain or North Africa the melancholy caravan, now so familiar, must move on. Not until four centuries had elapsed was Oliver Cromwell to open again the coasts of England to the enterprise of the Jewish race.

By the end of the thirteenth century three departments of specialised administration were already at work. One was the Exchequer, where most of the revenue was received and the accounts kept. The second was the Chancery, a general secretariat responsible for the writing and drafting of innumerable royal charters, writs, and letters. The third was the Wardrobe, with its separate secretariat, the Privy Seal, attached to the ever-moving royal Household, and combining financial and secretarial functions, which might range from financing a continental war to buying a pennyworth of pepper for the royal cook. The Chancellor, Burnell, was a typical product of the incipient Civil Service. His place, after his death, was taken by an

One of the earliest caricatures of a Jew. This drawing from a thirteenth-century manuscript in the Public Record Office, London, shows Aaron of Colchester, known as Filius Diaboli, *or Son of the Devil, who was involved in an offence against the forestry laws in 1277. On his chest is the "tablets of the law" badge which all Jews were compelled to wear prominently at the time.*

Exchequer official, Walter Langton, the Treasurer, who, like Robert Burnell, looked upon his See of Lichfield as a reward for skilful service rather than as a spiritual office.

Though most orthodox of churchmen, Edward I did not escape conflict with the Church. Anxious though he was to pay his dues to God, he had a far livelier sense than his father of what was due to Caesar, and circumstances more than once forced him to protest. The leader of the Church party was John Pecham, a Franciscan friar, Archbishop of Canterbury from 1279 to 1292. With great courage and skill Pecham defended what he regarded as the just rights of the Church and its independence against the Crown. At the provincial Council held at Reading in 1279 he issued a number of pronouncements which angered the King. One was a canon against plurality of clerical offices, which struck at the principal royal method of rewarding the growing Civil Service. Another was the order that all who produced royal writs to stop cases in ecclesiastical courts were threatened with excommunication.

Pecham bowed to Edward's anger and waited his time. In 1281, when another provincial Council was summoned to Lambeth, the King, suspecting mischief, issued writs to its members forbidding them to "hold counsel concerning matters which appertain to our crown, or touch our person, our state, or the state of our Council". Pecham was undeterred. He revived the principal legislation of the Reading Council, prefaced it with an explicit assertion of ecclesiastical liberty, and a month later wrote a remarkable letter to the King, defending his action. "By no human constitution," he wrote, "not even by an oath, can we be bound to ignore laws which rest undoubtedly upon divine authority." "A fine letter" was the marginal comment of an admiring clerk who copied it into the Archbishop's register.

Edward I's seal, dating from 1276, can now be seen in the British Museum.

Pecham's action might well have precipitated a crisis comparable to the quarrel between Becket and Henry II, but Edward seems to have quietly ignored the challenge. Moderation was observed, and in 1286 by a famous writ Edward wisely ordered his itinerant justices to act circumspectly in matters of ecclesiastical jurisdiction, and listed the kinds of case which should be left to Church courts. The dispute thus postponed was to outlive both Archbishop and King.

At the beginning of the reign relations between England and France were governed by the Treaty of Paris, which the baronial party had concluded in 1259. For more than thirty years peace reigned between the two countries, though often with an undercurrent of hostility. The disputes about the execution of the terms of the Treaty and the quarrel between English, Gascon, and French sailors in the Channel, culminating in a great sea-fight off Saint-Matthieu in 1293, need never have led to a renewal of war, had not the presence of the English in the south of France been a standing challenge to the pride of the French. Even when Philip the Fair, the French king, began to seek opportunities of provocation Edward was long-suffering and patient in his attempts to reach a compromise. Philip asked for the token surrender of the principal Gascon fortresses, as a recognition of his legal powers as overlord. Edward complied. But once Philip was in possession he refused to give them up again. Edward now realised that he must either fight or lose his French possessions.

By 1294 the great King had changed much from his early buoyant manhood. After the long, stormy years of sustaining his father he had reigned himself for nearly quarter of a century. Meanwhile his world had changed about him; he had lost his beloved wife Eleanor of Castile, his mother, Eleanor of Provence, and his two eldest infant sons. Burnell was now dead. Wales and Scotland presented grave problems; opposition was beginning to make itself heard and felt. Alone, perplexed, and ageing, the King had to face an endless succession of difficulties.

In June 1294 he explained the grounds of the quarrel with the French to what is already called "a Parliament" of magnates in London. His decision to go to war was accepted with approval — as has often been the case in more regularly constituted assemblies.

The war itself had no important features. There were campaigns in Gascony, a good deal of coastal raiding in the Channel, and a prolonged seige by the English of Bordeaux. Any enthusiasm which had been expressed at the outset wore off speedily under the inevitable increases of taxation. All wool and leather, the staple items of the English export trade, were impounded, and could only be redeemed by the payment of a customs duty of forty shillings on the sack. In September the clergy, to their great indignation, were ordered to contribute one-half of their revenues. The Dean of St Paul's, who attempted to voice their protests in the King's own terrifying presence, fell down in a fit and died. In November Parliament granted a heavy tax upon all movable property. As the collection proceeded a bitter and sullen discontent spread among all classes.

After October 1297 the French war degenerated into a series of truces which lasted until 1303. Such conditions involved expense little less than actual fighting. These were years of severe strain, both at home and abroad, and especially with Scotland. Although the King did not hesitate to recall recurrent Parliaments to Westminster and explained the whole situation to them, he did not obtain the support which he needed. Parliament was reluctant to grant the new taxes demanded of it.

The position of the clergy was made more difficult by the publication in 1296 of the Papal Bull *Clericis Laicos,* which forbade the payment of extraordinary taxation without Papal authority. At the autumn Parliament at Bury St Edmunds the clergy, under the leadership of Robert Winchelsea, the new Primate, decided that they were unable to make any contribution. Edward in his anger outlawed them and declared their lay fiefs forfeit. The Archbishop retaliated by threatening with excommunication any who should disobey the Papal Bull. For a time passion ran high, but eventually a calmer mood prevailed. By the following summer the quarrel was allayed, and the Pope had withdrawn his claims.

Edward was the more prepared to come to terms with the Church because opposition had already broken out in another quarter. He proposed to the barons that a number of them should serve in Gascony while he conducted a campaign in Flanders. This was ill-received. Humphrey de Bohun, Earl of Hereford and Constable of England, together with the Marshal, Roger Bigod, Earl of Norfolk, declared that their hereditary offices could only be exercised in the King's company. Such excuses deceived nobody. Both the Earls had personal grudges against the King, and — more importantly — they voiced the resentment felt by a large number of the barons who for the past twenty years had steadily seen the authority of the Crown increased to their own detriment. The time was ripe for a revival of the baronial opposition which a generation before had defied Edward's father.

Edward I dominates a thirteenth-century Parliament from his canopied throne, flanked by King Alexander III of Scotland and Prince Llewellyn of Wales. The Archbishop of Canterbury sits on the King's right: behind him stands the Master of the Rolls. The rank, function and importance of the members can be deduced from their position in the formal assembly, their hats, and the relative size of the figures. The illustration dates from 1523 and comes from the Wriothesley manuscript, which can be found in Windsor Castle.

Edward I travelled ceaselessly around his territories. The boats in the picture are from a contemporary illustration depicting the King's return from Gascony.

For the moment the King ignored the challenge. He pressed forward with his preparations for war, appointed deputies in place of Hereford and Norfolk, and in August sailed for Flanders. The opposition saw in his absence their long-awaited opportunity. They demanded the confirmation of those two instruments, Magna Carta and its extension, the Charter of the Forest, which were the final version of the terms extorted from John, together with six additional articles. By these no aid was to be imposed in future except with the consent of the community of the realm; corn, wool, and the like must not be impounded against the will of their owners; the clergy and laity of the realm must recover their ancient liberties; the two Earls and their supporters were not to be penalised for their refusal to serve in Gascony; the prelates were to read the Charter aloud in their cathedrals, and to excommunicate all who neglected it. In the autumn the two Earls, backed by armed forces, appeared in London and demanded the acceptance of these proposals. The Regency, unable to resist, submitted. The articles were confirmed, and in November at Ghent the King ratified them, reserving however certain financial rights of the Crown.

These were large and surprising concessions. Both King and Opposition attached great importance to them, and the King was suspected, perhaps with justice, of trying to withdraw from the promises he had given. Several times the baronial party publicly drew attention to these promises before Parliament, and finally in February 1301 the King was driven by the threats and arguments of a Parliament at Lincoln to grant a new confirmation of both Charters and certain further articles in solemn form.

By this crisis and its manner of resolution two principles had been established from which important consequences flowed. One was that the King had no right to despatch the feudal host wherever he might choose. This limitation sounded the death knell of the feudal levy, and inexorably led in the following century to the rise of indentured armies serving for pay. The second point of principle now recognised was that the King could not plead "urgent necessity" as a reason for imposing taxation without consent. A precedent had been set up, and a long stride had been taken towards the dependence of the Crown upon Parliamentary grants.

Edward to a greater extent than any of his predecessors had shown himself prepared to govern in the national interest and with some regard for constitutional form. It was thus ironical, and to the King exasperating, that he found the principles he had emphasised applied against himself. The baronial party had not resorted to war; they had acted through the constitutional machinery the King himself had taken so much pains to create. Thereby they had shifted their ground: they spoke no longer as the representatives of the feudal aristocracy, but as the leaders of a national Opposition. So the Crown was once again committed solemnly and publicly to the principles of Magna Carta, and the concession was made all the more valuable because remedies for actual recent abuses of the royal prerogative powers had been added to the original Charters.

In their fatal preoccupation with their possessions in France the English kings had neglected the work of extending their rule within the island of Great Britain. There had been fitful interference both in Wales and Scotland, but the task of keeping the frontiers safe had fallen mainly upon the shoulders of the local Marcher lords. Edward I was the first of the English kings to put the whole weight of the Crown's resources behind the effort of national expansion in the west and north, and to him is due the conquest of the independent areas of Wales and the securing of the western frontier. Edward, as his father's lieutenant, had experience of the Welsh. At the same time he had seen, with disapproving eye, the truculence of the barons of the Welsh Marches, who exploited their military privileges against the interests alike of the Welsh and English people. He resolved, in the name of justice and progress, to subdue the unconquered refuge of petty princes and wild mountaineers in which barbaric freedom had dwelt since remote antiquity, and at the same time to curb the privileges of the Marcher lords.

Edward I, utilising all the local resources which the barons of the Welsh Marches had developed in the chronic strike of many generations, conquered Wales in several years of persistent warfare, coldly and carefully devised, by land and sea. The forces he employed were mainly Welsh levies in his pay, reinforced by regular troops from Gascony and by one of the last appearances of the feudal levy; but above all it was by the terror of winter campaigns that he broke the power of the valiant Ancient Britons. By Edward's Statute of Wales the independent principality came to an end. The King's son Edward, born in Caernarvon, was proclaimed the first English Prince of Wales.

Edward I bestows the title of Prince of Wales on his son Edward in 1301. The Prince was born at Caernarvon, and Edward I used this fact to further his dynastic ambitions and secure the loyalty of the defeated Welsh. Edward II's neglected childhood is sometimes seen as a cause of his later misfortunes.

The Welsh wars of Edward reveal to us the process by which the military system of England was transformed from the age-long Saxon and feudal basis of occasional service to that of paid regular troops. For several reigns the principle of scutage had been agreeable alike to barons who did not wish to serve and to sovereigns who preferred a money payment with which to hire full-time soldiers. In the Welsh wars both systems are seen simultaneously at work, but the old is fading. Instead of liege service governments now required mercenaries, and for this purpose money was the solvent.

At the same time a counter-revolution in the balance of warfare was afoot. The mailed cavalry which from the fifth century had eclipsed the ordered tanks of the Legion were wearing out their long day. A new type of infantry raised from the common people began to prove its dominating quality. This infantry operated, not by club or sword or spear, or even by hand-flung missiles, but by an archery which, after a long development, concealed from Europe, was very soon to make an astonishing entrance upon the military scene and gain a dramatic ascendancy upon the battlefields of the Continent.

The investiture of the Prince of Wales at Caernarvon Castle in 1969. The castle was built to secure the position of the first Prince of Wales, with massive stone walls linking strong towers. Edward I copied this design from the Crusaders' castles he had seen in the Holy Land.

MEN AT ARMS

BETWEEN THE NORMAN CONQUEST in 1066 and the Black Death in 1348 there was only one period of domestic peace in England which lasted for more than thirty years. There was also much fighting across the Channel in France, culminating in the Hundred Years' War, which was in fact a series of wars beginning in the year 1337.

As different methods of fighting developed, castles changed. The first castles were of "motte and bailey" type, based on a mound and a ditch. The king's permission was needed to build a castle, but in times of strife some were built illegally. Later, stone towers, keeps, parapets and massive retaining (curtain) walls were more elaborate features in what became impressive buildings. Attackers had to breach the walls or lay siege to the defenders. Another less dramatic aspect of war was the application of economic pressure by ravaging lands and burning villages.

Military service was an essential element in the social system of the Middle Ages. Lords had to serve the king, knights their lords. Associated with the service, codes of chivalry laid down standards of courage and honour. The knight in armour on his horse is the image of chivalry which has passed down to posterity. Tournaments were used as a means of teaching knights the arts of warfare.

In the reign of Edward I (1272–1307) archers began to be used very successfully, and by 1327 English knights were instructed how to fight on foot. These tactics proved to be most effective in the Hundred Years' War, when unmounted men at arms and longbowmen inflicted heavy casualties on cumbersome opponents on horseback.

Although guns were known by 1327, they were small and awkward. It was not until the last decades of the fourteenth century that large siege guns were employed. As gunpowder came to be used, new kinds of military skills were required. The arts of war were never the same again.

SIEGES OF TOWNS AND CASTLES, as much to gain plunder as tactical victories, occupied most of the time spent in waging medieval wars. Walls had to be breached, moats filled in and gates broken into by battering-rams. Ingenious "siege engines" like the mangonel, a giant catapult, and the ballista, which had a sort of spoon for hurling boulders, were constructed. Huge wooden towers on wheels brought soldiers close to the castle walls in relative safety. Ladders on wheels were used too, sometimes with covers made of hides to protect the soldiers from the arrows, boiling oil or projectiles rained down on them. Sometimes attackers were able to enter castles through unguarded lavatory shafts. Often the besiegers waited for hunger to force the inmates to surrender, or undermined the walls by digging tunnels beneath them. They themselves could have difficulty in finding food and were likely to be surprised by an enemy army arriving to free the besieged. The picture above illustrates a siege in progress with opposing armies of archers. The most important English weapon was the longbow. It had an effective killing range of two hundred and fifty yards. Archery practice was compulsory for all able-bodied men in the Middle Ages, and the victories of Crécy, Poitiers and Agincourt were undoubtedly due to the English longbowmen.

PROTECTIVE ARMOUR and close formation in battle reduced the hazards of the infantry. But the weight of armour caused difficulty of movement, and if warriors broke ranks because the enemy feigned flight, they could easily be picked off by the cavalry. The picture (left) is taken from the Temple Pyx which is to be found in the Burrell Collection, Glasgow.

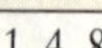

CHAUCER'S KNIGHT AND SQUIRE, seen above in the portraits from the Ellesmere Manuscript, represent the two faces of chivalry: military service, and courtly love. The biography of the "verray parfit, gentil Knyght" in Chaucer's The General Prologue to The Canterbury Tales *is a description of his character and of his achievements in war. The Squire's gives details of his handsome appearance and accomplishments, while mentioning that he became a Crusader in order to impress his lady.*

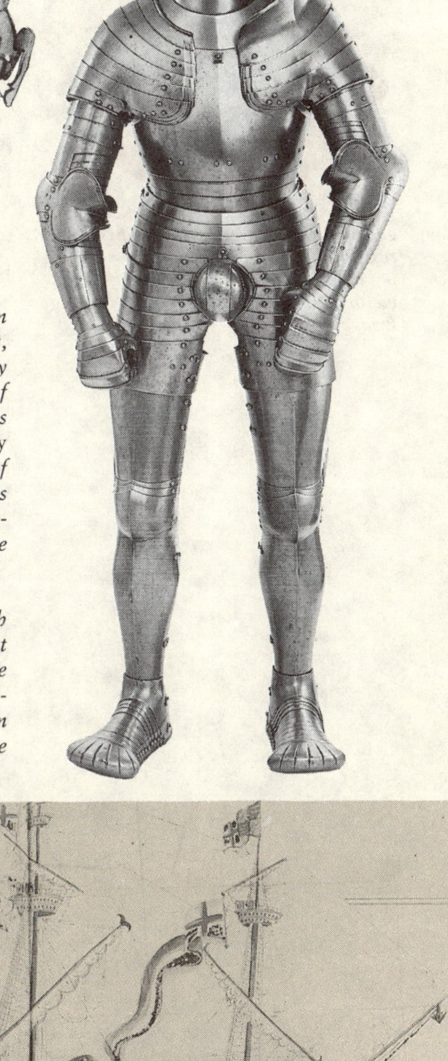

HENRY VIII'S ARMOUR, (right) which was made in his own workshops at Greenwich, can now be seen in the Tower of London. With the introduction of the deadly longbow, chain mail was superseded by armour made of overlapping plates of metal.

STRANGE MILITARY TECHNOLOGY like this horse-drawn battle chariot designed for speedy attack and retreat, could be more of a liability than an asset. The horses' armour marks them as vulnerable to attack.

GUNPOWDER WAS USED IN FIFTEENTH-CENTURY EUROPE, and a century earlier by the Chinese. Cannons had a limited use in the Middle Ages and their full potential was not realised until later. Gunpowder, however, was one of the two most important medieval inventions. The other was printing.

WARS AT SEA were common before Tudor times, but the only surviving battleship is the Mary Rose, *Henry VIII's flagship, which sank in Portsmouth harbour in July 1545. It has now been excavated and can be seen in Portsmouth. The ship was named after Henry's favourite sister, who was Queen of France briefly before being widowed; she later married the Duke of Suffolk. It is thought the ship capsized because the open gun ports were too close to the waterline; water surged in as the fully loaded ship went about.*

William Wallace, former outlaw and guerrilla fighter, mounted the first successful attacks on the English, thus paving the way for Robert the Bruce's great victory over the English at Stirling Bridge in 1297.

Here was a prize taken by the conquerors from their victims. In South Wales the practice of drawing the longbow had already attained an astonishing efficiency, of which one of the Marcher lords has left a record. One of his knights had been hit by an arrow which pierced not only the skirts of his mailed shirt, but his mailed breeches, his thigh, and the wood of his saddle, and finally struck deep into his horse's flank. This was a new fact in the history of war, which is also a part of the history of civilisation, deserving to be mentioned with the triumph of bronze over flint, or iron over bronze. For the first time infantry possessed a weapon which could penetrate the armour of the clanking age, and which in range and rate of fire was superior to any method ever used before, or ever used again until the coming of the rifle.

The great quarrel of Edward's reign was with Scotland. For long years the two kingdoms had dwelt in amity. In 1286 Alexander III of Scotland left as his heir his three-year-old granddaughter Margaret, known as the Maid of Norway. Now the bright project arose that the Maid of Norway should at the same moment succeed to the Scottish throne and marry Edward, the King's son. We can measure the sagacity of the age by the acceptance of this plan, by practically all the ruling forces in England and Scotland. It was a dream, and it passed as a dream. The Maid of Norway embarked in 1290 upon stormy seas, only to die before reaching land, and Scotland was bequeathed the problem of a disputed succession. From a dozen claimants, two men stood clearly forth, John Balliol and Robert Bruce.

Since the days of Henry II the English monarch had intermittently claimed an overlordship of Scotland, based on the still earlier acknowledgment of Saxon overlordship by Scottish kings. King Edward, whose legal abilities were renowned, now induced the Scots to accept him as arbitrator; and he, pursuing all the time a path of strict legality, consented to the task only upon the prior condition of the reaffirmation of his overlordship. The English King discharged his function as arbitrator with extreme propriety, and pronounced in 1292 in favour of John Balliol. In their distress the Scottish baronage accepted King Edward's award, but they also furnished the new King John with an authoritative council of twelve great lords to look after the rights of Scotland. Thus King Edward saw with disgust that all his fair-seeming success left him still confronted with the integrity of Scottish nationhood, with an independent and not a subject government.

At this very moment the same argument of overlordship was being pressed upon him by the formidable French King, Philip IV. Here Edward was the vassal, proudly defending feudal interests, and the French suzerain had the lawful advantage. Moreover, if England was stronger than Scotland, France was in armed power superior to England. This double conflict imposed a strain upon the financial and military resources of the English monarchy which it could by no means meet. The rest of Edward's reign was spent in a twofold struggle north and south, for the sake of which he had to tax his subjects beyond all endurance. He journeyed energetically to and fro between Flanders and the Scottish Lowlands. He racked the land for money. Nothing else mattered; and the embryonic Parliamentary system profited vastly by the repeated concessions he made in the hope of carrying opinion with him. He confirmed the bulk of the reforms wrung from John. With some exceptions among the great lords, the nation was with him in both his external efforts, but though time and again it complied with his demands it was not reconciled to the burden. Thus we see the wise law-reformer, forced to drive his people beyond their strength, and in this process to rouse oppositions which darkened his life and clouded his fame.

To resist Edward the Scots allied themselves with the French. Since Edward was at war with France he regarded this as an act of hostility. He summoned Balliol to meet him at Berwick. The Scottish nobles refused to allow their King to go, and from this moment war began. Edward struck with ruthless severity. He advanced on Berwick. The city, then the great emporium of northern trade, was unprepared, after a hundred years of peace, to resist attack. Palisades were hurriedly raised, the citizens seized such weapons as were at hand. The English army, with hardly any loss, trampled down these improvised defences, and Berwick was delivered to a sack and slaughter which shocked even those barbaric times. Berwick sank in a few hours from one of the active centres of European commerce to the minor seaport which exists today.

The gravestone of Gilbert Grenlau, who died in 1411, shows the characteristic Scottish two-edged sword known as the claymore. The tomb is in Kinkell, Aberdeenshire.

This act of terror quelled the resistance of the ruling classes in Scotland. Perth, Stirling, Edinburgh, yielded themselves to the King's march. Balliol surrendered his throne and Scotland was brought under English administration. But, as in Wales, the conqueror introduced not only an alien rule, but law and order, all of which were equally unpopular. The governing classes of Scotland had conspicuously failed, and Edward might flatter himself that all was over. It was only beginning. It has often been said that Joan of Arc first raised the standard of nationalism in the Western world. But over a century before she appeared an outlaw knight, William Wallace, arising from the recesses of southwest Scotland which had been his refuge, embodied, commanded, and led to victory the Scottish nation. Out of an unorganised mass of valiant fighting men he forged, in spite of cruel poverty and primitive administration, a stubborn, indomitable army, ready to fight at any odds and mock defeat.

Warenne, Earl of Surrey, was Edward's commander in the north. When the depredations of the Scottish rebels had become intolerable he advanced at the head of strong forces upon Stirling. At Stirling Bridge, near the Abbey of Cambuskenneth, in September 1297, he found himself in the presence of Wallace's army. Many Scotsmen were in the English service. One of these warned him of the dangers of trying to deploy beyond the long, narrow bridge and causeway which spanned the river. This knight pleaded calculations worthy of a modern staff officer. It would take eleven hours to move the army across the bridge, and what would happen, he asked, if the vanguard were attacked before the passage was completed? He spoke of a ford higher up, by which at least a flanking force could cross. But Earl Warenne would have none of these things. Wallace watched with measuring eye the accumulation of the English troops across the bridge, and at the right moment hurled his full force upon them, seized the bridgehead, and slaughtered the vanguard of five thousand men. Warenne evacuated the greater part of Scotland. His fortress garrisons were reduced one after the other. The English could barely hold the line of the Tweed.

It was beyond the compass of King Edward's resources to wage war with France and face the hideous struggle with Scotland at the same time. He sought at all costs to concentrate on the peril nearest home. He entered upon a long series of negotiations with the French king which were covered by truces repeatedly renewed, and reached a final Treaty of Paris in 1303. Though the formal peace was delayed for some years, it was in fact sealed by

Pictish and Scottish kings were crowned on the Stone of Scone, or Stone of Destiny, at the village of Old Scone in Scotland. In 1297 the stone was stolen by the English and Edward I had it incorporated inside the Coronation Chair, now to be seen in Westminster Abbey, London.

the arrangement of a marriage between Edward and Philip's sister, the young Princess Margaret, and also by the betrothal of Edward's son and heir, Edward of Caernarvon, to Philip's daughter Isabella. By these diplomatic arrangements Edward for two years was able to concentrate his strength against Scotland.

Edward, with the whole feudal levy of England, advanced against the Scots. The Battle of Falkirk in 1298, which he conducted in person, bears a sharp contrast to Stirling Bridge. Wallace, now at the head of stronger powers, accepted battle in a withdrawn defensive position. He had few cavalry and few archers; but his confidence lay in his spearmen. The armoured cavalry of the English vanguard were hurled back with severe losses from the spearpoints. But Edward, bringing up his Welsh archers in the intervals between horsemen of the second line, concentrated a hail of arrows upon particular points in the Scottish ranks, so that there were more dead and wounded than living men in these places. Into the gaps and over the carcasses, the knighthood of England forced their way. Once the Scottish order was broken the spearmen were quickly massacred. The slaughter ended only in the depths of the woods, and Wallace and the Scottish army were once again fugitives, hunted as rebels, starving, suffering the worst of human privations, but still in arms.

The Scots were unconquerable foes. It was not until 1305 that Wallace was captured, tried with full ceremonial in Westminster Hall, and hanged, drawn, and quartered at Tyburn. But the Scottish war was one in which, as a chronicler said, "every winter undid every summer's work". Wallace was to pass the torch to Robert Bruce.

In the closing years of Edward's life he appears as a lonely and wrathful old man. A new generation had grown up around him with whom he had slight acquaintance and less sympathy. Queen Margaret was young enough to be his daughter, and sided often with her stepchildren against their father. Few dared to oppose the King, but he had little love or respect in his family circle.

With Robert Bruce, grandson of the claimant of 1290, who had won his way partly by right of birth, but also by hard measures, the war in Scotland flared again. King Edward was old, but his willpower was unbroken. When the news came south to Winchester, where he held his Court, that Bruce had been crowned at Scone his fury was terrible to behold. He launched a campaign in the summer of 1306 in which Bruce was defeated and driven to take refuge on Rathlin Island, off the coast of Antrim. Here, according to the tale, Bruce was heartened by the persistent efforts of the most celebrated spider known to history. Next spring he returned to Scotland. Edward was now too ill to march or ride. Like the Emperor Severus a thousand years before, he was carried in a litter against this stern people, and like him he died upon the road. His last thoughts were on Scotland and on the Holy Land. He conjured his son to carry his bones in the van of the army which should finally bring Scotland to obedience, and to send his heart to Palestine with a band of a hundred knights to help recover the Sacred City. Neither wish was fulfilled by his futile and unworthy heir.

Edward I was the last great figure in the formative period of English law. His statutes, which settled questions of public order, assigned limits to the powers of the seigneurial courts, and restrained the sprawling and luxurious growth of judge-made law, laid down principles that remained fundamental to the law of property until the mid-nineteenth century. By these great enactments necessary bounds were fixed to the freedom of the Common Law which, without conflicting with its basic principles or breaking with the past, imparted to it its final form.

In the constitutional sphere the work of Edward I was not less durable. He had made Parliament — that is to say, certain selected magnates and representatives of the shires and boroughs — the associate of the Crown, in place of the old Court of Tenants in Chief. By the end of his reign it was fairly settled in the customs and traditions of England that "sovereignty", to use a term which Edward would hardly have understood, would henceforward reside, not in the Crown only, nor in the Crown and Council of the Barons, but in the Crown in Parliament.

Dark constitutional problems loomed in the future. The boundary between the powers of Parliament and those of the Crown was as yet very vaguely drawn. Parliament was still in its infancy.

Nevertheless the foundations of a strong national monarchy for a United Kingdom and of a Parliamentary Constitution had been laid. Long years of civil war, and despotism in reaction from anarchy, marred and delayed the development of its institutions. But when the traveller gazes upon the plain marble tomb at Westminster on which is inscribed, "Here lies Edward I, the Hammer of the Scots. Keep troth", he stands before the resting-place of a masterbuilder of British life, character, and fame.

Cambuskenneth Abbey was used as a supply depot by Robert the Bruce at Bannockburn.

CHAPTER 19

BANNOCKBURN

EDWARD II'S REIGN MAY FAIRLY BE REGARDED as a melancholy appendix to his father's and the prelude to his son's. A strong, capable King had with difficulty upborne the load. He was succeeded by a perverted weakling who despite an amiable interest in thatching and ditching and other serviceable arts, carried his friendship for his advisers beyond dignity and decency. Yet this was a reign in which forces of English nationhood, already alive and conscious under the old King, resumed their march at a quicker and more vehement step. In default of a dominating Parliamentary institution, the King's Council, as we have seen, seemed to be the centre from which the business of government could be controlled. On the death of Edward I the barons succeeded in gaining control of this mixed body of powerful magnates and competent Household officials. They set up a committee called "the Lords Ordainers", who represented the baronial and ecclesiastical interests of the State.

Portrait of the unfortunate King Edward II. He is said to have horrified his subjects by taking more interest in the rural crafts of thatching and ditching than he took in government.

Scotland and France remained the external problems confronting these new masters of government, but their first anger was directed upon the favourite of the King: Piers Gaveston, a young, handsome Gascon. There was a temper which would submit to the rule of a King, but would not tolerate the pretensions of his personal cronies. Edward and his favourite tried to stave off opposition by harrying the Scots. They failed, and in 1311 Gaveston was exiled to Flanders. Thence he was so imprudent as to return, in defiance of the Lords Ordainers. Besieged in the castle of Scarborough, Gaveston made terms with his foes. His life was to be spared; and on this they took him under guard. But other nobles, led by the Earl of Warwick, who had not been present at the agreement of Scarborough, overpowered the escort, seized the favourite and hewed off his head.

In spite of this, royal power remained formidable. Edward was still in control of government, although he was under the Ordainers' restraint. To wipe out his setbacks at home he resolved upon the conquest of the northern kingdom. A general levy of the whole power of England was set on foot to beat the Scots. A great army crossed the Tweed in the summer of 1314. Twenty-five thousand men, hard to gather, harder still to feed, with at least three thousand armoured knights and men-at-arms, under the nominal but nonetheless baffling command of Edward II, moved against the Scottish host. The new champion of Scotland, Robert the Bruce, now faced the vengeance of England. The Scottish army, of perhaps ten thousand men, was composed, as at Falkirk, mainly of hard, unyielding spearmen. But Bruce had pondered deeply upon the impotence of pikemen, however faithful, if exposed to the alternations of an arrow shower and an armoured charge. He therefore, with a foresight and skill which proves his military quality, took three precautions. First, he chose a position where his flanks were secured by impenetrable woods; secondly, he dug upon his front a large number of small round holes or "pottes", and covered them with branches and turfs as a trap for charging cavalry; thirdly, he kept in his own hand his small but highly trained force of mounted knights to break up any attempt at planting archers upon his flank. These dispositions made, he awaited the English onslaught.

The English army was so large that it took three days to close up from rear to front, and the ground available for deployment was little more than two thousand yards. On the morning of June 24 the English advanced, and a dense wave of steel-clad horsemen splashed and scrambled through the Bannock Burn, and charged uphill. Though much disordered by the "pottes", they came to deadly grip with the Scottish spearmen. "And when the two hosts so came together and the great steeds of the knights dashed into the Scottish pikes as into a thick wood there rose a great and horrible crash from rending lances and dying horse, and there they stood locked together for a space." As neither side would withdraw the struggle was prolonged and covered the whole front. The strong corps of archers could not intervene. When they shot their arrows into the air, they hit more of their

The fortress overlooking Stirling symbolised Scottish military resistance to England. Robert the Bruce won it and kept it for Scotland after the Battle of Bannockburn. Built originally in the thirteenth and fourteenth centuries, its present structure dates from the fifteenth.

The marriage of Edward II to the child, Isabella, daughter of the French King Philip IV, in 1308. She was twelve, he was twenty-four. She bore him four children but her hatred of his favourites, the Despensers, drove her back to France where she took Roger Mortimer as her lover. The pair invaded Britain, defeated the King and plotted his deposition, imprisonment and death.

own men than of the Scottish infantry. At length a detachment of archers was brought round the Scottish left flank. But Bruce's small cavalry force charged them with the utmost promptitude, and drove them back into the great mass waiting to engage, and now already showing signs of disorder. Confusion steadily increased. At length the appearance on the hills to the English right of the camp-followers of Bruce's army, waving flags and raising loud cries, was sufficient to induce a general retreat, which the King himself, with his numerous personal guards, was not slow to head. The retreat speedily became a rout. The Scottish spearmen hurled themselves forward down the slope, inflicting immense carnage upon the English even before they could recross the Bannock Burn. No more grievous slaughter of English chivalry ever took place in a single day.

In the long story of a nation we often see that capable rulers by their very virtues sow the seeds of future evil, and weak or degenerate princes open the pathway of progress. At this time the unending struggle for power had entered upon new ground. We have traced the ever-growing influence, and at times authority, of the permanent officials of the royal Household. This became more noticeable, and therefore more obnoxious, when the sovereign was not capable of overtopping them in policy or personality. The feudal baronage had striven successfully against kings. They now saw in the royal officials agents who stood in their way, yet at the same time were obviously indispensable to the widening aspects of national life. They could no more contemplate the abolition of these officials than their ancestors the destruction of the monarchy. The whole tendency of their movement was therefore in this generation to acquire control of an invaluable machine.

The Lords Ordainers, as we have seen, had control of the King's Council; but they soon found that many of the essentials of power still eluded their grasp. The high control of government had withdrawn itself from the Council into an inner citadel described as "the King's Wardrobe". There was the King, in his Wardrobe, with his favourites and indispensable functionaries, settling a variety of matters from the purchase of the royal hose to

A victory of Robert the Bruce over an English knight, Henry de Bohun, immediately before the Battle of Bannockburn. De Bohun attempted to attack Bruce who side-stepped at the last moment so that the English knight missed his mark and met his death instead. The encounter is described in lines which every Scottish schoolchild knows: "Bruce and de Bohun fightin' for the croon/ Bruce took his battle-axe and knocked de Bohun doon."

the waging of a continental war. Outside this select, secluded circle the rugged, arrogant, virile barons prowled morosely.

In this equipoise Parliament became of serious importance to the contending interests. Here at least was the only place where the case for or against the conduct of the central executive could be tried before something that resembled, however imperfectly, the nation. Thus we see in this ill-starred reign both sides operating in and through Parliament, and in this process enhancing its power. Parliament was called together no fewer than twenty-five times under King Edward II. It had no share in the initiation or control of policy. It was of course distracted by royal and baronial intrigue. Many of its knights and burgesses were but the creatures of one faction or the other. Nevertheless it could be made to throw its weight in a decisive manner from time to time. This therefore was a period highly favourable to the growth of forces in the realm which were to become inherently different in character from either the Crown or the barons.

Edward, for his part, began to build up a royalist party, at the head of which were the Despensers, father and son, both named Hugh. These belonged to the nobility, and their power lay on the Welsh border. By the favour of the King, they rose precariously amid the jealousies of the English baronage to the main direction of affairs. Against both of them the hatred grew, because of their self-seeking and the King's infatuation with the younger man. They were especially unpopular among the Marcher lords, who were disturbed by their restless ambitions in South Wales. In 1321 the Marcher lords and a party under Thomas of Lancaster, nephew of Edward I, joined hands with intent to procure the exile of the Despensers. The King for once showed energy and resolution. By speed of movement he defeated first the Marcher lords and then in the next year the northern barons at Boroughbridge in Yorkshire.

The Despensers and their King now seemed to have attained a height of power. But a tragedy with every feature of classical ruthlessness was to follow. One of the chief Marcher lords, Roger Mortimer, though captured by the King, contrived to escape to France. In 1324 Charles IV of France took advantage of a dispute in Gascony to seize the duchy, except for a coastal strip. Edward's wife Isabella, "the she-wolf of France", who was disgusted by his passion for Hugh Despenser, suggested that she should go over to France to negotiate with her brother Charles about the restoration of Gascony. There she became the lover and confederate of the exiled Mortimer. She now hit on the stroke of having her son, Prince Edward, sent over from England to do homage for Gascony. As soon as the fourteen-year-old prince, who as heir to the throne could be used to legitimise opposition to King Edward, was in her possession she and Mortimer staged an invasion of England at the head of a large band of exiles.

So unpopular and precarious was Edward's Government that Isabella's triumph was swift and complete, and she and Mortimer were emboldened to depose him. The end was a holocaust. In the furious rage which in those days led all who swayed the Government of England to a bloody fate the Despensers were seized and hanged at Bristol. For the King a more terrible death was reserved. He was imprisoned in Berkeley Castle, and by hideous methods which left no mark upon him was slaughtered. His screams as his bowels were burnt out by red-hot irons passed into his body were heard outside the prison walls, and awoke grim echoes which were long unstilled.

The finely sculpted effigy of King Edward II in Gloucester Cathedral may perhaps be interpreted as a sign of his wife's remorse for his murder. Isabella actually joined an order of nuns called the Poor Clares at the end of her life.

CHAPTER 20

SCOTLAND AND IRELAND

THE FAILURES OF THE REIGN OF EDWARD II had permanent effects on the unity of the British Isles. Bannockburn ended the possibility of uniting the English and Scottish Crowns by force. Across the Irish Sea the dream of a consolidated Anglo-Norman Ireland also proved vain. In Scotland, from Edward I's onslaught on Berwick, in 1296, the armed struggle had raged for twenty-seven years. It was not until 1323 that Robert the Bruce at last obliged the English to come to terms. Even then Bruce was not formally recognised as King of the Scots. This title, and full independence for his country, he gained by the Treaty of Northampton, sealed in 1328 after Edward's murder.

Portrait of the Scottish hero and king, Robert the Bruce, painted in 1633 by George Jamesone. It was commissioned in the year of Charles I's Scottish coronation and although not an authentic likeness, it represents an idealised view of the patriot and hangs in the National Portrait Gallery of Scotland.

A year later the saviour of Scotland was dead. While the Bruce had lived, his great prestige and the loyalty of his lieutenants served as a substitute for the institutions that united England. His death left the throne to his son, David II, a child of five. He was to reign for forty-two years, but no less than eighteen of them were spent outside his kingdom. For a long spell he was a refugee in France and loyalty to France led him to invade England. In 1346, the year of Crécy, he was defeated and captured at Neville's Cross, in County Durham. Eleven years of imprisonment followed before he was ransomed for a sum that sorely taxed Scotland.

David II was succeeded by his nephew Robert the High Steward, first king of a line destined to melancholy fame. For many generations the Stuarts, as they came euphoniously to be called, had held the hereditary office from which they took their name. Their claim to the throne was legitimate, but they failed to command the undivided loyalty of the Scots. The first two Stuarts, Robert II and Robert III, were both elderly men of no marked strength of character. The affairs of the kingdom rested largely in the hands of the magnates, whether assembled in the King's Council or dispersed about their estates. For the rest of the fourteenth century, and throughout most of the fifteenth, Scotland was therefore too deeply divided to threaten England. A united England, free from French wars, might have taken advantage of the situation, but by the mid-fifteenth century England was herself tormented by the Wars of the Roses.

Union of the Crowns was the obvious and natural solution. But the reinvigorated pride of Scotland offered an insurmountable obstacle. Hatred of the English was the mark of a good Scot. Though discontented nobles might accept English help and English pay, the common people were resolute in their refusal to bow to English rule in any form, while the memory of Bannockburn kept a series of notable defeats at the hand of the English from breeding despair or thought of surrender.

Destiny proved adverse to the house of Stuart. Dogged by calamity, they could not create enduring institutions comparable to those by whose aid the great Plantagenets tamed English feudalism. King Robert II sent his son, later James I, to be schooled in France. Off Flamborough Head in 1406 he was captured by the English, and taken prisoner to London. In the following month King Robert died, and for eighteen years Scotland had no monarch.

This fourteenth-century illuminated capital letter, from a manuscript in The British Library, shows David II of Scotland shaking the hand of King Edward III. Robert the Bruce had persuaded the Pope to allow Scottish kings to be anointed at their coronations and his son, David II, was thus Scotland's first anointed king.

Eventually the English Government was prepared to let King James I be ransomed and return to his country.

Captivity had not daunted James. He had conceived a justifiable admiration for the English monarch's position and powers, and on his arrival in Scotland he asserted his sovereignty with vigour. During his effective reign of thirteen years he ruthlessly disciplined the Scottish baronage. It was not an experience they enjoyed. At length a party of infuriated lords decided on revenge; in 1437 they found the opportunity to slay James by the sword. So died, and before his task had been accomplished, one of the most forceful of Scottish kings.

The throne once more descended to a child, James II, aged seven. After the inevitable tumults of his minority the boy grew into a popular and vigorous ruler. He had need of his gifts, for the "Black Douglases", descendants of Sir James Douglas, the faithful sword-arm of the Bruce, had now become over-mighty subjects and constituted a heavy menace to the Crown. For more than a century the Douglases, "Black" and "Red" had been among the foremost champions of Scotland, but their continual intrigues, both at home and at the English Court, incensed the young and high-spirited King. In 1452, when he had not long turned twenty-one, James invited the "Black" Douglas to Stirling. Under a safe-conduct he came; and there the King himself in passion stabbed him. The King's attendants finished his life.

But to cut down the chief of the Douglases was not to stamp out the family. Only in 1455 did he finally succeed, by burning their castles and ravaging their lands, in driving the leading Douglases over the Border. In England they survived for many years, to vex the house of Stuart with plots and conspiracies, abetted by the English Crown.

James II was now at the height of his power; but in 1460, while inspecting one of his primitive siege guns, the piece exploded, and he was killed by a flying fragment.

For the fourth time in little more than a century a minor inherited the Scottish Crown. James III was a boy of nine. As he grew up he showed some amiable qualities, but his reign, which lasted into Tudor times, was much occupied by civil wars and disorders, and its most notable achievement was the acquisition to Scotland, in lieu of a dowry, of Orkney and Shetland from the King of Denmark, whose daughter James married.

The palace of Scone (pronounced Skoon) stands on what is possibly the most historic site in Scotland. It was the capital of an ancient Pictish kingdom until AD 843 when Kenneth MacAlpin, King of the Scots, subdued the Picts and united the rival nations. Scottish kings, including Robert the Bruce in 1306, continued to be crowned at Scone.

The Declaration of Arbroath, *dated 1320, is the classic document stating Scottish independence. It is written in Latin and affirms this powerful national message: "For as long as one hundred men remain alive, we shall never under any conditions submit to the domination of the English."*

The disunity of the kingdom, fostered by English policy and perpetuated by the tragedies that befell the Scottish sovereign, was not the only source of Scotland's weakness. The land was divided in race, in speech, and in culture. The rift between Highlands and Lowlands was more than a geographical distinction. The Lowlands formed part of the feudal world, and, except in the west, in Galloway, English was spoken. The Highlands preserved a social order much older than feudalism. In the Lowlands the King of Scots was a feudal magnate; in the Highlands he was the chief of a loose federation of clans. He had, it is true, the notable advantage of blood kinship with the ancient Celtic kings. The Bruces were undoubted descendants of the family of the first King of Scots in the ninth century. For all Scots, Lowland and Highland alike, the royal house had therefore a sanctity which commanded reverence periods when obedience and even loyalty were lacking.

But reverence was not an effective instrument of government. In law and fact feudal authority remained far stronger than in England. The King's justice was excluded from a great part of Scottish life, and many of his judges were ineffective competitors with the feudal system. Over much of the kingdom feudal justice itself fought a doubtful battle with the more ancient clan law. The Highland chiefs might formally owe their lands and power to the Crown and be classified as feudal tenants in chief, but their

Irish reliquary made to contain a fragment of the True Cross for Turlough O'Connor, High King of Erin, in about 1130. The relic was set in the centre of The Cross and enclosed by a piece of transparent rock crystal.

real authority rested on the allegiance of their clansmen. Some clan chiefs, like the great house of Gordon, in the Highlands, were also feudal magnates in the neighbouring Lowlands. In the west the rising house of Campbell played either role as it suited them. They were to exercise great influence in the years to come.

Meanwhile the Scots peasant farmer and the thrifty burgess, throughout these two hundred years of strife, pursued their ways and built up the country's real strength in spite of the disputes among their lords and masters. The Church devoted itself to its healing mission, and many good bishops and divines adorn the annals of medieval Scotland. In the fifteenth century three Scottish universities were founded: St Andrew's, Glasgow and Aberdeen — one more than England had until the nineteenth century.

Historians of the English-speaking peoples have been baffled by medieval Ireland. Here dwelt one of the oldest Christian communities in Europe, distinguished by missionary endeavours and monkish scholarship while England was still a battlefield for heathen Germanic invaders. Until the twelfth century, however, Ireland had never developed the binding feudal institutions of state that were gradually evolving elsewhere. A loose federation of Gaelic-speaking rural principalities was dominated by a small group of clan patriarchs who called themselves kings. Over all lay the shadowy authority of the High King of Tara, which was a sacred hill surmounted by earthworks of great antiquity. Until about the year 1000 the High King was generally a member of the O'Neill family. The High Kings exercised no real central authority, and there were no towns of Irish founding from which government power could radiate. When the long, sorrowful story began of English intervention in Ireland the country had already endured the shock and torment of Scandinavian invasion. But although impoverished by the ravages of the Norsemen, and its accepted order of things greatly disturbed, Ireland was not remade. It was the Norsemen who built the first towns — Dublin, Waterford, Limerick, and Cork.

The High Kingship had been in dispute since the great Brian Boru — much lamented in song — had broken the O'Neill succession, only himself to be killed in his victory over the Danes at Clontarf in 1014. A century and a half later one of his disputing successors, the King of Leinster, took refuge at the Court of Henry II. He secured permission to raise help for his cause from among Henry's Anglo-Norman knights. It was a fateful decision for Ireland. In 1169 there arrived in the country the first progenitors of the Anglo-Norman ascendancy.

Led by Richard de Clare, Earl of Pembroke, and known as "Strongbow", the invaders were as much Welsh as Norman; and even today some of the commonest Irish names suggest a Welsh ancestry. Irish military methods were no match for the newcomers, and Strongbow, marrying the daughter of the King of Leinster, might perhaps have set up a new feudal kingdom in Ireland. But Strongbow was doubtful both of his own strength and of the attitude of his vigilant superior, Henry II. So the conquests were proffered to the King, and Henry briefly visited this fresh addition to his dominions.

The reviving power of the Papacy had long been offended by the traditional independence of the Irish Church. By Papal Bull in 1155 the overlordship of Ireland had been granted to the English king. The Pope at the time was Adrian IV, the only Englishman ever to be Pope. Here were foundations both spiritual and practical. But Henry had little time for Irish problems. He

Trim Castle, Co. Meath, was part of a chain of castles built by the Anglo-Norman nobles who needed to subdue Ireland. Richard II visited Trim with his relative Henry Bolingbroke, who later deposed him and became Henry IV.

left the affairs of the island to the Norman adventurers. It was a pattern often to be repeated.

The century that followed Henry II's visit marked the height of Anglo-Norman expansion. More than half the country was by now directly subjected to the knightly invaders. Among them Gerald of Windsor, ancestor of the Fitzgerald family, the branches of which, as Earls of Kildare, were for long to control large tracts of southern and central Ireland. There was also William de Burgh, brother of the great English Justiciar, and ancestor of the Earls of Ulster; and Theobald Walter, King John's butler, founder of the powerful Butler family of Ormond. But there was no organised colonisation and settlement. English authority was accepted in the Norse towns on the southern and eastern coasts, and the King's writ ran over a varying area of country surrounding Dublin. This hinterland of the capital was significantly known as "the Pale", which might be defined as a defended enclosure. Immediately outside lay the big feudal lordships, and beyond these were the "wild" unconquered Irish of the west. Two races dwelt in uneasy balance, and the division between them was sharpened when a Parliament of Ireland evolved towards the end of the thirteenth century. It was a Parliament in Ireland of the Anglo-Irish only.

Within a few generations of the coming of the Anglo-Normans, however, the Irish chieftains began to recover from the shock of new methods of warfare. They hired mercenaries to help them, originally in large part recruited from the Norse-Celtic stock of the Scottish isles, and regained for the Gaelic-speaking peoples wide regions of Ireland, and might have won more, had they not quarrelled among themselves.

Meanwhile a change of spirit had overtaken many of the Anglo-Norman Irish barons. These great feudatories were constantly tempted by the independent role of the Gaelic clan chiefs with whom they were frequently united by marriage. Their stock was seldom reinforced from England, except by English lords who wedded Irish heiresses, and then became absentee landlords. Gradually a group of Anglo-Irish nobles grew up, largely assimilated to their adopted land, and as impatient as their Gaelic peasants of rule from London.

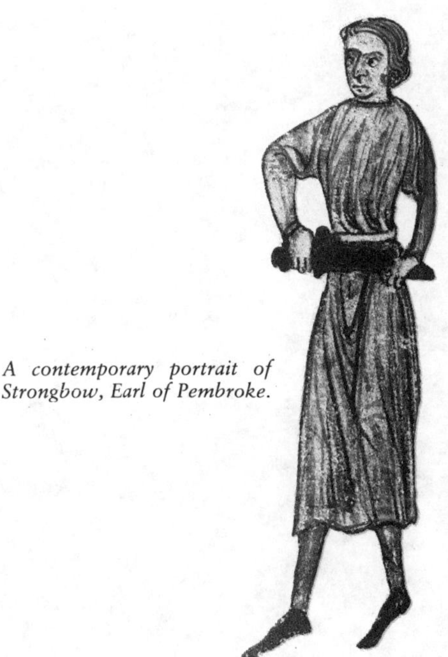

A contemporary portrait of Strongbow, Earl of Pembroke.

If English kings had regularly visited Ireland, the ties between the two countries might have been closely and honourably woven together. As it

This map shows the Pale area in Ireland in 1494. The word Pale means paling, or fence, and refers to the boundary of English legal jurisdiction in Ireland. It is from here that the expression "beyond the pale" is derived.

was, when the English king was strong English laws generally made headway; otherwise a loose Celtic anarchy prevailed. King John, in his furious fitful energy, twice went to Ireland, and twice brought the quarrelsome Norman barons and Irish chiefs under his suzerainty. Although Edward I never landed in Ireland English authority was then in the ascendant. Thereafter the Gaels revived. The shining example of Scotland was not lost upon them. The brother of the victor of Bannockburn, Edward Bruce, was called in by his relations among the Irish chiefs with an army of Scottish veterans. He was crowned King of Ireland in 1316, but after a temporary triumph was defeated and slain at Dundalk.

This victory of English arms did not mean a victory for English law, custom, or speech. The Gaelic reaction gathered force. In Ulster the O'Neills gradually won the mastery of Tyrone. In Ulster and Connaught the feudal trappings were openly discarded when the line of the de Burgh Earls of Ulster ended in 1333 with a girl. According to feudal law, she succeeded to the whole inheritance. In fact she was married to Edward III's second son, Lionel of Clarence. But in Celtic law women could not succeed to the chieftainship. The leading male members of the cadet branches of the de Burgh family accordingly "went Irish", snatched what they could of the inheritance, and assumed the clan names of Burke, or, after their founder, MacWilliam.

To preserve the English character of the Pale and of its surrounding Anglo-Norman lordships, a Parliament was summoned in the middle of the fourteenth century, but its enactments had little effect. In the Pale the old Norman settlers clung to their privileged position, but most of Ireland by now lay outside the Pale, under native chiefs who had practically no dealings with the representatives of the English kings.

By Tudor times the anarchic Ireland lay open to reconquest, and to the tribulations of reimposing English royal authority was to be added after Henry VIII's Reformation the fateful division of religious belief.

CHAPTER 21

THE LONGBOW

BENEATH THE SQUALID SURFACE OF EDWARD II'S REIGN there had nonetheless proceeded in England a marked growth of national power and prosperity. The English people stood at this time possessed of a commanding weapon: the longbow. Handled by the well-trained archer class, this brought into the field a yeoman type of soldier with whom there was nothing on the Continent to compare.

The power of the longbow and the skill of the bowmen had developed to a point where even the finest mail was no certain protection. At two hundred and fifty yards the arrow hail produced effects never reached again by infantry missiles at such a range until the American Civil War. The archer was a professional soldier, earning and deserving high pay. He went to war often on a pony, but always with a considerable transport for his comfort and his arrows. He carried with him a heavy iron-pointed stake, which, planted in the ground, afforded a deadly obstacle to charging horses. Behind this shelter a company of archers in open order could deliver a discharge of

This manuscript picture, dating from around 1400, shows both longbows and crossbows. The longbow was developed as a formidable weapon during the Welsh wars of Edward I.

arrows so rapid, continuous, and penetrating as to annihilate the cavalry attack. Moreover, in all skirmishing and patrolling, the trained archer brought his man down at ranges which had never before been considered dangerous in the whole history of war. Of all this the Continent, and particularly France, our nearest neighbour, was ignorant. In France the armoured knight and his men-at-arms had long exploited their ascendancy in war. The foot-soldiers who accompanied their armies were regarded as the lowest type of auxiliary. A military caste had imposed itself upon society in virtue of physical and technical assertion which the coming of the longbow must disprove. It was with a sense of unmeasured superiority that the English now looked out upon Europe.

The reign of King Edward III passed through several distinct phases. In the first he was a minor, and the land was ruled by his mother and her lover, Roger Mortimer. This Government, founded upon unnatural murder and representing only a faction in the nobility, was condemned to weakness at home and abroad. Its rule of nearly four years was marked by concession and surrender both in France and in Scotland. A treaty with France in March 1327 condemned England to pay a war indemnity, and restricted the English possession to a strip of land running from Saintes in Saintonge and Bordeaux to Bayonne, and to a defenceless enclave in the interior of Gascony. In May 1328 the "Shameful Treaty of Northampton" implied the abandonment of all the claims of Edward I in Scotland.

The anger which these events excited was widespread. The regime might however have maintained itself for some time but for Mortimer's quarrel with the barons he had so lately led. His desire to make his position permanent caused him to seek from a Parliament convened in October at Salisbury the title of Earl of March, in addition to the office he already held of Justice of Wales for life. Mortimer attended, backed by his armed retainers. But it then appeared that many of the leading nobles were absent, and among them Henry, Earl of Lancaster, uncle of the King, who held a counter-meeting in London. From Salisbury Mortimer, taking with him the young King, set forth in 1328 to ravage the lands of Lancaster, and in the disorders which followed he succeeded in checking the revolt.

Then Mortimer made an overweening mistake. In 1330 the King's uncle, the Earl of Kent, was deceived into thinking that Edward II was still alive. Kent made an ineffective attempt to restore him to liberty, and was executed. This event convinced Henry of Lancaster and other magnates that

Edward III had far more in common with his grandfather, Edward I, than with his effeminate father. This portrait showing a strong, alert character can be seen in the National Portrait Gallery, London.

it might be their turn to suffer next at Mortimer's hands. They decided to get their blow in first. All eyes were therefore turned to the young King. When fifteen, in 1328, he had been married to Philippa of Hainault. In June 1330 a son was born to him; he felt himself now a grown man who must do his duty by the realm. But effective power still rested with Mortimer and the Queen Mother. In October Parliament sat at Nottingham. Mortimer and Isabella, guarded by ample force, were lodged in the castle. It is clear that very careful thought and preparation had marked the plans by which the King should assert his rights. Were the King to succeed, Parliament was at hand to acclaim him. Mortimer and Isabella did not know the secrets of the castle. An underground passage led into its heart. Through this on an October night a small band of resolute men entered, surprised Mortimer and the Queen, and, dragging them along the subterranean way, delivered them to the King's officers. Mortimer was brought before the peers, accused of the murder in Berkeley Castle and other crimes, and, after condemnation by the lords, hanged on November 29. Isabella was consigned by her son to perpetual captivity at various country manors, and Edward made it his practice to pay her a periodic visit. She died nearly thirty years later. Upon these grim preliminaries the long and famous reign began.

English spinsters making yarn using carding tools to sort the wool fibres and distaffs to spin them into thread. There were about ten million sheep in England in the thirteenth century—more than three times the number of the human population—in order to meet the demand for English wool which was the best in Europe.

The guiding spirit of the new King was to revive the policy, assert the claims, and restore the glories of his grandfather. The quarrel with Scotland was resumed. Edward, the son of John Balliol, the nominee of Edward I, had become a refugee at the English Court. In 1332 Edward Balliol rallied his adherents and, with the secret support of Edward III, sailed from Ravenspur to Kinghorn in Fife. Advancing on Perth, he met and defeated the infant David's Regent at Dupplin Moor. Balliol received the submission of many Scottish magnates, and was crowned at Scone.

Within two months, however, he and his supporters were driven into England. Edward III was now able to make what terms he liked with the beaten Balliol. He was recognised by Balliol as his overlord and promised the town and shire of Berwick. In 1331 therefore Edward III advanced to besiege Berwick, and routed the Scots at Halidon Hill. This was a battle very different in character from Bannockburn. The power of the archers was allowed to play its part, and the exiled party re-established for a while their authority in their native land. Yet in exacting his concessions Edward III had overshot the mark; he had damned Balliol's cause in the eyes of all Scots. Meanwhile the descendants and followers of Robert Bruce took refuge in France. The contacts between Scotland and France and the constant aid given by the French Court to the Scottish enemies of England roused a deep antagonism. Thus the war in Scotland pointed the path to Flanders.

Here a new set of grievances formed a substantial basis for a conflict. The loss of all the French possessions, except Gascony, and the constant bickering on the Gascon frontiers, had been endured perforce since the days of John. But in 1328 the death of Charles IV without a direct heir opened a further issue. Philip of Valois assumed the royal power and demanded homage from Edward, who in his mother's right had a remote claim to the throne of France. This claim, by and with the assent and advice of the Lords Spiritual and Temporal, and of the Commons of England, he was later to advance in support of his campaigns.

The youthful Edward was less drawn to domestic politics than to foreign adventure and the chase. He was conscious moreover from the first of the advantage to be gained by diverting the restless energies of his nobles from internal intrigues and rivalries to the unifying purposes of a foreign war. This was also in harmony with the temper of his people. European adventure was previously regarded as a matter mainly of interest to a prince concerned with his foreign possessions or claims. Yet Edward III did not have to wring support from his Parliament for an expedition to France. On the contrary, nobles, merchants, and citizens vied with one another in pressing the Crown to act.

Taxes on wool helped to fund the army. This famous fourteenth-century woolmark shows a shepherd's crook beneath a woolsack.

The dynastic and territorial disputes were reinforced by a less sentimental but nonetheless powerful motive, which made its appeal to many Members of the Houses of Parliament. The wool trade with the Low Countries was the staple of English exports, and almost the sole form of wealth which rose above the resources of agriculture. The Flemish towns had attained a high economic development, based upon the art of weaving cloth. They depended for their prosperity upon the wool of England. But the aristocracy under the Counts of Flanders nursed French sympathies which recked little of the material wellbeing of the burghers, regarding them as dangerous and subversive folk whose growth in wealth and power conflicted with feudal ascendancy. Repeated obstructions were placed by the Counts of Flanders upon the wool trade, and each aroused the anger of those concerned on both sides of the Narrow Sea. The mercantile element in the English Parliament, already inflamed by running sea-fights with the French in the Channel, pleaded vehemently for action.

In 1336 Edward was moved to retaliate in a decisive manner. He decreed an embargo on all exports of English wool, thus producing a furious crisis in the Netherlands. The townspeople rose against the feudal aristocracy, and under Jacques Van Arteveldt, a warlike merchant of Ghent, gained control over a large part of the country. The victorious burghers, threatened by aristocratic and French revenge, looked to England for aid, and their appeals met with a hearty response. Thus all streams of profit and ambition flowed into a common channel at a moment when the floodwaters of conscious military strength ran high, and in 1337, when Edward repudiated his grudging homage to Philip VI, the Hundred Years' War began. It was never to be concluded; no general peace treaty was signed, and not until the Peace of Amiens in 1802, when the French royal heir was a refugee within these isles, did the English sovereign formally renounce his claims to the throne of the Valois and the Bourbons.

Edward slowly assembled an expeditionary army. This was not a feudal levy, but a paid force of picked warriors, recruited where and how their captains pleased. In consequence the knights and archers who gathered in the Cinque Ports formed one of the most formidable and efficient invading armies history had yet seen. These preparations were well-known in France, and the whole strength of the monarchy was bent to resist them.

Wool merchants lived prosperously, as this substantial house at Chipping Camden testifies. It was the home of William Gravel, a Cotswold wool dealer in the fourteenth century.

Philip VI looked first to the sea. All the resources of the French marine were strained to produce a fleet; even hired Genoese galleys appeared in the French harbours. In Normandy plans were mooted for a counter-invasion which should repeat the exploits of William the Conqueror. But Edward had not neglected sea power. His interest in the navy won him from Parliament early in his reign the title of "King of the Sea". He was able to marshal a fleet equal in vessels and superior in men. A great sea battle was necesssary before transport of the English army to France and its maintenance there was feasible. In the summer of 1340 the hostile navies met off Sluys, and a struggle of nine hours ensued. The French admirals had been ordered, under pain of death, to prevent the invasion, and both sides fought well; but the French fleet was decisively beaten and the command of the Channel passed into the hands of the invading power. The seas being now open, the army crossed to France.

Joined with the revolted Flemings, Edward's numbers were greatly augmented, and this combined force, which may have exceeded twenty thousand, undertook the first Anglo-Flemish siege of Tournai. The city was stubbornly defended, and as the grip of famine tightened upon the garrison the horrible spectacle was presented of the "useless mouths" being driven forth into no-man's-land to perish by inches without pity or relief. But the capture of this fortress was beyond Edward's resources in money and supplies. The power of the archers did not extend to stone walls; the first campaign of what was a great European war yielded no results, and a prolonged truce supervened.

This truce was imposed upon the combatants through lack of money, and carried with it no reconciliation. On the contrary, both sides pursued their quarrel in secondary ways. The French wreaked their vengeance on the burghers of the Netherlands, whom they crushed utterly, and Van Arteveldt met his death in a popular tumult at Ghent. The English retaliated as best they could. There was a disputed succession in Brittany, which they fomented with substantial aids. The chronic warfare on the frontiers of Gascony continued. Both sides looked forward to a new trial of strength. Well-trained men, eager to fight, there were in plenty, but to maintain them in the field required funds. How could these resources be obtained? The Jews had been exploited, pillaged, and expelled in 1290. The Florentine bankers, who had found the money for the first invasion, had been ruined by

This manuscript picture shows the French artist and scholar, Jean Froissart, writing his Chronicles *of French and English history in the fourteenth century. He has left a unique record of how royalty and the aristocracy lived.*

royal default. But now a fertile source was at hand. The wealthiest and best-organised commercial interest in England, the wool trade, was eager to profit from war. A monopoly of wool merchants was created, bound to export only through a particular town to be prescribed by the King from time to time in accordance with his needs and judgment. This system, which was called the Staple, gave the King a convenient and flexible control. By taxing the wool exports which passed through his hands at the Staple port he was assured of an important revenue independent of Parliament. Moreover, the wool merchants who held the monopoly formed a corporation interested in the war, dependent on the King, and capable of lending harmony in return for considerate treatment. This development was not welcomed by Parliament, where the smaller wool merchants were increasingly represented. They complained of the favour shown to the monopolists of the Staple, and they also pointed to the menace to Parliamentary power involved in the King's independent resources.

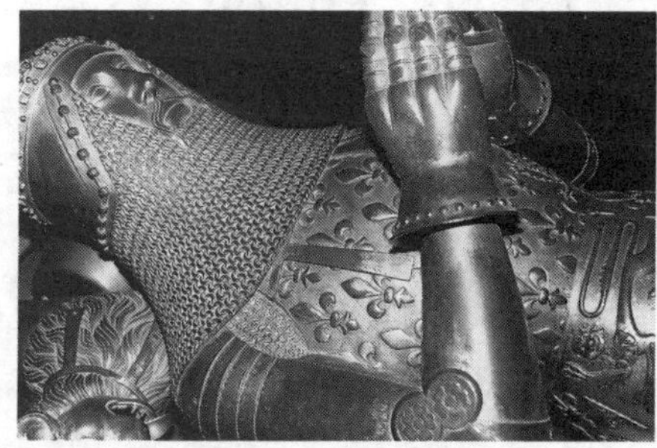

Edward, the Black Prince, who won his spurs at the battle of Crécy in 1346, is seen here magnificently attired in chain mail from his effigy in Canterbury Cathedral.

By the spring of 1346 Parliament had at length brought itself to the point of facing the taxation necessary to finance a new invasion. The army was reconstituted, more efficiently than before. In one wave 2,400 cavalry, 12,000 archers, and other infantry sailed, and landed unopposed at St Vaast in Normandy on July 12. The secret was well-kept; even the English army itself believed it was going to Gascony. The French could not for some time collect forces sufficient to arrest the inroads. Caen fell, and Edward advanced, burning and laying waste the country, to the very walls of Paris. But by this time a huge French force, probably three times as big as Edward's army, assembled in the neighbourhood of St Denis. Against such opposition, added to the walls of a fortified city, Edward's resources could not attempt to prevail. King Philip grimly invited him to choose upon which bank of the Seine he would fight a pitched battle.

The thrust had failed and the challenger was forced to quit the lists at a pace which covered sixty miles in four days. The French army moved on a parallel line to the southward and denied the Seine valley to the retreating English. They must now make for the Somme, and hope to cross between Amiens and the sea. But all the bridges were broken or held by the levies of Picardy. Edward and the English host, which had tried so audacious, even foolhardy, a spring, now seemed penned in a triangle between the Somme, the seashore, and the French mass. No means had been found to bring the fleet and its transports to any suitable harbour. To cross the Somme near the mouth was a desperate enterprise. The ford was very lengthy, and the tides, violent and treacherous, offered only a few precarious hours in any day.

Moreover, the passage was itself defended by strong forces popularly estimated to have been upwards of twelve thousand men. But since to pause was to perish, the King ordered his marshals to plunge into the water and fight their way across. The French resistance was spirited. The knighthood of Picardy rode out and encountered the English on the treacherous sands in the rising waters. By hard fighting, under conditions most deadly to men encased in mail, the passage was forced. At the landing the Genoese crossbowmen inflicted losses and delayed the deployment until the longbow asserted its mastery.

Thus did King Edward and his army escape, intensely convinced of the narrowness of their deliverance. That night they rejoiced. The countryside was full of food; the King gathered his chiefs to supper and afterwards to

THE BLACK DEATH

THE BLACK DEATH came from Asia in 1346, and was brought to Europe by Genoese ships trading with the Crimea. A bubonic plague, carried by fleas on black rats, it is said to have claimed no less than one third of Europe's population. It recurred, less devastatingly, in the 1360s and 1370s.

In England the first attack came in June 1348 at Melcombe Regis, now Weymouth, in Dorset, two years after the battle of Crécy. It was known at the time as "the great Mortality", and it hit at rich and poor alike. The newly appointed Archbishop of Canterbury died six days after his consecration, and within twelve months his two successors were dead too.

The Plague's biggest impact, however, was on the poor and powerless, who in many instances had their resistance lowered by malnutrition. According to an inscription in Ashwell church in Hertfordshire, "miserable, wild, distracted, only the dregs of the populace live to tell the tale".

The population continued to decline, if irregularly, for more than a century. The young were particularly vulnerable to the disease and the Plague of 1361 was known as "the pestilence of the children".

The Black Death's effects on agriculture and industry are contentious. It has been claimed that it brought agricultural expansion to an abrupt end; it certainly led to some villages and marginal farming land being abandoned. The shortage of labour tilted the economic balance in favour of labourers, yet there were some lords who continued to prosper and new wool producing towns flourished. Landowners turned from wheat farming to sheep, which required less labour, and seven years after the Plague forty thousand sacks of wool were being exported annually.

Society felt the impact, however, as it felt the impact of the Hundred Years' War. The ambitious prospered, and the relative economic position of the labourer improved. The whole social order was changing.

LONDON'S POPULATION was nearly halved by the Black Death, the first symptoms of which were raised pustules in the armpit and groin, followed by a high fever and mental confusion, then coma and death. An excavation (above) on the site of the Royal Mint near the Tower has revealed rows of graves which culminated in a large trench as the disease claimed more and more victims. A Flemish manuscript (below) records the plethora of burials undertaken by sorrowing friends and relatives. The reduction in England's work force changed medieval society: those who survived the Plague could command higher wages; also, since short-staffed landowners lured labourers away from their native villages, some workers were able to break their ties of bondage to the lords of the manor. Many people gained a wealth and freedom that they had never known before.

MEDICAL KNOWLEDGE WAS ELEMENTARY. *In these illustrations from a medieval medical manual (below), a physician sets his patients' dislocated limbs. Medical treatments centred around a need to balance four "humours" in the body: yellow bile (choler), black bile (melancholy), phlegm and blood. Medical expertise was rudimentary, and physic was considered useless unless linked to astrology.*

THE WHEEL OF FORTUNE *(above) symbolised the unjust and arbitrary nature of life. It could raise people to the heights of prosperity and happiness or hurl them to the depths of poverty, despair and death. In an age of political autocracy and medical ignorance, ordinary people felt they had little control over their own destiny. The wheel's power as an image of life on earth was intensified by the notorious torture wheel. St Catherine suffered on such a wheel and her name is commemorated in the popular firework.*

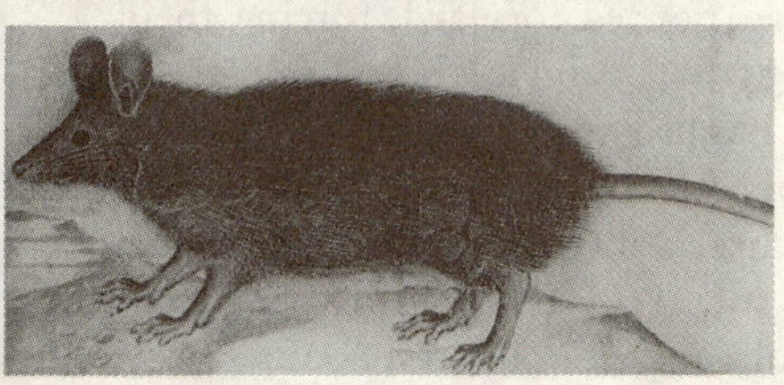

BLACK RATS AND THEIR FLEAS *brought the disease to England; later the infection was spread by human contact. The drawing above, by a fourteenth-century Italian artist, records one of the culprit species of Asian black rat. Although there was little knowledge of germs, the picture below shows that people had learnt to protect themselves from the infection by burning the clothes worn by the sick. By the seventeenth century overcrowding was connected with the spread of the disease.*

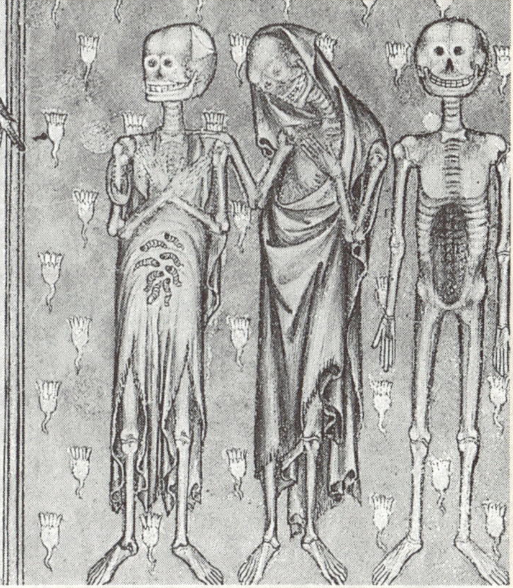

THE CONTEMPLATION OF DEATH *sharpened people's minds. The point is made in this fourteenth-century manuscript picture, now in the British Museum, that death comes even for kings. Fear and despair during the Plague years turned people's minds not only to religion but also to the quality of life on earth. Revolutionaries such as Wat Tyler and John Ball led the people in their demands for a more just society.*

prayer. But it was certain that they could not gain the coast without a battle at enormous odds. The King and the Prince of Wales, afterwards famous as the Black Prince, received all the offices of religion, and Edward prayed that the impending battle should at least leave him unstripped of honour. With daylight he marshalled about eleven thousand men in three divisions. Mounted upon a small palfrey, with a white wand in his hand, with his splendid surcoat of crimson and gold above his armour, he rode along the ranks. "He spoke so sweetly," says Froissart in his famous *Chronicle,* "and with such a cheerful countenance that all who had been dispirited were directly comforted by seeing and hearing him . . . They ate and drank at their ease . . . and seated themselves on the ground, placing their helmets and bows before them, that they might be the fresher when their enemies should arrive." Their position on the downs enjoyed few advantages, but the forest of Crécy on their flanks afforded protection and the means of a final stand.

King Philip at sunrise on this same Saturday, August 26, 1346, heard Mass in the monastery of Abbeville. He had crossed the Somme by bridge, and his whole army, gigantic for those times, rolled forward in their long pursuit. Four knights were sent forth to reconnoitre. About midday the King received their reports. The English were in battle array and meant to fight. He gave the sage counsel to halt for the day, bring up the rear, form the battleline, and attack on the morrow. But the thought of leaving, even for a day, this hated foe, who had for so many marches fled before them was unendurable to the French army. What surety had they that the morrow might not see their enemies decamped and the field bare? It became impossible to control the forward movement. All the roads and tracks from Abbeville to Crécy were black and glittering with marching columns. King Philip's orders were obeyed by some, rejected by most. While many great bodies halted obediently, still larger masses poured forward, forcing their way through the stationary or withdrawing troops, and at about five o'clock in the afternoon came face to face with the English army lying in full view on the broad slopes of Crécy. Here they stopped.

King Philip, arriving on the scene, was carried away by the ardour of the throng around him. The sun was already low; nevertheless all were determined to engage. There was a corps of six thousand Genoese crossbowmen in the van of the army. These were ordered to make their way through the masses of horsemen, and with their missiles break up the hostile array in preparation for the cavalry attacks. The Genoese had marched eighteen miles in full battle order with their heavy weapons and store of bolts. Fatigued, they made it plain that they were in no condition to do much that day. But the Count of Alençon, who had covered the distance on horseback, did not accept this remonstrance kindly. "This is what one gets," he exclaimed, "by employing such scoundrels, who fall off when there is anything for them to do." Forward the Genoese! At this moment, while the crossbowmen were threading their way to the front under many scornful glances, dark clouds swept across the sun and a short, drenching storm beat upon the hosts. A large flight of crows flew cawing through the air above the French in gloomy presage. The storm, after wetting the bowstrings of the Genoese, passed as quickly as it had come, and the setting sun shone brightly in their eyes and on the backs of the English. This, like the crows, was adverse, but it was more material. The Genoese, drawing out their array, gave a loud shout, advanced a few steps, shouted again, a third time

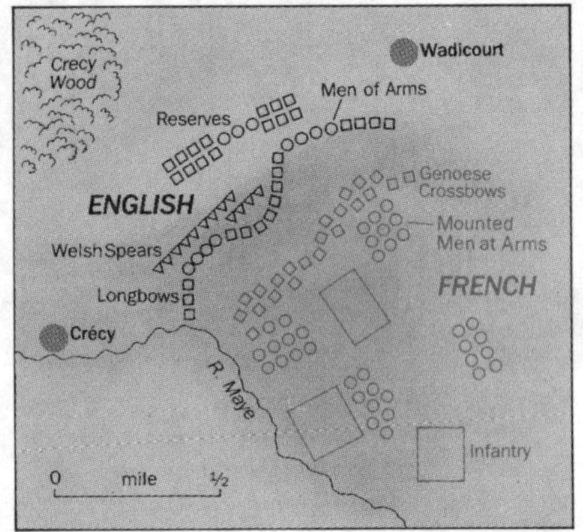

Map of the Battle of Crécy, at which the longbow won the day. It had a greater range than the crossbow and was easier to fire. The Genoese crossbowmen upon whom Philip VI of France depended were killed before they came within striking distance of the English.

This contemporary picture of a fourteenth-century siege shows the defenders pouring boiling oil and raining arrows and boulders on their attackers. They also have a stone attached to a rope, to swing against the covered vehicles attempting to bring the enemy close to the castle walls.

advanced, and discharged their bolts. Unbroken silence had wrapped the English lines, but at this the archers, six or seven thousand strong, ranged on both flanks, who had hitherto stood motionless, advanced one step, drew their bows to the ear, and came into action. They "shot their arrows with such force and quickness," says Froissart, "that it seemed as if it snowed."

The effect upon the Genoese was annihilating; at a range which their own weapons could not attain they were in a few minutes killed by thousands. The ground was covered with feathered corpses. Reeling before this blast of missile destruction, the like of which had not been known in war, the survivors recoiled in rout upon the eager ranks of the French cavalry which stood just out of arrowshot. "Kill me those scoundrels," cried King Philip in fury, "for they stop up our road." Whereupon the front line of the French cavalry rode among the retreating Genoese, cutting them down with their swords. In doing so they came within the deadly distance. The arrow snowstorm beat upon them, piercing their mail and smiting horse and man. Valiant squadrons from behind rode forward into the welter, and upon all fell the arrow hail, strewing the field with horses and richly dressed warriors. A hideous disorder reigned. And now Welsh and Cornish light infantry, slipping through the chequered ranks of the archers, came forward with long knives and, "slew many, at which the King of England was afterwards exasperated". Many a ransom was cast away in those moments.

In this slaughter fell King Philip's ally, the blind King of Bohemia, who bade his knights fasten their bridles to his in order that he might strike a blow with his own hand. Thus entwined, he charged forward in the press. Man and horse they fell, and the next day their bodies were found still linked. The main attack of the French now developed. The Count d'Alençon and the Count of Flanders led heavy cavalry charges upon the English line. Evading the archers as far as possible, they sought the men-at-arms, and French, German, and Savoyard squadrons actually reached the Prince of Wales's division. The enemy's numbers were so great that those who fought about the Prince sent to the windmill, whence King Edward directed the

Rodin's dramatic sculpture "The Burghers of Calais" is famous throughout the world. Copies can be seen in Paris, London, Washington and Calais. It was made between 1884 and 1895.

battle, for reinforcements. But the King would not part with his reserves, saying, "Let the boy win his spurs" — which in fact he did.

When night fell, Philip found himself with no more than sixty knights. He was slightly wounded by an arrow, and his horse had been shot under him.

"The English now looked upon the field as their own and their enemies as beaten and King Edward, who all that day had not put on his helmet, then came down from his post, and, with his whole battalion, advanced to the Prince of Wales, whom he embraced in his arms and kissed, and said, 'Sweet son, God give you good perseverance. You are my son, for most loyally have you acquitted yourself this day.'"

On the Sunday morning fog enshrouded the battlefield, and Edward sent a strong force of five hundred lancers and two thousand archers to learn what lay upon his front. These met the columns of the French rear, still marching up from Rouen to Beauvais in ignorance of the defeat, and fell upon them. After this engagement the bodies of 1,542 knights and esquires were counted on the field. Later this force met with the troops of the Archbishop of Rouen and the Grand Prior of France, who were similarly unaware of the event, and were routed with much slaughter. "It has been assured to me for fact," says Froissart, "that . . . . there were slain, this Sunday morning, four times as many as in the battle of the Saturday." This astounding victory of Crécy ranks with Blenheim, Waterloo, and the final advance in the last summer of the Great War as one of the four supreme achievements of the British Army.

Edward marched through Montreuil and Etaples to Boulogne, passed through the forest of Hardelot, and opened the siege of Calais. Calais presented itself to English eyes as the hive of that swarm of privateers who were the endless curse of the Channel. Here on the nearest point of the Continent England had long felt a festering sore. The siege lasted for nearly a year. Every new art of war was practised; the bombards flung cannonballs against the ramparts with terrifying noise; elaborate barriers of piles stopped the French light craft, which sought to evade the sea blockade by creeping along the coast. All reliefs by sea and land failed. But the effort of maintaining the siege strained the resources of the King to an extent we can hardly conceive. When the winter came his soldiers demanded to go home, and the fleet was on the verge of mutiny. In England, Parliament was morose in demeanour and reluctant in supply. Moreover, the siege had hardly begun when King David of Scotland, in fulfilment of the alliance with France, led his army across the Border. But the danger was foreseen, and at Neville's Cross, just west of the city of Durham, the English won a decisive victory which removed the Scottish danger for a generation.

Calais held out for eleven months. Famine at length left no choice to the besieged. They sued for terms. The King was so embittered that when at his demand six of the noblest citizens presented themselves in their shirts, barefoot, emaciated, he was for cutting off their heads. The warnings of his advisers that his fame would suffer in history by so cruel a deed left him obdurate. But Queen Philippa, great with child, who had followed him to the war, fell down before him in an edifying, and perhaps prearranged, tableau of Mercy pleading with Justice. So the burghers of Calais who had devoted themselves to save their people were spared, and even kindly treated. Calais, then, was the fruit, and the sole territorial fruit so far, of the exertions, prodigious in quality, of the whole power of England in the war with France. But Crécy had a longer tale to tell.

CHAPTER 22

THE BLACK DEATH

While feats of arms and strong endeavours held the English mind a far more deadly foe was marching across the continents to their doom. Christendom has had no catastrophe equal to the Black Death. This plague in the course of twenty years destroyed at least one-third of Europe's entire population. The privations of the people, resulting from ceaseless baronial and dynastic wars, presented an easy conquest to disease. The records in England tell more by their silence than by the shocking figures which confront us wherever records were kept. We read of lawsuits where all parties died before the cases could be heard; of monasteries where half the inmates perished; of the Goldsmiths' Company, which had four Masters in a year. These are detailed indications. But far more convincing is the gap which opens in all the local annals of the nation. A whole generation is slashed through by a hideous severance.

The character of the pestilence was appalling. The disease itself, with its frightful symptoms, the swift onset, the blotches, the hardening of the glands under the armpit or in the groin, these swellings which no poultice could resolve, these tumours which, when lanced, gave no relief, the horde of virulent carbuncles which followed the dread harbingers of death, the delirium, the insanity which attended its triumph, the blank spaces which opened on all sides in human society, stunned and for a time destroyed the life and faith of the world. This affliction, added to all the severities of the Middle Ages, was more than the human spirit could endure. The Church, smitten like the rest in body, was wounded grievously in spiritual power. If a God of mercy ruled the world, what sort of rule was this? Such was the challenging thought which swept upon the survivors. Weird sects sprang up, and plague-haunted cities saw the gruesome procession of flagellants, each lashing his forerunner to a dismal dirge, and ghoulish practices glare at us from the broken annals. It seemed to be the death-rattle of the race.

At length the plague abated its force. The tumours yielded to fomentations,

Flagellants' procession. An illustration from northern Europe shows an austere religious sect scourging its members with whips in the hope, perhaps, that public penance would ward off the ravages of the dreaded Plague.

and recoveries became more frequent; the resistant faculties of life revived. The will to live triumphed. The scourge passed, and a European population, too small for its clothes, heirs to much that had been prepared by more numerous hands, turned with unconquerable hope to the morrow.

The calamity which fell upon mankind reduced their numbers and darkened their existence without abating their quarrels. The war between England and France continued in a broken fashion, and the Black Prince, the most renowned warrior in Europe, became a freebooter. Grave reasons of State had been adduced for Edward's invasion of France in 1338, but the character of the Black Prince's forays in Aquitaine can vaunt no such excuses. Nevertheless they produced a brilliant military episode.

In 1355 King Edward obtained from Parliament substantial grants for the renewal of active war. An ambitious strategy was adopted. The Black Prince would advance northward from the English territories of Gascony and Aquitaine towards the Loire. His younger brother, John of Gaunt, Duke of Lancaster, struck in from Brittany. The two forces were to join for a main decision. But all this miscarried. The Black Prince found himself, with forces shrunk to about four thousand men, forced to retire with growing urgency before the advance of a French royal army twenty thousand strong. So grim were his straits that he proposed, as an accommodation, that he and the army should be allowed to escape to England. These terms were rejected by the French; King John of France was resolved to avenge Crécy and finish the war at a stroke. Forced against all odds to fight, the haggard band of English marauders who had carried pillage and arson far and wide were drawn up at Poitiers in array and position chosen by consummate insight. The flanks were secured by forests; archers commanded the only practicable passage.

Ten years had passed since Crécy, and French chivalry and high command alike had brooded upon the tyranny of that event. They had been forced to accept the fact that horses could not face the arrow storm. King John was

The Battle of Poitiers of 1355 is famous not only as a great English victory but for the chivalrous treatment given by the Black Prince to his royal captive, John of France. However, in later years the Black Prince's name became a byword for cruelty.

certain that all must attack on foot, and he trusted to overwhelming numbers. But the great merit of the Black Prince is that he did not rest upon the lessons of the past. He understood that the masses of mail-clad footmen who now advanced upon him in such towering numbers would not be stopped as easily as the horses. Archery alone, however good the target, would not save him. He must try the battle of manoeuvre and counter-attack. He therefore did the opposite to what military convention, based upon the then known facts, would have pronounced right.

The French nobility left their horses in the rear. The Black Prince had all his knights mounted. The French chivalry, encumbered by their mail, plodded ponderously forward amid vineyards and scrub. Many fell before the arrows, but the arrows would not have been enough at the crisis. It was the English spear and axe men who charged in the old style upon ranks disordered by their fatigue of movement and the accidents of the ground. At the same time, a strong detachment of mounted knights, riding round the French left flank, struck in upon the harassed and already disordered attack. The result was a slaughter as large and a victory as complete as Crécy, but with even greater gains. King John of France and the flower of his nobility were captured or slain. The Black Prince, whose record is dented by many cruel acts of war, showed himself a paladin of the age when, in spite of the weariness and stresses of the desperate battle, he treated the captured monarch with all the ceremony of his rank, seated him in his own chair in the camp, and served him in person. Thus by genius, valour, and chivalry he presents himself in a posture which history has not failed to salute.

King John was carried to London. Like King David of Scotland before him, he was placed in the Tower, and upon this personal trophy, in May 1360, the Treaty of Brétigny was concluded. By this England acquired, in addition to her old possession of Gascony, the whole of Henry II's possessions in Aquitaine in full sovereignty, Edward I's inheritance of Ponthieu, and the city of Calais. A ransom was fixed for King John at three million crowns. This was eight times the annual revenue of the English Crown in peacetime.

At Crécy France had been beaten on horseback; at Poitiers she was beaten on foot. These two terrible experiments against the English bit deep into French thought. A sense of hopelessness overwhelmed the French Court and army. How could these people be beaten? A similar phase of despair had swept across Europe a century earlier after the menacing battles of the Mongol invasions. But, as has been wisely observed, the trees do not grow up to the sky. A great French hero appeared in Bertrand du Guesclin, who, by refusing battle and acting through sieges and surprises, rallied the factor of time to the home side. The triumph and the exhaustion of England were simultaneously complete. It was proved that the French army could not beat the English, and that England could not conquer France. The main effort of Edward III, though crowned with all the military laurels, had failed.

The years of the war with France are important in the history of Parliament. The need for money drove the Crown and its officials to summoning it frequently. This led to rapid and important developments. One of the main functions of the representatives of the shires and boroughs was to petition for the redress of grievances, and to draw the attention of the King and his Council to urgent matters. The stress of war forced the Government to take notice of these petitions of the Commons of England, and the fact that the Commons now petitioned as a body in a formal way, and asked, as they did

Edward III and some of the first of the twenty-five knights-companion of the Order of the Garter. The Order was installed in 1348.

in 1327, that these petitions should be transformed into Parliamentary statutes, distinguishes the lower House from the rest of Parliament. Under Edward I the Commons were not an essential element in a Parliament, but under Edward III they assumed a position distinct, vital, and permanent. The separation of the Houses now appears. The Lords had come to regard themselves not only as the natural counsellors of the Crown, but as enjoying the right of separate consultation within the framework of Parliament itself. In 1343 the prelates and magnates met in the White Chamber at Westminster, and the knights and burgesses adjourned to the Painted Chamber to discuss the business of the day. Here too, in this Parliament, for the first time, the figure of a Speaker emerged. He was not on this occasion a Member of the House, and for some time to come the Commons generally spoke through an appointed deputation. But by the end of the reign the role of the Speaker was recognised, and the Crown became anxious to secure its own nominees for this important and prominent office.

The concessions made by Edward III to the Commons mark a decisive stage. He consented that all aids should be granted only in Parliament. He accepted the formal drafts of the Commons' collective petitions as the preliminary bases for future statutes, and by the time of his death it was recognised that the Commons had assumed a leading part in the granting of taxes and the presentation of petitions. Naturally the Commons stood in awe of the Crown. There was no long tradition of authority behind them, and there was no suggestion that either they or Parliament as a whole had any right of control or interference in matters of administration and government. They were summoned to endorse political settlements, to vote money, and to voice grievances; but the permanent acceptance of Parliament as an essential part of the machinery of government, and of the Commons as its vital foundation, is the lasting work of the fourteenth century.

Against Papal agents feeling was strong. The interventions of Rome in the days of John, the submissiveness of Henry III to the Church, the exactions of the Papal tax collectors, the weight of clerical influence within the Household and the Council, all contributed to the growing criticism of the Church. Moreover, this declining power had perforce abandoned its sacred traditional seat in Rome, and was now installed under French influence in enemy territory at Avignon. During these years Parliament passed statutes forbidding appeals to be carried to the Papal Council for matters recognisable in the royal courts and restricting its power to make appointments in the Church of England. It is true that these statutes were only fitfully enforced, as dictated by diplomatic demands, but the drain of the war left little money for Rome, and the Papal tax collectors gleaned the country to little avail during the greater part of the reign.

The renewal in 1369 of serious fighting in Aquitaine found England exhausted and disillusioned. The clergy claimed exemption from taxation, and they could often flaunt their wealth in the teeth of poverty and economic dislocation. Churchmen were ousting the nobility from public office and anti-clerical feeling grew in Parliament. The King was old and failing and a resurgence of baronial power was due. John of Gaunt set himself to redress the balance in favour of the Lords by a carefully planned political campaign against the Church. Ready to his hand lay an unexpected weapon. In the University of Oxford, the national centre of theological study and learning, arguments for Church reform set forth by a distinguished Oxford scholar

MEDIEVAL MONUMENTS

Despite the disasters of plague and civil war, the Middle Ages were a time of conscientious craftsmanship, Gothic splendour and scholarly dedication.

SALISBURY CATHEDRAL, WILTSHIRE

BODIAM CASTLE, SUSSEX, *(above)* survives as an impressive monument to a period when comfort became almost as important as defence to the builders of castles, and when splendour as well as courage was expected of a knight-at-arms (left). In the fourteenth century, the residential quarters were carefully planned rather than fitted haphazardly within the fortifications as was previously the case. They were also designed to minimise the danger of mutiny amongst the retainers within the walls.

OLD SOAR MANOR, KENT, *belonged to the Colepepper family. Of their medieval home now only the chapel and the solar (right) remain. The "solar" was the name given to the owner's private chamber. To this he was able to withdraw from the communal life of the main hall through an adjoining door. This solar was heated by its own fireplace, and there is evidence that the windows were originally not glazed, but shuttered.*

RUFFORD OLD HALL, LANCASHIRE, *built in the 1480s, is an outstanding example of an English house of that period. Its great hall (below) would have served as a dining hall for the whole household, and as sleeping quarters for the servants. At the far end of the hall stands a movable screen which was used to shield the diners on the high table from draughts. One of the few such screens to survive intact, it is covered with intricate Gothic carving. The roof also is exceptionally ornate, being built with hammerbeams: braced struts that project at right angles from the walls to support the wooden rafters.*

STOKESAY CASTLE, SHROPSHIRE, *(left) is a fortified manor house, rather than a castle. Its fortifications could have resisted only the most casual marauder. In the twelfth century it was the home of the de Say family, from whom the house takes its name. They are believed to have built the north tower, now surmounted by some sixteenth-century timber-work.*

CHIPPING CAMPDEN, GLOUCESTERSHIRE, *was a principal centre of the Cotswold wool trade in the Middle Ages. Here its fourteenth-century buildings (left) may be glimpsed through the arches of the timber-roofed market hall.*

CHESTER, CHESHIRE, *retains major buildings in almost every style from the days when the Romans first built its still-surviving wall. Its most distinctive medieval feature is The Rows (right). Its double-level walkways, with shops both at street and first-floor level, date back to the fourteenth century.*

ALFRISTON, SUSSEX, *retains a number of buildings dating from medieval times. The Old Clergy House, (below) the first building ever bought by the National Trust, has timbers still blackened from the smoke of the fourteenth-century central hearth. In the priests' time, the rammed chalk floor would have been spread with rushes and sweetening herbs.*

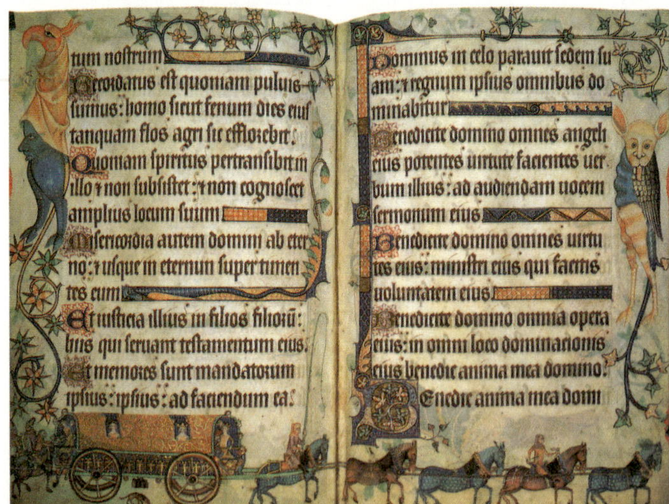

tum nostrum
Recordatus est quoniam pulvis
sumus: homo sicut fenum dies eius
tanquam flos agri sic efflorebit.
Quoniam spiritus pertransibit in
illo et non subsistet: et non cognoscet
amplius locum suum
Misericordia autem domini ab eterno:
et usque in eternum super timen
tes eum
Et iusticia illius in filios filiorum:
his qui seruant testamentum eius.
Et memores sunt mandatorum
ipsius: ipsius: ad faciendum ea.

Dominus in celo parauit sedem su
am: et regnum ipsius omnibus do
minabitur
Benedicite domino omnes angeli
eius potentes uirtute facientes uer
bum illius: ad audiendam uocem
sermonum eius
Benedicite domino omnes uirtu
tes eius: ministri eius qui facitis
uoluntatem eius
Benedicite domino omnia opera
eius: in omni loco dominacionis
eius benedic anima mea domino.
Benedic anima mea domi

MEDIEVAL MANUSCRIPTS *were often decorated with pictures of life in the town and country. The Luttrell Psalter (above) was made in the early fourteenth century, and the Reaping Calendar (left), some seventy years later. Both can be seen in the British Library's collection at the British Museum, London.*

Duncan Fosters RESTAURANT
FOR SALE
Alkit TAILORS
Alkit

CANTERBURY CATHEDRAL, KENT, *was built on the site of St Augustine's Saxon cathedral. This twelfth-century window (above) portrays Archbishop Thomas Becket, who was murdered here in 1170.*

WESTMINSTER ABBEY, LONDON, *(right) was founded by the Saxon king, St Edward the Confessor, but owes much of its final form to the Plantagenet Henry III, whose part in its history is commemorated in this painting (above). St Edward was never to enter the Abbey alive. He died a few days after its consecration, and was buried near the high altar. His Norman successor, William the Conqueror, chose to be crowned in Westminster Abbey.*

THE WILTON DIPTYCH, NATIONAL GALLERY, LONDON, *(right) is an altarpiece named after Wilton House, Wiltshire, its home from 1700 to 1929. It depicts Richard II being presented to the infant Jesus by John the Baptist, St Edward the Confessor, and St Edmund the Martyr. Despite the French influence, it may have been painted in England, probably between 1395 and Richard's deposition in 1399.*

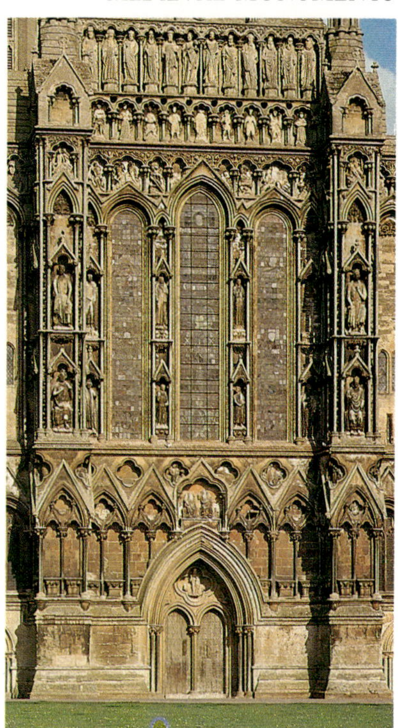

WELLS CATHEDRAL, SOMERSET, *was the first English cathedral to be built entirely in the Gothic style. The unique scissor arches (left) were built in the fourteenth century after cracks appeared in the tower wall. The west façade (above) was designed as a gallery to display nearly four hundred figures.*

HEREFORD CATHEDRAL, HEREFORD AND WORCESTER, *contains the largest chained library in the world. It has fifteen hundred books, each of them secured against theft by a chain attached to the front cover (above). Fifty-two books are incunabula—that is, printed before 1500—two by William Caxton.*

KING'S COLLEGE, CAMBRIDGE, was founded by Henry VI in 1440 for boys from the school he had founded at Eton to continue their ecclesiastical studies. The truly magnificent fan-vaulted ceiling of its chapel crowns one of the major monuments of medieval architecture. Henry VI personally specified the dimensions of the chapel, which he wanted to outshine any other in Cambridge, but it was not completed until 1515, under Henry VIII, who was ultimately responsible for many of the more ornate features of the building.

named Wyclif attracted attention. Wyclif was indignant at the corruption of the Church, and saw in its proud hierarchy and absolute claims a distortion of the true principles of Christianity. He declared that dominion over men's souls had never been delegated to mortals. The final appeal was to Heaven, not to Rome. Also, the King, as the Vicar of God in things temporal, was as much bound by his office to curb the material lavishness of the clergy as the clergy to direct the spiritual life of the King.

Wyclif's doctrine opened deep rifts. It involved reducing the powers of the Church temporal in order to purify the Church spiritual. John of Gaunt was interested in the first, Wyclif in the second. The Church was opposed to both. Gaunt and Wyclif entered into alliance. Gaunt busied himself in packing the new Parliament, and Wyclif lent moral support by running about from church to church preaching against abuses. But counter-forces were also aroused. The bishops, recognising in Wyclif Gaunt's most dangerous supporter, arraigned him on charges of heresy at St Paul's. Gaunt, coming to his aid, encountered the hostility of the London mob. The ill-matched partnership fell to pieces.

Church "abuses" covered a variety of practices, among them the sale of pardons and so-called sacred relics to gullible peasants; the acquisition of personal wealth by Church officials; and the behaviour of wanton priests. Many manuscripts of the fourteenth and fifteenth centuries cast a highly critical light on these practices.

It was at this same point that Wyclif's enduring influence began. He resolved to appeal to the people. Church abuses and his own reforming doctrines had attracted many young students. He organised his followers into bands of poor preachers, who, like those of Wesley in a later century, spread the doctrines of poverty and holiness for the clergy throughout the countryside. He wrote English tracts, of which the most famous was *The Wicket*, which were passed from hand to hand. Finally, with his students he took the tremendous step of having the Bible translated into English.

"Cristen men and wymmen, old and yonge, shulden studie fast in the Newe Testament, for it is of ful autorite, and opyn to undirstonding of simple men, as to the poyntis that be moost nedeful to salvacioun . . . ."

The spirit of early Christianity now revived the English countryside with a keen, refreshing breeze after the weariness of sultry days. But the new vision opened to rich and poor alike profoundly disturbed the decaying society to which it was vouchsafed. The powers of Church and State were soon to realise their danger.

The long reign had now reached its dusk. The glories of Crécy and Poitiers had faded. The warlike King, whose ruling passions were power and fame, who had been willing to barter prerogatives to obtain money for foreign adventure, was now in old age a debtor to time and fortune. He saw the wide conquests which his sword and his son had made in France melt like snow at Easter. A few coastal towns alone attested the splendour of victories long to be cherished in the memories of the island race. Queen Philippa, his loving wife, had died in 1369. Even before her death the old King had fallen under the consoling thrall of Alice Perrers, a lady of indifferent extraction, but of remarkable wit and capacity, untrammelled by scruple or by prudence. The spectacle of the famous King in his sixties, infatuated by an illicit love, jarred upon the touchy temper of the times. Here was something less romantic than the courtly love that had been symbolised in 1348 by the founding of the Order of the Garter. Nobles and people alike would not extend to the mistress of the King's old age the benefits of the commanding motto of the Order, *Honi soit qui mal y pense*.

The King, at length worn down by war, business, and pleasure, subsided into senility. He had reached the allotted span. The last decade of his reign was disparaging to his repute. Apart from Alice, he concentrated his remaining hopes upon the Black Prince; but this great soldier was also brought low by the fatigues of war, and was sinking fast in health. In 1376 the Prince expired, leaving a son not ten years old as heir apparent to the throne. Mortally stricken, Edward III retired to Sheen Lodge, where Alice encouraged him to dwell on tournaments, the chase, and wide plans when he should recover. But hostile chroniclers have it that when the stupor preceding death engulfed the King she took the rings from his fingers and other movable property and departed for some time to extreme privacy. We have not heard her tale, but all accounts, alas! confirm that King Edward died deserted by all, and that only the charity of a local priest procured him the protection and warrant of the Church in his final expedition.

The Black Prince's son was recognised as King by general assent on the very day his grandfather died, no question of election being raised, and the Crown of England passed to a minor.

CHAPTER 23

KING RICHARD II AND THE SOCIAL REVOLT

Richard II is shown in this portrait of about 1390 in regalia at Westminster Abbey. Many portraits of this scholarly, artistic king survive, and most share a recognisable resemblance.

JOHN OF GAUNT, DUKE OF LANCASTER, uncle of the King, was head of the Council of Regency and ruled the land, but it was the impact and the shadow of the Black Death that dominated the scene. The pang of almost mortal injury still throbbed, but with it crept a feeling that there was for the moment more room in the land. A multitude of vacant places had just been filled, and many men in all classes had the sense of unexpected promotion and enlargement about them.

The Black Death had struck a world already in movement. Ever since the Crown had introduced the custom of employing wage-earning soldiers instead of the feudal levy the landed tie had been dissolving. Why should not the noble or knight follow the example of his liege lord? Covenants in which a small landowner undertook to serve a powerful neighbour, "except against the King", became common. The restriction would not always be observed. The old bonds of mutual loyalty were disappearing.

In medieval England the lords of the manors had often based their prosperity on a serf peasantry, whose status and duties were enjoined by long custom and enforced by manorial courts. Around each manor a closely bound and self-sufficient community revolved. Although there had been movement of labour and interchange of goods in the thirteenth and early fourteenth centuries, development had been relatively slow and the break-up of the village community gradual. The time had now come when the compartments of society and toil could no longer preserve their structure. The convulsion of the Black Death violently accelerated this deep and rending process. Nearly one-third of the population being suddenly dead, smallholdings were deserted, and many manors were denuded of the peasantry who had served them from time immemorial. Ploughmen and labourers found themselves in high demand, and were competed for on all sides. They in their turn sought to better themselves, or at least to keep their living equal with the rising prices.

But their masters saw matters differently. They repulsed fiercely demands

The Malvern Hills in Worcestershire look much as they did in the fourteenth century when the writer, William Langland, fell asleep there and dreamt "The Vision of William concerning Piers the Plowman." The book which he subsequently wrote divided society into groups of "winners" and "wasters" and raised dangerous questions about social equality.

for increased wages; they revived ancient claims to forced or tied labour. The pedigrees of villagers were scrutinised with a care hitherto only bestowed upon persons of quality. In turn assertions of long-lapsed authority, however good in law, were violently resisted by the country folk. They formed unions of labourers to guard their interests. There were escapes of villeins from the estates, like those of the slaves from the southern states of America in the 1850s. Some landlords in their embarrassment offered to commute the labour services they claimed and to procure obedience by granting leases to smallholders.

The turmoil through which all England passed affected the daily life of the mass of the people in a manner not seen again in our social history till the Industrial Revolution of the nineteenth century. Here was a case in which a Parliament based upon property could have a decided opinion. The Statute of Labourers in 1351 was the first important attempt to fix wages and prices for the country as a whole. In the aggravated conditions following the pestilence Parliament sought to enforce these laws as fully as it dared. "Honorary justices of labour", drawn from the rural middle classes, were appointed to try offenders. Between 1351 and 1377 nine thousand cases of breach of contract were tried before the Common Pleas. In many parts the commissioners, who were active and biased, were attacked by the inhabitants. Unrest spread wide and deep.

One of the first illustrations to William Langland's "Piers Plowman" is of a fourteenth-century plough drawn by oxen. The latter seem unwilling workers: the ploughman's assistant has to goad them with a pointed stick.

The people were not without the means of protesting against injustice, nor without the voice to express their discontent. Among the lower clergy the clerks with small benefices had been severely smitten by the Black Death. In East Anglia alone eight hundred priests had died. The survivors found that their stipends remained unaltered in a world of rising prices, and that the higher clergy were completely indifferent to this problem of the ecclesiastical proletariat. At the fairs, on market day, preachers, especially among the friars, collected and stirred crowds.

Many vehement agitators, among whom John Ball is the best known, gave forth a stream of subversive doctrine. The country was full of broken soldiers, disbanded from the war, and all knew about the longbow and its power to kill nobles, however exalted and well armed. The preaching of revolutionary ideas was widespread, and a popular ballad expressed the response of the masses:

When Adam delved, and Eve span,
Who was then a gentleman?

This was a novel question for the fourteenth century, and awkward at any time. The rigid, time-enforced framework of medieval England trembled to its foundations.

All rolled forward to the terrifying rebellion of 1381. It was a social upheaval, spontaneous and widespread, arising in various parts of the country from the same causes, and united by the same sentiments. That all this movement was the direct consequence of the Black Death is proved by the fact that the revolt was most fierce in those very districts of Kent and the East Midlands where the death rate had been highest. It was a cry of pain and anger from a generation shaken out of submissiveness.

Throughout the summer of 1381 there was a general ferment. Beneath it all lay organisation. Agents moved round the villages, in touch with a "Great Society" which was said to meet in London. In May violence broke out in Essex. It was started by an attempt to make a second and more stringent

John Ball addressing a crowd outside the city walls of London, from a manuscript now in the British Museum.

collection of the poll tax which had been levied in the previous year. The turbulent elements in London took fire, and a band under one Thomas Faringdon marched off to join the rebels. Walworth, the mayor, faced a strong municipal opposition which was in sympathy and contact with the rising. In Kent, after an attack on Lesnes Abbey, the peasants marched through Rochester and Maidstone, burning manorial and taxation records on their way. At Maidstone they released the agitator John Ball from the episcopal prison, and were joined by a military adventurer with gifts and experience of leadership, Wat Tyler.

The King's Council was bewildered and inactive. Early in June the main body of rebels from Essex and Kent moved on London. Here they found support. For three days the city was in confusion. Two members of the King's Council, Simon Sudbury, the Archbishop of Canterbury and Chancellor, and Sir Robert Hales, the Treasurer, were dragged from the Tower and beheaded on Tower Hill; the Savoy palace of John of Gaunt was burnt; Lambeth and Southwark were sacked. But loyal citizens rallied round the mayor, and at Smithfield the young King faced the rebel leaders.

Among the insurgents there seems to have been a general loyalty to the sovereign. Their demands were reasonable but disconcerting. In particular they asserted that no man ought to be a serf or do labour services to a seigneur, but pay fourpence an acre a year for his land and not have to serve any man against his will. While the parley was going on Tyler was first wounded by Mayor Walworth and then smitten to death by one of the King's esquires. As the rebel leader rolled off his horse, dead in the sight of the great assembly, the King met the crisis by riding forward alone with the cry, "I will be your leader. You shall have from me all you seek. Only follow me to the fields outside." But the death of Tyler proved a signal for the wave of reaction. The leaderless bands wandered home and spread a vulgar lawlessness through their counties. They were pursued by reconstructed authority. Vengeance was wreaked.

The Great Gate to the Abbey of Bury St Edmunds gives an indication of the Abbey's wealth and size. The peasants of the rich grain and wool producing area of East Anglia had the strength and independence to question the authority of the manorial system. The Church was unpopular with the peasants because it demanded tithes, a tenth of their grain, while the lords of the manor exacted forced labour on their own lands.

The rising had spread throughout the southwest. There were riots in Bridgwater, Winchester, and Salisbury. In Hertfordshire the peasants rose against the powerful and hated Abbey of St Albans, and marched on London under Jack Straw. There was a general revolt in Cambridgeshire, accompanied by burning of rolls and attacks on episcopal manors. The Abbey of Ramsey, in Huntingdonshire, was attacked. In Norfolk and Suffolk, where the peasants were richer and more independent, the irritation against legal villeinage was stronger. The Abbey of Bury St Edmunds was a prominent object of hatred, and the Flemish woollen-craftsmen were murdered in Lynn. Waves of revolt rippled on as far north as Yorkshire and Cheshire, and to the west in Wiltshire and Somerset.

But after Tyler's death the resistance of the ruling classes was organised. Letters were sent out to the royal officials commanding the restoration of order, and justices gave swift judgment upon insurgents. The King, who accompanied Chief Justice Tresilian on the punitive circuit, pressed for the observance of legal forms in the punishment of rebels. The warlike Bishop, le Despenser, of Norwich, used armed force in the Eastern Counties in defence of Church property, and a veritable battle was fought at North Walsham. Nevertheless the reaction was, compared to modern examples, very restrained. Not more than a hundred and fifty executions are recorded in the rolls. In January 1382 a general amnesty, suggested by Parliament,

Container, known as a "pyx", for the wafers used in the Communion service. Wyclif's questioning of the teachings of the established Church led his followers to doubt the doctrine of transubstantiation — the belief that the bread and wine consumed during the Eucharist not only symbolised, but actually became, the body and blood of Christ. These doubts were very dangerous to the Church because they challenged its absolute authority and asserted the right of each individual to be guided by his or her own conscience.

was proclaimed. But the victory of property was won, and there followed the unanimous annulment of all concessions and a bold attempt to recreate intact the manorial system of the early part of the century.

Yet for generations the upper classes lived in fear of a popular rising and the labourers continued to combine. The legal aspect of serfdom became of little importance, and the development of commutation went on at an accelerated pace after 1349. Such were the more enduring legacies of the Black Death. The revolt, which to the historian is but a sudden flash of revealing light on medieval conditions among the poorer classes, struck with lasting awe the imagination of its contemporaries.

In the charged, sullen atmosphere of the England of the 1380s Wyclif's movement, or "Lollardy", as it came to be called, gathered wide momentum. But, faced by social revolution, English society was in no mood for Church reform. Wyclif's "poor preachers" bore the stigma of having fomented the troubles, and although Wyclif was not directly responsible the result was disastrous to his cause. The landed classes gave silent assent to the ultimate suppression of the preacher by the Church. Wyclif's old opponent, Courtenay, had become Archbishop after Sudbury's murder. He acted with speed. The doctrines of the reformer were officially condemned. The bishops were instructed to arrest all unlicensed preachers, and the Archbishop himself descended upon Oxford and held a convocation in the chapter house of what is now Christ Church. The chief Lollards were sharply summoned to recant. Hard censure fell upon Wyclif's followers. They blenched and bowed. Wyclif found himself alone. His attack on Church doctrine as distinct from Church privilege had lost him the support of Gaunt. His popular preachers and the beginnings of English Bible-reading could not build a solid party against the dominant social forces.

Yet Wyclif, who died in 1384, had stirred the conscience of his age. By his frontal attack on the Church's absolute authority over men in this world, by his implication of the supremacy of the individual conscience, and by his challenge to ecclesiastical dogma Wyclif had called down upon himself the thunderbolts of repression. But the cause, lost in his day, impelled the tide of the Reformation. Lollardy was driven beneath the surface. The Church, strengthening its temporal position by alliance with the State, brazenly repelled the first assault; but its spiritual authority bore henceforward the scars and enfeeblement resulting from the conflict.

The King was now growing up. His keen instincts and precocious abilities were sharpened by all that he had seen and done. In the crisis of the Peasants' Revolt, by his personal action he had saved the situation on a memorable occasion, and it was the King's Court and the royal judges who had restored order when the feudal class had lost their nerve. It was not till he was twenty that Richard determined to be complete master of his Council. By then John of Gaunt, Viceroy of Aquitaine, had quitted the realm to pursue abroad interests which included personal claims to the kingdom of Castile. Richard's Household and the Court around it were deeply interested in his assumption of power. Its chiefs were the Chancellor, Michael de la Pole, Chief Justice Tresilian, and Alexander Neville, Archbishop of York. Behind them Simon Burley, Richard's tutor and close intimate, was probably the guide. A group of younger nobles threw in their fortunes with the Court. Of these the head was Robert de Vere, Earl of Oxford, who now played a part resembling that of Gaveston under Edward II. The King, the fountain of honour, spread his favours among his adherents, and de Vere was soon created Duke of Ireland. This was plainly a political challenge to the magnates of the Council. Ireland was a reservoir of men and supplies, beyond the control of Parliament and the nobility, which could be used for the mastery of England.

The accumulation of Household and Government offices by the clique around the King and his effeminate favourite affronted the feudal party, and to some extent the national spirit. As so often happens, the opposition found in foreign affairs a vehicle of attack. Lack of money, fear of asking for it, and above all no military leadership, had led the Court to pacific courses. The nobility were at one with the Parliament in decrying the unmartial Chancellor and the hedonism of the Court. War must be waged with France; and on this theme in 1386 a coherent front was formed against the Crown. Parliament was led to appoint a commission of five ministers and nine lords, of whom the former Councillors of Regency were the chiefs. The Court bent before the storm of Pole's impeachment. A purge of the Civil Service, supposed to be the source alike of the King's errors and of his strength, was instituted; and we may note that Geoffrey Chaucer, his equerry, but famous for other reasons, lost his two posts in the Customs.

When the commissioners presently compelled the King to dismiss his personal friends Richard in deep distress sought to marshal his forces for civil war. Irish levies, Welsh pikemen, and above all Cheshire archers from his own earldom, were gathering to form an army. Upon this basis of force Tresilian and four other royal judges pronounced that the pressure put upon him by the Lords Appellant, as they were now styled, and the Parliament, was contrary to the laws and Constitution of England. This judgment, the legal soundness of which is undoubted, was followed by a bloody reprisal. The King's uncle, Gloucester, together with other heads of the baronial oligarchy, denounced the Chief Justice and those who had acted with him, including de Vere and the other royal advisers, as traitors to the realm. The lords of the Council were still able to command the support of Parliament. Moreover, they resorted to arms. Gloucester, with an armed power, neared

John of Gaunt sits at the right hand of his host, King John I of Portugal. The festivities were connected with the marriage of John of Gaunt's daughter to a Portuguese prince. The marriage was a sign of John of Gaunt's political importance, and the picture reveals a number of interesting features such as the use of drinking cups covered with lids to prevent the addition of poison.

London. Richard, arriving there first, was welcomed by the people. They displayed his red and white colours, and showed attachment to his person, but they were not prepared to fight the advancing baronial army. In Westminster Hall the three principal Lords Appellant, Gloucester, Arundel, and Warwick, with an escort outside of three hundred horsemen, bullied the King into submission.

De Vere escaped to Chester and raised an armed force to secure the royal rights. With this, in December 1387, he marched towards London. But now appeared in arms the Lords Appellant, and also Gaunt's son Henry. At Radcot Bridge, in Oxfordshire, Henry and they defeated and broke de Vere. The favourite fled overseas. The King was now at the mercy of the proud faction which had usurped the rights of the monarchy. They disputed long among themselves whether or not he should be deposed and killed. It was Henry, the young military victor, who pleaded for moderation, possibly because his father's claim to the throne would have been overridden by the substitution of Gloucester for Richard.

The Lords Appellant, as divided as they were, shrank from deposing and killing the King; but they drew the line at nothing else. They forced him to yield at every point. Cruel was the vengeance that they wreaked upon the upstart nobility of his circle and his legal adherents. Parliament was summoned to give countenance to the new regime. On the appointed day the five Lords Appellant, in golden clothes, entered Westminster Hall arm-in-arm. "The Merciless Parliament" opened its session, which, though it asserted the fact of feudal power, also proclaimed the principle of parliamentary control. The fact vanished in the turbulence of those days, but the principle echoed down into the seventeenth century.

Chief Justice Tresilian and four of the others who had promulgated at Nottingham the doctrine of Royal Supremacy were hanged, drawn, and quartered at Tyburn. The royal tutor, Burley, was not spared. Richard, forced not only to submit but to assent to the slaughter of his friends, buried himself as low as he could in retirement.

We must suppose that this treatment produced a marked impression upon his mind. It falls to the lot of few mortals to endure such ordeals. He brooded upon his wrongs, and also upon his past mistakes. He saw in the triumphant lords men who would be tyrants not only over the King but over the people. He laid his plans for revenge and for his own rights with far more craft than before. For a year there was a sinister lull.

On May 3, 1389, Richard took action which none of them had foreseen. Taking his seat at the Council, he asked blandly to be told how old he was. On being answered that he was three-and-twenty he declared that he had certainly come of age, and that he would no longer submit to restrictions upon his rights which none of his subjects would endure. He would manage the realm himself and choose his own advisers; he would be King indeed.

This stroke was immediately successful. The King's sympathisers, William of Wykeham and Thomas Brantingham, were restored to their posts as Chancellor and Treasurer. King's nominees were added to those of the Appellants on the judicial bench. Letters from the King to the sheriffs announced that he had assumed the government, and the news was accepted by the public with an unexpected measure of welcome.

Richard used his victory with prudence and mercy. In October 1389 John of Gaunt returned from Spain, and his son, Henry, now a leading personage,

The manuscript of the Roman de la Rose *was made in France in the late fifteenth century and is now in the Bodleian Library, Oxford. This illustration shows courtly love in an age of chivalry. Knights take leave of their maidens before riding to battle.*

was reconciled to the King. The terrible combination of 1388 had dissolved. The machinery of royal government, triumphant over faction, resumed its sway, and for the next eight years Richard governed England in the guise of a constitutional and popular King.

This was an age in which the masses were totally excluded from power, and when the ruling classes, including the new middle class, even in their most deadly quarrels, always united to keep them down. Richard has been judged and his record declared by the socially powerful elements which overthrew him; but their verdict upon his character can only be accepted under reserve. That he sought to subvert and annul the constitutional rights which the rivalries of factions and of Church and baronage had unconsciously but resolutely built up cannot be denied; but whether this was for purposes of personal satisfaction or in the hope of fulfilling the pledge which he had made in the crisis of the Peasants' Revolt, "I will be your leader," is a question not to be incontinently brushed aside. He had solemnly promised the abolition of serfdom. He had proposed it to Parliament. He had been overruled. He had a long memory for injuries and also for obligations.

The patience and skill with which Richard accomplished his revenge are most striking. For eight years he tolerated the presence of Arundel and Gloucester, not, as before, as the governors of the country, but still in high positions. Meanwhile he sought to strengthen himself by gathering Irish resources. In 1394 he went with all the formality of a Royal Progress to Ireland, and for this purpose created an army dependent upon himself, which was to be useful later in overawing opposition in England. When he returned his plans were far advanced. After the death of his first wife, Anne, he had married in 1396 the child Isabelle, daughter of Charles VI of France. Upon this a truce or pact of amity and non-aggression for thirty years was concluded with France. A secret clause laid down that if Richard were in future to be menaced by any of his subjects the King of France would come to his aid. The King gained immensely by his liberation from the obligation

CHAUCER'S ENGLAND

GEOFFREY CHAUCER, son of a wine merchant, was born in 1343 and died in 1400. He is now remembered for his poetry, but in his time he was a successful civil servant, diplomat and courtier. Chaucer wrote his poems in the "English tongue" which "all understanden" and, as a result, it is easy to recall today the spirit of his century. It was a troubled period. There was the Black Death and then, in 1381, the Peasants' Revolt culminated in a dramatic meeting between Richard II and the rebels. The revolt was crushed but serfdom was in decline and yeoman farmers were acquiring new wealth and influence.

At about the same time, the reformer, John Wyclif, was criticising the Established Church and monasticism, and was accused of preaching heresy.

In his *Canterbury Tales*, which present a canvas of a whole society, Chaucer includes the clergy. His portraits of Church officials provide a gallery of misfits and rogues, but true saintliness is found in his humble ploughman and village parson.

Pilgrimages were part of the medieval way of life. Some were linked to holy days, some to sacred places, and a pilgrimage to the shrine of Thomas Becket at Canterbury is the framework of Chaucer's tales. Pilgrimages could be cheerful, rewarding or hazardous, an opportunity for crime or an expression of religious devotion. Chaucer's pilgrims and the tales they tell form an introduction to English literature as we know it today.

One of the most striking figures among Chaucer's pilgrims is his knight: "That from the time that he first began To ride abroad, he loved chivalry, Truth and honour, freedom and courtesy."

In 1478, about a century after Chaucer wrote them, William Caxton, the first English printer, produced the *Canterbury Tales*. The introduction of printing was a landmark in the late medieval world. The diffusion of information which it brought about helped to lead people into a new age.

CHAUCER'S PILGRIMS ride from Canterbury to London, past a contemporary background of castles and churches. The picture above comes from John Lydgate's story, The Siege of Thebes, *presented in 1420 as a sequel to Chaucer's* Canterbury Tales.

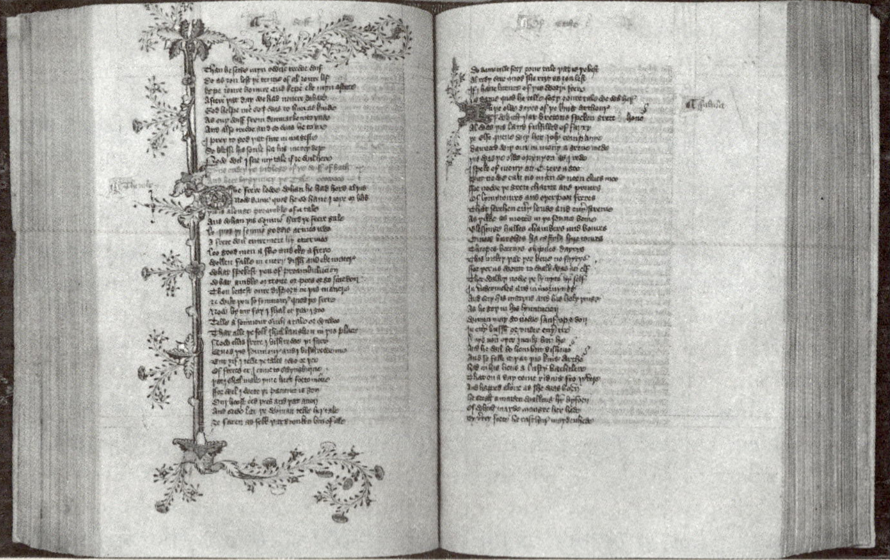

THE CANTERBURY TALES (above) in a manuscript dating from 1420, is now in the National Trust Egremont Collection at Petworth House. The copy originally belonged to the Percy family in Northumbria. These twenty-four tales completed by Chaucer before his death are his masterpiece: he had intended to make each of his twenty-nine "sondry folk" tell two stories on the outward journey, and two more to shorten the homeward stretch. In the book, the pilgrims hold a storytelling competition, organised by Harry Bailly, the forthright landlord of the Tabard Inn at Southwark, and the prize is to be a dinner at the losers' expense. Chaucer's patron was the scholarly Richard II, seen in the narrative painting of the Peasants' Revolt (right) by Froissart. King Richard is depicted twice, riding a richly caparisoned horse. On the left of the picture he witnesses the Lord Mayor of London's murder of the rebel leader Wat Tyler. On the right he addresses the armed labourers and offers to replace their dead hero by leading them himself.

FAT LITTLE CHAUCER *(above) admitted to having a paunch, loved his food and was a connoisseur of wine. From his boyhood, when he served as a page to Prince Lionel, he had been connected with the Court, and his wife Philippa was John of Gaunt's sister-in-law. No English poet is more appealing. His portraits of his oddly assorted collection of pilgrims are as alive today as they were over six centuries ago.*

THE SHRINE OF THOMAS BECKET *at Canterbury Cathedral (below) was sought by millions of pilgrims. December and July were the most popular months as they were the anniversaries of the saint's murder and canonisation, but Chaucer's pilgrims set off in spring and their journey is filled with its life and freshness. The Pilgrims' Way can still be traced from Winchester eastward along the high ridge of the North Downs. Rochester was an important overnight stop for pilgrims like Chaucer's who travelled from London.*

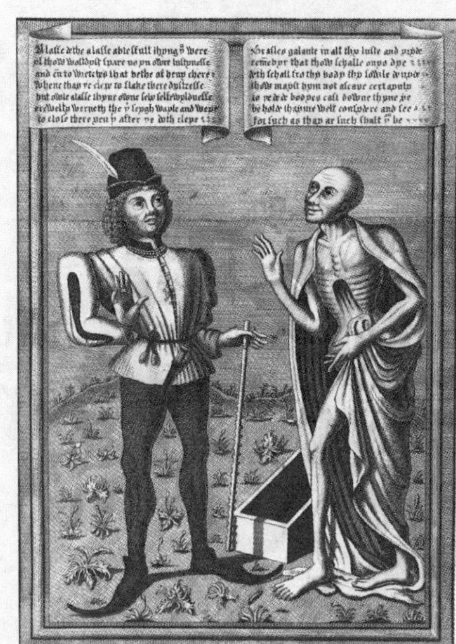

"DETHE AND THE GALANTE" *is the title of the sinister illustration shown above. Its subject is reminiscent of the brilliant story told by Chaucer's crafty Pardoner, a Church official who sold pardons to those gullible enough to believe that their sins would then be forgiven. In his Tale, three young rowdies seek to find and kill Death, who has robbed them of their companions in the years of pestilence. They meet an ancient robed figure who tells them where to find gold. In their anxiety to avoid sharing their fortune, each youth plots to kill his fellows. Inevitably, all find death.*

PRINTING WAS INVENTED IN EUROPE *in 1450: there had been printing earlier in China. William Caxton set up a printing press, like the one shown in the picture above, in 1476. Chaucer's works were written to be read aloud, and even today they still benefit from being heard, but when Caxton produced a printed edition he ensured a more lasting heritage.*

Anne of Bohemia on her deathbed. Richard II's popular queen died of the Plague at Sheen in 1394, after twelve years of marriage. Richard's grief at her death was overwhelming. He put off the funeral for more than two months, in order that the mourning ceremony might be as magnificent as possible.

of making a war, which he could only sustain by becoming the beggar and drudge of Parliament. So hard had Parliament pressed the royal power, that we have the unique spectacle of a Plantagenet king lying down and refusing to pull the waggon farther over such stony roads. But this did not spring from lack of mental courage or from narrowness of outlook. It was a necessary feature in the King's far-reaching designs.

The Irish expedition had been the first stage towards the establishment of a despotism; the alliance with France was the second. The King next devoted himself to the construction of a compact, efficient Court party. Both Gaunt and his son and Mowbray, Earl of Norfolk, one of the former Appellants, were now rallied to his side, partly in loyalty to him and partly in hostility to Arundel and Gloucester. New men were brought into the Household. Sir John Bushy and Sir Henry Greene represented the Parliamentary class, the inevitable arbiter of the feuds between Crown and aristocracy. In January 1397 Parliament was summoned to Westminster, where under deft and at the same time resolute management it showed all due submission. Thus assured, Richard decided at last to strike.

Arundel and Gloucester, though now somewhat in the shade, must have considered themselves protected by time from the consequences of what they had done in 1388. Chief Justice Tresilian, the tutor Burley, and other victims of that bloodbath seemed distant memories. It was with amazement that they saw the King advancing upon them in cold hatred rarely surpassed among men. Arundel and some others of his associates were declared traitors and accorded only the courtesy of decapitation. Warwick was exiled to the Isle of Man. Gloucester, arrested and taken to Calais, was there murdered by Richard's agents; and this deed, not being covered by constitutional forms, bred in its turn new retributions. A stigma rested henceforward on the King similar to that which had marked John after the murder of Arthur. But for the moment he was supreme as no King of all England had been before, and still his wrath was unassuaged.

Parliament was called only to legalise these events. It was found that there was nothing it would not do for the King. Never has there been such a Parliament. With ardour pushed to suicidal lengths, it suspended almost

THE MEDIEVAL TOWN

In his book, Makers of the Realm, *Sir Arthur Bryant presents this fascinating picture of life in a medieval town.*

The first sight the traveller had of a medieval town was its towers and spires on the horizon, with, perhaps, a castle on higher ground. Boundary stones beside the highroad marked the beginning of its land — the arable strips of the "town field" with hired labourers working on them, and the great meadow along the river where the cattle grazed under the gaze of cowherds. Entry was through a stone archway and a vast wooden gate, closed from sundown to sunrise by a porter who collected the corporation's tolls. The streets were narrow and winding, with upper storeys overhanging the cobbled roadways till they almost touched. From them gilded signs swung and creaked in the wind, while apprentices bawled out the wares set out on the benches before the open doors. Through these could be seen journeymen working at their trade. The shouting was terrific, the hoofs and iron-rimmed wheels on the cobblestones made a perpetual hammering, and the bells of the churches and monasteries kept pealing and chiming. The stink, too, was overwhelming, especially in the streets occupied by tanners and butchers. For mutual protection and cooperation all the bakers and cookshops tended to be in one street, the mercers in another, the goldsmiths, shoemakers or saddlers in another. Leading out of them were narrow alleys giving on to stables and laystalls and the fetid, tumbledown hovels of the poorer artisans and labourers.

In the centre of the town were the fine stone houses of the richer citizens, the guildhall with its belfry-tower, and the market place — a square or broad street, like modern Oxford's Cornmarket, with a cross where the town crier made public announcements with bell or horn. Here, too, were the stocks, where offenders were pelted with filth and rotten fruit, and the ducking stool for scandalmongers. On market days the surrounding countryside poured in to sell its produce, doubling the population for a few noisy hours and filling the cookhouses and taverns.

every constitutional right and privilege gained in the preceding century. It raised the monarchy upon a foundation more absolute than even William the Conqueror had claimed. All that had been won by the nation through the crimes of John and the degeneracy of Edward II, all that had been conceded or established by the two great Edwards, was relinquished. And the Parliament, having done its work with this destructive thoroughness, ended by consigning its unfinished business to the care of a committee of eighteen persons. As soon as Parliament had dispersed Richard had the record altered by inserting words that greatly enlarged the scope of the committee's work. If his object was not to do away with Parliament, it was at least to reduce it to the role it had played in the days of Edward I.

This detail of a white hart, from the right-hand back panel of the Wilton Diptych in the National Gallery, was adopted by Richard as his own personal symbol or badge. The sensitive drawing seems highly appropriate to this doomed, artistic king.

The relations between Richard and Gaunt's son, Henry, the King's cousin and contemporary, now passed through drama into tragedy. Henry believed himself to have saved the King from being deposed and murdered in the crisis of 1388. Very likely this was true. Since then he had dwelt in familiarity and friendship with Richard. These two young men had lived their lives in fair comradeship; the one was King, the other, as son of John of Gaunt, stood near the throne and nearer to the succession.

A quarrel arose between Henry and Thomas Mowbray, now Duke of Norfolk. Henry accused Mowbray of treasonable language. Conflicting reports of what had been said were laid before Parliament. Each, when challenged, gave the lie to the other. Trial by battle appeared the correct solution. The famous scene took place in September 1398. The lists were drawn; but the King, exasperating the spectators of all classes who had gathered in high expectation to see the sport, forbade the combat, and exiled Mowbray for life and Henry for a decade. Both lords obeyed the royal commands. Mowbray soon died; but Henry, astounded by what he deemed ingratitude and injustice, lived and schemed in France.

The year which followed was an unveiled despotism, and Richard, so patient till his vengeance was accomplished, showed restlessness and perplexity, profusion and inconsequence, in his function. He sped about the kingdom beguiling the weeks with feasts and tournaments, while the administration was left to minor officials at Westminster. Financial stringency followed royal extravagance, and forced loans and heavier taxes angered the merchants and country gentry.

During 1398 there were many in the nation who awoke to the fact that a servile Parliament had in a few weeks suspended many of the fundamental rights and liberties of the realm. For some time they had had no quarrel with the King. They now saw him revealed as a despot. Not only the old nobility, who in the former crisis had been defeated, but all the gentry and merchant classes were aghast at the triumph of absolute rule. Nor did their wrath arise from love of constitutional practices alone. They feared, perhaps with many reasons not known to us, that the King, now master, would rule over their heads, resting himself upon the submissive shoulders of the mass of the people. They felt again the terror of the social revolution which they had tasted so recently in the Peasants' Revolt. A solid amalgamation of interest, temper, and action united all the classes which had raised or found themselves above the common level. Here was a king, now absolute, who would, as they muttered, let loose the mob upon them.

In February of 1399 died old John of Gaunt, "time-honoured Lancaster". Henry, in exile, succeeded to vast domains, not only in Lancashire and the

Henry IV receives the Dukes of Exeter and Surrey at Chester. This French manuscript from the early fifteenth century shows Henry, the figure wearing the Russian-style hat, to have been a physically commanding presence.

north but scattered all over England. Richard, pressed for money, declared his cousin disinherited. This challenged the position of every property-holder. And forthwith, by a fatal misjudgment of his strength and of what was stirring in the land, the King set out in May upon a punitive expedition to assert the royal authority in Ireland. He left behind him a disordered administration, deprived of troops, and a land violently incensed against him. News of the King's departure was carried to Henry. The moment had come; the coast was clear, and the man did not tarry. In July, Henry of Lancaster, as he had now become, landed in Yorkshire, declaring that he had only come to claim his lawful rights as heir to his venerated father. He was immediately surrounded by adherents, particularly from the Lancaster estates, and the all-powerful northern lords, led by the Earl of Northumberland. From York Henry marched across England, amid general acclamation, to Bristol, and just as Isabella had hanged Hugh Despenser upon its battlements, so now did Henry of Lancaster exact the capital forfeit from William Scrope, Earl of Wiltshire, Bushy, and Greene, King Richard's ministers and representatives.

It took some time for the news to reach King Richard in the depths of Ireland. He hastened back, though baffled by stormy seas. Having landed in England on July 27, he made a rapid three weeks' march through North Wales in an attempt to gather forces. What he saw convinced him that all was over. The whole structure of his power, so patiently and subtly built up, had vanished as if by enchantment. The Welsh, who would have stood by him, could not face the advancing power of what was now all England. At Flint Castle he submitted to Henry, into whose hands the whole administration had now passed. He rode through London as a captive; he was lodged in the Tower. His abdication was extorted; his death had become inevitable. The last of all English kings whose hereditary right was indisputable disappeared forever beneath the portcullis of Pontefract Castle. Henry, by and with the consent of Parliament and the Lords Spiritual and Temporal, ascended the throne as Henry IV, and thereby opened a chapter of history destined to be fatal to the medieval baronage.

The character of Richard II and his place in the regard of history remain an enigma. The injuries and cruelties which he suffered at the hands of his uncle Gloucester and the high nobility may perhaps be the key to understanding him. Some historians have felt that he was prepared not only to exploit parliamentary and legal manoeuvres against the governing classes, but perhaps even that he would use social forces then and for many generations utterly submerged. At any rate, the people for their part, long cherished some such notion of him. These unhappy folk, already to be numbered by the million, looked to Richard with hopes destined to be frustrated for centuries. All through the reign of Henry IV the conception they had formed of Richard was idealised. He was deemed, whether rightly or wrongly, a martyr to the cause of the weak and poor. Statutes were passed declaring it high treason even to spread the rumour that he was still alive.

We have no right in this modern age to rob him of this shaft of sunlight which rests upon his harassed, hunted life. There is however no dispute that in his nature fantastic error and true instinct succeeded each other with baffling rapidity. He was capable of more than human cunning and patience, and also of foolishness. He fought four deadly duels with feudal aristocratic society. In 1398 he was supreme; in 1399 he was destroyed.

CHAPTER 24

THE USURPATION OF HENRY BOLINGBROKE

All power and authority fell to King Henry IV, and all who had run risks to place him on the throne combined to secure his right, and their own lives. But the opposite theme endured with strange persistency. His right in blood was not valid while Richard lived, nor even afterwards when lineage was scrutinised. But other rights existed. The right of conquest, on which he was inclined to base himself, was discarded by him upon good advice. But the fact that he was acclaimed by the Parliament summoned in Richard's name, added to a near right by birth, afforded a broad though challenged foundation for his reign.

All historians concur that he was manly, capable, and naturally merciful. He who had benefited most from the violent spasm and twist of fortune which had overthrown Richard was the least vindictive against Richard's adherents. He had been wronged and ill-used; yet he showed a strong repugnance to harsh reprisals. In the hour of his accession he was still the bold knight, surprisingly moderate in success, averse from bloodshed, affianced to growing constitutional ideas, and always dreaming of ending his life as a Crusader. But the sullen, turbulent march of events frustrated his tolerant inclinations and eventually soured his generous nature.

Henry IV's face, in effigy at Canterbury Cathedral, shows something of the strength and determination of his father, John of Gaunt. Shakespeare represents him as perpetually anxious to retain his barons' allegiance, and as a nagging father to his fun-loving son.

From the outset Henry depended upon Parliament to make good by its weight the defects in his title, and rested on the theory of the elective, limited kingship rather than on that of absolute monarchy. He was therefore alike by mood and need a constitutional king. Here we see a memorable advance in practice.

Parliament itself must not however be deemed a fountain of wisdom and virtue. It could be packed or swayed. "The Made Parliament", and "the Merciless Parliament", were fresh in memory. Moreover, the Commons, while acting with vigour, preferred to base themselves upon petition rather than resolution, thus throwing the responsibility definitely upon the most exalted ruling class. Significantly they appealed to the King not to judge of any matter from their debates or from the part taken in them by various Members, but rather to await the collective decision of the House. However, they strongly pressed the doctrine of "grievances before supply", and although Henry refused to accept this claim he was kept so short of money that in practice it was largely conceded. During this time therefore parliamentary power over finance was greatly strengthened. Not only did it supply the money by voting the taxes, but it began to follow its expenditure, and to require and to receive accounts from the high officers of the State. Nothing like this had been tolerated by any of the kings before. These great advances in the polity of England were the characteristics of Lancastrian rule, and followed naturally from the need the House of Lancaster had to buttress its title by public opinion and constitutional authority. Thus Parliament in this early epoch appears to have gained ground never held again till the seventeenth century.

But although the spiritual and lay Estates had seemed to choose the sovereign, and the history of these years furnished precedents which lawyers

The word "Lollard" meant "Babbler", one who muttered prayers. People who challenged accepted beliefs were seen as a threat to property and the established order. In fact, the Lollards, followers of Wyclif, were forerunners of the Protestants who insisted on the importance of the individual conscience. This picture records the execution of the Lollard leader, Sir John Oldcastle, who was burnt to death after being dragged through the streets on a hurdle.

of the Stuart period carefully studied, the actual power of Parliament at this time must not be overstated. The usurpation of Henry IV, was an act of feudal violence and rebellion, covered up by declaratory statutes. Parliament was not the author, but only the apprehensive registrar of the results of both martial and baronial struggles. It had nonetheless been declared upon parliamentary authority, although at Henry's insistance, that the Crown should pass to the King's eldest son, and to his male issue after him. Thus what had been the English usage was overridden by excluding an elder line, the Mortimers, dependent on a female link.

On one issue indeed, half social, half religious, King and Parliament were heartily agreed. The Lollards' advocacy of a Church purified by being relieved of all wordly goods did not command the assent of the clergy. They resisted with wrath and vigour. Lollardy was in essence a challenge first to the Church and then to the wealthy. The lords saw that their own estates stood on no better title than those of the Church. They joined with the clergy in defence of their property. Very severe laws were now enacted against the Lollards. The King declared, in full agreement with Parliament, that he would destroy heresies with all his strength, and in 1401 a terrible statute, *De Heretico Comburendo*, condemned relapsed heretics to be burnt alive. Thus did orthodoxy and property make common cause.

But the Estates of the Realm considered that their chief immediate safeguard lay in the blotting out of the eclipsed faction. The slowness of communication had enabled one set of forces to sweep the country while the opposite had hardly realised what was happening. Now they in their turn began to move. Five of the six former Lords Appellant, finding themselves in the shade, formed with friends of Richard II a plot to seize the usurping prince at Windsor. Henry evaded their trap, and the conspiracy received no genuine support. All the mercy of Henry's temper could not moderate the prosecution now enforced by those who shared his risks. Indeed in a year his popularity was almost destroyed by what was held to be his weakness in dealing with rebellion and attempted murder. Yet we must understand that he was a braver, stronger man than these cruel personages below him.

The unsuccessful revolt was fatal to the former King. A sanctity dwelt about his person, and all the ceremonial and constitutional procedure which enthroned his successor could not rob him of it. This chafed and gnawed the party in power. Richard's death was announced in February 1400. Whether, as the Government suggested, he went on hunger strike, or whether more direct methods were used, is unknowable. The walls of Pontefract have kept their secret. But far and wide throughout England spread the tale that he had escaped, and that in concealment he awaited his hour to bring the common people of the time to the enjoyment of their own.

All this welled up against Henry Bolingbroke. He faced continual murder plots. In Wales, Owen Glendower, who was a remarkable man, of considerable education, carried on a war which was the constant background of English affairs till 1409. The King was also forced to fight continually against the Scots. After six years of harassment we are told that his natural magnanimity was worn out, and that he yielded himself to the temper of his supporters and of his Parliament in cruel deeds. It may well be so.

His most serious conflict was with the Percys. These lords of the Northern Marches, the old Earl of Northumberland and his fiery son Hotspur, had for nearly three years carried on the defence of England against the Scots almost entirely at their own expense. They could no longer bear the burden. The Earl presented a bill for £60,000. The King, in bitter poverty, could offer but £40,000. Behind this was a longer tale. The Percys had played a great part in placing Henry on the throne. But Edmund Mortimer, Hotspur's brother-in-law, had joined Glendower in rebellion, and the family were now under suspicion. They held a great independent power, and an antagonism was perhaps inevitable. Hotspur raised the standard of revolt. But at Shrewsbury on July 21, 1403, Henry overcame and slew him in a small, fierce battle. The old Earl, who was marching to his son's aid, was forced to submit, and pardon was freely extended to him. This clemency was no doubt due to the lack of any other means of defending the Border against the Scots.

Two years later, with his son's death at heart, Northumberland rebelled again, and this time the conspiracy was far-reaching. Archbishop Scrope of York and Thomas Mowbray, Earl of Nottingham, were his principal confederates. The programme of the rebellion was reform, and all personal issues were avoided. Once again Henry marched north, and once again he was successful. Northumberland was driven across the Border. Scrope and Mowbray fell into the hands of the King's officers, and Henry, in spite of the appeals of the Archbishop of Canterbury, allowed them to be beheaded after a summary trial. Scrope's execution caused a profound shock throughout the land, and many compared it with the murder of Thomas Becket. At the same time the King's health failed. He was said to be smitten with leprosy, and this was attributed to the wrath of God. The diagnosis at least was incorrect, but he was physically a broken man. Henceforward his reign was a struggle against death as well as life.

The Battle of Shrewsbury, depicted in a manuscript dating from 1480, owned by the Earl of Warwick. The Percy family had gained much experience in fighting the Scots; Henry IV's inability to pay them turned their skills against him. The leaders of the two sides had formerly been allies in the events which brought Henry to the throne four years earlier. This picture portrays the death of Hotspur, the young Percy heir, as he is contemptuously cut off in his prime by the future King Henry V.

Harlech Castle as it exists today. This mighty thirteenth-century stronghold was captured by the Welsh leader, Owen Glendower, in 1401. Years later the castle was used as a refuge by the warlike queen of Henry VI, Margaret of Anjou, and her young son, Edward.

He still managed to triumph in the Welsh war, and Owen Glendower was forced back into his mountains. But Parliament took all advantages from the King's necessities. He yielded himself and his burdens with the constitutional deference of a modern sovereign. They pressed him hard, and in all the ways most intimately galling. Foreigners were to be expelled. A Council must be nominated by the King which included the parliamentary leaders. The accounts of Government expenses were subject to a parlimentary audit. The King's own Household was combed and remodelled by unfriendly hands. The new Council demanded even fuller powers. The King pledged himself to govern only by their advice. By these submissions Henry became the least of kings. But he had transferred an intolerable task to others. They had the odium and the toil. They were increasingly unworthy of the trust.

A new figure now came upon the scene. Henry's eldest son, the Prince of Wales, showed already an extraordinary force and quality. He had led the charge against Hotspur at Shrewsbury. He had gained successes in Wales. As his father's health declined he was everywhere drawn into State business. Pressed by his adherents to take over the Government from the failing hands of an invalid, he demanded that the King should abdicate in his favour. Henry Bolingbroke, though tottering, repulsed the proposal with violent indignation. There was a stern confrontation of father and son at Westminster in 1411. The King's partisans appeared to be the more numerous or more resolute. The Prince withdrew abashed. There can be no doubt that the dying sovereign still gripped convulsively the reins of power. Misgovernment and decrepitude remained for a while successfully enthroned. In 1412, when the King could no longer walk and scarcely ride, he was with difficulty dissuaded by his Council from attempting to command the troops in Aquitaine. He lingered through the winter, talked of a Crusade. In March 1413, when praying in Westminster Abbey, he had a prolonged fit, from which he rallied only to die in the Jerusalem Chamber.

Thus the life and reign of King Henry IV exhibit to us another instance of the vanities of ambition and the harsh guerdon which rewards its success. He had had wrongs to avenge and a cause to champion. He hardly dared at first to aim at the Crown, but he had played the final stake to gain it. He had found it less pleasing when possessed. Not only physically but morally he sank under its weight. But none can say he had not reason and justice behind his actions, or that he was not accepted by the country at large.

CHAPTER 25

THE EMPIRE OF HENRY V

A GLEAM OF SPLENDOUR now falls across the dark, troubled story of medieval England. Henry V was King at twenty-five. He felt, as his father had never done, sure of his title. The romantic stories of his riotous youth and sudden conversion to gravity and virtue must not be pressed too far. If he had thus yielded to the vehement ebullitions of his nature this was no more than a pastime, for always since boyhood he had been held in the grasp of grave business.

In the surging realm, with its ailing King, all men had for some time looked to him; and succeeding generations have seldom doubted that according to the standards of his day he was all that a king should be. His face, we are told, was oval, with a long, straight nose, ruddy complexion, dark, smooth hair, bright eyes, mild as a dove's when unprovoked, but lion-like in wrath; his frame was slender, yet well-knit, strong, and active. His disposition was orthodox, chivalrous, and just. He came to the throne at a moment when England was wearied of feuds and brawls and yearned for unity and foreign conquest. As was even then usual, Parliament wrapped this up in phrases of opposite import. Bishop Beaufort opened the session of 1414 with a sermon upon "Strive for the truth unto death" and the exhortation "While we have time, let us do good to all men." This was understood to mean the speedy invasion of France.

An unknown artist depicted Henry V in the latest fashions of the fifteenth century: hair shaved from the neck and above the ears to form a neat cap, a fur-trimmed robe, and rings and chain of office to indicate wealth and power. The young king died seven years after his famous victory at Agincourt. The portrait can now be seen in the National Portrait Gallery, London.

The Commons were thereupon liberal with supply. The King on his part declared that no law should be passed without their assent. A wave of reconciliation swept the land. The King declared a general pardon. He negotiated with the Scots for the release of Hotspur's son, and reinstated him in the Earldom of Northumberland. He brought the body, or reputed body, of Richard II to London, and reinterred it in Westminster Abbey, with pageantry and solemn ceremonial. A plot formed against him on the eve of his setting out for the wars was suppressed, by all appearance with ease and national approval, and with only a handful of executions. In particular he spared his cousin, the young Edmund Mortimer, Earl of March, who had been named as the rival king, and through whose family much that was merciless was to follow later.

At Henry V's accession the Orleanists had gained the decisive power at the Court of the witless French King, Charles VI, and unfurled the oriflamme against the Duke of Burgundy. The Burgundians, in their distress, were prepared to acknowledge Henry as King of France. When he led the power of England across the Channel he could therefore count upon the support of a large part of what is now the French people.

During the whole of 1414 Henry V was absorbed in warlike preparations by land and sea. He reorganised the fleet. Instead of mainly taking over and arming private ships, as was the custom, he, like Alfred, built many vessels for the Royal Navy. He had at least six "great ships", with about fifteen hundred smaller consorts. The expeditionary army was picked and trained with special care; six thousand archers, of whom half were mounted infantry, were the bulk and staple of the army, together with two thousand five hundred noble, knightly, or otherwise substantial warriors in armour, each with his two or three attendants and aides.

On August 11, 1415, the English army landed without opposition at the mouth of the Seine. Harfleur was besieged and taken by the middle of September. The King was foremost in prowess:

"Once more unto the breach, dear friends, once more;
Or close the wall up with our English dead."

However, the attrition of the siege, and disease, which levied its unceasing toll on these medieval camps, had already wrought havoc in the English expedition. The main power of France was now in the field. The Council of War, on October 5, advised returning home by sea.

Henry V reorganised the navy as part of his meticulous preparations for war in France. This manuscript illustration shows a ship of about 1415, the date of the Battle of Agincourt.

But the King, leaving a garrison in Harfleur, and sending home several thousand sick and wounded, resolved, with about a thousand knights and men-at-arms and four thousand archers, to traverse the French coast in a hundred-mile march to his fortress at Calais, where his ships were to await

The cannon was invented in the fourteenth century and used in siege warfare in the fifteenth, when this French manuscript was made. The archers shooting from the turrets seem to be obvious targets: the slit-like window openings offered more protection, but longbows were unwieldy to shoot from them.

him. All the circumstances of this decision show that his design was to tempt the enemy to battle. This was not denied him. He crossed the Somme at Béthencourt. On October 20 he camped near Péronne. He was now deeply plunged into France. With the grim courtesies of chivalric war, the French heralds came to the English camp and inquired, for mutual convenience, by which route His Majesty would desire to proceed. "Our path lies straight to Calais," was Henry's answer. This was not telling them much, for he had no other choice. He must cut his way through the French army, perish, or surrender. When one of his officers, Sir Walter Hungerford, deplored the fact "that they had not but one ten thousand of those men in England that do no work today", the King rebuked him and revived his spirits in a speech to which Shakespeare has given an immortal form:

"If we are marked to die, we are enough
To do our country loss; and if to live,
The fewer men, the greater share of honour."

"Wot you not," he actually said, "that the Lord with these few can overthrow the pride of the French?" He and the few lay for the night at the village of Maisoncelles, maintaining utter silence and the strictest discipline. The French headquarters were at Agincourt, and it is said that they kept high revel and diced for the captives they should take.

The English victory of Crécy was gained against great odds upon the defensive. Poitiers was a counterstroke. Agincourt was a vehement assault. The French, whose numbers have been estimated at about twenty thousand, were drawn up in three lines of battle, of which a proportion remained mounted. With justifiable confidence they awaited the attack of less than a third their number. Mounted upon a small grey horse, with a richly jewelled crown upon his helmet, and wearing his royal surcoat of leopards and lilies, the King drew up his array. The archers were disposed in six wedge-shaped formations, each supported by a body of men-at-arms. At the last moment Henry sought to avoid so desperate a battle. Heralds passed to and fro. He offered to yield Harfleur and all his prisoners in return for an open road to Calais. The French prince replied that he must renounce the Crown of France. On this he resolved to dare the last extremity. The whole English army, even the King himself, dismounted and sent their horses to the rear; and shortly after eleven o'clock on St Crispin's Day, October 25, he gave the order, "In the name of Almighty God and of Saint George, Avaunt Banner in the best time of the year, and Saint George this day be thine help." The archers kissed the soil in reconciliation to God, and, crying loudly, "Hurrah! Hurrah! Saint George and Merrie England!" advanced to within three hundred yards of the heavy masses in their front. They planted their stakes and loosed their arrows.

The French were once again unduly crowded upon the field. Neither their crossbowmen nor their cannon could fire effectively. Under the arrow storm they in their turn moved forward down the slope, plodding heavily through a ploughed field already trampled into a quagmire. Still at thirty deep they felt sure of breaking the line. But once again the longbow destroyed all before it. Horse and foot alike went down; a long heap of armoured dead and wounded lay upon the ground, over which the reinforcements struggled bravely, but in vain. In this grand moment the archers slung their bows, and, sword in hand, fell upon the reeling squadrons and disordered masses. Then the Duke of Alençon rolled forward with the whole second line, and a stubborn hand-to-hand struggle ensued, in which the French prince struck down with his own sword Humphrey of Gloucester. The King rushed to his brother's rescue, and was smitten to the ground by a tremendous stroke; but in spite of the odds Alençon was killed, and the French second line was beaten hand-to-hand by the English chivalry and yeomen leaving large numbers of prisoners in the assailants' hands.

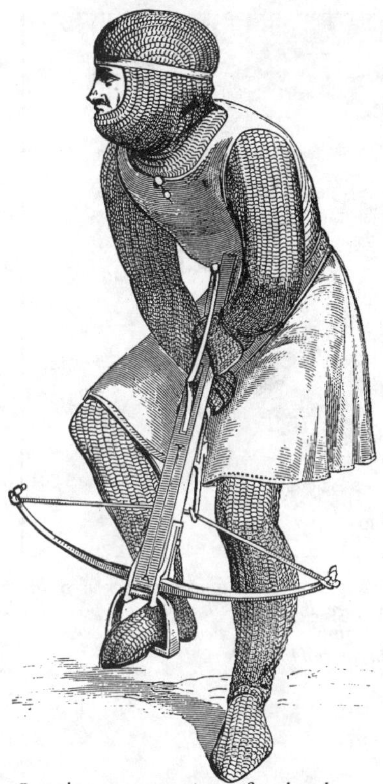

Crossbows were easier to fire than longbows from arrow slits, but precious seconds were lost in rewinding them before each subsequent firing.

At this moment the French camp-followers, who had wandered round the English rear, broke pillaging into the camp and stole the King's crown, wardrobe, and Great Seal. The King, believing himself attacked from behind, issued the dread order to slaughter the prisoners. Then perished the flower of the French nobility, many of whom had yielded themselves to easy hopes of ransom. The desperate character of this act, and of the moment, supplies what defence can be found for its ferocity. It was not in fact a necessary recourse. The French third line quitted the field without attempting to renew the battle in any serious manner. Henry now saw his path to Calais clear before him. But far more than that: he had trodden underfoot at once the corpses of the slain and the willpower of the French monarchy, by a feat of arms which, however it may be tested, must be held unsurpassed.

The victory of Agincourt made Henry the supreme figure in Europe, and when in 1416 the Holy Roman Emperor, Sigismund, visited London in an effort to effect a peace, he recognised Henry as King of France. But there followed long, costly campaigns and sieges which outran the financial resources of the island and gradually cooled its martial ardour. A much larger expedition crossed the Channel in 1417. After a hard, long siege Caen was taken; and one by one every French stronghold in Normandy was reduced in successive years. After hideous massacres in Paris, led by the Burgundians, Orleanist France was utterly defeated, not only in battle, but in the war. In May 1420, by the Treaty of Troyes, Charles VI recognised Henry as heir to the French kingdom upon his death and as Regent during his life. The English King undertook to govern with the aid of a council of Frenchmen, and to preserve all ancient customs. He was accorded the title "King of England and Heir of France". To implement and consolidate these triumphs he married Charles's daughter Catherine, a comely princess, who bore him a son long to reign over impending English miseries.

This was the boldest bid the English ever made in Europe. Henry V was no feudal sovereign of the old type with a class interest which overrode social

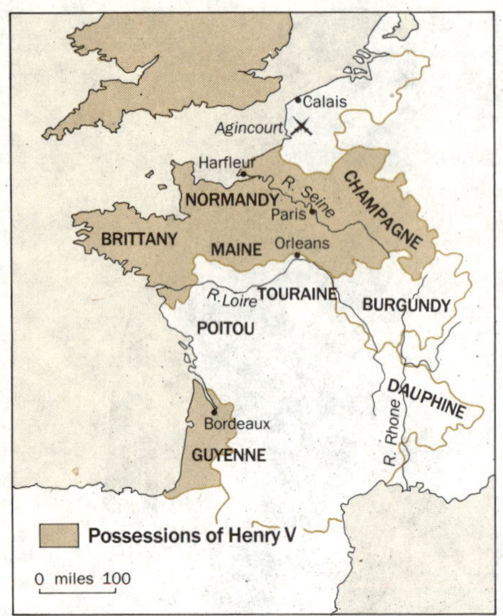

Henry V's victory at Agincourt increased his French empire and made him the most powerful European monarch. However, his possessions proved impossible to hold.

and territorial barriers. He was entirely national in his outlook: he was the first king to use the English language in his letters and his messages home from the front; his triumphs were gained by English troops; his policy was sustained by a Parliament that could claim to speak for the English people. For it was the union of the country gentry and the rising middle class of the towns, working with the Common Lawyers, that gave the English Parliament thus early a character and a destiny that the States-General of France and the Cortes of Castile were not to know. Henry stood, and with him his country, at the summit of the world.

He was himself endowed with the highest attributes of manhood. Ruthless he could be on occasion, but the chroniclers prefer to speak of his generosity and of how he made it a rule of his life to treat all men with consideration. He disdained in State business evasive answers. "It is impossible" or "It shall be done" were the characteristic decisions which he gave. He was more deeply loved by his subjects of all classes than any king has been in England. Under him the English armies gained an ascendancy which for centuries was never to be seen again.

But glory was, as always, dearly bought. The imposing Empire of Henry V was hollow and false. Where Henry II had failed his successor could not win. When Henry V revived the English claims to France he opened the greatest tragedy in our medieval history. Agincourt was a glittering victory, but the wasteful and useless campaigns that followed more than outweighed its military and moral value, and the miserable, destroying century that ensued casts its black shadow upon Henry's heroic triumph.

And there is also a sad underside to the brilliant life of England in these years. If Henry V united the nation against France he set it also upon the Lollards. We can see that the Lollards were regarded not only as heretics, but as what we should now call Christian Communists. They had secured as their leader Sir John Oldcastle, a warrior of renown. They threatened nothing less than a revolution in faith and property. Upon them all domestic hatreds were turned by a devout and credulous age. It seemed frightful beyond words that they should declare that the Host lifted in the Mass was a dead thing, "less than a toad or a spider". Nor did the constancy of these

TAKING A BATH

Bathing was not always a simple matter of turning on the taps. Here are the details given by Edith Rickert in 1460.

If your lord wishes to bathe and wash his body clean, hang sheets round the roof, every one full of flowers and sweet green herbs, and have five or six sponges to sit or lean upon, and see that you have one big sponge to sit upon, and a sheet over so that he may bathe there for a while, and have a sponge also for under his feet, if there be any to spare, and always be careful that the door is shut. Have a basin full of hot fresh herbs and wash his body with a soft sponge, rinse him with fair rosewater, and throw it over him; then let him go to bed; but see that the bed be sweet and nice; and first put on his socks and slippers that he may go near the fire and stand on his foot-sheet, wipe him dry with a clean cloth, and take him to bed to cure his troubles.

A stained glass window from Brandiston Hall in Norfolk.

The Making of a Medicinable Bath

Boil together hollyhock, mallow, wall pellitory and brown fennel, danewort, St John's wort, centaury, ribwort and camomile, heyhove, heyriff, herb-benet, bresewort, smallage, water speedwell, scabious, bugloss, and wild flax which is good for aches — boil withy leaves and green oates together with them, and throw them hot into a vessel and put your lord over it and let him endure it for a while as hot as he can, being covered over and closed on every side; and whatever disease, grievance or pain ye be vexed with, this medicine shall surely make you whole, as men say.

martyrs to their convictions, or their strange, horrible executions allay the public rage. Oldcastle himself after a feeble insurrection in 1414, fled to the hills of Herefordshire, was captured at length, and suffered in his turn. This degradation lies about Henry and his times, and our contacts with his personal nobleness and prowess, though imperishable, are marred.

In the full tide of power and success Henry died at the end of August 1422 of a malady contracted in the field, probably dysentery, against which the medicine of those times could not make head. When he received the Sacrament and heard the penitential psalms, at the words "Build thou the walls of Jerusalem," he spoke, saying, "Good Lord, thou knowest that my intent has been and yet is, if I might live, to re-edify the walls of Jerusalem." This was his dying thought.

He died with his work unfinished. He had once more committed his country to the murderous dynastic war with France. He had been the instrument of the religious and social persecution of the Lollards. Perhaps if he had lived the normal span his power might have become the servant of his virtues and produced the harmonies and tolerances which mankind so often seeks in vain. But Death drew his scythe across these prospects. The gleaming King, cut off untimely, went to his tomb amid the lamentations of his people, and the Crown passed to his son, an infant nine months old.

CHAPTER 26

JOAN OF ARC

A BABY WAS KING OF ENGLAND, and two months later, on the death of Charles VI, was proclaimed without dispute the King of France. Bedford and Gloucester, his uncles, became Protectors, and with a Council comprising the heads of the most powerful families attempted to sustain the work of Henry V. A peculiar sanctity enshrined Henry VI, the hero's son. Nurses, teachers, and presently noble guardians, carefully chosen for the boy's education and welfare, were authorised to use "reasonable chastisement" when required. But this was little needed, for the child had a mild, virtuous, honest and merciful nature. His piety knew no bounds, and was, with hunting and a taste for literature, the stay and comfort of his long, ignominious, and terrifying pilgrimage. He was physically weak, and through his mother inherited the mental infirmities of Charles VI. He was feeble alike in body and mind, unwise and unstable in his judgments, profuse beyond his means to his friends, uncalculating against his enemies, so tender-hearted that it was even said he would let common thieves and murderers live, yet forced to bear the load of innumerable political executions. Flung about like a shuttlecock between the rival factions; presiding as a helpless puppet over the progressive decay of English society and power; hovering bewildered on the skirts of great battles; three times taken prisoner on the field; now paraded with all kingly pomp before Parliaments, armies, and crowds, now led in mockery through the streets, now a captive, now a homeless fugitive, hiding, hunted, hungry; afflicted from time to time by phases of total or partial idiocy, he endured in the fullest measure for nearly fifty years the extreme miseries of human existence, until the hand of murder despatched him to a world which he was sure would be better, and could

This portrait of Henry VI can be seen in the National Portrait Gallery, London.

hardly have been worse than that he had known. Yet with all his shame of failure and incompetence, and the disasters these helped to bring upon his country, the English people recognised his goodness of heart and rightly ascribed to him the quality of holiness. In many parts of the country he was venerated both as a saint and martyr.

At the time of the great King's death, a successor of the highest military quality was found in his brother, John, Duke of Bedford, who went to France as Regent and commander in chief. The death, in October 1422, of the French king, who had signed the Treaty of Troyes, while it admitted the English infant to the kingship of France, nevertheless exposed his title to a more serious challenge. South of the Loire, except of course in Gascony, the Dauphin ruled. Many sieges and much ravaging distressed the countryside. In 1421 the French and their Scottish allies defeated the English at Baugé, but other considerable actions ended in English victories. At Cravant, in August 1423, the French were again aided by a strong Scots contingent. These Scotsmen were animated by a hatred of the English which stood out above the ordinary feuds. But the English archers, with their Burgundian allies, shot most of them down. At Verneuil a year later this decision was repeated. The French, having had some success, were inclined to retire behind the Loire, but the rage of the Scots was uncontrollable. They forced a battle, and were nearly all destroyed by the arrow storm. Douglas, Buchan, and other Scottish chieftains fell upon the field, and so grievous was the slaughter of their followers that it was never again possible to form in these wars a separate Scottish brigade.

Portrait by Fouquet of Charles VII of France. His legitimacy was questioned, and when his father died in 1422 the French Crown passed to the infant king, Henry VI of England. Charles's claims to the French throne were taken more seriously after Joan of Arc impelled him to be crowned in Rheims Cathedral. He owed his throne to her military victories, but when she needed his help, he deserted her.

The English attempt to conquer all vast France with a few thousand archers led by warrior nobles, with hardly any money from home, and little food to be found in the ruined regions, reached its climax in the triumph of Verneuil. There seemed to the French to be no discoverable way to contend against these rugged, lusty violent islanders, with their archery, their flexible tactics, and their audacity. Yet the Dauphin stood for France, and everywhere, even in the subjugated provinces, a dull, deep sense of nationality, centred upon him. By 1429, however, the defects of the Dauphin, the exhaustion of the French monarchy, and the disorder and misery of the realm had reached a pitch where all hung in the balance.

There now appeared upon the ravaged scene an Angel of Deliverance, the most splendid of France's heroes, the most beloved of her saints, the most inspiring of all her memories, the peasant Maid, the ever-shining, ever-glorious Joan of Arc. In the poor, remote hamlet of Domrémy, on the fringe of the Vosges Forest, she served at the inn. She rode the horses of travellers, bareback, to water. She wandered on Sundays into the woods, where there were shrines, and a legend that some day from these oaks would arise one to save France. In the fields where she tended her sheep the saints of God, who grieved for France, rose before her in visions. St Michael himself appointed her, by right divine, to command the armies of liberation. Joan shrank at first from the awful duty, but when he returned attended by St Margaret and St Catherine, patronesses of the village church, she obeyed their command. There welled in the heart of the Maid a pity for the realm of France, sublime, perhaps miraculous, certainly invincible.

She found the most stubborn obstacle in her own family. Her father was scandalised that she should wish to ride in male attire among rough soldiers. But the saints no doubt felt bound to set her fair upon her course. She convinced Baudricourt, governor of the neighbouring town, that she was inspired. He recommended her to a Court ready to clutch at straws. She made a perilous journey across France. She was conducted to the King's presence in the immense stone pile of Chinon. There, among the nobles and courtiers in the great hall, under the flaring torches, she at once picked out the King, who had purposely mingled with the crowd. "Most noble Lord Dauphin," she said, "I am Joan the Maid, sent on the part of God to aid you and the kingdom, and by His order I announce that you will be crowned in the city of Rheims." The aspersion that he was a bastard had always troubled Charles, and when the Maid picked him out among the crowd he was profoundly moved. Alone with him, she spoke of State secrets which she must either have learnt from the saints or from other high authority. She asked for an ancient sword which she had never seen, but which she described minutely before it was found. She fascinated the royal circle. When they set her astride on horseback in martial guise it was seen that she could ride. As she couched her lance the spectators were swept with delight.

Policy now, if not earlier, came to play a part. The supernatural character of the Maid's mission was spread abroad. To make sure that she was sent by Heaven and not from elsewhere, she was examined by a committee of theologians, by the Parlement of Poitiers, and by the whole Royal Council. She was declared a virgin of good intent, inspired by God. Indeed, her answers were of such a quality that the theory has been put forward that she had for some time been carefully trained for her mission.

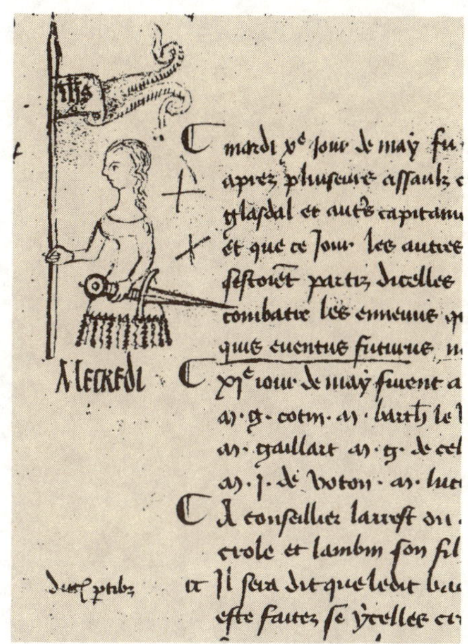

This sketch of Joan of Arc armed for battle, made by a clerk of the Parliament of Paris, is the only known drawing to have been made of her during her lifetime. It appears in the margin of a history of the siege of Orleans.

Orleans in 1429 lay under the extremities of siege. A few thousand English were slowly reducing the city by an incomplete blockade. Their self-confidence and prestige hardened them to pursue the attack of a fortress deep in hostile territory, whose garrison was four times their number. The Maid now claimed to lead a convoy to the rescue. In armour plain and without ornament, she rode at the head of the troops. She restored their spirits; she broke the spell of English dominance. She captivated not only the rough soldiery but their hard-bitten leaders. Her plan was simple. She would march straight into Orleans. But the experienced captain, Dunois, a bastard of the late Duke of Orleans, had not proposed to lead his convoy by this dangerous route. As the Maid did not know the map, he embarked his supplies in boats, and brought her by other ways into the besieged town. She was received with rapture. But the convoy, beaten back by adverse winds, was forced after all to come in by the way she had prescribed; and in fact it marched for a whole day between the redoubts of the English while they gaped at it dumbfounded.

The report of a supernatural visitant sent by God to save France, which inspired the French, clouded the minds and froze the energies of the English. The sense of awe, and even of fear, robbed them of their assurance. Upon her invocation the spirit of victory changed sides. She called for an immediate onslaught upon the besiegers, and herself led the storming parties against them. Wounded by an arrow, she plucked it out and returned to the charge. She mounted the scaling-ladders and was hurled half stunned into the ditch. Prostrate on the ground, she commanded new efforts. "Forward, fellow-countrymen! God has delivered them into our hands." The siege was broken, Orleans saved. The English retired in good order, and the Maid prudently restrained the citizens from pursuing them into the open country.

Joan now was head indeed of the French army; it was dangerous even to dispute her decisions. The contingents from Orleans would obey none but her. She led the assault upon Jargeau, thus opening the Loire above Orleans. In June 1429 she marched with the army that gained the victory of Patay. She told Charles he must march on Rheims to be crowned upon the throne of his ancestors. The idea seemed fantastic: Rheims lay deep in enemy country. But under her spell he obeyed, and everywhere the towns opened their gates before them and the people crowded to his aid. With all the pomp of victory and faith, with the most sacred ceremonies of ancient days, Charles was crowned at Rheims. By his side stood the Maid, resplendent, with her banner proclaiming the Will of God. If this was not a miracle it ought to be.

Joan now became conscious that her mission was exhausted; her "voices" were silent; she asked to be allowed to go home. But all adjured her to remain. The French captains who conducted the actual operations, though restive under her military interference, were deeply conscious of her value to the cause. A half-hearted attack was made upon Paris. Joan advanced to the forefront and strove to compel victory. She was severely wounded and the leaders ordered the retreat. When she recovered she again sought release. They gave her the rank and revenue of an earl.

But the attitude both of the Court and the Church was changing towards Joan. After her "twenty victories" the full character of her mission appeared. It became clear that she served God rather than the Church, and France rather than the Orleans party. Indeed, the whole conception of France seems to have sprung and radiated from her. Thus the powerful particularist interests which had hitherto supported her were estranged. Meanwhile she planned to regain Paris for France. When in May 1430 the town of Compiègne revolted against the decision of the King that it should yield to the English, Joan with only six hundred men attempted its succour. She had no doubt that the enterprise was desperate. It took the form of a cavalry sortie across the long causeway over the river. The enemy, at first surprised, rallied, and a panic among the French ensued. Joan, undaunted, was bridled from the field by her friends. She still fought with the rearguard across the causeway. The two sides were intermingled. The fortress itself was imperilled. Its cannon could not fire upon the confused melee. Flavy, the governor, whose duty it was to save the town, felt obliged to pull up the drawbridge in her face and leave her to the Burgundians.

Rheims Cathedral was the scene of Charles VII's magnificent coronation in 1429. His French subjects regarded the consecration as a visible sign from God that he was their legitimate ruler.

She was sold to the rejoicing English for a moderate sum. To Bedford and his army she was a witch, a sorceress, a harlot, a foul imp of black magic, at all costs to be destroyed. But it was not easy to frame a charge; she was a prisoner of war, and many conventions among the warring aristocrats protected her. The spiritual arm was therefore invoked. The Bishop of Beauvais, the learned doctors of Paris, pursued her for heresy. The gravamen was that by refusing to disown her "voices" she was defying the judgment and authority of the Church. For a whole year her fate hung in the balance, while careless, ungrateful Charles lifted not a finger to save her. Joan recanted under endless pressure, but in her cell the inexorable saints appeared to her again. Entrapping priests set her armour and man's clothes before her; with renewed exaltation she put them on. From that moment she was declared a relapsed heretic and condemned to the fire. Amid an immense concourse she was dragged to the stake in the marketplace of Rouen. High upon the pyramid of faggots the flames rose towards her, and the smoke of doom wreathed and curled. She raised a cross made of firewood, and her last word was "Jesus!" History has recorded the comment of an English soldier who witnessed the scene. "We are lost," he said. "We have burnt a saint." All this proved true.

Joan was a being so uplifted from the ordinary run of mankind that she finds no equal in a thousand years. The records of her trial present us with facts alive today through all the mists of time. Out of her own mouth can she be judged in each generation. She embodied the natural goodness and valour of the human race in unexampled perfection. Unconquerable courage, infinite compassion, the virtue of the simple, the wisdom of the just, shone forth in her. She glorifies as she freed the soil from which she sprang.

Joan of Arc perished on May 30, 1431, and thereafter the tides of war flowed remorselessly against the English. The boy Henry was crowned in Paris in December amid chilly throngs. The whole spirit of the country was against the English claim. Bedford died, and was succeeded by lesser captains. The French gained a series of battles. Here they caught the English men-at-arms on one side of the river while their archers were on the other; there by a cannonade they forced a disjointed English attack. The French artillery now became the finest in the world. Numberless castles which the English still held now fell in a few days to smashing bombardment. All northern France, except Calais, was reconquered. The valiant Talbot, Earl of Shrewsbury, was killed with most of his English in his foolhardy Battle of Castillon in 1453. The surviving English made terms to sail home from La Rochelle. By the end of that year, through force or negotiation, the English had been driven off the Continent. Of all their conquests they held henceforward only the bridgehead of Calais.

Joan of Arc tied to the stake at Rheims, where she was burnt on May 30, 1431. Her integrity and humour made it difficult for the judges to convict her and she faced death so courageously that even her enemies were profoundly moved. Joan was canonised in 1924, and George Bernard Shaw wrote a play about her. The manuscript from which this illustration is taken is now in the Bibliotheque Nationale, Paris.

CHAPTER 27

YORK AND LANCASTER

AS HENRY VI GREW UP HIS VIRTUES and simpleness became equally apparent. The Council had in his childhood made a great show of him, brought him to ceremonies, and crowned him with solemnity both in London and Paris. His consequence was maintained by the rivalry of the nobles, and by the unbounded hopes of the nation. As the disastrous years in France unfolded he was pressed continually to assert himself. At fifteen he was already regularly attending Council meetings. He was allowed to exercise a measure of prerogative both in pardons and rewards. Before he was eighteen he had absorbed himself in the foundation of his colleges at Eton and Cambridge, but in public affairs he showed a feebleness of mind and spirit and a gentleness of nature which were little suited to the fierce rivalries of a martial age. Opinion and also interests were divided upon him. Flattering accounts of his remarkable intelligence were matched by other equally biased tales that he was an idiot. Modern historians confirm the less complimentary view. At the hour when a strong king alone could recreate the balance between the nation and the nobility, the throne was occupied by a devout simpleton suited alike by his qualities and defects to be a puppet.

These were evil days for England. The Crown was beggarly, the nobles rich. The people were unhappy and unrestful rather than unprosperous. The empire so swiftly gained upon the Continent was being cast away by an

Henry VI and his forceful bride, Margaret of Anjou. She had the soundness of mind and spirit which Henry lacked. The English were so eager to secure her as queen that they agreed secretly to return the province of Maine to France as part of the marriage contract.

incompetent and self-enriching oligarchy, and revenues which might have sent irresistible armies to beat the French were engrossed by the Church.

The loss of France, as it sank in year by year, provoked a deep, sullen rage throughout the land. This passion stirred not only the nobility, but the archer class, with their admiring friends in every village. Where were the glories of Crécy and Poitiers? Where were the fruits of famous Agincourt? All were squandered, or indeed betrayed, by those who had profited from the overthrow and murder of good King Richard. There were not lacking agitators and preachers who prepared a national and social upheaval by reminding folk that the true line of succession had been changed by violence. All this was an undercurrent, though nonetheless potent. Slowly, ceaselessly, there grew in the land, not only among the nobility and gentry, strong parties which presently assumed both shape and organisation. Meanwhile the princes of the House of Lancaster disputed among themselves. After Bedford's death in 1435 the tension grew between Gloucester and the Beauforts. Cardinal Beaufort, Bishop of Winchester, and one of the legitimised sons of John of Gaunt's third union, was himself the richest man in England, and a prime master of such contributions as the Church thought it prudent to make to the State. Meddling little with the ill-starred conduct of affairs, the Beauforts and their associate, William de la Pole, Earl of Suffolk, maintained by peaceful arts and critical detachment an influence to which the martial elements were often forced to defer. The power of this faction was in 1441 turned in malice upon the Duke of Gloucester, weakened as he was by the record of maladministration and ill-success in France. He was now wedded to the fair Eleanor Cobham, who had long been his mistress. She was singled out for attack, and was accused with much elaboration of lending herself to the black arts. She had made, it was alleged, a wax figure of the King, and had exposed it from time to time to heat, which wasted it away. Her object, according to her accusers, was to cause the King's life to waste away too. She was declared guilty. Barefoot, in penitential garb, she was made to walk for three days through the London streets, and then consigned to perpetual imprisonment with reasonable maintenance. Her alleged accomplices were put to death. This was of course a trial of strength between the parties and a real injury to Gloucester.

Humphrey, Duke of Gloucester, was a man of great culture and the first important English patron of the new learning. The Bodleian Library, Oxford, (above) was founded by him and in 1444 he was honoured with the title of Founder of the Oxford University Library.

At twenty-three it was high time that King Henry should marry. Each of the Lancastrian factions was anxious to provide him with a queen; but Cardinal Beaufort and his brothers, with their ally, Suffolk, prevailed over the Duke of Gloucester. Suffolk was sent to France to arrange a further truce, and it was implied in his mission that he should treat for a marriage between the King of England and Margaret of Anjou, niece of the King of France. This remarkable woman added to rare beauty and charm a masterly intellect and a dauntless spirit. Like Joan the Maid, though without her inspiration or her causes, she knew how to make men fight. Even from the seclusion of her family her qualities became well-known. Was she not then the mate for this feeble-minded King? Would she not give him the force that he lacked? And would not those who placed her at his side secure a large and sure future for themselves?

Suffolk was well aware of the delicacy and danger of his mission. He produced from the King and the lords an assurance that if he acted to the best of his ability he should not be punished for ill consequences, and that any errors proved against him should be pardoned in advance. Thus fortified he addressed himself to his task with a zeal which proved fatal to him. The father of Margaret, René of Anjou, was not only cousin of the French King and his favourite counsellor, but in his own right King of Jerusalem and of Sicily. These magnificent titles were not sustained by practical enjoyments. Jerusalem was in the hands of the Turks, he did not own a square yard in Sicily, and half his patrimony of Anjou and Maine was for years held by the English army. Suffolk was enthralled by Margaret. He made the match; and in his eagerness, by a secret article, agreed with formal authority that Maine should be the reward of France. So strong was the basic power of Gloucester's faction, so sharp was the antagonism against France, so loud were the murmurs that England had been betrayed in her wars, that the clause was guarded as a deadly secret. The marriage was solemnised in 1445 with such splendour as the age could afford. The King was radiantly happy, the Queen faithfully grateful. But the secret slumbered uneasily.

During the six years following the condemnation of his wife in 1441 Gloucester had been living in retirement, collecting books for Oxford University Library, which he founded. His enemies at this grave juncture resolved upon his final overthrow. Suffolk and Edmund Beaufort, nephew of the Cardinal, supported by the Dukes of Somerset and Buckingham, with the Queen in their midst and the King in their charge, arrested Gloucester when he came to a Parliament summoned at St Edmondsbury. Seventeen days later Gloucester's corpse was displayed, so that all could see there was no wound upon it. The manner of Edward II's death was too well-known for this proof to be accepted. It has however been suggested that his death was induced by choler and amazement at the ruin of his fortunes.

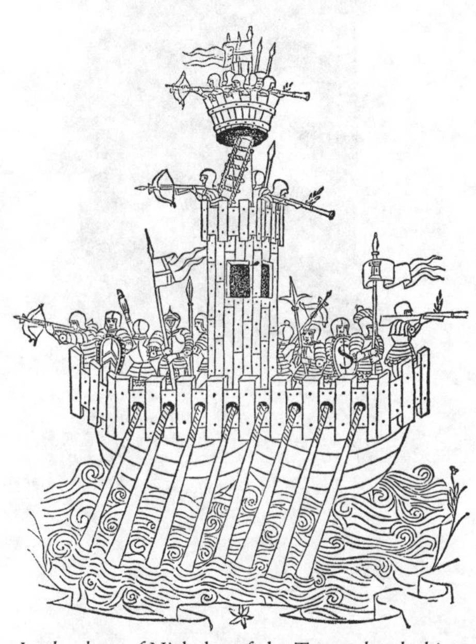

In the days of Nicholas of the Tower *battleships provided several platforms on the mainmast for archers as seen in this contemporary impression.*

It soon appeared that immense forces of retribution were on foot. When in 1448 the secret article for the cession of Maine became public through its occupation by the French, anger was expressed on all sides. England had paid a province, it was said, for a princess without a dowry. At the root of the fearful civil war soon to rend the land there lay this national grief and wrath at the ruin of empire. All other discontents fused themselves with this. The House of Lancaster had usurped the throne, had ruined the finances, had sold the conquests, and now had stained its hands with foul murder. From these charges all men held the King absolved alike by his good heart and silly head.

Edmund Beaufort, now Duke of Somerset, became commander of the army in France. The officer commanding the fortresses which were to be ceded to France refused to deliver them. The French armies advanced and took with a strong hand all that was now denied. Suffolk, who had remained at home, was impeached. Striving, as in honour bound, to save him, Henry burked the proceedings by sending him in 1450 into a five years' exile. When the banished Duke was crossing the Channel with his attendants and treasure, the *Nicholas of the Tower*, the largest warship in the Royal Navy, bore down upon him and carried him on board. He was received by the captain with the ominous words "Welcome, traitor", and two days later he was lowered into a boat and beheaded by six strokes of a rusty sword. It is a revealing sign of the times that a royal ship should seize and execute a royal minister who was travelling under the King's special protection.

In June and July a rising took place in Kent. Jack Cade, a soldier of capacity and bad character, home from the wars, gathered several thousand men, and marched on London. He was admitted to the city, but on his

The Bear and the Ragged Staff was the badge of the powerful Earl of Warwick and his successors, including Warwick the Kingmaker in the Wars of the Roses. Much later, it was used by Robert Dudley, Earl of Leicester, the favourite of Queen Elizabeth I.

executing Lord Say, the Treasurer, in Cheapside, after a mob trial, the citizens turned against him, his followers dispersed under terms of pardon, and he himself was pursued and killed. This success restored for the moment the authority of the Government, and Henry enjoyed a brief interlude in which he devoted himself anew to his colleges, and to Margaret, who had gained his love and obedience.

As the process of expelling the English from France continued fortresses fell, towns and districts were lost, and their garrisons for the most part came home. The speed of this disaster contributed powerfully to shock English opinion and to shake not only the position of individual ministers but the very foundations of the Lancastrian dynasty. England became full of what we should call "ex-Service men", who did not know why they had been beaten, but were sure they had been mishandled. The nobles, in the increasing disorder, were glad to gather these hardened fighters in bands almost amounting to private armies. The Earl of Warwick, perhaps the greatest landowner, had thousands of dependants who ate what was called "his bread", and of these a large proportion were organised troops proud to display his badge of the Bear and the Ragged Staff. Cash and ambition ruled and the land sank rapidly towards anarchy. The King was a helpless creature, and no prop for any man. Parliament, both Lords and Commons, was little more than a clearing-house for the rivalries of nobles.

A statute of 1429 had fixed the county franchise at the forty-shilling freeholder. In the preamble to the Act it was alleged that the participation in elections of too great a number of people "of little substance or worth" had led to homicides, riots, assaults, and feuds. This was a backward but enduring step. Yet never for centuries had the privilege of Parliament stood so high. Never for centuries was it more blatantly exploited.

The force of law was appropriated by intrigue. Baronial violence used or defied legal forms with growing impunity. The Constitution was turned against the public. No man was safe in life or lands, or even in his humblest

LOVE AND MARRIAGE IN THE FIFTEENTH CENTURY

In his famous English Social History *G.M. Trevelyan gave this introduction to the Paston letters, which give an illuminating insight into family life in the fifteenth century.*

The fifteenth century was the first in which the upper classes of both sexes customarily wrote letters — in "English tongue". Education had clearly made great strides since the time when kings and barons had set their seals and inked their crosses to documents they had not the skill to read. The best-known collection of letters from the period are those written by the Paston family who lived in Norfolk.

Such letters were not written for pastime or gossip, but had some practical purpose in view, usually of law, business or local politics. But they tell us by the way something of family life, love and marriage. The extreme deference that children were made to show to their parents, the hardness of home and school discipline, the constant "belashing" of boys and girls and of servants will perhaps cause no surprise. But to some readers, accustomed to think of the Middle Ages as a period of chivalry and love, it may come as a shock to realise that, in the knightly and gentle class, the choice of partners for marriage had normally nothing whatever to do with love; often the bride and bridegroom were small children when they were pledged for life, and even if adults, they were sold by their parents to the highest bidder. The Pastons and other county families regarded the marriages of their children as counters in the game of family aggrandisement, useful to buy money and estates, or to secure the support of powerful patrons. If the victim destined for the altar resisted, rebellion was crushed — at least in the case of a daughter or a female ward — with physical brutality almost incredible. Elizabeth Paston, when she hesitated to marry a battered and ugly widower of fifty, was for nearly three months on end "beaten once a week or twice, sometimes twice in one day, and her head broken in two or three places". Such were the methods of her mother Agnes, a highly religious and respectable controller of the large Paston household. Many parents seem to have cared very little who married their children, provided they themselves got the money.

However, even in the society of the prosaic Pastons we have epistolary record of at least two love marriages. In the first case, that of Margery Brews and John Paston in 1477, the girl right, except through the protection of his local chief. The celebrated Paston Letters show that England, enormously advanced as it was in character and civilisation, was relapsing from peace and security into barbaric confusion. The roads were insecure. The King's writ was denied or perverted. The royal judges were flouted or bribed. The powers of Parliament could be turned this way and that as the factions gripped it. Yet the suffering, toiling, unconquerable community had moved far from the days of Stephen and Maud. There was public opinion. There was a collective moral sense. There were venerated customs. Above all there was a national spirit.

It was upon this community that the agonies of the Wars of the Roses were now to fall. We must not underrate either the great issues which led to the struggle, or the conscious, intense, prolonged efforts made to avert it. The need of all men and their active desire was for a strong and capable Government. Some thought this could only be obtained by aiding the established regime. Others had for a long time been secretly contending that a usurpation had been imposed upon them which had now become incompetent. The claims and hopes of the opposition to the House of Lancaster were embodied in Richard, Duke of York. According to established usage he had prior right to the Crown. York was the grandson of Edmund, Duke of York, a younger brother of John of Gaunt. As the great-grandson of Edward III he was the only other person besides Henry VI with an unbroken legitimate male descent from Edward III, but in the female line he had a superior claim through his descent, via the Mortimers, from Gaunt's elder brother, Lionel of Clarence. Around York and beneath him there gathered an immense party of discontent, which drove him hesitantly to demand a place in the Government, and eventually the throne itself.

A Yorkist network grew up in all parts of the country, but mainly in the south and west of England, in Kent, in London, and in Wales. It was significant that Jack Cade, at the head of the Kentish insurgents, had pretended to the name of Mortimer. It was widely believed that the Yorkists

won over her soft-hearted mother to the romantic view. Here, in the original spelling, is Margery's love letter to John while the matter was still being negotiated, not very hopefully, on the usual purely financial ground.

"Right reverent and wurschypfull, and my ryght wele-beloved Voluntyne [Valentine] . . . My lady my moder hath labored the mat[t]er to my ffadur full delygently, but she can no more gete [*viz.* she can get no more dowry provided with me] than ye knowe of, for the wheche God knowythe I am full sory. But yf that ye loffe [love] me, as I tryste verely that ye do, ye will not leffe [leave] me therefor."

Her next letter on the same situation, though not very grammatical, is as moving as anything in English prose (I give it in modernised spelling).

"Wherefore, if ye could be content with that good [*viz.* that amount of dowry] and my poor person, I would be the merriest maiden on ground. And if ye think not yourself so satisfied, or that ye might have much more good as I have understood by you before; good, true and loving Valentine, that ye take no such labour upon you as to come [any] more for that matter but let it pass and never be spoken of, as I may be your true lover and bedewoman during my life. . ."

These entwined lovers appear as a detail of a fifteenth-century tapestry now on view in the Victoria and Albert Museum, London.

had procured the murder of Suffolk. Blood had thus already flowed between the Houses of Lancaster and York.

In these conditions the character of Richard of York deserves close study. He was a virtuous, law-respecting, slow-moving, and highly competent prince. Every office entrusted to him by the Lancastrian regime was ably and faithfully discharged. He would have been content with the government of Calais and what was left of France, but being deprived of this for the sake of Somerset he accepted the government of Ireland. Not only did he subdue part of that island, but he won the goodwill of the Irish people. Thus we see on the one side a weak King with a defective title in the hands of personages discredited by national disaster, and now with blood-guilt upon them, and on the other an upright and wise administrator supported by a nationwide party and with some superior title to the Crown.

Anyone who studies the argument which now tore the realm will see how easily honest men could convince themselves of either cause. When King Henry VI realised that his right to the throne was impugned he was mildly astonished. "Since my cradle," he said, "I have been King. My father was King; his father was King. You have all sworn fealty to me on many occasions, as your fathers swore it to my father." But the other side declared that oaths not based on truth were void, that wrong must be righted, that successful usurpation gained no sanctity by time, that the foundation of the monarchy could only rest upon law and justice, that to recognise a dynasty of interlopers was to invite rebellion whenever occasion served, and thus dissolve the very frame of English society; and, finally, that if expediency were to rule, who could compare the wretched half-wit King, under whom all was going to ruin, with a prince who had proved himself a soldier and a statesman of the highest temper and quality?

The Chapel of King's College, Cambridge, has a beautiful fan-vaulted ceiling and is a typical example of the late Gothic, or Perpendicular style of architecture. Arches have become less pointed and they meet in star-shaped patterns at the vault.

All England was divided between these two conceptions. Although the Yorkists predominated in the rich south, and the Lancastrians were supreme in the warlike north, there were many interlacements and overlaps. While the townsfolk and the mass of the people, upon the whole, abstained from active warfare in this struggle of the upper classes and their armed retainers, and some thought "the fewer nobles the better", their own opinion was also profoundly divided. They venerated the piety and goodness of the King; they also admired the virtues and moderation of the Duke of York. The attitude and feeling of the public weighed heavily with both contending factions. Thus Europe witnessed the amazing spectacle of nearly thirty years of war, conducted with hardly the sack of a single town, and with the mass of the common people little affected and the functions of local government very largely maintained.

In 1450 the ferment of discontent and rivalries drew the Duke of York into his first overt act. He quitted his government in Ireland and landed unbidden in Wales. During the Parliamentary session of the following year a member of the Commons, one Young, boldly proposed that the Duke of York should be declared heir to the throne. This demand was formidable, not only for its backing, but for its good sense. The King had now been married for six years and had no child. Ought he not, men asked at this time, to designate his successors? If not York, whom then? The Beauforts, Gaunt's legitimised bastards, had been barred from the succession by the Act of 1407. But the King, animated certainly by Margaret, refused to abandon his hope of progeny, and, as soon as the Parliament had dispersed, sent the presumptuous Young to the Tower. At this time, also, he broke with the Duke of York, who retired to his castle on the borders of Wales.

Disgusted by the Government's failure to restore order and justice at home and to prevent military disasters in France, York became more and more convinced that the Beaufort party, which dominated the weak-willed King, must be driven from power. Prayers and protests had failed; there remained the resort to arms. Accordingly, on February 3, 1452, York sent an address to the citizens of Shrewsbury, accusing Somerset of the disgrace in France and of "labouring continually about the King's Highness for my undoing." On this he marched from Shrewsbury towards London, with an army of several thousand men. The response was disappointing. London closed its gates against his emissaries. The King was carried by Margaret, Somerset, and the Lancastrian interests to Blackheath, with a superior force. Civil war seemed about to begin.

Ludlow Castle, on the border of Wales, was the home of Richard, Duke of York. Between 1453 and 1455 he took over the Government of the country during the King's temporary insanity.

Every effort was made to prevent bloodshed. Parleys were unending. In the event York dispersed his forces and presented himself unarmed and bareheaded before King Henry, protesting his loyalty, but demanding redress. Since he was supported by the Commons and half the nation was providently behind him, the King promised that "a sad and substantial Council" should be formed, of which he should be a member. The Court had still to choose between Somerset and York. The Queen decided the issue in Somerset's favour. He was appointed Constable of Calais, garrisoned by the only regular troops in the pay of the Crown, and was in fact for more than a year at the head of affairs both in France and at home.

Then in quick succession a series of grave events occurred. The Earl of Shrewsbury's attempt to reconquer Gascony failed and Somerset, the chief commander, bore the burden of defeat. In this situation the King went mad. He recognised no one, not even the Queen. For another fifteen months he remained entirely without comprehension. The pious Henry had been withdrawn from the worry of existence to a land of merciful oblivion where he gaped and drivelled over the bristling realm.

When these terrible facts became known, Queen Margaret aspired to be Protector. But the adverse forces were too strong for the Lancastrian party. Moreover, she had another preoccupation. On October 13 she gave birth to a son. This event inevitably hardened the hearts of all men. Hitherto neither side had been inclined to go to extremes. If Lancaster ruled during the life of Henry, York would succeed at his death, and both sides could accommodate themselves to this natural and lawful process. Now it seemed that there would be a Lancastrian ascendancy for ever.

The insanity of the King defeated Somerset: he could no longer withstand York. Norfolk, one of York's supporters, presented a petition against him to the Council and in December 1453 he was committed to the Tower. The strength of York's position bore him to the Protectorate. He moved by parliamentary means and with great moderation, but he was not to be withstood. He had not long to show his qualities, but an immediate improvement in the administration was recognised. He set to work with cool vigour to restore order throughout the land and he did not hesitate to imprison several of his own adherents, among them the Earl of Devonshire, for levying private war. If he refrained from bringing Somerset to trial, this was only from mercy. His party were astounded at his tolerance. When the Government was in his hands, when his future was marred by the new heir to the Crown, when his power or his life might be destroyed at any moment by the King's recovery, he kept absolute faith with right and justice. Here then is his monument and justification. He stands before history as a patriot ready to risk his life to protect good government, but unwilling to raise his hand against the State in any personal interest.

Surprises continued. At Christmas 1454 when he seemed to have sunk into permanent imbecility, Henry suddenly regained all his faculties. He inquired whether he had been asleep. Margaret showed him his son, and told him she had named him Edward. Hitherto he had looked with dull eyes upon the infant. Now he was as good as he had ever been. He sent his almoner to Canterbury with a thank-offering, and declared himself "in charity with all the world", remarking that he "only wished the lords were too".

CHAPTER 28

THE WARS OF THE ROSES

In the spring of 1455 the red rose of Lancaster bloomed again. York ceased legally to be Protector from the moment that the King's mental recovery was known. Queen Margaret took the helm. Somerset was not only released but restored to his key position. York retired to Sandal in Yorkshire, and, being joined by the Earls of Warwick and Salisbury, together with a large company of nobles, he denounced Somerset as the man who, having lost Normandy and Guienne, was now about to ruin the whole kingdom. York's lords agreed upon a resort to arms. With three thousand men they marched south. At the same time the Duke of Norfolk appeared at the head of several thousand Yorkists, and Shrewsbury and Sir Thomas Stanley of a few thousands more. All these forces moved towards London, with St Albans as their point for concentration. The King, the Queen, Somerset, and the Court and Lancastrian party, with their power, which numbered less than three thousand men, moved to Watford to meet them.

St Albans was an open town. The ancient, powerful monastery there had prevented the citizens from "girding themselves about with a great wall", lest they should become presumptuous. For this reason it was a convenient

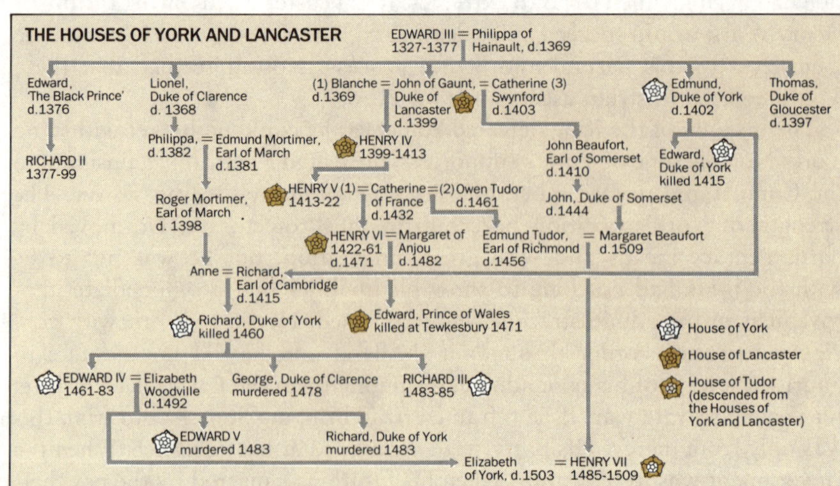

The descendants of Edward III formed the Houses of York and Lancaster. The Yorkist leaders in the Wars of the Roses were Richard, Duke of York and his son, Edward IV. The Lancastrians were headed by Henry VI but his dauntless queen, Margaret of Anjou, was the power behind the throne.

rendezvous. Here the King's army arrived, and the royal standard was unfurled. York, Salisbury, and Warwick did not wait for the heavy reinforcements that were approaching them. They saw that their forces had the advantage and that hours counted. This time there was a fight. It was a collision rather than a battle; but it was nonetheless decisive. The royal troops were put to flight. Somerset was killed "fighting for a cause which was more his own than the King's". The King himself was slightly wounded by an arrow, but took refuge in a tradesman's house. There presently the Duke of York came to him, and, falling upon his knees, assured him of his fealty and devotion. Not more than three hundred men perished in this clash at St Albans, but these included an extraordinary proportion of the nobles on the King's side. The rank and file were encouraged to spare one another; the leaders fought to the death.

The Yorkist triumph was complete. They had now got the King in their hands. Margaret and her child had taken sanctuary. The victors declared their devotion to the royal person and rejoiced that he was rid of evil counsellors. Upon this Parliament was summoned in the King's name.

Historians have shrunk from the Wars of the Roses, and most of those who have catalogued their events have left us only a melancholy and disjointed picture. We are however in the presence of the most ferocious and implacable quarrel of which there is factual record. The individual actors were bred by generations of privilege and war, into which the feudal theme had brought its peculiar sense of honour, and to which the Papacy contributed such spiritual sanction as emerged from its rivalries and intrigues. It was a conflict in which personal hatreds reached their maximum, and from which mass effects were happily excluded. There must have been many similar convulsions in the human story. None however has been preserved with characters at once so worldly and so expensively chiselled.

Needless causes of confusion may be avoided. Towns must not be confused with titles. The mortal struggle of York and Lancaster did not imply any antagonism between the two well-known English counties. York was in fact the stronghold of the Lancastrians, and the Yorkists founded their strength upon the Midlands and the south of England. The ups and downs of fortune were so numerous and startling, the family feuds so complicated, the impact of national feeling in moments of crisis so difficult to measure, that it has been the fashion to disparage this period. Only Shakespeare has portrayed its savage yet heroic lineaments. He does not attempt to draw conclusions, and for dramatic purposes telescopes events and campaigns. Let us now set forth the facts as they occurred.

St Albans was the first shedding of blood in strife. The Yorkists gained possession of the King. But soon we see the inherent power of Lancaster. They had the majority of the nobles on their side, and the majesty of the Crown. In a few months they were as strong as ever. Continual trials of strength were made. There were risings in the country and grim assemblies of Parliament. Legality, constitutionalism, and reverence for the Crown were countered, but not yet overthrown, by turbulent and bloody episodes. The four years from 1456 to 1459 were a period of uneasy truce. Then in 1459 fighting broke out again. A gathering near Worcester of armed Yorkists dispersed in the presence of the royal army and their chiefs scattered. York returned to Ireland, and Warwick to his captaincy of Calais, in which he had succeeded Somerset.

MEDIEVAL MERCHANT GUILDS

THERE WAS A MARKED DIFFERENCE in the Middle Ages between the towns and the countryside, though the town was never far from the country and had plenty of green in it.

Towns grew in the twelfth century with the expansion of trade, and the earliest town records go back to this period. The most important records were charters, usually granting market privileges and freedom from tolls. By the end of the century London, by far the biggest town, had an official described as a mayor.

Trade was in the hands of merchants, big and small, and some of it was carried on at fairs. For regular trade in most towns other than London there was a guild to which merchants had to belong. They came together not only to control local trade but also to feast and pray. They had customs and they had rules. They were also expected to charge a "just" price for what they sold. In the thirteenth century, craft guilds, such as that of artisan tailors, also came into existence. They set standards and prices and determined the pattern of apprenticeship. In most crafts apprentices had to serve for seven years. The apprenticeship system for young people still survives in this country, although in a very different form, in the twentieth century.

The guilds helped to organise pageants and processions. They staged Mystery or Miracle Plays, performed by apprentices on carts in the streets.

Foreign merchants in England had their own organisations, as did English merchants abroad. William Caxton, before he turned to printing, was a prosperous silk merchant and head of English merchants in Bruges. For a time this was a so-called Staple town, an authorised trading centre through which English wool had to make its way after 1313, for selling, and for taxation purposes. Other Staple towns included, at various times, Calais and Antwerp.

A GUILD WAS AN ASSOCIATION OF TRADERS who united for the protection of their mutual interests. No person outside the guild could buy or sell without its permission. Guilds not only controlled trade, but also played an important part in local and cultural life. Trade went hand in hand with the town's possession of a charter, which was granted by the king in return for taxes, and exempted the inhabitants from the bondage of the lord of the manor. The guilds founded schools, organised charities and a merchant-banking system, appointed their own officials and administered justice according to their own courts and laws. Lavenham Guildhall (above) in Suffolk retains its medieval appearance.

CRAFTSMEN PROVED THEIR SKILLS to a guild master, as can be seen in this picture in which the work of a mason and a carpenter is being examined. Craft guilds grew up later than merchant guilds, sometimes in reaction to the latter's restrictive practices.

MYSTERY PLAYS were acted by apprentices of the "misters" or trade guilds. Their subjects were always moral or Biblical. Some well-known examples of these early plays are Noah's Fludde, The Second Shepherd's Play *and* Everyman. *They are still acted today in Wakefield, Coventry, Chester and London. The picture on the left is from a recent production by the London Medieval Players.*

RAW WOOL FOR THE FOREIGN MARKET *had to go through a centre known as The Staple in Flanders or Northern France. Here the quality of the wool was graded, prices were fixed, and customs duties levied for the English Crown. From the fourteenth century, wool exports were increasingly controlled by the Merchants of the Staple, whose insignia are shown above. However, the ravaging of the countryside in Northern France, and the destruction of the vineyards in Gascony, disrupted trade later in the century. The Staple system had encouraged the manufacture and production of woollen cloth in England, so that trade in textiles became more important than trade in wool itself as the century went by. The picture on the left shows a cargo ship being loaded in a Flemish port while others sail into the harbour.*

SIGNS ADVERTISED THE WARES *of medieval shops. The sun emblem shown below indicates a goldsmith's premises. Prosperous merchants often bought gold with their surplus cash and deposited it at the goldsmith's for safekeeping. Some medieval shop signs are still in use. For instance, the barber's red-and-white striped pole represents a bandaged limb, and was the symbol used by the barber-surgeon in olden times.*

IMPRESSIVE CEREMONIES ACCOMPANIED *official guild business. The picture above, by Holbein, commemorates Henry VIII's granting of a prestigious charter in 1541 to the Company of Barber-Surgeons in London. The guildsmen kneel in order of rank about the King. The dignitaries are attired in livery, and the guild's fine tapestries are clearly shown.*

This sallet, or battle helmet, dates from 1460, when the Wars of the Roses started in earnest with the Battle of Wakefield. It can now be seen in the Victoria and Albert Museum, London.

War began in earnest in July 1460. York was still in Ireland; but the Yorkist lords under Warwick, holding bases in Wales and at Calais, with all their connections and partisans, supported by the Papal Legate and some of the bishops, and, on the whole, by the Commons, confronted the Lancastrians and the Crown at Northampton. Henry VI stood entrenched, and new cannon guarded his line. But when the Yorkists attacked, Lord Grey of Ruthven, who commanded a wing, deserted him and helped the Yorkists over the breastworks. The royal forces fled in panic. King Henry VI remained in his tent, "sitting alone and solitary". The victors presented themselves to him, bowing to the ground. As after St Albans, they carried him again to London, and, having him in their power once more, ruled in his name. The so-called compromise in which all the Estates of the Realm concurred was then attempted. Henry was to be King for life; York was to conduct the government and succeed him at his death. The King in bondage had disinherited his own son. All who sought a quiet life for the nation hailed this arrangement. But the settlement defied the fact that Queen Margaret, with the Prince of Wales, was at liberty at Harlech Castle, in Wales. The Queen fought on.

With her army of the north and of north Wales Margaret advanced to assert the birthright of her son. The Duke of York, disdaining to remain in the security of Sandal Castle until his whole strength was gathered, marched against her. At Wakefield on December 30, 1460, the first considerable battle of the war was fought. The Lancastrians, with superior forces, caught the Yorkists by surprise, when many were foraging, and a frightful rout and massacre ensued. The old Earl of Salisbury, caught during the night, was beheaded immediately by Lord Exeter. Margaret's hand has been discerned in this severity. The heads of the three Yorkist nobles were exposed over the gates and walls of York. The great Duke's head, with a paper crown, grinned upon the landscape, summoning the avengers.

Hitherto the struggle had been between mature, comfortable magnates, deeply involved in State affairs and trying hard to preserve some limits. Now a new generation took charge. There was a new Lord Clifford, a new Duke of Somerset, above all a new Duke of York, all in their twenties, sword in hand, with fathers to avenge and England as the prize. When York's son, hitherto Earl of March, learnt that his father's cause had devolved upon him he did not shrink. He fell upon the Earl of Wiltshire and the Welsh Lancastrians, and on February 2, 1461, at the Battle of Mortimer's Cross, near Hereford, he beat and broke them up. "No quarter" was again the word. Among those executed after the battle was Owen Tudor, a harmless notable, who, with the axe and block before him, hardly believed that he would be beheaded until the collar of his red doublet was ripped off. His grandson, as will be seen, would carry on the quarrel.

The victorious Yorkists under their young Duke now marched to help the Earl of Warwick, who had returned from Calais and was being hard pressed in London; but Queen Margaret forestalled him, and on February 17, at the second Battle of St Albans, she inflicted upon Warwick a bloody defeat. Warwick, who was at this time the real leader of the Yorkist party, with many troops raised abroad and with the latest firearms and his own feudal forces, had carried the captive King with him and claimed to be acting in his name. But Margaret's onset took him by surprise. Warwick and Norfolk escaped; half their army was slaughtered. King Henry had been carted to the scene. There, beneath a large tree, he watched what happened with legitimate and presently unconcealed satisfaction. Two knights of high renown in the French war, one the redoubtable Sir Thomas Kyriel, had been appointed as his warders. They were to make sure no harm came to him. They therefore remained with him under his tree, and all were surrounded by the victorious army. Among the many captains of consequence whom Margaret put to death in cold blood the next morning these two cases needed special consideration. King Henry said he had asked them to bide with him and that they had done so for his own safety. Queen Margaret produced her son Edward, now seven years old, to whose disinheritance the King had perforce consented, and asked this child, already precociously fierce, to pronounce. "Their heads should be cut off" was the ready answer. As Kyriel was being led away to his fate he exclaimed, "May the wrath of God fall on those who have taught a child to speak with such words." Thus was pity banished from all hearts, and death or vengeance was the cry.

Edward IV's portrait shows the good-looking young man who, in 1461, was proclaimed King at Westminster. His grandfather, father and elder brother all perished in the Wakefield bloodbath.

Margaret now had her husband safe back in her hands, and with him the full authority of the Crown. The road to London was open, but she did not choose to advance upon it. The fierce hordes she had brought from the north had already disgraced themselves by their ravages far and wide along their line of march. They had roused against them the fury of the countryside. The King's friends said, "They deemed that the Northern men would have been too cruel in robbing if they had come to London." The city was, upon the whole, steadfast in the Yorkist cause, but it was also said, "If the King and Queen had come with their army to London they would have had all things as they wished." We cannot judge the circumstances fully. Edward of York was marching with the triumphant army of Mortimer's Cross night and day to reach London. Warwick had joined him in Oxfordshire with the survivors of St Albans. Perhaps King Henry pleaded that the capital should not become a battlefield, but at any rate Margaret and her advisers did not dare to make it so. Flushed with victory, laden with spoil, reunited with the King, the Lancastrians retired through Dunstable to the north, and thus disguised the fact that their Scottish mercenaries were already jogging home with all that they could carry.

This was the turning-point in the struggle. Nine days after the second Battle of St Albans Edward of York entered London. The citizens, who might have submitted to Margaret and the King, now hailed the Yorkists with enthusiasm. They thanked God and said, according to Gregory's *Chronicle*, "Let us walk in a new vineyard, and let us make a gay garden in the month of March, with this fair white rose and herb, the Earl of March." It was a vineyard amid thorns. The pretence of acting in the King's name could serve no longer. The Yorkists had become without disguise traitors and rebels against the Crown. But the mood of the youthful warrior who had triumphed and butchered at Mortimer's Cross recked little of this charge. As he saw it, his father had been ruined and killed through respect for the majesty of Henry VI. He and his friends would palter no longer with such conceptions. Forthwith he claimed the Crown; and such was the feeling of London and the strength of his army, now upon the spot, that he was able to make good show of public authority for his act. He declared himself King, and on March 4, 1461, was proclaimed at Westminster with such formalities as were possible. Henceforward he declared that the other side were guilty of treason, and that he would enforce upon them every penalty.

Bamburgh Castle, in Northumberland, was one of the three northern strongholds which sheltered Margaret of Anjou and her armies in 1462.

These assertions must now be made good, and King Edward IV marched north to settle once and for all with King Henry VI. Near York the Queen, with the whole power of Lancaster, confronted him not far from Tadcaster, by the villages of Saxton and Towton. Some accounts declare that a hundred thousand men were on the field, the Yorkists having forty and the Lancastrians sixty thousand; but later authorities greatly reduce these figures.

The Lancastrians held a good position on rising ground, their right flank being protected by the flooded stream of the Cock. Although Edward's army was not complete and the Duke of Norfolk's wing was still approaching, he resolved to attack. The battle began in a blinding snowstorm, which drove in the faces of the Lancastrians. The wind gave superior range to the archery of the attack and the Lancastrian shafts fell short, while they themselves suffered heavily. Under this pressure the decision was taken to advance downhill upon the foe. For six hours the two sides grappled furiously, with varying success. At the height of the battle Warwick is said to have dismounted and slain his horse to prove to his men he would not quit them alive. But all hung in the balance until late in the afternoon, when the arrival of the Duke of Norfolk's corps upon the exposed flank of the Lancastrians drove the whole mass into retreat, which soon became a rout.

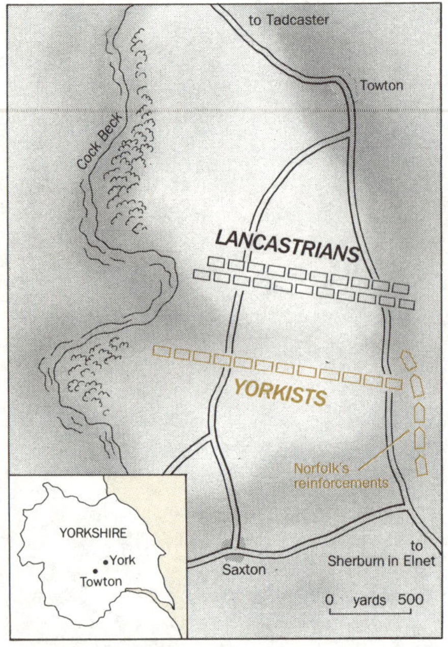

Snow, wind and the flooded River Cock made fighting difficult for both sides at the Battle of Towton in 1461. Victory for the Yorkists was, however, assured when supporting troops arrived with the Duke of Norfolk.

Now the Cock beck, hitherto a friend to Lancaster, became an enemy. The bridge towards Tadcaster was blocked with fugitives. Many thousands of men, heavily armoured, plunged into the swollen stream, and were drowned in such numbers that hideous bridges were formed of the corpses and some escaped thereby. The pursuit was carried on far into the night. Margaret and her son escaped to York, where King Henry had been observing the rites of Palm Sunday. Gathering him up, the imperious Queen set out with her child and a cluster of spears for the Scottish border. The bodies of thousands of Englishmen lay upon the field. The flower of the Lancastrian nobility and knighthood fell. For all prisoners there was but death. When Edward reached the town of York his first task was to remove the heads of his father and others of Margaret's victims from the battlements and to replace them with those of his noblest captives. Three months later, on June 28, he was crowned King at Westminster, and the Yorkist triumph seemed complete. It was followed by wholesale proscriptions and confiscations. Parliament in November 1461 passed an Act of Attainder which, surpassing all previous severities, lapped a hundred and thirty-three notable persons in its sweep. Not only the throne but one-third of the estates in England changed hands.

After Towton the Lancastrian cause was sustained by the unconquerable will of Queen Margaret. Never had her tenacity and rarely have her vicissitudes been surpassed in any woman. Apart from the sullen power of Lancaster in the north, she had the friendly regard of two countries, Scotland and France. Both had felt the heavy arm of England in former reigns; both rejoiced at its present division and weakness.

Margaret, as Queen of England and Princess of France, was an outstanding personage in the west of Europe. Her qualities of courage and combativeness, her commanding, persuasive personality, her fury against those who had driven her and her husband from the throne, produced from this one woman's willpower a long series of desperate, forlorn struggles after the main event had been decided. English national interests did not enter her mind. She had paid her way with Scotland by the surrender of Berwick. She then clinched a bargain with Louis XI by mortgaging Calais to him for twenty thousand gold livres.

In 1462 Margaret, after much personal appeal to the Courts of France and Scotland, found herself able to land with a power, and whether by treachery or weakness the three strongest northern castles, Bamburgh, Alnwick, and Dunstanburgh, opened their gates to her. Louis XI had lent her the services of a fine soldier, Pierre de Bréze, who under her spell spent his large fortune in her cause. In the winter of 1462, therefore, King Edward gathered his Yorkist powers, and, carrying his new train of artillery by sea to Newcastle, began the sieges of these lost strongholds. The heavy cannon played havoc with the masonry of the castles. All three fortresses fell in a month.

The behaviour of Edward at this moment constitutes a solid defence for his character. This young King, sure of his position, now showed a clemency unheard of in the Wars of the Roses. Not only did he pardon the Lancastrian nobles who were caught in the fortresses, but he made solemn pacts with them and took them in his full confidence. The Duke of Somerset and Sir Ralph Percy, on swearing allegiance were not merely allowed to go free, but restored to their estates. Percy was even given the guardianship of two of the castles. Somerset, son of the eminent minister slaughtered in the first Battle of St Albans, was admitted to even higher favour. Having made his peace, he was given a high command and a place in the inner councils of the royal army. In this new position at first he gave shrewd military advice, and was granted special pensions by the King.

The Wars of the Roses did not much affect the lives of ordinary people. These farm labourers are reasonably well-clothed. The view now held by historians is that this was a time of relative affluence for the workers.

Edward's magnanimity and forgiveness were ill repaid. When Margaret returned with fresh succours from France and Scotland in 1463 Percy opened the gates of Bamburgh to the Scots, and Alnwick was betrayed about the same time by a soured Yorkist officer, Sir Ralph Grey. Meanwhile Queen Margaret, with King Henry in her hands, herself besieged the castle of Norham, on the Tweed, near Berwick. Once again Edward and the Yorkists took the field, and the redoubtable new artillery, at that time esteemed as much among the leading nations as atomic weapons are today, was carried to the north. The great guns blew chunks off the castles. Margaret fled to France, while Henry buried himself amid the valleys and the pious foundations of Cumberland. This was the final parting of King Henry VI and his

Norham Castle in Northumberland was captured by the Lancastrians in 1464. In the previous century it had held out against the attack of Robert the Bruce.

Queen. Margaret took the prince with her on her travels. These were remarkable. With the Duke of Exeter, six knights, and her faithful Pierre de Brézé she landed at Slys, and appealed to the renowned chivalry of the house of Burgundy. She came "without royal habit or estate", she and her seven waiting-women had only the clothes they were wearing. Brézé paid for their food. Still, she was treated even in this adverse Court with royal honours.

Edward's clemency had been betrayed by Percy, but he did not withdraw his confidence from Somerset. The King was a man capable of the most bloody deeds when compelled, as he thought, by necessity, and at the same time eager to practise not only magnanimity, but open-hearted confidence. The confidence he showed to Somerset led him into deadly perils.

When in the autumn of 1462 he went to the north, Somerset and two hundred of his own men were his bodyguard. At Northampton, where bitter memories of the battle lingered, the townsfolk were first astounded and then infuriated to see this bearer of an accursed name in company with their Yorkist sovereign. Only King Edward's personal exertions saved his new-found follower from being torn to pieces. After this he found it necessary to provide other employment for Somerset.

He was sent to Holt Castle, in Denbighshire. The brawl at Northampton we must suppose convinced Somerset that even the King could not protect him from his Yorkist foes. At Christmas 1463 he deserted Edward and returned to the Lancastrian side.

Again the banner of Lancaster was raised. Somerset joined King Henry. Alnwick and Bamburgh still held out. Norham and Skipton had been captured, but now Warwick's brother Montagu with a substantial army was in the field. On April 25, 1464, at Hedgeley Moor, near Alnwick, he broke and destroyed the Lancastrian revolt. The leaders perished on the field, or afterwards on the block.

Edward's experiment of mercy in this quarrel was now at an end, and the former rigours were renewed in their extreme degree. Somerset, defeated with a small following at Hexham on May 15, 1464, was beheaded the next morning. Before this month was out in every Yorkist camp Lancastrian nobles and knights by dozens and half-dozens were put to death. There was nothing for it but to still these unquiet spirits.

This drawing of Henry Tudor as a young man shows him with an alert, watchful expression. The hardships he had suffered as a small boy left their mark on his character. In later years, contemporaries described him as "subtle", by which they meant that he possessed great cunning and intelligence.

Meanwhile the diplomacy of the English Crown had effected a fifteen years' truce with the King of Scotland, and was potent both at the Courts of France and Burgundy. Margaret remained helpless at Bar-le-Duc. Poor King Henry was at length tracked down near Clitheroe, in Lancashire, and conveyed to London. This time there was no ceremonial entry. With his feet tied by leather thongs to the stirrups, and with a straw hat on his head, the futile but saintly figure around whom such storms had beaten was led three times round the pillory, and finally hustled to the Tower, whose gates closed on him – yet not, this time, for ever.

With the fall of Alnwick only one fortress in the whole kingdom still resisted. The castle of Harlech, on the western sea, alone flaunted the Red Rose. Harlech stood a siege of seven years. When it surrendered in 1468 there were found to be but fifty effective men in the garrison. With two exceptions, they were admitted to mercy. Among them was a child of twelve, who had survived the rigours of the long blockade. His name was Richmond. He was the grandson of Owen Tudor, and the future founder of the Tudor dynasty.

CHAPTER 29

THE ADVENTURES OF EDWARD IV

KING EDWARD IV HAD MADE GOOD his right to the Crown upon the field. He was a soldier and a man of action; in the teeth of danger his quality was at its highest. Long marches, hazardous decisions, the marshalling of armies, the conduct of battles, seemed his natural sphere. The worse things got, the better he became. But the opposite was also true. He was at this time a fighting man and little more, and when the fighting stopped he had no serious zest for sovereignty. The land was fair; the blood of youth coursed in his veins; all his blood debts were paid. With goodwill he sheathed his sharp sword. It had won him his crown; now to enjoy life.

In the first part of his reign England was therefore ruled by the two brothers, Warwick, and Montagu, Earl of Northumberland. They believed they had put the King on the throne, and meant him to remain there while they governed. The King did not quarrel with this. History has scolded this prince of twenty-two for not possessing immediately the statecraft and addiction to business for which his office called. Edward united contrasting characters. He loved peace; he shone in war. But he loved peace for its indulgences rather than its dignity. His pursuit of women, combined with hunting, feasting, and drinking to fill his life. Let Warwick and Northumberland and other anxious lords carry the burden of State, and let the King be merry. For a while this suited all parties. The victors divided the spoil; the King had his amusements, and his lords their power and policy.

Elizabeth Woodville, the widow of a Lancastrian knight, was Edward's beautiful but dangerous choice of Queen. Her relatives, whom Edward raised to positions of power, made enemies among the established aristocracy.

Thus some years slipped by, while the King, although gripping from time to time the reins of authority, led in the main his life of ease, until in 1464 he strayed from the broad, sunlit glades of royal libertinage onto the perilous precipices of romance and marriage.

One day the King a-hunting was carried far by the chase. He rested for the night at a castle. In this castle a lady of quality, niece of the owner, had found shelter. Elizabeth Woodville was the widow of a Lancastrian knight, Sir John Grey, "in Margaret's battle at St Albans slain". Her mother, Jacquetta of Luxembourg, had been the youthful wife of the famous John, Duke of Bedford, and after his death she had married his steward, Sir Richard Woodville, later created Earl Rivers. This condescension so far below her station caused offence to the aristocracy. She was fined £1,000 as a deterrent to others. Nevertheless she lived happily ever after, and bore her husband no fewer than thirteen children, of whom Elizabeth, an austere woman, upright, fearless, chaste and fruitful, was one. She and her two sons were all under the ban of the attainder which disinherited the adherents of Lancaster. The chance of obtaining royal mercy could not be missed. The widow bowed in humble peitition before the youthful conqueror, and, like the tanner's daughter of Falaise, made at first glance the sovereign her slave. The Lady Elizabeth, however, observed the strictest self-restraint, which only enhanced the passion of the King. He gave her all his love, and when he found her obdurate he besought her to share his Crown. He spurned the counsels of prudence and worldly wisdom. But he was well aware of the dangers of his choice. His marriage in 1464 with Elizabeth Woodville was a secret guarded in deadly earnest. The statesmen at the head of the Government, while they smiled at what seemed an amorous frolic, never dreamt it was a solemn union.

Warwick's plans for the King's future had been different. Isabella of Spain, or preferably a French princess, were brides who might greatly forward the interests of England. A royal marriage in those days might be a bond of peace between neighbouring states or the means of successful war. Warwick used grave arguments and pressed the King to decide. Edward seemed strangely hesitant, however, and dwelt upon his objections until the minister, who was also his master, became impatient. Then at last the truth was revealed to all: he had for five months been married to Elizabeth Woodville. Here then was the occasion which sundered him from the valiant Kingmaker. Fourteen years older, but also in the prime of life, Warwick had deep roots in England, and his popularity was unbounded. The Londoners looked to him. He held the power. But no one knew better than he that there slept in Edward a tremendous warrior, capable when roused of attempting and of doing all.

The King too, for his part, began to take more interest in affairs. Queen Elizabeth had five brothers, seven sisters, and two sons. By royal decree he raised them to high rank, or married them into the greatest families. He went so far as to marry his wife's fourth brother, at twenty, to the Dowager Duchess of Norfolk, aged eighty. Eight new peerages came into existence in the Queen's family. It must be remembered that at this time there were but sixty peers, of whom not more than fifty could ever be got to Parliament on one occasion. The arrival of a new nobility who had done nothing notable in the war and now surrounded the indolent King was not merely offensive, but politically dangerous to Warwick and his proud associates.

But the clash came over foreign policy. In this sad generation England, lately the master, had become the sport of neighbouring states. Her titled refugees, from one faction or the other, beset the Courts of Western Europe. The Duke of Burgundy had been shocked to learn one morning that a Duke of Exeter and several other high English nobles were actually begging their bread at the tail of one of his progresses. Ashamed to see such a slight upon his class, he provided them with modest dwellings and allowances. Similar charities were performed by Louis XI to the unhappy descendants of the victors of Agincourt. Margaret with her retinue of shadows was welcomed in her pauper stateliness both in Burgundy and France. At any moment either power, now become formidable as England had waned, might support the exiled faction in good earnest and pay back the debts of fifty years before by an invasion of England. It was the policy of Warwick and his connections to make friends with France, by far the stronger power, and thus obtain effective security. In this mood they hoped to make a French match for the King's sister. Edward took the opposite line. With the instinct which afterwards ruled our island for so many centuries, he sought to base English policy upon the second strongest state in Western Europe. He could no doubt argue that to be the ally of France was to be in the power of France, but to be joined with Burgundy was to have the means of correcting if not of controlling a French action. Amid his revelries and other hunting he nursed a conqueror's spirit.

The King therefore, to Warwick's chagrin and alarm, in 1468 married his sister Margaret to Charles the Bold, who had in 1467 succeeded as Duke of

In this manuscript picture from the Bodleian Library, Oxford, Margaret of Burgundy kneels in prayer with her ladies. She was Edward IV's sister, whom he had married to Charles the Bold. Edward IV avoided a dynastic marriage for himself, but forced one on his sister.

Burgundy. Thus not only did these great lords, who at the constant peril of their lives and by all their vast resources had placed him on the throne, suffer slights by the creation of a new nobility, but they had besides to stomach a foreign policy which they believed would be fatal to England, to the Yorkist party, and to themselves. What help could Burgundy give if France, joined to the House of Lancaster, invaded England? What would happen to them, their great estates, and all who depended upon them in such catastrophe?

The offended chiefs took deep counsel together. Edward continued to enjoy his life with his Queen, and now and again with others. His attention in public matters was occupied mainly with Lancastrian plots and movements, but underneath and behind him a far graver menace was preparing. The Nevilles were at length ready to try conclusions with him. Warwick's plan was singular in its skill. He had gained the King's brother, Clarence, to his side by whispering that but for the upstart Woodvilles he might succeed Edward as King. As bond it was secretly agreed that Clarence should marry Warwick's daughter Isabella.

Richard Neville, Earl of Warwick, is shown here with symbols from his crest, the Dun Cow and the Eagle of Monthernes. He was better known as "the Kingmaker", and his plans for Edward's future included a dynastic marriage with a French or Spanish princess.

When all was ready Warwick struck. A rising took place in the north. Thousands of men in Yorkshire under the leadership of various young lords complained in arms about taxation. The "thrave", a levy paid since the days of Athelstan, became suddenly obnoxious. But other grievances were urged, particularly that the King was swayed by "favourites". The King was now forced to go to the north. Except his small bodyguard he had no troops of his own, but at Nottingham he awaited the Earls of Pembroke and Devon, both new creations of his own, who had marshalled the levies of Wales and the west. As soon as the King had been enticed northward, Warwick and Clarence, who had hitherto crouched at Calais, came to England with the Calais garrison. Warwick published a manifesto supporting the northern rebels, "the King's true subjects" as he termed them, and urged them "with piteous lamentation to be the means to our Sovereign Lord the King of remedy and reformation". He was joined by many thousands of Kentish men and was received with great respect in London. But before he and Clarence could bring their forces against the King's rear the event was decided. The northern rebels intercepted Pembroke and Devon, and at Edgcott, near Banbury, defeated them with a merciless slaughter, a hundred and sixty-eight knights, squires, and gentlemen either falling in the fight or being executed thereafter. Both Pembroke and later Devon were beheaded.

The King, trying to rally his scattered forces at Olney, in Buckinghamshire, found himself in the power of his great nobles. His brother, Richard of Gloucester, known to legend as "Crookback" because of his alleged deformity, seemed his only friend. At first Edward attempted to rally Warwick and Clarence to their duty, but in the course of conversation he was made to realise that he was their captive. With bows and ceremonies they explained that his future reign must be in accordance with their advice. He was conveyed to Warwick's castle at Middleham, and there kept in honourable but real restraint. At this moment therefore Warwick the Kingmaker had actually the two rival Kings, Henry VI and Edward IV, both his prisoners, one in the Tower and the other at Middlesham. To make the lesson even plainer, Lord Rivers, the Queen's father, and John Woodville, her brother, were arrested and executed at Kenilworth without any pretence of trial. Thus did the old nobility deal with the new.

But the relations between Warwick and the King did not admit of such simple solutions. Warwick had struck with suddenness and for a while no one realised what had happened. As the truth became known, the Yorkist nobility viewed with astonishment and anger the detention of their brave, victorious sovereign, and the Lancastrians everywhere raised their heads in the hopes of profiting by the Yorkist feud. The King found it convenient in his turn to dissemble. He professed himself convinced that Warwick and Clarence were right. He undertook to amend his ways, and after he had signed free pardons to all who had been in arms against him he was liberated. Thus was a settlement reached between Warwick and the Crown. King Edward was soon again at the head of forces, defeating Lancastrian rebels and executing their leaders, while Warwick and all his powerful connections returned to their posts, proclaimed their allegiance, and apparently enjoyed royal favour. But all this was on the surface.

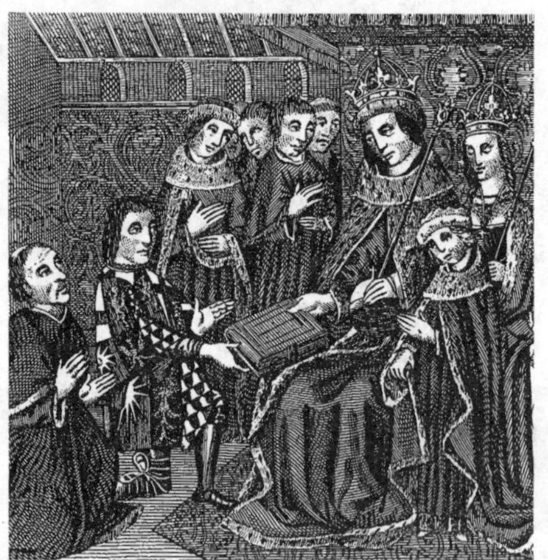

Earl Rivers presents a book to his patron, his son-in-law Edward IV. The resentment felt by the nobility towards Rivers and his family brought tragic consequences.

In March 1470, under the pretence of suppressing a Lancastrian rebellion in Lincolnshire, the King called his forces to arms. At Losecoat Field he defeated the insurgents, who fled; and in the series of executions which had now become customary after every engagement he obtained a confession which accused both Warwick and Clarence of treason. The evidence is fairly convincing; for at this moment they were conspiring against Edward, and shortly afterwards refused to obey his express order to join him. The King, with troops fresh from victory, turned on them all of a sudden. They fled, astounded that their own methods should be retorted upon themselves. They sought safety in Warwick's base at Calais, but Lord Wenlock, whom he had left as his deputy, refused to admit them. The Kingmaker found himself by one sharp twist of fortune deprived of almost every resource he had counted upon as sure. He in his turn presented himself at the French Court as a suppliant.

But this was the best luck Louis XI had ever known. Now here in France were the leaders of both the parties that had disputed England for so long. With gusto the stern, hard-pressed Louis set himself to the task of reconciling and combining these opposite forces. At Angers he confronted Margaret and her son, now a fine youth of seventeen, with Warwick and Clarence, and proposed brutally to them that they should join together with his support to overthrow Edward. At first both parties recoiled. Nor can we wonder. A river of blood flowed between them. She had beheaded Warwick's father Salisbury, slain his uncle York and his cousin Rutland. He for his part had butchered the two Somersets, the Earl of Wiltshire, and many of her devoted adherents. In 1459 Margaret had declared Warwick attainted. In 1460 he had branded her son as bastard. But they both hated Edward and were the champions of a generation which could not accept defeat. And here, as indeed for a time it proved, appeared the means of speedy triumph.

Warwick had a fleet. He had the sailors in all the seaports of the south coast. He knew he had but to go or send his summons to large parts of England for the people to take arms at his command. Margaret represented the House of Lancaster, stubborn as ever. They agreed to forgive and unite. They took solemn oaths at Angers upon a fragment of the Holy Cross, which luckily was available. The confederacy was sealed by the betrothal of Margaret's son to Warwick's younger daughter, Anne. No one can blame Margaret because in the ruin of her cause she reluctantly forgave injuries and welcomed the Kingmaker's invaluable help. She had never swerved from her faith. But for Warwick the transaction was unnatural and brutal.

Moreover, he overlooked the effect on Clarence of the new marriage he had arranged for his daughter Anne. A son born of this union would have had a great hope of uniting torn, tormented England. It was reasonable to expect the birth of an heir to these prospects. But Clarence had been swayed in his desertion of his brother by thoughts of the Crown, and although he was now named as the next in succession after Margaret's son the value of his chance was no longer high. Edward had been staggered by his brother's conduct. He did not however allow his personal resentment to influence his action. A lady in attendance upon the new Duchess of Clarence proved to be a discreet and accomplished emissary. She conveyed to Clarence soon after he fled from England that he had only to rejoin his brother for all to be pardoned and forgotten. The new agreement between Warwick and Margaret decided Clarence to avail himself of this offer, but not immediately. He must have been a great dissembler; for Warwick was no more able to forecast his action in the future than his brother had been in the past.

This picture of ships of the time of Edward IV shows platforms both at the prow and at the stern for the positioning of guns.

Warwick now repeated the process he had used a year before. Fitzhugh, his cousin, started a new insurrection in Yorkshire. Edward gathered some forces and, making little of the affair, marched against the rebels. Warned by Charles of Burgundy, he even expressed his wish that Warwick would land. He seems to have been entirely confident. But never was there a more swift un-deception. Warwick and Clarence landed at Dartmouth in September 1470. Kent and other southern counties rose in Warwick's behalf. He marched to London. He brought the miserable Henry VI from his prison in the Tower, placed a crown on his head, paraded him through the capital, and seated him upon the throne.

At Nottingham Edward received alarming news. The major part of his kingdom seemed to have turned against him. Suddenly he learnt that while the northern rebels were moving down upon him and cutting him from his Welsh succours, and while Warwick was moving northward with strong forces, the Marquis of Montagu, Warwick's brother, hitherto faithful, had made his men throw up their caps for King Henry. When Edward heard of Montagu's desertion, and also of rapid movements to secure his person, he deemed it his sole hope to fly beyond the seas. He had but one refuge — the Court of Burgundy; and with a handful of followers he cast himself upon his brother-in-law. Charles the Bold was also cautious. He had to consider the imminent danger of an attack by England and France united. Until he was sure that this was inevitable he temporised with his royal refugee relation. But when it became clear that the policy of Warwick was undoubtedly to make war upon him in conjunction with Louis XI he defended himself by an obvious manoeuvre. He furnished King Edward secretly with about twelve hundred Flemish and German soldiers and ships and money for a descent.

Meanwhile the Kingmaker ruled England, and it seemed that he might long continue to do so. He had King Henry VI a puppet in his hand. The unhappy man, a breathing ruin sitting like a sack upon the throne, with a crown on his head and a sceptre in his hand, received the fickle caresses of Fortune with the same mild endurance which he had shown to her malignities. Statutes were passed in his name which annihilated all the disinheritances and attainders of the Yorkist Parliament. The banished nobles or the heirs of the slain returned from poverty and exile to their ancient seats. Meanwhile all preparations were made for a combined attack by England and France on Burgundy, and war became imminent.

This contemporary picture of the Battle of Barnet shows the pike as a formidable weapon. The battleground was a mass of confusion due to a thick fog and in the melee, Warwick was slain.

But while these violent transformations were comprehensible to the actors, and the drama proceeded with apparent success, the solid bulk of England on both sides was incapable of following such too-quick movements and reconciliations. Almost the whole population stood wherever it had stood before. Their leaders might have made new combinations, but ordinary men could not believe that the antagonism of the Red and the White Rose was ended. It needed but another shock to produce an entirely different scene. It is significant that, although repeatedly urged by Warwick to join him and her husband in London, and although possessed of effective forces, Margaret remained in France, and kept her son with her.

In March 1471 Edward landed with his small expedition at Ravenspur, a port in Yorkshire now washed away by the North Sea, but then still famous for the descent of Henry of Bolingbroke in 1399. Edward, fighting for his life, was, as usual, at his best. York shut its gates in his face, but, like Bolingbroke, he declared he had only come to claim his private estates, and bade his troops declare themselves for King Henry VI. Accepted and nourished on these terms, he set forth on his march to London. Montagu, with four times his numbers, approached to intercept him. Edward, by extraordinary marches, manoeuvred past him. All Yorkist lords and adherents in the districts through which he passed joined his army. He was strong enough to proclaim himself King again. The Kingmaker, disconcerted by the turn of events, sent repeated imperative requests to Margaret to come at once, and at Coventry stationed himself in King Edward's path. Meanwhile his brother Montagu followed Edward southward, only two marches behind. In this dire strait Edward had a resource unsuspected by Warwick. He knew Clarence was his man. Clarence was moving from Gloucestershire with considerable forces, ostensibly to join Warwick; but Edward, slipping round Warwick's flank, as he had outmarched and outwitted Montagu, placed himself between Warwick and London, where Clarence could make his junction with him.

Both sides now concentrated all their strength. Edward entered London, and was cordially received by the bewildered citizens. Henry VI, who had actually been made to ride about the streets at the head of six hundred horsemen, was relieved from these exertions and taken back to his prison in the Tower. The decisive battle impended on the North Road, and at Barnet on April 14, 1471, Edward and the Yorkists faced Warwick and the house of Neville, with the new Duke of Somerset, and important Lancastrian allies.

Throughout England no one could see clearly what was happening, and the Battle of Barnet, which resolved their doubts, was itself fought in a fog. The lines of battle overlapped; Warwick's right turned Edward's left flank, and vice versa. The Kingmaker, stung perhaps by imputations upon his physical courage, fought on foot. Lord Oxford, a prominent Lancastrian, commanding the overlapping Lancastrian left, found himself successful in his charge, but lost in the mist. Little knowing that the whole of King Edward's rear was open to his attack, he tried to regain his own lines and arrived in the rear of Somerset's centre. The badge of a star and rays on his banners was mistaken by Warwick's troops for the sun and rays of King Edward. Warwick's archers loosed upon him. The mistake was discovered, but in those days of treason and changing sides it only led to another blunder. It was assumed that he had deserted. Oxford, in his uncertainty, rode off into the gloom. Somerset, on the other flank, had already been routed. Warwick, with the right wing, was attacked by the King and the main Yorkist power. Here indeed it was not worthwhile to ask for mercy. Warwick, outnumbered, his ranks broken, sought to reach his horse but was overtaken by the Yorkists and battered to death. He had been the foremost champion of the Yorkist cause. By his depraved abandonment of all the causes for which he had sent so many men to their doom he had deserved death; and for his virtues, which were distinguished, it was fitting that it should come to him in honourable guise.

On the very day of Barnet Margaret at last landed in England. Somerset, the fourth Duke, with his father and elder brother to avenge, met her and became her military commander. On learning that Warwick was slain and his army beaten and dispersed, the hitherto indomitable Queen had her hour of despair. Sheltering in Cerne Abbey, near Weymouth, her thought was to return to France; but now her son, the Prince of Wales, nearly eighteen, in whose veins flowed the blood of Henry V, was for fighting for the Crown or death. Margaret once again rallied her spirits. Her only hope was to reach the Welsh border, where strong traditional Lancastrian forces were already in arms. The Kingmaker aberration had been excised. The struggle was once again between Lancaster and York. Edward strove to cut Margaret off from Wales. Both armies marched incessantly. The Lancastrians succeeded in reaching the goal first, but only with their troops in a state of extreme exhaustion. Edward, close behind, pressed on, and on the May 4 brought them to battle at Tewkesbury.

This battle was simple in its character. The two sides faced each other in the usual formation of three sectors, right, centre, and left. Somerset commanded Margaret's left, Lord Wenlock and the Prince of Wales the centre, and Devon her right. King Edward exercised a more general command. The Lancastrian position was strong; "in front of their field were so evil lanes, and deep dykes, so many hedges, trees, and bushes, that it was right hard to approach them here and come to hands." Apparently the Lancastrian plan was to await the attack which the Yorkists were eager to deliver. However, Somerset saw an opportunity for using one of the "evil lanes" to pierce the Yorkist centre, and either without consulting the other generals or in disagreement with them, he charged forward and gained a momentary success. But King Edward had foreseen his weakness in this quarter. He

Aerial view of the town of Tewkesbury, Gloucestershire. The battle fought here in 1471 ended Margaret of Anjou's hopes and killed her young, courageous son, Edward. It also sealed the fate of Henry VI; the Yorkists put him to death.

manfully withstood the irruption upon his main body, and two hundred spears he had thrown out wide as a flank guard fell upon Somerset at a decisive moment and from a deadly angle. The Lancastrians' wing recoiled in disorder. The Yorkists advanced all along the line. In their turn they fell upon their enemies' now unguarded flank, and the last army of the House of Lancaster broke into ruin. Somerset evidently felt that he had not been supported at the critical moment. Before flying from the field he dashed out Wenlock's brains with his mace.

The Lancastrians were scattered or destroyed. Somerset and many other notables who thought themselves safe in sanctuary were dragged forth and decapitated. The Prince of Wales, fighting valiantly, was slain on the field. Margaret was captured and kept for a show. She remained in captivity, moved from place to place, until ransomed by Louis XI. Eleven years after Tewkesbury she died in poverty in her father's Anjou.

A carving in Bristol Cathedral shows two peasants killing a pig. Despite the ravages of Civil War, ordinary people were better off than ever before in the fifteenth century, and farming enjoyed a time of prosperity.

After the battle Richard of Gloucester had hastened to London. He had a task to do at the Tower. As long as the Prince of Wales lived King Henry's life had been safe, but with the death of the last hope of Lancaster his fate was sealed. On the night of May 21 the Duke of Gloucester visited the Tower with full authority from the King, where he probably supervised the murder of the melancholy spectator who had been the centre of fifty years of cruel contention. When King Edward and his victorious army entered London, always their partisan, the triumph of the Yorkist cause was complete.

The rest of the reign of Edward IV may be told briefly. The King was now supreme. His foes and his patrons alike were dead. He was now a matured and disillusioned statesman. Victorious and unchallenged, he set himself to practise the utmost economy in everything except his personal expenses, and to avoid any policy which might drive him to beg from Parliament. He had a new source of revenue in the estates of the attainted Lancastrians. Thus so long as there was peace the King could pay his way. But the nobility and the nation sought more. They wanted to reconquer France. They looked back across their own miseries to the glories of Agincourt, Poitiers, and Crécy. The King was expected to produce results in this sphere. It was his intention to do the least possible. Nevertheless he obtained from Parliament considerable grants for a war in alliance with Burgundy against France.

In 1475 he invaded France, but advanced only as far as Picquigny, near Amiens. There he parleyed. Louis XI shared his outlook. He too saw that kings might grow strong and safe in peace. The kings sought peace and found it. Louis offered Edward a lump sum of 75,000 crowns, and a yearly tribute of 50,000, almost enough to balance the royal budget and make him independent of Parliament. Edward closed on the bargain, and signed the Treaty of Picquigny. But Charles the Bold, his ally of Burgundy, took it amiss. At Péronne, in full assembly, with all the English captains gathered, he declared that he had been shamefully betrayed by his ally. A most painful impression was created; but the King put up with it. He went back home and drew for seven successive years this substantial payment for not harrying France, and at the same time he pocketed most of the monies which Parliament had voted for harrying her.

At this date the interest of these transactions centres mainly upon the character of Edward IV, and we can see that though he had to strive through fierce deeds and slaughter to his throne he was at heart a lover of ease. It by no means follows that his policy was injurious to the realm. A long peace was needed for recovery from the horrible civil war. On his death he was the first King since Henry II to leave not debts but a fortune.

There came one day when he had to call Parliament together. His quarrel was with his brother Clarence. Although the compact made between these brothers before Barnet and Tewkesbury had been strictly kept, Edward never trusted Clarence again. Nothing could burn out from his mind the sense that Clarence was a traitor who had betrayed his cause and his family at one decisive moment and had been rebought at another. Clarence for his part knew that the wound was unhealed but he was a magnificent prince, and he sprawled buoyantly over the land. He flouted the King, defying the royal courts; he executed capital sentences upon persons who had offended him in private matters. He may have discovered the secret of Edward's alleged pre-contract of marriage with Eleanor Butler which Richard of Gloucester was later to use in justifying his usurpation. Certainly if Edward's marriage to Elizabeth Woodville were to be proved invalid for this reason Clarence was the next legitimate heir, and a source of danger to the King. In January 1478 Edward's patience was exhausted. He called Parliament to condemn Clarence. He adduced a formidable catalogue of crimes and affronts to the throne, constituting treason. Parliament accepted the King's view. They adjudged Clarence worthy of death, and left the execution in the hands of the King.

Clarence was already in the Tower. How he died is much disputed. Some say the King gave him his choice of death. Certainly Edward did not intend to have a grisly public spectacle. According to Shakespeare the Duke was drowned in a butt of malmsey wine. This was certainly the popular legend. At any rate no one has attempted to prove any different tale.

Other fortunes had attended Richard of Gloucester. Shortly after the death of Henry VI he married Anne Neville, daughter of the dead Kingmaker and co-heiress to the vast Warwick estates. This union excited no enthusiasm; for the succession to the Crown seemed plain and secure. The King himself was only forty, and Queen Elizabeth had produced not only five daughters, but two fine boys. In 1483 one was twelve and the other nine. In another ten years the Yorkist triumph would have become permanent. But here Fate intervened. In April 1483, after only ten days' illness, this strong King was cut down in his prime. It may well have been appendicitis. He died unprepared except by the Church, and his faithful brother Richard saw himself suddenly confronted with an entirely new view of his future.

Mary of Burgundy, shown above, was Edward IV's niece and the daughter of his wealthy ally, Charles the Bold. The fact that each side in the Wars of the Roses had a continental ally probably helped to prolong the years of conflict. Support for the Lancastrians, of course, came from Anjou.

CHAPTER 30

RICHARD III

THE KING DIED SO SUDDENLY that all were caught by surprise. His eldest son, Edward, dwelt at Ludlow, on the Welsh border, under the care of his uncle, the second Lord Rivers. A Protector was inevitable and Richard of Gloucester, the King's brother, renowned in war, grave and competent in administration, enriched by Warwick's inheritance and many other great estates, stood forth without compare, and had been nominated by the late King himself. Around him gathered most of the old nobility. They viewed with general distaste the idea of a king whose grandfather,

This portrait of Richard III, one of the most controversial characters in history, is now in the National Portrait Gallery. Was crookbacked Richard really the murderer of his nephews or was he a just King whose reputation was wrecked by Tudor propaganda? The question has exercised the minds of historians through the ages and has been examined by Josephine Tey in her detective story The Daughter of Time.

though a knight, had been a mere steward to one of their own order. They deplored a minority and thereafter the rule of an inexperienced boy-king. They were however bound by their oaths and by the succession in the Yorkist line that their own swords had established.

One thing at least they would not brook: Queen Elizabeth and her low-born relations should no longer have the ascendancy. On the other hand, Lord Rivers at Ludlow had possession of the new King. For three weeks both parties eyed one another and parleyed. It was agreed in April that the King should be crowned at the earliest moment, but that he should come to London attended by not more than two thousand horsemen. Accordingly this cavalcade, headed by Lord Rivers and his nephew, Grey, rode through Shrewsbury and Northampton. They had reached Stony Stratford when they learnt that Gloucester and his ally, the Duke of Buckingham, were only ten miles behind them. They turned back to Northampton to greet the two Dukes, apparently suspecting no evil. Richard received them amicably; they dined together. But with the morning there was a change.

Rivers and Grey were immediately made prisoners and Richard then rode to Stony Stratford, arrested the commanders of the two thousand horse, forced his way to the young King, and told him he had discovered a design on the part of Lord Rivers and others to seize the Government and oppress the old nobility. On this declaration Edward V took the only positive action recorded of his reign. He wept. Well he might.

The next morning Duke Richard presented himself again to Edward. He embraced him as an uncle; he bowed to him as a subject. He announced himself as Protector. He dismissed the two thousand horsemen to their homes; their services would not be needed. To London! To the coronation! Thus this melancholy procession set out.

The Queen, who was already in London, had no illusions. She took sanctuary at once with her other children at Westminster, making a hole through the wall between the church and the palace to transport such personal belongings as she could gather.

The report that the King was in duress caused a commotion in the capital. But Lord Hastings reassured the Council that all was well and that any disturbance would only delay the coronation, upon which the peace of the realm depended. The Archbishop of York, who was also Chancellor, tried to reassure the Queen. He even gave her the Great Seal as a kind of guarantee. He was not in any plot, but only an old fool playing for safety first and peace at any price. Presently, frightened at what he had done, he managed to get the Great Seal back.

The King arrived in London only on May 4, and the coronation, which had been fixed for that date, was necessarily postponed. He was lodged at the Bishop of London's palace, where he received the fealty of all the lords, spiritual and temporal. But the Protector and his friends argued that it would be more fitting to the royal dignity to dwell in one of his own castles. The Tower was a residence not only commodious but at the same time safe from any popular disorder. To this decision the lords of the Council gave united assent, it not being either easy or safe to disagree. With much ceremony and protestations of devotion the child of twelve was conducted to the Tower, and its gates closed behind him.

London was in a ferment, and the magnates gathered there gazed upon each other in doubt and fear. The next step in the tragedy concerned Lord

Hastings. He had played a leading part in the closing years of Edward IV. After the King's death he had been strong against the Woodvilles; but he was the first to detach himself from Richard's proceedings. It did not suit him that all power should rapidly be accumulating in Richard's hands. He began to be friendly with the Queen's party, still in the sanctuary of Westminster Abbey. Of what happened next all we really know is that Hastings was abruptly arrested in council at the Tower on June 13 and beheaded without trial on the same day. Meanwhile Richard's trusted lieutenant, Sir Richard Ratcliffe, had collected Lords Rivers, Vaughan, Grey, and the commanders of the two thousand horse from the castles in which they were confined. He cut off their heads a few days after Hastings had suffered.

The Queen and her remaining son still sheltered in sanctuary. Richard felt that it would be more natural that the two brothers should be together under his care, and he moved the Council to request the Queen to give him up. Having no choice, the Queen submitted, and the little prince of nine was handed over in Westminster Hall to the Protector, who embraced him affectionately and conducted him to the Tower, which neither he nor his brother was ever to leave again.

Richard's northern bands were now approaching London in considerable numbers, and he felt strong enough to take his next step. The coronation of Edward V had been postponed several times. Now a preacher named Shaw, brother of the Lord Mayor of London, one of Richard's partisans, was engaged to preach a sermon at St Paul's Cross. Taking his text from the Book of Wisdom, "Bastard slips shall not take deep root", he impugned Edward IV's marriage with Elizabeth Woodville upon a number of grounds, including sorcery, violation of the alleged previous betrothal to Eleanor Butler, and the assertion that the ceremony had been performed in an unconsecrated place. He argued from this that Edward's children were illegitimate and that the Crown rightly belonged to Richard. Richard now appeared, accompanied by Buckingham, evidently expecting to be publicly acclaimed; but the people remained mute, and only some of the Duke's servants threw up their caps, crying, "King Richard!"

Nevertheless on June 25 Parliament met, and after receiving a roll declaring that the late King's marriage with Elizabeth was no marriage at all and that Edward's children were bastards it petitioned Richard to assume the Crown. With becoming modesty Richard persistently refused; but when Buckingham assured him of Parliament's determination that the children of Edward should not rule, and if he would not serve the country they would be forced to choose some other noble, he overcame his conscientious scruples. The next day he was enthroned, with much ceremony. At the same time the forces, about five thousand strong, which Ratcliffe had sent from the north were reviewed in Finsbury Fields.

The coronation of King Richard III was fixed for July 6, and was celebrated with all possible pomp and splendour. Particular importance was attached to the religious aspect. Archbishop Bourchier placed the crowns on the heads of the King and Queen; they were anointed with oil; they received the Sacrament in the presence of the assembly, and finally repaired to a banquet in Westminster Hall.

The King now had a title acknowledged and confirmed by Parliament, and upon the theory of the bastardy of Edward's children he was also the lineal successor in blood. Yet from this very moment there began that

The Great Seal of Richard III. Seals were often used instead of signatures to give authorisation to orders issued by the king.

The tragic story of the princes in the Tower was the subject of this famous painting by Millais (1829–96) in Victorian times.

marked distrust and hostility of all classes towards King Richard III which all his arts and competence could not allay. It is contended by the defenders of King Richard that the Tudor version of these events has prevailed. But the English people who lived at the time and learnt of the events day by day formed their convictions two years before the Tudors gained power, or were indeed a prominent factor. Richard III held the authority of government. He told his own story with what facilities were available, and he was spontaneously and almost universally disbelieved. Indeed, no fact stands forth more unchallengeable than that the overwhelming majority of the nation was convinced that Richard had used his power as Protector to usurp the Crown and that the princes had disappeared in the Tower.

No man had done more to place Richard upon the throne than the Duke of Buckingham, and upon no one had the King bestowed greater gifts and favours. Yet during these first three months of Richard's reign Buckingham from being his chief supporter became his mortal foe. His motives are not clear. Perhaps he feared for his own safety, for was he not himself of royal blood descended both through the Beauforts and Thomas of Woodstock from Edward III? Buckingham's mind was also troubled by the knowledge that all the ceremony and vigour with which Richard's ascent to the throne had been conducted did not affect the general feeling that he was a usurper.

Meanwhile Richard began a progress from Oxford through the Midlands. At every city he laboured to make the best impression, righting wrongs, settling disputes, granting favours, and courting popularity. Yet he could not escape the sense that behind the displays of gratitude and loyalty there lay an unspoken challenge to his kingship. There was little concealment of this in the south. In London, Kent, Essex, and throughout the Home Counties feeling already ran high against him, and on all men's lips was the demand that the princes should be liberated. Richard did not as yet suspect Buckingham, who had parted from him at Gloucester, of any serious disaffection. But he was anxious for the safety of his crown. How could he maintain it while his nephews lived to provide a rallying point for any combination of hostile forces against him? So we come to the principal crime ever afterwards associated with Richard's name. His interest is plain. His character was ruthless. It is certain that the helpless children in the Tower were not seen again after the month of July 1483.

The Bloody Tower where the young princes were kept at the Tower of London. High-born prisoners lived there in comfort, and it is possible that the young princes were installed for protection, rather than for any more sinister reason.

The popular demand for the release of the princes was now followed by a report of their death. When, how, and by whose hand the deed had been done was not known. But as the news spread like wildfire a kind of fury seized upon many people. Although accustomed to the brutalities of the long civil wars, the English people of those days still retained the faculty of horror; and once it was excited they did not soon forget. A modern dictator can easily lead the public on from day to day, destroying all persistency of thought and aim, so that memory is blurred by the multiplicity of daily news. But in the fifteenth century the murder of the two young princes by the very man who had undertaken to protect them was regarded as an atrocious crime, never to be forgotten or forgiven. In September Richard in his progress reached York, and here he created his son Prince of Wales, thus in the eyes of his enemies giving confirmation to the darkest rumours.

Buckingham had now become the centre of a conspiracy throughout the west and south of England against the King. He had reached a definite decision about his own claims to the Crown. He seems to have assumed that the princes in the Tower were either dead or doomed. He met at this time Margaret, Countess of Richmond, survivor of the Beaufort line, and recognised that even if the house of York were altogether set aside both she and her son Henry Tudor, Earl of Richmond, stood between him and the Crown. The Countess of Richmond, presuming him to be still Richard's right-hand man, asked him to win the King's consent to a marriage between her son Henry of Richmond and one of King Edward's daughters, Elizabeth, still in sanctuary with her mother at Westminster. Buckingham saw that such a marriage would unite the claims of York and Lancaster, bridge the gulf that had parted England for so long, and enable a tremendous front to be immediately formed against the usurper.

The ruins of Minster Lovell, near Burford, are a tourist attraction for visitors to the Cotswolds. Francis Lovell was created viscount by Richard III in 1483. The Lovells were one of the turncoat families of the Wars of the Roses: John Lovell, Francis's father, had been a Lancastrian.

His preparations were for a general rising on October 18. He would gather his Welsh forces at Brecknock; the southern and western counties would take up arms; and Henry, Earl of Richmond, with the aid of the Duke of Brittany, would land with a force of five thousand men in Wales. But the anger of the people at the rumoured murder of the princes deranged this elaborate plan.

In Kent, Wiltshire, Sussex, and Devonshire there were risings ten days before the appointed date; Henry of Richmond was forced to set sail from Brittany in foul weather on October 12, so that his fleet was dispersed; and when Buckingham unfurled his flag at Brecknock the elements took sides against him too. A terrific storm flooded the Severn valley, and he found himself penned on the Welsh border and unable, as he had planned, to join the rebels in Devonshire.

Richard acted with the utmost vigour. He had an army and he marched against rebellion. The sporadic risings in the south were suppressed. Buckingham's forces melted away, and he himself hid from vengeance. Richmond reached the English coast at last with only two ships, and sailed westward waiting for a sign which never came. At Plymouth he warily made further inquiries, as a result of which he sailed back to Brittany. Buckingham, with a high price on his head, was betrayed to Richard, who lost not an hour in having him slaughtered. A crop of executions followed, and the King seemed to have established himself securely upon his throne.

He proceeded in the new year to inaugurate a series of enlightened reforms in every sphere of government. Parliament again legislated copiously after a long interval. Commerce was protected by a series of well-meant if ill-judged Acts, and a land law was passed to regulate "uses", or, as we should now say, trusts. Attempts were made to please the clergy by confirming their privileges, endowing new religious foundations, and extending the patronage of learning. Much care was taken over the shows of heraldry and pageantry; magnanimity was shown to fallen opponents, and petitioners in distress were treated with kindness. But all counted for nothing. The hatred roused against him throughout the land remained sullen and quenchless.

An impulsive gentleman, one Collingbourne, formerly Sheriff of Worcester, was so much incensed against the King that he had a doggerel rhyme he had composed nailed on the door of St Paul's:

The Catte, The Ratte, and Lovell our dogge
Rulyth all Englande under a Hogge.

Catesby, Ratcliffe, Viscount Lovell, and Richard, whose badge was a boar, saw themselves affronted. But it was not only for this that Collingbourne

SPORTS AND PASTIMES

HISTORIANS HAVE RECENTLY become just as much interested in leisure as in work. The distinction between the two is new, however. The first hunters needed to find food: the first craftsmen created objects to get personal satisfaction and pleasure.

Play separated different sections of society in the Middle Ages at least as much as work. The privilege of hunting in the forest belonged to the king alone, although he could grant it to others. Every man was entitled to hunt game on his own land, but there were relatively few landed men. Poaching was a serious crime.

The chase was a favourite pastime during the late Middle Ages, and there were merchants as well as landlords who enjoyed both hunting and hawking. Boar hunts and stag hunts were sometimes the subject of popular poems. Queen Elizabeth hunted until she was nearly seventy and other women shared her toughness and her enthusiasm for the chase.

Indoor pastimes included chess and draughts, and there were now books to read. Children played with dolls and toy soldiers, with spinning tops and skipping-ropes. At Court it was fashionable to compose tunes and the words to go with them. Henry VIII himself was an accomplished writer of songs, and his daughter Elizabeth was renowned for her spirited dancing.

Popular spectator sports included bull- and bear-baiting, and cockfighting, while football of various kinds was played in most parts of the country. Some of these pastimes had their critics, but in 1550 one austere clergyman commended fishing, fowling, hunting and hawking. Dr Andrew Boord, whose *Breviary of Health* was published in 1542, recommended as exercise "playing at the tennis, or casting a bowl, or poising weights or plummets of lead in your hands . . . to open your pores and to augment natural heat."

HUNTING, HAWKING AND HARE-COURSING were the most popular outdoor sports. In The Devonshire Hunting Tapestry (above) the modish young hunter on the left releases a falcon to kill the duck "put up" by a beater. The tapestry was made in Flanders in the fifteenth century. Other outdoor activities like dancing round the maypole were associated with seasonal celebrations and anniversaries such as on November 17, when special jousting games marked the occasion of Elizabeth' accession. Morris dancing and wrestling matches took place at fairs; for centuries archer practice for the young and fit was require by law. Some Elizabethan children's game survive today, for example, Hide and Seek and Blind Man's Buff, and songs such as "London Bridge is falling down."

BOARD GAMES LIKE CHESS, *tables (backgammon) and shove-groat, similar to our shove-ha'penny, occupied the long evenings. These chess figures made from walrus ivory were found in the Isle of Lewis and date from the twelfth century.*

GAMBLING GAMES *mixed pleasure with business, judging by the coins lying on the table in this picture from the Manchester City Art Gallery. A game of poker called "primero" is in progress; versions of rummy and whist were also played. The queen in modern packs of cards reflects early origins: the pointed head-dress was fashionable in the sixteenth century.*

FISHING WAS MORE THAN A PASTIME *in Tudor England. The twice-weekly "fish days" and the Lenten fast made it compulsory for people to eat fish. A family who lived inland had no option but to eat smoked or salted fish unless they could catch it fresh. March and April were the leanest months; it was too late for the meat slaughtered before Christmas, and too early for the Spring crops.*

REAL TENNIS OR ROYAL TENNIS *was a game played in an enclosed court with a small leather ball stuffed with hair or linen. Women did not play this game, possibly because of the strength needed to strike a ball which hardly bounced. A genuine Tudor tennis court is still in use at Hampton Court Palace, where Henry VIII was a keen player.*

FOOTBALL COULD CAUSE RIOTS, *hardly surprisingly, since there were no rules. It was played by apprentices in the streets of towns like Gloucester where this carving in the cathedral (left) depicts an energetic running tackle. There were no team games or athletic sports except at wakes and festivals, where informal running races were organised. Women competitors could be debarred on the grounds of being hunchbacked or bandy-legged.*

Processional cross found at Bosworth. It was probably carried into battle by supporters of Richard III and abandoned in the ensuing defeat. The cross can now be seen at the headquarters of the Society of Antiquaries in London.

suffered an agonising death at the end of a year. He was undoubtedly a rebel, actively engaged in conspiracy.

A terrible blow now fell upon the King. In April 1484 his only son, the Prince of Wales, died at Middleham, and his wife, Anne, whose health was broken, could bear no more children. Henry Tudor, Earl of Richmond, now became obviously the rival claimant and successor to the throne. Richmond, "the nearest thing to royalty the Lancastrian party possessed", was a Welshman, whose grandfather, Owen Tudor, executed by the Yorkists in 1461, had married, if indeed he married, Henry V's widow, Catherine of France, and whose father Edmund had married the Lady Margaret Beaufort. Thus Richmond could trace his descent through his mother from Edward III, and on his father's side had French royal blood in his veins as well as a shadowy claim to descent from the legendary ancient kings of Britain, including King Arthur. His life had been cast amid ceaseless trouble. For seven years of childhood he had been besieged in Harlech Castle. At the age of fourteen he was forced to flee to Brittany. Thereafter exile and privation had been his lot. These trials had stamped themselves upon his character, rendering him crafty and suspicious. This, however, did not daunt a proud spirit nor cloud a wise and commanding mind.

All hopes in England were now turned towards Richmond, who after the failure of Buckingham's rebellion had returned to Brittany. Richard offered a large sum of money for the surrender of his rival, and during the illness of the Duke of Brittany the Breton Minister, Landois, was disposed to sell the valuable refugee. Richmond, however, suspecting the danger, escaped in the nick of time, galloping into France, where he was well received.

As the months passed, many prominent Englishmen, both Yorkist and Lancastrian, withdrew themselves from Richard's baleful presence, and made their way to Richmond, who from this time forth stood at the head of a combination which might well unite all England. His great hope lay in the marriage with Edward IV's eldest daughter Elizabeth. But in this quarter Richard had not been idle. Before the rebellion he had taken steps to prevent Elizabeth slipping out of sanctuary and England. In March 1484 he made proposals to the Dowager Queen, Dame Elizabeth Grey as he called her, of reconciliation. In a solemn deed witnessed not only by the Lords Spiritual and Temporal, but in addition by the Lord Mayor of London and the Aldermen, Richard promised "on his honour as a King" to provide maintenance for her and to marry her daughters suitably to gentlemen. In spite of the past the Queen had to trust herself to this. She abandoned the match for her daughter with Richmond. She quitted sanctuary. She and the elder princesses were received at Richard's Court and treated with exceptional distinction. At the Christmas revels at Westminster in 1484 it was noticed that the changes of dress provided for Dame Elizabeth Grey and her daughters were almost royal in style and richness. The stigma of bastardy so lately inflicted upon Edward's children, and the awful secret of the Tower, were banished. Although the threat of invasion was constant, gaiety and dancing ruled the hour.

In March 1485 Queen Anne died, probably from natural causes. Rumours were circulating that Richard intended to marry his niece Elizabeth himself, in order to keep her out of Richmond's way. This incestuous union could have been achieved by Papal dispensation, but Richard disavowed all intention of it, both in Council and in public. And it is indeed hard to see how his position could have been strengthened by marrying a princess whom he had declared illegitimate.

All through the summer Richmond's expedition was preparing at the mouth of the Seine, and the exodus from England of substantial people to join him was unceasing. The suspense was wearing to Richard. He felt he was surrounded by hatred and distrust, and that none served him but from fear or hope of favour. His dogged, indomitable nature had determined him to make for his Crown the greatest of all his fights. He fixed his headquarters in a good central position at Nottingham. Commissions of muster and array were ordered to call men to arms in almost every county. He stationed relays of horsemen every twenty miles permanently along the great roads to bring news and carry orders with an organised swiftness hitherto unknown in England. Richard himself ceaselessly patrolled the Midland area, endeavouring by strength to overawe and by good government to placate his sullen subjects. He set forth his cause in a vehement proclamation, denouncing "one, Henry Tydder, son of Edmund Tydder, son of Owen Tydder", of bastard blood both on his father's and mother's side, who of his ambition and covetousness pretended to the Crown, "to the disinheriting and destruction of all the noble and worshipful blood of his realm forever". But this fell cold.

On August 1 Richmond embarked at Harfleur with his Englishmen, Yorkist as well as Lancastrian, and a body of French troops. A fair wind bore him down the Channel. He evaded the squadrons of "Lovell our dogge", doubled Land's End, and landed at Milford Haven on August 7. Kneeling, he kissed the ground, signed himself with the Cross, and gave the order to advance in the name of God and St George. He had only two thousand men; but such were his assurances of support that he proclaimed Richard forthwith usurper and rebel against himself. The Welsh were gratified by the prospect of one of their race succeeding to the Crown of mighty England. The ancient Britons would come back into their own. Richmond displayed not only the standard of St George, but the Red Dragon of Cadwallader. With five thousand men he now moved eastward.

The Duke of Norfolk's death in the early stages of the Battle of Bosworth Field disheartened Richard's troops. This portrait, by an unknown artist, is inscribed with the message given to Norfolk before Bosworth — "Jockey of Norfolk be not too bold, For Dickon thy master is bought and sold."

The King gathered his army and marched to meet his foe. At this moment the attitude of the Stanleys became of decisive importance. They had been entrusted by the King with the duty of intercepting the rebels should they land in the west. Sir William Stanley, with some thousands of men, made no attempt to do so. Richard thereupon summoned Lord Stanley, the head of the House, to his Court, and when that potentate declared himself "ill of the sweating sickness" he seized Lord Strange, his eldest son, to hold him answerable with his life for his father's loyalty. This did not prevent Sir William Stanley from making friendly contact with Richmond. But Lord Stanley, hoping to save his son, remained till the last moment uncertain.

The Duke of Norfolk and Percy, Earl of Northumberland, were Richard's principal adherents, and "the Catte and the Ratte", had no hope of life but in their master's victory. On August 17, thus attended, the King set forth towards Leicester at the head of his army. Their ordered ranks, four abreast, with the cavalry on both flanks and the King mounted on his great white charger in the centre, made a formidable impression upon beholders. And when on Sunday, August 21, this whole array came out of Leicester to meet Richmond near the village of Market Bosworth it was certain that a decisive battle impended on the morrow.

Appearances favoured the King. He had ten thousand disciplined men

This statue at the entrance to Hampton Court represents the red dragon of Cadwallader. Henry Tudor was supported by five thousand Welshmen at the Battle of Bosworth Field, where he gained the Crown.

under the royal authority against Richmond's hastily gathered five thousand rebels. But at some distance from the flanks of the main army, on opposite hilltops, stood the respective forces, mainly from Lancashire and Cheshire, of Sir William Stanley and Lord Stanley, the whole situation resembling, as has been said, four players in a game of cards. Richard, according to the Tudor historians, although confessing to a night of frightful dreams, harangued his captains in magnificent style. "Dismiss all fear. . . . Every one give but one sure stroke and the day is ours. What prevaileth a handful of men to a whole realm? As for me, I assure you this day I will triumph by glorious victory or suffer death for immortal fame." He then gave the signal for battle, and sent a message to Lord Stanley that if he did not fall on forthwith he would instantly decapitate his son. Stanley, forced to this bitter choice, answered proudly that he had other sons. The King gave orders for Strange's execution. But the officers so charged thought it prudent to wait. "My lord, the enemy is past the marsh. After the battle let young Stanley die."

But even now Richmond was not sure what part Lord Stanley and his forces would play. When, after archery and cannonade, the lines were locked in battle, all doubts were removed. The Earl of Northumberland, commanding Richard's left, stood idle at a distance. Lord Stanley's force joined Richmond. The King saw that all was lost, and, shouting "Treason! Treason!" hurled himself into the thickest of the fray in the desperate purposes of striking down Richmond with his own hand. He actually slew Richmond's standard-bearer, and laid low Sir John Cheney, a warrior renowned for his bodily strength. He is said even to have reached Richmond and crossed swords with him. But at this moment Sir William Stanley's three thousand, "in coats as red as blood", fell upon the struggling Yorkists. The tides of conflict swept the principals asunder. Richmond was preserved, and the King, refusing to fly, was borne down and slaughtered.

Richard's crown, which he wore to the last, was picked out of a bush and placed upon the victor's head. The Duke of Norfolk was slain fighting bravely; Ratcliffe was killed; Catesby, after being allowed to make his will, was executed on the field; and Henry Tudor became King of England. Richard's corpse, naked, and torn by wounds, was bound across a horse, with his head and long hair hanging down, bloody and hideous, and in this condition borne into Leicester for all men to see.

Bosworth Field may be taken as closing a long chapter in English history. Though risings and conspiracies continued throughout the next reign, the strife of the Red and White Rose had in the main come to an end. Neither won. A solution was reached in which the survivors of both causes could be reconciled. The marriage of Richmond with the adaptable Princess Elizabeth produced the Tudor line, in which both Yorkists and Lancastrians had a share. The revengeful ghosts of two mangled generations were laid forever. Richard's death also ended the Plantagenet line. For over three hundred years this strong race of warrior and statesmen kings, whose gifts and vices were upon the highest scale, whose sense of authority and empire had been persistently maintained, now vanished from the fortunes of the island. The Plantagenets and the proud, exclusive nobility which their systems evolved had torn themselves to pieces. As Coeur de Lion said of his House, "From the Devil we sprang and to the Devil we shall go."

The crown of York is the emblem shown on the flag in this heraldic sign.

At Bosworth the Wars of the Roses reached their final milestone. In the next century the subjects of the Tudors liked to consider that the Middle

Ages too had come to a close in 1485, and that a new age had dawned with the accession of Henry Tudor. Modern historians prefer to point out that there are no sharp dividing lines in this period of our history, and Henry VII carried on and consolidated much of the work of the Yorkist kings. Certainly the prolongation of strife, waste, and insecurity in the fifteenth century had aroused in all classes an overpowering desire for strong, ordered government. The parliamentary conception which had prevailed under the House of Lancaster had gained many frontiers of constitutional rights. However, not until the seventeenth century were the old maxims, "Grievances before supply", "the Crown the servant and not the master of the State", brought again into the light, and, as it happened, the glare of a new day. The stir of the Renaissance, the storm of the Reformation, hurled their new problems on the bewildered but also re-inspired mortals of the new age upon which England entered under the guidance of the wise, sad, careful monarch who inaugurated the Tudor dictatorship as King Henry VII.

CHAPTER 31

THE TUDOR DYNASTY

For a generation and more the English monarchy had been tossed on the rough waters of a disputed succession. On August 22, 1485, in the person of Henry VII, a new dynasty mounted the throne. Henry's first task was to induce magnates, Church, and gentry to accept the decision of Bosworth and to establish himself as King. He was careful to be crowned before facing the representatives of the nation, thus resting his title first upon conquest, and only secondly on the approbation of Parliament. Then he married, as had long been planned, the heiress of the rival house, Elizabeth of York.

Portrait of Henry VII, the first Tudor king, which hangs in the National Portrait Gallery.

Lack of money had long weakened the English throne, but Henry now possessed a valuable inheritance in the great estates of the Lancastrian kings, whose heir he was. The north country estates of Richard, Duke of Gloucester, were his by right of conquest, and later the treason and execution of Sir William Stanley, who had been discontented with his rewards after Bosworth, brought spacious properties in the Midlands into the royal hands. Henry was thus assured of a settled income.

But this was not enough. It was essential to regulate the titles by which land was held in England. The rapid succession of rival monarchs had produced a feeling of insecurity among landowners. Execution and death in battle had shattered the power of the great feudal houses. The survivors and the mass of smaller landed gentry were in constant danger of losing their estates by actions in the law courts started by personal enemies and based on past allegiances or treacheries. It was difficult to find a man whose family had not supported a losing side at some point or other during the civil wars. All this was extremely dangerous to Henry, for if the landowners were insecure about the legal possession of their property they might follow another usurper if one should appear. Legislation was therefore passed stating that all who gave their allegiance to the King for the time being—that is, to the King upon the throne—should be secure in their lives and property. This idea of an actual King as distinct from a rightful King was

The medieval town of Bruges was a centre of the wool trade between England and Flanders. The town retains much of its sixteenth-century character today.

characteristic of the new ruler. Sure of himself, Henry did not shrink from establishing his power upon a practical basis.

Then there were the frontiers. Throughout the history of medieval England there runs a deep division between north and south. In the south a more fully advanced society dwelt in a rich countryside, with well-developed towns and a prosperous wool trade with Flanders and Italy. The Wars of the Roses had been a serious threat to this organised life, and it was in the south that Henry found his chief support. In the words of a chronicler, "he could not endure to see trade sick". He secured favourable terms for merchants who traded with the Netherlands and representatives of their class cooperated with him in Parliament. Henry's careful attention to this body sprang from a real community of interests, the need for settled government. If this was despotism, it was despotism by consent.

The north was very different. Great feudal houses like the Percys dominated the scene. The land was mountainous and barren, the population lawless and turbulent. The King's authority was often ignored and sometimes flouted. The long tradition of Border warfare with the Scots, the ballads of cattle-raids and the burning of villages still survived. Richard, Duke of Gloucester, had been popular in these parts. In a rough-and-ready fashion he had governed well. Henry had not only to preserve order and authority in these regions, but to establish a secure frontier against the Scots.

It was impossible to govern England from London in the fifteenth century. It was essential to delegate authority. Councils were accordingly established to administer the northern parts and the Welsh Marches. Trusted servants were given wide powers of administration, and new officials who owed everything to their master and were trained in the law now for the first time had the ascendancy over the old nobles. Such were men like Henry Wyatt in the north, captain of the key castle of Berwick, and Edmund Dudley in the south; and from them and their like the Sidneys, Herberts, Cecils, and Russells were descended.

The threat of internal disorder marched with the menace from beyond the sea. Henry had to keep ceaseless watch for the invasion of pretenders. The Court of Burgundy was a centre of plots against him, the Duchess being the sister of Richard III. Twice she launched pretenders against the Tudor regime. The first was Lambert Simnel, who finished ingloriously as a scullion in the royal kitchens. The second and more formidable was Perkin Warbeck, collector of taxes at Tournai and the son of a boatman, put forward as the younger of the princes murdered in the Tower. Backed by discontented Yorkist nobles in Ireland, by Burgundian money, Austrian and Flemish troops, and Scottish sympathy, Warbeck remained at large for seven years, plotting openly. Thrice he attempted to seize the English throne. But the classes who had backed the King since Bosworth were staunch. Warbeck's invasion of Kent was repulsed, his attack from Scotland penetrated only four miles across the Border, and a Cornish rising in 1497 which he joined melted away. He fled to sanctuary, whence he was taken to London and kept in custody. Two years later, he was executed, after confessing his guilt, on the scaffold at Tyburn. The affair ended in ignominy and ridicule, but the danger had been a real one.

Henry had many reasons to feel his throne shake a little beneath him. The Wars of the Roses had weakened English authority in Wales, but it was in Ireland that their effects were most manifest. The dynastic struggle had been eagerly taken up in Ireland; there were Lancastrians and Yorkists among the great Anglo-Irish families, and there were Lancastrian and Yorkist cities in the English Pale around Dublin and among remote outposts of the Englishry like Limerick and Galway. But all this turmoil was a mere continuation of clan feuds. The Butler family, under its hereditary chief, the Earl of Ormonde, was Lancastrian. The Fitzgeralds, led by the Earl of Kildare in Leinster and the Earl of Desmond in Munster, both having close alliances of blood and marriage with the native chiefs, were Yorkist in sympathy, because they thus had hoped to promote their own aggrandisement. Sir Edward Poynings, appointed Lord Deputy of Ireland in 1494, tried to limit their powers of mischief. He persuaded the Irish Parliament at Drogheda to pass the celebrated Poynings' Law, subordinating the Irish Parliament to the English, which was not repealed for three hundred years and remained a grievance till the twentieth century.

This portrait of Henry VII's mother, the Lady Margaret Beaufort, hangs in St John's College, Cambridge, which she founded in 1509.

Kildare himself was attained and sent over to London; but Henry was too wise to apply simple feudal justice to so mighty an offender, with his fighting clan on the outskirts of Dublin, and cousins, marriage-kin, and clients all over the island. The charges against the great Earl were serious enough. Apart from his suspect favour to Perkin Warbeck, had he not burnt down the cathedral of Cashel? The Earl admitted it, but excused himself in a fashion that appealed to the King. "I did, but I thought that the Archbishop was inside." Henry VII accepted the inevitable with a dictum that is famous, if not authentic. "Since all Ireland cannot govern the Earl of Kildare, let the Earl of Kildare govern all Ireland." Kildare was pardoned, married to the King's cousin, and sent back to Ireland, where he succeeded Poynings as Lord Deputy.

Power in Ireland still rested on the ability to call out and command a sufficiency of armed men. In this the English King exercised a potent and personal influence. He could clothe with the royal insignia and status of Deputy any great noble who could muster and control the fighting men, or by raising Butlers and Burkes make it impossible for even a Kildare to control the great clan chiefs. This precarious and shifting balance was for a while the only road to establishing a central government. No English king had yet found how to make his title of "Lord of Ireland" any more real than his title of "King of France".

But a powerful ally was at hand. Artillery, which had helped to expel

THE ENGLISH AT TABLE

This Italian view of English eating habits comes from Andreas Franciscus's Itinerarium Britanniae *circa 1497.*

They eat very frequently, at times more than is suitable, and are particularly fond of young swans, rabbits, deer and sea birds. They often eat mutton and beef, which is generally considered to be better here than anywhere else in the world. This is due to the excellence of their pastures. They have all kinds of fish in plenty and great quantities of oysters which come from the seashore. The majority, not to say everyone, drink that beverage [beer] I have spoken of before, and prepare it in various ways. For wine is very expensive, as the vine does not grow in the island; nor does the olive, and the products of both are imported from France and Spain.

Cooking was a long and complicated process in medieval times. Most people ate more than is considered necessary today, and took great trouble with colourings and flavourings.

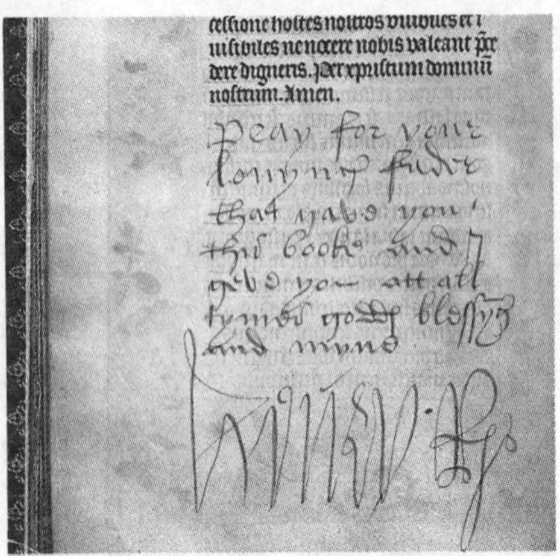

"Pray for your loving father that gave you this book and I give you at all times Godd's blessing and myne. Henricus Rex." King Henry VII wrote this touching prayer in his daughter Margaret's prayer book.

the English from France, now aided their incursion into Ireland. Cannon spoke to Irish castles in a language readily understood. But the cannon came from England. The Irish could use but could not make them. Here for a time was the key to an English control over Irish affairs. Now in the advance of culture precedence was regulated by gunpowder.

Henry's dealings with Scotland are also characteristic of his shrewd judgment. An ugly situation arose when King James IV lent his support to the Pretender Perkin Warbeck. Henry's first move was to shake the position of the Scottish king by shipping armaments through Berwick to the baronial opponents of the Crown. But his ultimate aims were constructive. He signed a truce which was confirmed by treaty, and took the first steps to unite England and Scotland by marrying his daughter Margaret to James in 1502, and there was peace in the north until after his death.

With France too his policy was eminently successful. He realised that more could be gained by the threat of war than by war itself. Henry summoned Parliament to consent to taxation for a war, and proceeded to gather together a small army, which crossed to Calais in 1492 and besieged Boulogne. At the same time he entered into negotiations with the French king, who, unable to face Spain, the Holy Roman Emperor, and England simultaneously, was compelled to buy him off. Henry gained both ways. Like Edward IV, he pocketed not only a considerable subsidy from France, but also the taxes collected in England for war.

The most powerful new monarchy in Europe was Spain, recently forged into a strong state by the united efforts of Ferdinand of Aragon and Isabella of Castile and their successful warfare against the Moors. Their marriage marked the unification of the country. From 1489, when Henry's eldest son, Arthur, was betrothed to their daughter, Catherine, England and Spain worked steadily together to secure booty from France—Spain in the form of territory, Henry as the annual tribute in cash, which amounted in the earlier years to about a fifth of the revenues of the Crown.

Henry VII as a statesman was imbued with the new, ruthless political ideas of Renaissance Europe. His youth as an exile in foreign Courts had taught him much. He had watched marriage negotiations, treaties, the hire of professional men-at-arms to fight the battles of Louis XI and Charles of Burgundy, the regulation of trade, the relations between the national monarchies of France and the territorial nobility, between Church and State. He sharpened his Welsh shrewdness with the refinements of practical politics, which were then reaching a high development among the Latin races. Indeed, his main interest, apart from an absorbing passion for administration, was foreign policy. He maintained the first permanent English envoys abroad. Diplomacy, he considered, was no bad substitute for the violence of his predecessors, and early, accurate, and regular information was essential to its conduct.

Internally he strove to establish a strong monarchy moulded out of native institutions, working almost always by adaptation, modifying old forms ever so slightly, rather than by crude innovation. Without any fundamental constitutional change administration was established again on a firm basis. The King's Council was given parliamentary authority to examine persons with or without oath, and condemn them, on written evidence alone, in a manner foreign to the practice of the Common Law. The Court of Star Chamber met regularly at Westminster, with the two chief justices in attendance. It was originally a judicial committee of the King's Council, trying cases which needed special treatment because of the excessive might of one of the parties or the novelty or enormity of the offence. The complaints of the weak and oppressed against the rich and mighty, cases of retainer which involved keeping private armies of liveried servants, and of embracery, which means corruption of juries—all these became their sphere.

But the main function of the King's Council was to govern rather than to judge. A small inner committee conducted foreign affairs. Another managed the finances; treasurers were now appointed who were answerable personally to the King. And at the centre was the King himself, often authorising or auditing expenditure, even the most trifling, with great sprawling initials which may still be seen at the Record Office in London. Henry VII was probably the best businessman to sit upon the English throne.

He was also a remarkably shrewd picker of men. Few of his ministers came from the hereditary nobility: Richard Fox, Bishop of Winchester, Chief Minister, and the most powerful man in England after the King, had been a schoolmaster at Hereford before he met Henry in Paris, and they became companions in exile. Edmund Dudley was an under-sheriff of the City of London, who came under the King's notice in connection with the regulation of the Flanders wool trade. John Stile, who invented the first diplomatic cipher, began his career as a grocer or a mercer (weaver). Richard Empson was the son of a sieve-maker.

Like other princes of his age, Henry built and altered. His chapel at Westminster and his palace at Richmond were superb monuments of his architectural taste. Though personally frugal, he maintained a calculated pageantry; he wore magnificent clothes, superb jewels, and moved in public under a canopy of state, waited upon by noblemen, with a Court where about seven hundred persons dined daily in the Tower at his expense, entertained by jesters, minstrels, huntsmen, and his famous leopards.

How far Henry VII was a conscious innovator is in dispute among historians. Even during the last years of the Wars of the Roses the Yorkist sovereigns were preparing the foundations of a new, powerful, and centralised State. Under Henry VII these hopes became realities. His achievement lay in transmuting medieval institutions into the organs of modern rule. He built his power amid the ruins and ashes of his predecessors. He thriftily and carefully gathered what seemed in those days a vast reserve of

The Henry VII Chapel in Westminster Abbey displays the refinement that was typical of this sensitive king, and the quality of workmanship that he demanded.

This famous view of King's College, Cambridge, shows the Backs, the area along the River Cam behind the college buildings. King's College was founded by Henry VI but largely constructed during the reign of Henry VII.

liquid wealth. He trained a body of efficient servants. He magnified the Crown without losing the cooperation of the Commons. He identified prosperity with monarchy.

Almost all existing portraits of Henry VII are based upon a single death-mask, tending to give him a hard and grave appearance, which does not tally with any contemporary description. The picture in the National Portrait Gallery is however dated four years before his death; and here his quick, hard grey eyes look out from an arched setting. Delicate, well-kept hands rest lightly upon the bottom of the frame. His lips are set tight, with a faint smile breaking the corners. There is an air of disillusionment, of fatigue, of unceasing vigilance, and above all of sadness and responsibility. Such was the architect of the Tudor monarchy, who was to lead England out of medieval disorder into greater strength and broader times.

CHAPTER 32

KING HENRY VIII

Henry VIII as a baby. He was the second son of Henry VII and was expected to enter the Church. Not brought up to be King, he spent his youth pursuing scholarly and musical interests.

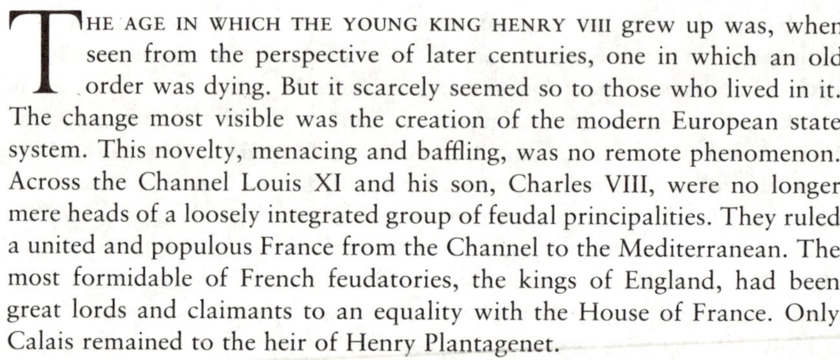

THE AGE IN WHICH THE YOUNG KING HENRY VIII grew up was, when seen from the perspective of later centuries, one in which an old order was dying. But it scarcely seemed so to those who lived in it. The change most visible was the creation of the modern European state system. This novelty, menacing and baffling, was no remote phenomenon. Across the Channel Louis XI and his son, Charles VIII, were no longer mere heads of a loosely integrated group of feudal principalities. They ruled a united and populous France from the Channel to the Mediterranean. The most formidable of French feudatories, the kings of England, had been great lords and claimants to an equality with the House of France. Only Calais remained to the heir of Henry Plantagenet.

Meanwhile the House of Burgundy, which had for nearly a century disputed the authority of the kings of France, had come to an end with the death of Charles the Bold in 1477, and Louis XI contrived to lay hands on Burgundy itself. All the rest of the Burgundian inheritance passed through the marriage of Mary of Burgundy to Maximilian, the Holy Roman Emperor. Henceforth the Habsburgs controlled the duchies, counties, lordships, and cities that the Dukes of Burgundy had, with craft and fortune, acquired in the Netherlands and Belgium. Now Habsburg and Valois confronted one another on the northeastern frontiers of France. It was the opening of a long struggle.

One medieval State seemed to defy this process of aggregation and concentration. The Holy Roman Empire was visibly in dissolution. But for two generations past the Emperor had been the head of the House of Habsburg, and what arms could not do diplomacy and luck did. As Emperor, Maximilian had married the greatest heiress in Europe. The Habsburgs thus began to act on the maxim of gaining major victories by marriage. In the next generation the Archduke Philip married an even greater heiress, the Infanta Joanna, heir to Castile, Aragon, Sicily, and Naples. It was her sister who had accelerated the rise of the Tudors by marrying Prince Arthur and after him King Henry VIII.

In this world of growing power the King of England had to move and act with far fewer resources than his neighbours. His subjects numbered not many more than three millions. He had smaller revenues, no standing army. And yet by the mere proximity of France and the Imperial Netherlands England was forced to play a part in European politics.

In this changing world, the old politics, the old tried recipes of war and victory that had stood English kings in good stead for so long, were of little avail. So for a century the rulers of England had to move warily, threatened with disaster and conscious of dangerous weakness if any shift of continental politics should leave England alone in face of France or Spain.

Until the death of his elder brother, Prince Arthur, Henry had been intended for the Church. He had therefore been brought up by his father in an atmosphere of learning. Much time was devoted to serious studies—Latin, French, Italian, theology, music—and also to bodily exercise, to the sport of jousting, at which he excelled, to tennis, and hunting the stag.

Henry was a tall, redheaded man who preserved the vigour and energy of ancestors accustomed for centuries to the warfare of the Welsh Marches. His massive frame towered above the throng, and those about him felt in it a sense of concealed desperation, of latent force and passion. A French ambassador confessed that he could never approach the King without fear of personal violence. Although Henry appeared to strangers open, jovial, and trustworthy, with a bluff good-humour which appealed at once to the crowd, even those who knew him most intimately seldom penetrated the inward reserve which allowed him to confide freely in no one. To those who saw him often he seemed almost like two men, one the merry monarch of the hunt and banquet, the friend of children, the patron of every kind of sport, the other the cold, acute observer of the audience chamber or the Council, watching vigilantly, refusing except under the stress of great events to speak his own mind. On his long hunting expeditions (which sometimes lasted for weeks) when the courier arrived with papers, he swiftly left his companions of the chase and summoned the "counsellors attendant" for what he was wont to call "London business".

Bursts of restless energy and ferocity were combined with extraordinary patience and diligence. Deeply religious, Henry regularly listened to sermons lasting between one and two hours, and wrote more than one theological treatise of a high standard. He was accustomed to hear five Masses on Church days, and three on other days, served the priest at Mass himself, and always did penance on Good Friday. His zeal in theological controversy earned him from the Pope the title of "Defender of the Faith". An indefatigable worker, he digested a mass of dispatches, memoranda, and plans each day. He wrote verses and composed music. He chose as his advisers men for the most part of the meanest origin: Thomas Wolsey, the son of a poor and rascally butcher of Ipswich, whose name appears on the borough records for selling meat unfit for human consumption; Thomas Cromwell, a small attorney; Thomas Cranmer, an obscure lecturer in divinity. Like his father he distrusted the hereditary nobility, preferring the discreet counsel of men without a wide circle of friends.

Early in his reign he declared, "I will not allow anyone to have it in his power to govern me." As time passed his wilfulness hardened and his temper worsened. His rages were terrible to behold. There was no noble head in the country, he once said, "but he would make it fly", if his will were crossed. Many were indeed to fly in his thirty-eight years on the throne.

Catherine of Aragon was the daughter of the premier royal family in Europe. Months of bargaining had preceded her marriage in 1501 with the Prince Arthur of England. Following Arthur's death in 1502, negotiations were reopened with Catherine's father, and only when the Pope gave a special dispensation was she permitted to marry her brother-in-law, Henry VIII, who was five years younger than she was.

This enormous man was the nightmare of his advisers. Once a scheme was fixed in his mind he could seldom be turned from it. The only secret of managing him, both Wolsey and Cromwell disclosed after they had fallen, was to see that dangerous ideas were not permitted to reach him. But arrangements of this sort could not be complete. His habit was to talk to all classes—barbers, huntsmen, his "yeoman cook to the King's mouth"—and particularly anyone, however humble, connected with the sea, to ferret out opinions. Each summer he went on progress through the country, keeping close to the mass of his subjects, whom he understood so well.

Almost his first act, six weeks after the death of his father in 1509, was to marry his brother Arthur's widow, Princess Catherine of Aragon. He was aged eighteen and she was five years older. She had made great efforts to fascinate him, and succeeded so well that while Ferdinand of Aragon and Henry VII had made plans for the match long beforehand, and had obtained from the Pope a dispensation for a marriage within the degrees of affinity prohibited by the Church, there can be no doubt that Henry was eager to complete the proceedings. During the first fifteen years of his reign, until she reached the age of thirty-eight, Catherine remained, apart from three or four short lapses, the mistress of his affections, restrained his follies, and in her narrow way helped to guide public affairs between the intervals of her numerous confinements. Henry settled down to married life very quickly, in spite of a series of misfortunes. The Queen's first baby was born dead, just after Henry's nineteenth birthday; another died soon after birth a year later. In all there were to be five such disappointments.

King Henry continued the alliance with his father-in-law, Ferdinand of Aragon, which had brought both honour and wealth to England. He supported the Pope, and was sent the Golden Rose, the highest distinction which could be conferred on any Christian prince. He deliberated with his father's grave counsellors—and under their guidance pursued for a short time the policy which his father had always favoured—isolation, provided that France continued to pay tribute. But Henry was on the edge of the vortex of Europe's new politics. Should he plunge in? The richest cities of Europe had changed hands many times during the last few years, paying tribute on each occasion. Frontiers were altering almost from month to month. Ferdinand had conquered the Kingdom of Naples, and the two French border provinces of Cerdagne and Roussillon. Other princes had done nearly as well. Amid the alluring vistas of conquest which opened up before Henry his father's aged counsellors remained obstinately men of peace. Henry VIII now determined that their policy should be reversed.

For some time he had been watching Dean Wolsey of Lincoln, a discovery of the Marquis of Dorset, whose sons had been to Magdalen College School at Oxford when Wolsey was the master there. Dorset had provided Wolsey with several livings. The young priest then obtained a post as chaplain to the Governor of Calais. Besides academic learning Wolsey possessed a remarkable aptitude for negotiation and finance and Henry VII, sensing his abilities, had taken him over from the Governor and employed him on minor official business abroad. He was promoted by Henry VIII to the Council Board in November 1509, with the office of almoner to the royal Household. He was then aged thirty-six.

Two years later Wolsey's growing influence may be perceived in the decision to join the Holy League against France. He was put in charge of preparations for the war, and his former pupil, the young Marquis of Dorset, was commander in chief. Henry planned to reconquer Bordeaux while King Ferdinand invaded Navarre, an independent kingdom lying athwart the Pyrenees, and the Pope and the republic of Venice operated against the French armies in Italy. It was 1512, and the first time since the Hundred Years' War that an English army had campaigned in Europe.

Ferdinand took the whole of Navarre. But the English expedition failed. The style of warfare they had learnt in the Wars of the Roses, with longbows and ponderously armed mounted men, had become obsolete on the Continent. Both Ferdinand and the French employed professional infantry, Swiss and Austrian, who advanced at a great pace in solid squares with eighteen-foot pikes bristling in every direction. The primitive firearms of the day, known as arquebuses, were too heavy and slow-firing to inflict serious damage on these fast-moving squares. Ferdinand sent a great deal of military advice to Henry, and suggested that he should use his gathered wealth to procure an overwhelming professional force of his own. But, before Henry could adopt this plan, Dorset's army disintegrated. After negotiations lasting throughout the winter of 1512-13 Ferdinand and the Venetians deserted Henry and the Pope and made peace with France. The Holy League, they concluded, had proved futile as a political combination.

In England the responsibility for these failures was cast on the new adviser, Wolsey. The lay members of the Council had from the beginning opposed a war policy managed by a priest and had intrigued to get rid of him. But Henry VIII and the Pope never wavered. Pope Julius II, who had been besieged by a French force in Rome, had excommunicated the entire French army, and now grew a beard—an adornment then out of fashion—and swore he would not shave until he was revenged on the King of France. Henry, not to be outdone, also grew a beard. It was auburn, like his hair. He arranged to hire the Imperial artillery and the greater part of the Austrian army, to serve under the royal standard of England.

This scene from the Great Tournament Roll of Westminster shows Henry VIII jousting before Catherine of Aragon at the tournament held in February 1511 to celebrate the birth of their son, Henry, Prince of Wales. The little prince lived for only seven weeks.

Holbein's drawing of Henry VIII in a characteristic pose shows his father, Henry VII, in the background. An ambassador described Henry as "the handsomest potentate I have ever set eyes on; above the usual height, with a round face so very beautiful that it would become a pretty woman."

These arrangements, though costly, were brilliantly successful. Under Henry's command, the English, with Austrian mercenaries, routed the French in August 1513 at the Battle of the Spurs, so called because of the rapidity of the French retreat. Bayard, the most famous knight in Europe, was captured, together with a host of French notables. Tournai, the richest city of all northeast France, surrendered at the mere sight of the Imperial artillery, and was occupied by an English garrison. To crown all, Queen Catherine, acting as Regent of England, sent great news from the north.

To aid their French ally the Scots in the King's absence had crossed the Tweed in September and invaded England with an army of fifty thousand men. Thomas Howard, Earl of Surrey, son of Richard III's Duke of Norfolk, slain at Bosworth, and still under the family attainder, was nonetheless entrusted with the command. This skilful veteran, knowing every inch of the ground, did not hesitate to march round the Scottish army, and, although outnumbered by two to one, placed himself between the enemy and Edinburgh, at Flodden Field. Both armies faced their homeland. The whole of Scotland, Highland and Lowland alike, drew out with their retainers in the traditional circles of spearmen, and around the standard of their king, James IV. The English archers once again directed upon these redoubtable masses a long, intense, and murderous arrow storm. Moreover, the bills or axes in the hands of English infantry were highly effective against the Scottish spears in hand-to-hand assault, while the English cavalry awaited the chance of piercing the gaps caused by slaughter. Among the dead was King James. This was the last great victory gained by the longbow. Surrey was rewarded by the restoration of the Norfolk dukedom. In Scotland a year-old child succeeded to the throne as James V. His mother, the Regent, was Henry's sister Margaret, and peace now descended on the northern border for the greater part of the reign.

CHAPTER 33

CARDINAL WOLSEY

During the autumn of 1513 the French were hard pressed from all sides. Wolsey, through the Emperor, hired a Swiss army, which invaded Burgundy. Dijon was captured. The French had no troops of their own which could resist the Swiss, and hired fresh mercenaries from abroad. Henry had every intention of renewing his campaign in France in 1514, but his successes had not been to the liking of Ferdinand of Spain. Ferdinand now set about making a separate peace with France, into which he also tried to draw the Emperor Maximilian.

Faced with the defection of his allies, Henry was quick to obtain a favourable peace treaty with France, thereby securing exactly double the amount of annual tribute that had been paid to his father. The crowning event of the peace was the marriage between Henry's young sister, Mary, and Louis XII himself. She was seventeen, he was fifty-two. The story runs that she extracted from her brother the promise that if she married this time for diplomacy she would be free next time to marry for love. Promise or no promise, that is what she did. She was Queen of France for three months; then, as queen dowager, and to Henry's displeasure, she cut short her widowhood by marrying Charles Brandon, Duke of Suffolk. The marriage ultimately bore tragic fruit: a grandchild was Lady Jane Grey, who was for ten days to be Queen of England.

Among those who had crossed with the bridal retinue to France was a young girl named Mary Boleyn. She was one of three nieces of the Duke of Norfolk, all of whom successively engaged the dangerous love of Henry VIII. Mary and her sister Anne had been educated in France at an expensive academy attached to the French Court. On her return to England Mary married William Carey, a Gentleman of the Bedchamber, and before long became the King's mistress. Her father was upon this favour created Lord Rochford, while her sister, Anne, continued her studies in France.

Wolsey was richly rewarded for the foreign successes. He received the Bishopric of Lincoln during the course of the negotiations; then, after the peace terms were settled, the Archbishopric of York; and, a year later, in September 1515, a cardinal's hat. As these ecclesiastical honours did not give Wolsey sufficient civil authority, Henry also created him Lord Chancellor.

For fourteen years Wolsey in the King's name was the effective ruler of the realm. He owed his position not only to his great capacity for business, but to his considerable personal charm. He had "an angel's wit", one of his contemporaries wrote, for beguiling and flattering those whom he wished to persuade. In the King's company he was brilliant, convivial, and "a gay seeker out of new pastimes". All this commended him to his young master. Other would-be counsellors resented the Cardinal's arrogance, and envied his ever-growing wealth. At the height of his influence Wolsey kept a thousand servants, and his palaces surpassed the King's in splendour. He loaded profitable favours upon his relations, including his illegitimate son, who held eleven Church appointments, and their incomes, while still a boy. These counts against him gradually added up in the course of years. But for the time being—and it was for a long time, as chief ministers go—he successfully held in his grasp an accumulation of power that has probably never been equalled in England.

The King's popularity rose with the achievements of his reign. There were many of course who grumbled at the war taxes imposed during the previous two years; but as Wolsey managed to tap new sources of revenue, Henry's subjects were taxed much more lightly than any other subjects in Europe. Successes abroad enabled Wolsey to develop principles of centralised government. During the years that he was Lord Chancellor Parliament met only once, for two sessions spreading over three months in all. The Court of Star Chamber grew more active. It evolved methods copied from Roman law, and persons who could give evidence were simply brought in for interrogation, one by one, often without even the formality of an oath. Justice was swift, fines were heavy, and no one in England was so powerful that he could afford to flout the Star Chamber. When a common soldier of the Calais garrison once sent his wife to complain of his treatment by the Lord Deputy of Calais she received a full hearing. The new generation grown up after the Wars of the Roses was accustomed to royal law and order, and determined that it should prevail.

Henry VIII found an institution ready to his hand in the unpaid Justice of the Peace, the local squire or landlord, and taught him to govern. Rules and regulations of remarkable complexity were given to the Justice to administer; and later in the century Justices' manuals were produced, which

Portrait of Cardinal Wolsey at the height of his power. The son of an Ipswich butcher, Wolsey rose to be a cardinal at the age of forty-one. For seventeen years he ruled both King and kingdom, but in 1530 he died, discredited because he could not obtain the King's divorce.

covered almost every contingency which could arise in country life. The Tudors were indeed the architects of an English system of local government which lasted almost unchanged until Victorian times. Unpaid local men, fearless and impartial, because they could rely on help from the King, dealt with small matters, sitting in the villages often in twos and threes. Bigger matters such as roads and bridges and sheep-stealing came before quarter sessions in the appropriate town.

It was a rough justice that the country gentlemen meted out, and friendship and faction often cut across the interests of both the nation and the Crown. If in the main they carried the directions of the Crown to the people, the Justices could also on occasion, by turning a deaf ear to official advice, express popular resistance to the royal will. What they did in the counties they could also sometimes do in the House of Commons. Wolsey saw the dangers of the situation and preferred to work out his policy without the unappreciative counsel of Parliament. Later, Henry VIII learnt to handle the Commons with discretion, though even then resistance was not unknown. But in spite of occasional friction, and even riot and rebellion in the countryside, it was on the whole a working partnership.

Within a few years of his accession Henry embarked upon a programme of naval expansion, while Wolsey concerned himself with diplomatic manoeuvre. Henry had already constructed the largest warship of the age, the *Great Harry*, of fifteen hundred tons, with seven tiers one above the other, and an incredible array of guns. Under the King's care the fleet was built up and he ordered the admiral to send word to him in minute detail "how every ship did sail", and was not content until England commanded the Narrow Seas. Wolsey's arrangements for the foreign service were hardly less remarkable. A system of couriers and correspondents was organised over Western Europe, through whom, centuries later, news was received in England as quickly as during the wars of Marlborough or Wellington. The diplomatic service which Henry VII had organised with such care was used as a nucleus, supplemented by the ablest products of the New Learning at Oxford. The dispatches of this period, at the height of the Renaissance, are as closely knit and coloured as any in history; each event—the size of armies, rebellions in Italian cities, movements within the College of Cardinals, taxes in France—is carefully weighed and recorded. Wolsey was thus a powerful factor and balancing weight in Europe.

The zenith of this brilliant period was reached at the Field of the Cloth of Gold in June 1520, when Henry crossed the Channel to meet his rival, Francis I of France, for the first time. Henry's main perplexity was, we are told, about his appearance; he could not decide how he would look best, in his beard or clean-shaven. At first he yielded to Catherine's persuasion and shaved. But he soon regretted he had done so and grew the beard again. It reached its full luxuriance in time to create a great impression in France.

At the Field of the Cloth of Gold, near Guisnes, the jousting and feasting, the colour and glitter, the tents and trappings, dazzled all Europe. It was the last display of medieval chivalry. Many noblemen, it was said, carried on their shoulders their mills, their forests, and their meadows. But Henry and Francis failed to become personal friends. Henry, relying on his great physical strength, challenged Francis to a wrestling match. Francis seized him in a lightning grip and put him on the ground. Henry went white with passion, but was held back. Although the ceremonies continued Henry

Henry VIII's embarkation at Dover, in 1520, for his famous meeting with Francis I of France at the Field of the Cloth of Gold, near Calais.

could not forgive such a personal humiliation. He was, in any case, already negotiating with Francis's enemy, the new Emperor Charles V, who had lately succeeded his grandfather, Maximilian. Within a month he had concluded an alliance with the Emperor, thus forfeiting the French tribute. When the Emperor declared war on Francis, English wealth was squandered feverishly on an expedition to Boulogne and subsidies to mercenary contingents serving with the Emperor. Wolsey had to find the money. When Kent and the eastern counties rose against a capital levy imposed by Wolsey in the second year of war, and absurdly misnamed the "Amicable Grant", the Government had to beat a retreat, the campaign was abandoned, and Wolsey got the King's consent to make secret overtures for peace to Francis.

These overtures were Wolsey's fatal miscalculation; only six weeks later the Imperial armies won an overwhelming victory over the French at Pavia, in northern Italy. But although Francis himself was taken prisoner and crushing terms of peace were imposed on France, England did not share in the spoils. The blame was clearly Wolsey's, and the King decided that perhaps the Cardinal had been given too free a hand. He insisted on visiting the great new college which Wolsey was building at Oxford, destined to become Christ Church. When he arrived he was astonished at the vast sums which were being lavished upon the masonry. "It is strange," he remarked to the Cardinal, "that you have found so much money to spend upon your college and yet could not find enough to finish my war."

Up till now he had been inseparable from Wolsey. In 1521 he had sent to the scaffold the Duke of Buckingham, son of Richard III's Buckingham, for leading the opposition of the displaced nobility to the King's chosen Chancellor. But after Pavia Henry began to have second thoughts. Perhaps, he decided, Wolsey would have to be sacrificed to preserve the popularity of the monarch. Then there was Queen Catherine. In 1525 she was aged forty. At the Field of the Cloth of Gold, five years before, King Francis had mocked at her behind the scenes, saying she was already "old and deformed". A typical Spanish princess, she had matured and aged rapidly; it was clear that she would bear Henry no male heir. Either the King's illegitimate son, the Duke of Richmond, now aged six, would have to be appointed by Act of Parliament, or perhaps England might accept Catherine's child, Mary, now aged nine, as the first Queen of England in her own right since Matilda. Would England tolerate being ruled by a woman? Might Mary

TUDOR HOMES AND GARDENS

EVEN BEFORE KING HENRY VIII established the Tudor dynasty there were many signs that manor houses were becoming more comfortable than they had been, places to live in rather than to defend. There were more private apartments and more agreeable rooms. In smaller houses, too, the size of halls was reduced. There was often elegant timberwork, both in town and country houses.

There are many surviving Tudor houses, big and small, which are gems, some constructed from materials acquired when the monasteries were dissolved. The period has been described as "the age of the household", and by the end of the Tudor period some of the houses were elaborate and fanciful with rich interior details. Country living was more attractive to aristocrats and gentlemen than living in town, and the household was the centre of an estate.

The parson William Harrison noted in his *Description of England*, 1587, that even cottages were acquiring chimneys. Previously, smoke could only escape through open windows or a hole in the roof. The increase in chimneys was partly due to the introduction of coal, which emitted "sulphurous fumes".

"Every man almost is a builder," wrote Harrison. "How they pull down, how they enlarge, how they restrain, how they add to, how they take from" were main preoccupations. In four widely separated counties—Derbyshire, Shropshire, Essex and Somerset—more new country houses were built between 1570 and 1620 than in any other half-century.

There was a delight in flower gardens, too. Earlier, gardens had been used chiefly for growing food. Now, often in walled gardens, flowers were planted neatly in rows or in squares, herbs were tended, hedges were started (often, of course, to enclose land) and mazes were created.

HOUSES GREW MORE HOMELY *in Tudor times. The stronger government imposed after the Wars of the Roses meant that they no longer needed to be fortified strongholds. Little Moreton Hall (above) is a Tudor "black and white" house, built between 1559 and 1580. Brick was increasingly used as a building material, particularly when there were local shortages of timber. Houses usually looked attractive inside as they now contained some elaborate furnishings. There were more rooms, often including a "solar", or family room, upstairs, and a "long gallery" in the roof. Walls were covered in carved panels, and ceilings had mouldings. Large windows were made possible by the availability of cheaper glass.*

FURNITURE WAS STILL SPARSE. *A table and stools furnish this panelled dining room, but most people still stood up to eat their meals, and although pewter plates began to replace tin and wooden platters, most dinner "plates" were simply thick slices of bread called "trenchers", which were eaten afterwards. The main meal was taken at 11.00 a.m. and lasted several hours. Supper was a lighter repast which was eaten at about 5.00 p.m.*

COLOURFUL NEEDLEWORK *brightened all but the poorest homes. Carpets were now regularly traded from the East, as were tapestries*

TABLEWARE BECAME GRANDER, *like this tigerware pottery jug which has silver-gilt mounts and an ornately worked lid. Although more eating utensils were used in Tudor times, forks were still rare.*

GARDENS WERE GEOMETRIC AND FORMAL, *as the plan shown above indicates. Square or rectangular plots are outlined by clipped box hedges. A stonework balustrade encloses the flowerbeds and a man waters them by means of a primitive spray pump. Hives for bees have been placed in the far corner: flowers needed to be pollinated, and honey provided sweetening. The picture is taken from the 1586 edition of* The Gardener's Labyrinth *by Thomas Hill. The Italianate cherub fountain in a marble pool at Hatfield House (below) is a typical Tudor garden feature, as is the knot garden in the background. Knot gardens were formed by lines of box hedges planted and trimmed to look like laced ribbons. The ground beneath was often coloured red with crushed bricks, or white with powdered chalk, to make the patterns stand out.*

FAMILIES WERE LARGE *though many infants did not survive. Lord and Lady Cobham, shown with their family and Lord Cobham's sister, were luckier than most. The eldest of their six children is six years old in the picture, so there can have been few infant deaths in their family. The cherries, grapes and peaches on the table would have cost more than steak in Elizabethan times. The children eat fruit and play with their pets. Lord Cobham was Warden of the Cinque Ports and the parrot on the table was probably a gift from one of his seafaring friends.*

from Flanders. Most housewives knew how to embroider, and some created scenes of everyday life like this Tudor stag hunt.

Hampton Court Palace in Middlesex. Wolsey gave this very desirable residence to Henry VIII in 1525, hoping to secure the King's favour. The palace had a thousand rooms, with two hundred and eighty beds kept always ready in anticipation of visitors.

not turn out very like her Spanish mother, not acceptable to the free English, who had obeyed Henry VII and Henry VIII because they wished to obey?

To the monarch these great questions of State were questions in which conscience, his sensual passions and his care for the stability of the realm were all fused together. They perplexed Henry for two more years. The first step, clearly, was to get rid of Catherine. In May 1527 Cardinal Wolsey, acting as Papal Legate and with the collusion of the King, held a secret ecclesiastical court at his house in Westminster. He summoned Henry to appear before him, charged with having married his deceased brother's wife within the degrees of affinity prohibited by the laws of the Church. Henry's authority had been a Bull of dispensation obtained by Ferdinand and Henry VII in 1503, which said in effect that since the marriage between Catherine and Arthur had not been consummated Catherine was not legally Henry's deceased brother's wife and Henry could marry her. Although Catherine maintained to her dying day that her marriage with Arthur had not been consummated nobody was convinced. They had lived under the same roof for seven months.

The ceilings and wall paintings of Wolsey's private apartments inside Hampton Court Palace are an indication of the building's opulence.

The court decided that the point should be submitted to a number of the most learned bishops in England. Several bishops replied however that provided Papal dispensation had been secured such a marriage was perfectly lawful. Henry then tried to persuade Catherine herself that he and she had never been legally married, that they had lived in mortal sin for eighteen years. He added that as he intended to abstain from her company in future he hoped she would retire far from Court. Catherine burst into tears and firmly refused to go away.

About a fortnight later Wolsey crossed the Channel to conduct prolonged negotiations for a treaty of alliance with France. While Wolsey was away Henry became openly infatuated with Anne Boleyn. He had had mistresses before, but never openly. The appearance at Court of a lady with whom he spent hours at a time created an extraordinary stir. Since she had returned from school in France Anne had grown into a vivacious, witty woman of twenty-four, very slender and frail, with beautiful black eyes and thick black hair, so long that she could sit on it, which she wore flowing loose over her shoulders. She had a fiery temper, was outspoken and domineering, and although not generally liked soon gained a small following, many of them noted for their leanings towards the new religious doctrines of Luther. We first hear of Anne Boleyn at Court in a dispatch of the Imperial ambassador dated August 16, 1527, four months after Henry had begun proceedings for the annulment of his marriage. Did he plan the divorce and then find Anne? Or had he arranged to marry Anne from the beginning? We shall never know, for Henry was very secretive. "Three may keep counsel," he observed a year or two later, "if two be away; and if I thought my cap knew my counsel I would cast it into the fire and burn it." His love letters were secured by Papal agents, and are now in the Vatican library, but, while prettily phrased, they are undated, and disclose little except that Anne Boleyn kept him waiting for nearly a year.

Portrait by Clouet of Francis I of France, Henry's magnificent rival. When Francis built the Château of Fontainebleau, Henry responded by building a splendid palace near Epsom, in Surrey. He called it Nonsuch, for there was "None such" to compare with it.

Together Anne and Henry arranged to send a special royal ambassador to Pope Clement VII, independently of the resident ambassador chosen by Wolsey, to seek not only annulment of the King's marriage, but also a dispensation to marry again at once. Two entirely different sets of instructions were prepared; one made no mention of the proposed new marriage and was to be shown to Wolsey as he passed through Compiègne on his way to Rome; the other was the one on which the ambassador was to act. Wolsey was shown the dummy instructions as arranged, and at once saw that they had been drafted by ignorant laymen. He hurried home to have the instructions altered, and thus learnt all. But although he now took over the management of the negotiations, every expedient proved fruitless. The Papal Legate, Cardinal Campeggio, who was sent to England to hear the case, used all possible pretexts to postpone a decision. Italy had fallen to the Habsburgs and the Pope was now practically a prisoner of Charles V, who was determined that Henry should not divorce his aunt.

This broke Wolsey. New counsellors were called in. A follower of the Duke of Norfolk, Stephen Gardiner, was appointed Secretary to the King. Soon after this appointment Thomas Cranmer, a young lecturer in divinity at Cambridge and a friend of the Boleyns, made a suggestion to Gardiner, that the question whether the King had ever been legally married should be submitted to the universities of Europe. The King at once took up the idea. Cranmer was sent for and complimented. Letters and messengers were dispatched to all the universities in Europe. At the same time the King had the writs sent out for a Parliament, the first for six years, to strengthen his hand in the great changes he was planning. Norfolk and Gardiner, not Wolsey, completed the arrangements. Wolsey retired in disgrace to his diocese of York, which he had never visited.

On October 9, 1529, Wolsey's disgrace was carried a step farther by an indictment in the King's Bench under one of the Statutes of Praemunire, passed in the reign of Richard II. These Acts of Parliament were designed to uphold the jurisdiction of the royal courts against the Church courts, and had been one of Wolsey's favourite instruments for exacting money for the King for technical offences. They provided that anyone who obtained in the court of Rome or elsewhere any transfers of cases to Rome, processes, sentences of excommunication, Bulls (edicts or decrees), instruments, or "any other things whatsoever which touch the King, against him, his Crown and regalty, or his realm", should lose the royal protection and forfeit all his goods to the King. While the proceedings were going forward in King's Bench, Norfolk and Suffolk came to Wolsey to take away the Great Seal as a mark that he was no longer Lord Chancellor. When they had gone with the seal the great Cardinal was found seated, weeping and lamenting his misfortunes.

Portrait of Anne Boleyn, from the National Portrait Gallery. Anne was one of the three nieces of the Duke of Norfolk to catch the eye of Henry VIII. The others being Anne's sister Mary, and her cousin, Catherine Howard.

Anne was determined to ruin him. She had set her heart on York Place, the London residence of the Archbishops of York, which was, she decided, of a convenient size for her and Henry; large enough for their friends and entertainments, yet too small to permit Queen Catherine to live there also. Anne and her mother took the King to inspect York Place, and Henry was incensed by the wealth which he found. The judges and learned counsel were summoned and the King asked how he could legally obtain possession of York Place, which had been regarded as belonging to the Archbishops of York in perpetuity.

The judges advised that Wolsey should make a declaration handing over York Place to the King and his successors. A judge of the King's Bench was accordingly sent to Wolsey. A member of his household, George Cavendish, has left an account of the Cardinal's last days. According to him Wolsey said, ". . . May I do it with justice and conscience, to give that thing away from me and my successors which is none of mine?" The judge explained how the legal profession viewed the case. Then said the Cardinal, "I will in no wise disobey, but most gladly fulfil and accomplish his princely will and pleasure in all things, and in especial in this matter, inasmuch as ye, the fathers of the law, say that I may lawfully do it. Howbeit I pray you show his Majesty from me, that I most humbly desire his Highness to call to his most gracious remembrance that *there is both Heaven and Hell.*"

Henry cared nothing for the fulminations of a Cardinal. Threats merely made him take more sweeping measures. The charge under Praemunire was supplemented by a charge of traitorous correspondence with the King of France, conducted without the King's knowledge. Wolsey was found guilty.

As the Cardinal journeyed back to London, where the cell in the Tower used by the Duke of Buckingham before his execution was again being placed in readiness, he fell ill, and when he neared Leicester Abbey for the night he told the monks who came out to greet him, "I am come to leave my bones among you." About eight in the morning two days later he sank into a last decline, murmuring to those gathered at the bedside, "If I had served God as diligently as I have done the King He would not have given me over in my grey hairs." Soon afterwards he died; and they found beneath his shirt, which was of very fine linen, another shirt of hair next to his body. This shirt of hair was unknown to all his servants except his chaplain.

The high offices of State were conferred on a new administration: Gardiner secured the Bishopric of Winchester, the richest See in England; Norfolk became President of the Council, and Sir Thomas More Lord Chancellor. The King applied the Great Seal himself to documents of State. With the death of the Cardinal political interests hitherto submerged made their bid for power. The ambition of the country gentry to take part in public affairs in London, the longing of an educated, wealthy Renaissance England to cast off the tutelage of priests, the naked greed and thirst for power of rival factions, began to shake and agitate the nation. Henry was now thirty-eight years old.

CHAPTER 34

THE BREAK WITH ROME

Cranmer's idea of an appeal to the universities about Henry VIII's marriage to Catherine had proved a success, and the young lecturer was rewarded with an appointment as Ambassador to the Emperor. Even the University of Bologna, in the Papal States, declared that the King was right and that the Pope could not set aside so fundamental a law. Many others concurred: Paris, Toulouse, Orleans, Padua, Ferrara, Pavia, Oxford, and Cambridge. The King had known all along that he was right, and here, it seemed, was final proof. He determined to mark his displeasure with the Pope by some striking measure against the power of the Church in England. Why, he asked, was the right of Sanctuary allowed to obstruct the King's justice? Why were parsons permitted to hold more than one living while underpaid substitutes did the work for the absentees? Why did Italians enjoy the revenues of English bishoprics? Why were the clergy demanding fees for probate on wills and gifts on the death of every parishioner? The King would ask his learned Commons to propose reforms.

Gateway of Trinity College, Cambridge, with a statue of Henry VIII, the college's founder.

A committee was formed of all the lawyers in the House, and they drafted the necessary Bills in record time. The House of Lords, where the bishops and abbots still had more votes than the lay peers, agreed to Bills reforming sanctuaries and abolishing mortuary fees, which affected the lower clergy only, but when the Probate Bill came up to the Lords the Archbishop of Canterbury "in especial", and all the other bishops in general, both frowned and grunted. Fisher, Bishop of Rochester, a representative of the old school, warned the Lords that religious innovation would bring social revolution in its train. He pointed to the national Bohemian revolt led by John Huss.

"My lords," he said, "you see daily what Bills come here from the Commons house, and all is for the destruction of the Church. For God's sake see what a realm the kingdom of Bohemia was; and when the Church went down, then fell the glory of the kingdom."

The Commons soon heard of this bold speech, and thirty leading members went off to complain to the King. Sharp exchanges took place before the Probate Bill could be forced through the Lords, and rancour grew. Thus from the outset the Reformation House of Commons acquired a corporate spirit, and during its long life, longer than any previous Parliament, eagerly pursued any measure which promised revenge against the bishops for what it deemed their evasion and duplicity over the Probate Bill. Hostility to the episcopate smouldered, marking the Commons for more than a hundred years.

Martin Luther (1483–1546), the fearless German ex-monk, teacher and founder of the Protestant Reformation. This wood-cut portrait shows Luther six years before his death.

The King was already delighted with what they had done, but he made it clear at once that he remained fully orthodox in matters of doctrine, that he was merely adhering to the principle of John Colet and other leading divines whom he had known in his youth, that men could be Catholic though critical of Papal institutions. "If Luther," he declared, "had confined himself to denouncing the vices, abuses, and errors of the clergy, instead of attacking the sacraments of the Church and other divine institutions, we should all have followed him." After this blunt though reasoned statement the negotiations in Rome for annulling the King's marriage encountered even greater obstacles. But Henry all his life was only spurred by opposition, and he determined to show he was in earnest.

During December 1530 the Attorney-General charged the whole body of the clergy with breaking the fourteenth-century Statutes of Praemunire and Provisors by acquiescing in Wolsey's many high-handed actions in his role as Papal Legate. Henry, after defeating the bishops in the matter of probate by enlisting the support of Parliament, knew that Convocation, the assembly of the bishops, would not defy him. When the Papal Nuncio intervened, without allowing him even to open his mouth, they begged him to leave them in peace, since they had not the King's leave to speak with him. In return for a pardon for contravening Praemunire and Provisors the King extracted large sums from Convocation, £100,000 from the province of Canterbury and £19,000 from York. The clergy also acknowledged that the King was "their especial Protector, one and supreme lord, and, as far as the law of Christ allows, even supreme head".

Parliament, which had been prorogued from month to month since the great doings about probate in 1529, was now recalled to hear and disseminate the royal view on the divorce. Lord Chancellor More came down to the House and read out the opinions of twelve foreign universities and showed a hundred "books" drawn up by doctors of strange regions, all agreeing that the King's marriage was unlawful. Then the Lord Chancellor said, "Now you of this Commons house may report in your counties what you have seen and heard, and then all men shall openly perceive that the King hath not attempted this matter of will or pleasure, as some strangers report, but only for the discharge of his conscience and surety of the succession of his realm."

Throughout these proceedings Queen Catherine remained at Court. The King, although he rode and talked openly with Anne, left Catherine in charge of his personal wardrobe. Anne was furiously jealous, but for months the King refused to abandon his old routine. A new attempt was then made by the Boleyn party to persuade Catherine to renounce her rights. On June 1, 1531, she was waited on by Norfolk, Suffolk, Gardiner, Anne's father—now Earl of Wiltshire—and several others. As before she refused to renounce anything. Finally, about the middle of July, Anne took the King on a long hunting expedition, away from Windsor Castle, longer than any they had ever made together. Catherine waited, day after day, until a month had gone by. At last a messenger came: the King would come back. But his Majesty did not wish to see the Queen; she was commanded to retire instantly to Wolsey's former palace at Moor, in Hertfordshire. Henceforward she and her daughter Mary were banished from Court.

The winter of 1531-2 was marked by the tensest crisis of Henry's reign. A form of excommunication, or even interdict, had been drafted in Rome, ordering the King to cast off his concubine Anne within fifteen days, only the penalties being left blank. The shadow of Papal wrath hung over England. But, as in the dark days in the early part of the reign, after the failure of the Bordeaux expedition, the King pursued his inflexible course to the end. Opposition merely confirmed him in his plans. "The Annates Bill" was drafted as a fighting measure, in case the worst occurred. It armed the King for a greater struggle with the Papacy than had preceded Magna Carta. If the Court of Rome, its preamble ran, endeavoured to wield excommunication, interdict, or process compulsory in England, then all manner of sacraments and divine service should continue to be administered, and the interdict should not by any prelate or minister be executed or divulged. If anyone named by the King to a bishopric were restrained by Bulls from Rome from accepting office he should be consecrated by the Archbishop, or anyone named to an Archbishopric. And the Annates [the first year's income which the bishops were required to pay to Rome on consecration], a mainstay of the Papal finances, were limited to five per cent of their former amount.

This was the most difficult Bill which Henry ever had to steer through Parliament. He was obliged to go down to the House of Lords himself at least three times, and even then seemed likely to fail, until he thought of an entirely new expedient—the first public division of the House. "Those among the Members who wished for the King's welfare and the prosperity of the kingdom (as they call it) should stand on one side of the House and those who opposed the measure on the other. For fear of the King's indignation a number of them went over," and with considerable amendment the Bill was passed.

The next step was to make the clergy submit to the royal supremacy. Henry got the Commons to prepare a document called the Supplication against the Ordinaries, directed against the authority of Church courts. "Ordinaries" was the legal term for bishops and their deputies who enjoyed rights of jurisdiction. Although Convocation was truculent at first, making submission only in vague and ambiguous terms, Henry refused to compromise, and at the third attempt they agreed to articles of his own, making him effective master of the Church in England. On the very afternoon these articles were submitted for the royal consent, May 16, 1532, Sir Thomas More resigned the Lord Chancellorship as a protest against royal supremacy in spiritual affairs. He had tried to serve his sovereign faithfully in everything; now he saw that Henry's courses must inevitably conflict with his own conscientious beliefs.

Thus the English Reformation was a slow process. An opportunist king measured his steps as he went, until England was wholly independent of administration from Rome. Wolsey had done much to prepare the way. He

Thomas More, Henry's Chancellor (an office traditionally known as "The Keeper of the King's Conscience"), and his family, in Chelsea. This portrait is by R. Lockey and can be seen in the National Portrait Gallery.

THE NEW HORIZONS

ENGLAND IN THE FIFTEENTH CENTURY seemed to continental Europeans to be an unattractive country, inordinately proud of itself. According to a prestigious Venetian ambassador, Englishmen were "great lovers of themselves and of everything belonging to them: they think that there are no other men but themselves and no other world but England".

The huge changes in thought and culture which took place in Europe at that time were, however, bound to have implications for England. The flowering of the arts—the Renaissance—began in Italy, and Germany was the seedbed of the Reformation, the questioning of old religious beliefs. The tide of thought was directing attention away from God towards the study of men and women, and *their* works.

In England new horizons opened up in art, literature and music. Henry VIII took up "the new" and was prepared to spend money building palaces and patronising the arts; Hans Holbein painted many portraits at Court besides the King's and was principal designer at a great pageant at Greenwich in 1527; gentlemen like Sir Thomas Wyatt wrote poems, and the Chapel Royal provided good music.

This broader outlook also affected people's attitudes to the Church, and especially the monasteries, which were criticised for being too wealthy and unspiritual. Matters came to a head in 1530 when Henry VIII quarrelled with the Church of Rome and founded a separate Church of England with himself as supreme head. This heralded the English Reformation.

It was during the reign of Elizabeth I that English culture really flowered, encouraged by a more open education system, by greater social mobility and by more sophisticated and more varied tastes. The Queen was flattered and praised in words, pictures and music. It was Edmund Spenser who first called her Gloriana, and his wonderful epic poem *The Faerie Queen* was dedicated to Queen Elizabeth.

INTELLECTUAL ENQUIRY began to give thinking people in the sixteenth century a new perspective of the world. The desire for individual self-fulfilment here on earth was one of the hallmarks of the Renaissance. Another was a delight in beauty, and a third the desire to explore. "The Ambassadors" (above) by Hans Holbein shows two French diplomats who were clearly explorers of the new horizons: navigational, astronomical and musical instruments are depicted in the background, and the peculiar object in the foreground is a falling skull. It seems likely that the painter was conducting experiments in perspective; the distortion vanishes if the original is held level with the eyes. Holbein was closely associated with the Protestant Reformation. He designed woodcuts for Luther's translation of the New Testament and illustrated Tyndale's Bible. After his appointment as court painter to Henry VIII, Holbein lived in London.

THE IDEAL SOCIETY OF UTOPIA, located on an imaginary island which, although inhabited by pagans, possessed perfect government, was described by Sir Thomas More in his book Utopia, *published in 1516. The name in Greek means* No Place. *In Utopia, land was held in common by all adults, men and women were educated equally, and there was religious toleration. In England, however, the aristocracy held nearly all the land, few women were educated and religious toleration did not exist.*

ENJOYMENT OF LIFE ON EARTH was the keynote of the age and of this painting by Marcus Gheeraerts (right) which records the Tudor Court's glittering finery. It shows Elizabeth I being carried in procession to a wedding at Blackfriars. In the foreground is the bridegroom's father, the Earl of Worcester, and it is thought that he commissioned the picture. Elizabeth and her courtiers made frequent journeys, known in those days as "progresses", round her kingdom.

THE

THERE WERE MANY ENGLISH TRANSLATIONS OF THE BIBLE *in the sixteenth century, thus enabling more people to understand the Christian message. Previously, the church services and Bibles were in Latin. Below is the title page of the first printed edition of the English Bible, translated by Tyndale's former colleague, Coverdale, and published in 1535.*

BIBLIA
The Bible/that
is, the holy Scripture of the
Olde and New Testament, faithfully and truly translated out
of Douche and Latyn
in to Englishe.

M.D.XXXV.

S.paul.II. Tessa.III.
Praie for us, that the worde of God maie
haue fre passage, and be glorified.&c.

S.paul Col. III.
Let the worde of Christ dwell in you plen
teously in all wysdome &c.

Josue I.
Let not the boke of this lawe departe
out of thy mouth, but exercyse thyselfe
therin daye and nighte &c.

EDUCATION WAS A KEY TO ADVANCEMENT. *Christ Church College, Oxford (above) was built by Wolsey in 1525 and originally called Cardinal College. It has a huge quadrangle, for Wolsey intended to outdo all others. The bottom of the tower was built in Wolsey's time, but the top and much of the formal façade of the College were added by Wren in the seventeenth century.*

ADVANCES BY GEOGRAPHERS *led to a better understanding of the world's physical nature. The object above is an armillary sphere dated 1568. It is basically a reconstruction of the globe in skeletal form, in which the metal rings revolve on a central axis within a wooden horizon. The rings represent the equator, the tropics and the Arctic and Antarctic Circles.*

Thomas Cranmer was appointed Archbishop of Canterbury in December 1531 and, within a month, the first breach had been made between England and Rome. Cranmer's greatest memorial is The Book of Common Prayer. In Mary Tudor's reign he was burnt at the stake for his Protestant beliefs. His portrait, painted by Holbein, hangs in the National Portrait Gallery.

had supported the Papacy during some of its most critical years, and in return had been allowed to exercise wide and sweeping powers which were usually reserved to the Pope himself. England therefore was accustomed to Papal jurisdiction being vested in one of its own priests, and this made it easier to transfer it to the Crown. Wolsey had also brought Papal authority in his own person nearer to men's lives than it had ever been, and this unsought familiarity bred dislike. The death in August of the old Archbishop of Canterbury opened further possibilities and problems. Henry did not hasten to appoint a successor. He had to consider how far he could go. If there were a struggle could any of his bishops be trusted to forget the oath which they had sworn to the Pope at their consecration? Would there be a rebellion? Would the Emperor, Queen Catherine's nephew, invade England from the Low Countries? Could the King rely on French neutrality?

In order to weigh these factors at firsthand the King went over to Boulogne with only a few friends, including Anne Boleyn, for personal discussion with Francis I. He returned reassured. Confident that he could carry through even the most startling appointment to Canterbury, he recalled Cranmer from his embassy. Cranmer had been married twice, the second time in Germany after ordination, in the new German fashion for priests, to the niece of a well-known Lutheran. Since the marriage of priests was still illegal in England, Cranmer's wife went ahead in disguise. Cranmer himself arrived in London in the middle of December. A week later he was offered the Archbishopric of Canterbury. He accepted. Henceforward, until Henry died, Cranmer's wife was always hidden, and if she accompanied him was obliged, according to popular repute, to travel with the luggage in a vast chest specially constructed to conceal her.

A month later Henry secretly married Anne Boleyn. Historians have never discovered for certain who performed the ceremony, or where. Undoubtedly, in the eyes of the Roman Catholic world, Henry VIII committed bigamy, for his marriage had not yet been annulled by any court. He simply assumed he had never been legally married at all, and left the lawyers and clergy to put the matter right afterwards.

Cranmer became Archbishop in the traditional manner. At the King's request Bulls had been obtained from Rome by threatening the Papacy with a rigorous application of the Act of Annates. Cranmer swore to obey the Pope with the usual oath, though reservations were made before and afterwards, and he was consecrated with the full ceremonial. This was important: the man who was to carry through the ecclesiastical revolution had thus been endowed with full authority by the Pope. Two days afterwards, however, a Bill was introduced into Parliament vesting in the Archbishop of Canterbury the power, formerly possessed by the Pope, to hear and determine all appeals from the ecclesiastical courts in England. The judgments of the English courts were not to be affected by any Papal verdict or by excommunication, and any priest who refused to celebrate divine service or administer the sacraments was made liable to imprisonment. This momentous Bill, which abolished what still remained of Papal authority in England, passed through Parliament in due course, and became known as the Act of Appeals. The following month Henry himself wrote a letter describing his position as "King and Sovereign, recognising no superior in earth but only God, and not subject to the laws of any earthly creature." The breach between England and Rome was complete.

Having established his supremacy, Henry proceeded to exploit it. In March 1533 Convocation was asked two questions: Was it against the Law of God, and not open to dispensation by the Pope, for a man to marry his brother's wife, he being dead without issue, but having consummated the marriage? Answer by the prelates and clergy present: Yes. By Bishop Fisher of Rochester: No. Was Prince Arthur's marriage with Queen Catherine consummated? Answer by the clergy: Yes. By the Bishop: No. Thereupon the Bishop was arrested and committed to the Tower. About ten days later the Duke of Norfolk with royal commissioners waited on Queen Catherine at Ampthill. Every sort of reason was advanced why she should renounce her title voluntarily. She was blocking the succession. Her daughter would not be accepted by the country as Queen, and England might be plunged in chaos if she continued her unreasonable obstruction. If she resigned a great position would still be open to her. She refused to resign. Then she was informed of the decisions of Convocation. Steps would be taken to deprive her of the rank of Queen. She was determined to resist. But the Commissioners had still another announcement to make. Catherine was in any case Queen no longer, for the King was already married to Anne Boleyn.

Thus Henry's secret marriage became known. A fortnight later Cranmer opened a court at Dunstable, and sent a proctor to Ampthill citing Catherine to appear. She refused. In her absence the Archbishop pronounced judgment. Catherine's marriage with Henry had existed in fact but not in law; it was void from the beginning; and five days afterwards the marriage with Anne was declared valid. Queen Anne Boleyn was crowned on June 1 in Westminster Abbey.

The following month it became clear that the new Queen was expecting a child. As the confinement approached Henry remained with her at Greenwich, and took the greatest care she should not be disturbed. A magnificent and valuable bed, which had formed part of a French nobleman's ransom, was brought forth, and in it on September 7, 1533, the future Queen Elizabeth was born.

Although bonfires were lighted there was no rejoicing in Henry's heart. A male heir had been his desire. After he had defied the whole world, perhaps committed bigamy, and risked deposition by the Pope and invasion,

This engraving of Greenwich Palace was made by James Basire in 1767 when the town boasted the most splendid royal buildings anywhere in Britain.

here was only a second daughter. "Do you wish to see your little daughter?" the old nurse asked, according to one account. "My daughter! My daughter!" replied the King in a passion. "You old devil, you witch, don't dare to speak to me!" He galloped at once away from Greenwich, away from Anne, and in three days had reached Wolf Hall, in Wiltshire, the residence of a worthy old courtier, Sir John Seymour, who had a clever son in the diplomatic service and a pretty daughter, a former maid of honour to Queen Catherine. Jane Seymour was about twenty-five, and although she was attractive no one considered her a great beauty. But she was gay, and generally liked, and Henry fell in love with her.

Jane Seymour was Henry VIII's favourite wife. "Sweet Jane is dead," he is reputed to have mourned, when she died two weeks after the birth of her son, the future Edward VI.

After the birth of Elizabeth criticism of the King and his ecclesiastical measures could no longer be stifled. If the choice was to be between two princesses, men said, then why not choose Mary, the legitimate one? The King would have none of this argument. An Act was passed vesting the succession in Elizabeth. In March 1534 every person of legal age, male or female, throughout the kingdom was forced to swear allegiance to this Act and renounce allegiance to all foreign authority in England. The clergy were prohibited from preaching unless specially licensed; a bidding prayer was prescribed for use in all churches, containing the words, "Henry VIII being immediately next unto God, the only and supreme head of this Catholic Church of England, and Anne his wife, and Elizabeth daughter and heir to them both, our Princess." To publish or pronounce maliciously by express words that the King was a tyrant or heretic was made high treason. As the brutality of the reign increased many hundreds were to be hanged, disembowelled, and quartered on these grounds.

Fisher of Rochester and Sir Thomas More, who both refused the oath, were confined in the Tower for many months. At his trial More offered a brilliant defence, but the King's former trust in him had now turned into vengeful dislike. Under royal pressure the judges pronounced him guilty of treason. While Fisher was in the Tower the Pope created seven cardinals, of whom one was "John, Bishop of Rochester, kept in prison by the King of England". Directly Henry heard the news he declared in anger that he would send Fisher's head to Rome for the Cardinal's hat. Fisher was executed in June 1535 and More in July. Their fate is a black stain on Henry's record. Shortly afterwards Henry was excommunicated and in theory deprived of his throne by the Pope.

The resistance of More and Fisher to the royal supremacy in Church government was a noble and heroic stand. They realised the defects of the existing Catholic system, but they hated and feared the aggressive nationalism which was destroying the unity of Christendom. They saw that the break with Rome carried with it the threat of a despotism freed from every fetter. More stood forth as the defender of all that was finest in the medieval outlook. He represents to history its universality, its belief in spiritual values, and its instinctive sense of other-worldliness. Henry VIII with cruel axe decapitated not only a wise and gifted counsellor, but a system which, though it had failed to live up to its ideals in practice, had for long furnished mankind with its brightest dreams.

The King was still paying court to Jane Seymour when it became known that Anne was expecting another baby. But this time Henry refused to have anything to do with her. She was haggard and ill and had lost her freshness. Rumours were current at Court that he had only spoken to her ten times in three months, although formerly he could hardly bear to be separated from her for an hour. Anne became distracted with anxiety, and was obsessed with fears of a rising in favour of Catherine and Mary. Without consulting the King or his Council, she sent messages to Mary through her governess, making all sorts of promises if Mary would swear to the Act of Succession and renounce her claim to the throne. Promises were followed by threats; but Mary refused to give way. Soon afterwards Anne's uncle, the Duke of Norfolk, strode into the room and told her that Henry had had a serious accident out hunting. In her grief and alarm she nearly fainted. Five days later she miscarried.

The King, instead of pitying her, gave way to an uncontrollable outburst of rage. He visited her, repeating over and over again, "I see that God does not mean me to have male children." Anne replied that it was not her fault she had failed to bear another child. She had been frightened when she heard of the King's fall; besides, she loved him so passionately, with so much more fervour than Catherine, that it broke her heart when she saw that he gave his love to others. At this allusion to Jane the King left the room in a towering passion, and refused for days to see her.

Execution scenes were commonplace in Henry VIII's time. Yet "good King Harry" was popular to the end of his reign. After the disturbances of the Wars of the Roses, it was a period of peace and prosperity.

Jane Seymour was installed at Greenwich. Through her serving-man, who had been taken into the pay of the Imperial ambassador, we have a story of the royal courtship.

One day the King sent a page down from London with a purse full of gold and a letter in his own handwriting. Jane kissed the letter, but returned it to the page unopened. Then, falling on her knees, she said, "I pray you beseech the King to understand by my prudence that I am a gentlewoman of good and honourable family, without reproach, and have no greater treasure in the world than my honour, which I would not harm for a thousand deaths. If the King should wish to make me a present of money, I beg him to do so when God shall send me a husband to marry." The King was greatly pleased. She had, he said, displayed high virtue, and to prove that his intentions were wholly worthy of her he promised not to speak to her in future except in the presence of her relations.

In January 1536 Queen Catherine died. If the King was minded to marry again he could now repudiate Queen Anne without raising awkward questions about his earlier union. It was already rumoured by the Seymour party that in her intense desire for an heir Queen Anne had been unfaithful to the King with several lovers. If proved, this offence was capital. The Queen had accordingly been watched, and one Sunday two young courtiers, Henry Norris and Sir Francis Weston, were seen to enter the Queen's room, and were, it was said, overheard making love to her. Next day a parchment was laid before the King empowering a strong panel of counsellors and judges to investigate and try every kind of treason. The King signed. On Tuesday the Council sat all day and late into the night, but as yet there was not sufficient evidence.

The following Sunday a certain Smeaton, a gentleman of the King's chamber, who played with great skill on the lute, was arrested as the Queen's lover. Smeaton subsequently under torture confessed to the charge. On Monday Norris was among the challengers at the May Day tournament at Greenwich, and as the King rode to London after the jousting he called Norris to his side and told him what was suspected. Although Norris denied everything he also was arrested and taken to the Tower.

That night Anne learnt that Smeaton and Norris were in the Tower. The following morning she was requested to come before the Council. Although her uncle, the Duke of Norfolk, presided at the examination, no Queen of England, Anne complained afterwards, could have been treated with such brutality. At the conclusion of the proceedings she was placed under arrest, and kept under guard until the tide turned to take her upriver to the Tower. So quickly had the news spread that large crowds collected along the river bank, and were in time to watch her barge rowing rapidly upstream with a detachment of the guard and her uncle Norfolk on board. At the Traitor's Gate she was handed over to the Constable of the Tower.

The same evening, at York Place when the Duke of Richmond, the King's bastard son, came as usual to say goodnight to his father, the King burst into tears. "By God's great mercy," he said, "you and your sister Mary have escaped the hands of that damned poisonous strumpet. She was plotting to poison you both."

Henry then tried to forget his shame and disgrace in a ceaseless round of feasting.

On Friday morning the special commissioners of treason appointed the previous week, including Anne Boleyn's father, the Earl of Wiltshire, and the entire bench of judges except one, formed the court for the trial of Anne's lovers. A special jury consisting of twelve knights had been summoned, and found the prisoners guilty. They were sentenced to be hanged, drawn, and quartered, but execution was deferred until after the trial of the Queen. This opened the following Monday in the Great Hall of the Tower. Twenty-six peers—half the existing peerage—sat on a raised dais under the

ANNE BOLEYN'S LAST LETTER TO HENRY VIII

Anne Boleyn, Henry's second wife and the mother of Queen Elizabeth I, wrote this passionate, intelligent and eloquent letter to the King from the Tower, shortly before her execution.

Sir,

Your Grace's displeasure and my imprisonment are things so strange unto me, as what to write, or what to excuse, I am altogether ignorant. Whereas you send unto me willing me to confess a truth, and to obtain your favour by such a one whom you know to be mine ancient professed enemy. I no sooner conceived this message by him, than I rightly conceived your meaning; and if, as you say, confessing a truth indeed may procure my safety, I shall with all willingness and duty perform your command.

But let not your Grace ever imagine that your poor wife will ever be brought to acknowledge a fault where not so much as a thought thereof proceeded. And to speak a truth, never prince had wife more loyal in all duty, and in all true affection, than you have ever found in Anne Boleyn. . . . You have chosen me from a low estate to be your queen and companion, far beyond my desert or desire. If then you found me worthy of such honour, good your Grace, let not any light fancy or bad counsel of mine enemies withdraw your princely favour from me; neither let that unworthy stain of a disloyal heart towards your good Grace, ever cast so foul a blot on your most dutiful wife, and the infant princess, your daughter.

Let me receive an open trial, for my truth shall fear no open shame. But if you have already determined of me; and that not only my death, but an infamous slander, must bring you the enjoying of your desired happiness; then I desire of God that he will pardon your great sin.

My last and only request shall be, that myself may only bear the burden of your Grace's displeasure, and that it may not touch the innocent souls of those poor gentlemen who, as I understand, are likewise in strait imprisonment for my sake. If ever I have found favour in your sight, if ever the name of Anne Boleyn hath been pleasing in your ears, then let me obtain this request. . . . From my doleful prison in the Tower, this 6th of May. Your loyal and ever faithful wife,

ANNE BOLEYN

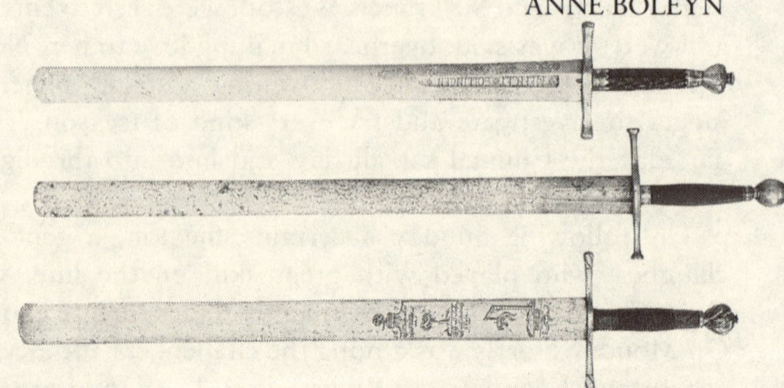

Double-bladed, two-handed sword of the type requested by Anne Boleyn for her execution on May 19, 1536. The Constable of the Tower recorded that ". . . this lady has much joy in her death."

presidency of the Duke of Norfolk. The Lord Mayor and a deputation of aldermen attended, with members of the public, by the King's command, in the well of the hall. The Queen was brought in by the Lieutenant of the Tower, to listen to the indictment by the Attorney General. She was charged with being unfaithful to the King; promising to marry Norris after the King was dead; giving Norris poisoned lockets for the purpose of poisoning Catherine and Mary; and other offences, including incest with her brother. The Queen denied the charges vigorously, and replied to each one in detail. The peers retired, and soon returned with a verdict of guilty. The Duke of Norfolk pronounced sentence: the Queen was to be burnt or beheaded, at the King's pleasure.

Anne received the sentence with calm and courage. She declared that if the King would allow it she would like to be beheaded like the French nobility, with a sword, and not with an axe. Her wish was granted; but no executioner could be found in the King's dominions to carry out the sentence with a sword and it was found necessary to postpone the execution while an expert was borrowed from St Omer.

St. George's Chapel, Windsor, the burial place of Henry VIII and Jane Seymour. It houses the Garter memorabilia, and is famous for its fan-vaulted roof.

During Thursday night Anne slept little. Distant hammering could be heard from the courtyard of the Tower as a scaffold was erected for the execution. In the morning the public were admitted to the courtyard, and the Lord Chancellor entered soon afterwards, with Henry's son, the Duke of Richmond, Cromwell, and the Lord Mayor and aldermen.

The headsman was already waiting, leaning on his heavy two-handed sword, when the Constable of the Tower appeared followed by Anne in a beautiful night robe of heavy grey damask trimmed with fur, showing a crimson kirtle beneath. She had chosen this garment in order to leave her neck bare. A large sum had been given to her to distribute in alms among the crowd. "I am not here," she said to them simply, "to preach to you, but to die. Pray for the King, for he is a good man and has treated me as well as could be. I do not accuse anyone of causing my death, neither the judges nor anyone else, for I am condemned by the law of the land and die willingly." Then she took off her pearl-covered headdress, revealing that her hair had been carefully bound up to avoid impeding the executioner.

"Pray for me," she said and knelt down while one of the ladies in waiting bandaged her eyes. Before there was time to say a Paternoster she bowed her head, murmuring in a low voice, "God have pity on my soul," as the executioner stepped forward and slowly took his aim. "God have mercy on my soul," she repeated. Then the great blade hissed through the air, and with a single stroke his work was done.

As soon as the execution was known Henry appeared in yellow, with a feather in his cap, and ten days later was privately married to Jane Seymour at York Place. Jane proved to be the submissive wife for whom Henry had always longed. Anne had been too dominating and too impulsive. "When that woman desires anything," one of the ambassadors had written of Anne two years before her execution, "there is no one who dares oppose her, or could do so if he dared, not even the King himself." Jane was the opposite, gentle though proud; and Henry spent a happy eighteen months with her. She was the only Queen whom Henry regretted and mourned, and when she died, still aged only twenty-seven, a fortnight after the birth of her first child, the future Edward VI, Henry had her buried with royal honours in St George's Chapel at Windsor. He himself lies near her.

Silver-gilt chalice from Dolgelly, Wales. Ecclesiastical lands and treasures, such as this, made Henry VIII's policy of dissolving the monasteries very profitable.

CHAPTER 35

THE END OF THE MONASTERIES

THOUGH ALL HAD BEEN BLISS AT COURT while Jane was Queen, rural England was heavy with discontents. Henry was increasingly short of revenue and Church properties offered a tempting prize. Just before Anne's trial he had gone down to the House of Lords in person to recommend a Bill suppressing those smaller monasteries which contained fewer than twelve monks. There were nearly four hundred of them, and the combined rent of their lands amounted to a considerable sum. The religious orders had for some time been in decline, and parents were becoming more and more averse to handing over their sons to the cloisters. At some houses the monks had given up all hope of carrying on, and squandered the endowments, cutting down woods, pawning the plate, and letting the buildings fall into disrepair. Grave irregularities had been discovered by the ecclesiastical Visitors over many years. The idea of suppression was not altogether new: Wolsey had suppressed several small houses to finance his college at Oxford, and the King had since suppressed over twenty more for his own benefit. Parliament made little difficulty about winding up the smaller houses, when satisfied that their inmates were either to be transferred to large houses or pensioned off. During the summer of 1536 royal commissioners toured the country, completing the dissolution as swiftly as possible.

The King had now a new chief adviser. Thomas Cromwell, in turn mercenary soldier in Italy, cloth agent, and moneylender, had served his apprenticeship in statecraft under Wolsey, but he had also learnt the lessons of his master's downfall. Ruthless, cynical, Machiavellian, Cromwell was a man of the New Age. His ambition was matched by his energy and served by a penetrating intelligence. He made no effort to inherit the pomp of the fallen Cardinal. Nevertheless Cromwell's were more solid achievements. In the administration of the realm he devised new methods to replace the institutions he found at hand. Before his day government policy had for centuries been both made and implemented in the royal Household. Though Henry VII had improved the system, he had remained in a sense a medieval king. Thomas Cromwell thoroughly reformed policy during his ten years of power, and when he fell in 1540 it was already carried out by government departments, operating outside the Household. Cromwell is thus the uncommemorated architect of our great departments of State.

As First Minister Cromwell handled the dissolution of the monasteries with conspicuous, cold-blooded efficiency. It was a step which appealed to the well-to-do. The high nobility and country gentry acquired on favourable terms all kinds of fine estates. Sometimes a neighbouring merchant, or a syndicate of City men and courtiers, bought or leased the confiscated lands. Throughout the middle classes there was great irritation at the privileges and wealth of the Church. They resented the undue proportion of the national income engrossed by those who rendered no economic service. The King was thus assured of the support of Parliament and the prosperous classes. Most of the displaced monks, nearly ten thousand in all, faced their

A cartoon of 1534 shows Henry VIII suppressing Pope Clement VII, ably assisted by Cromwell and Archbishop Cranmer. Bishops Fisher and Pole try to defend the Pope.

lot with relief or fortitude, assisted by substantial pensions. Some even married nuns, and many became respectable parish clergy. By the sale or lease of monastic properties the Crown gained a million and a half pounds—a huge sum for those days, though probably much less than the properties were worth. The main result of this transaction was in effect, if not in intention, to commit the landed and mercantile classes to the Reformation settlement and the Tudor dynasty.

The immediate impact on the masses is more difficult to judge. There does not seem to have been any widespread unemployment or distress among the sturdy proletariat, but many poor, weak, and ailing folk, especially in the north, who had found their only succour in the good works of the monastic orders, were left untended for a long time. In the north also, where the old traditions died hard, the new order aroused stiffer resistance than in the south, and the new lay landlord could be harsher than his clerical predecessor.

In the field of religious belief the Reformation brought profound change. The Bible now acquired a new and far-reaching authority. The older generation considered that Holy Writ was dangerous in the hands of the unlearned and should only be read by priests. "I never read the Scripture," said the Duke of Norfolk, "nor never will read it. It was merry in England afore the new learning came up." But complete printed Bibles, translated into English by Tyndale and Coverdale, had appeared for the first time late in the autumn of 1535, and were now running through several editions.

Portrait of Thomas Cromwell. He had served Wolsey, but while Wolsey used diplomacy, Cromwell was more ruthless in achieving his ends. He was a lawyer and moneylender, who had travelled in Italy when young and had studied The Prince, *Machiavelli's famous guide to the use of despotic power.*

These remained the basis of later editions, including the Authorised Version prepared in the reign of James I. The Government enjoined the clergy to encourage Bible reading, and, as the King's vicegerent in spiritual affairs, Cromwell ordered the Paternoster and Commandments to be taught in the mother tongue instead of in Latin. Next year *The Institution of a Christian Man*, prepared by Cranmer for popular edification, displayed a distinct leaning to the New Opinion. Here indeed was a change and a revelation. The country folk were deeply agitated, particularly in the fiercely Catholic and economically backward north.

In the autumn, when the new taxes came to be assessed after Michaelmas, farmers and yokels collected in large numbers throughout the north of England and Lincolnshire, swearing to resist the taxes and maintain the old order in the Church. The revolt, which took the name of "the Pilgrimage of Grace", was spontaneous. Its leader, a lawyer named Robert Aske, had his position thrust upon him. The nobles and higher clergy took no part. Although the rebels greatly outnumbered the loyal levies, and the King had no regular troops except the yeomen of the guard, Henry at once showed what Wolsey had called his "royal stomach". He refused to compromise with rebellion. When his Commissioners of Taxes were taken prisoners by the rebels in Lincolnshire he sent a terrifying message:

"This assembly is so heinous that unless you can persuade them to disperse and send a hundred of their ringleaders with halters round their necks to the Lieutenant to do with them as shall be thought best . . . we see no way to save them. For we have already sent . . . the Duke of Suffolk, our Lieutenant . . . with a hundred thousand men, horse and foot, in harness, with munitions and artillery. . . ."

After this the Commissioners reported that the common people as a whole were prepared to allow him for this once to have the first-fruits and the tenths [tithes] from the clergy, together with the subsidy he was demanding. "But, he shall have no more money of the commons during his life, nor shall he suppress no more abbeys." They protested against the King's choice of counsellors, and demanded the surrender of Cromwell, Cranmer, and four bishops who were suspected of heresy.

The King replied with vigour. "Concerning choosing of Counsellors, I never have read, heard, nor known that princes' counsellors and prelates should be appointed by rude and ignorant common people. . . . How presumptuous then are ye, the rude commons of one shire, and that one of the most brute and beastly of the whole realm, and of least experience, to find fault with your Prince. . . . As to the suppression of religious houses, know that this is granted us by all the nobles, spiritual and temporal, of this our realm, by Act of Parliament, and not set forth by any counsellors upon their mere will and phantasy as you full falsely would persuade our realm." If they did not submit, the King added, they with their wives and children would be utterly destroyed by the sword.

In early 1537 the rebellion collapsed as quickly as it had arisen, but Henry determined to make examples of the ringleaders. Seventy were hanged as traitors at Carlisle Assizes alone, and when Norfolk, the victorious general, seemed inclined to clemency the King sent word that he desired a large number of executions. Altogether some two hundred and fifty of the insurgents were put to death.

The rebels had objected to the taxes and suppression of the monasteries.

Henry now replied by tightening up the collection of taxes, and began suppressing the larger monasteries the moment the revolt was put down. As a further blow to the old school in September 1538 the Government directed that every parish in the country should purchase a Bible, to be set up in each church, where the parishioners might most commodiously resort to the same and read it. Six copies were set up in St Paul's, and multitudes thronged the cathedral all day to read them, especially, we are told, when they could get any person that had an audible voice to read aloud.

Up to this point Thomas Cromwell had consistently walked with success. But he now began to encounter the conservatism of the older nobility. They were more than content with the political revolution, but they wanted the Reformation to stop with the assertion of the royal supremacy, and they opposed the doctrinal changes of Cranmer and his following. The Duke of Norfolk headed the reaction, and the King, who was rigidly orthodox, except where his lusts or interests were stirred, agreed with it. Stephen Gardiner, Bishop of Winchester, was the brain behind the Norfolk party. Its leaders took pains to point out that France and the Emperor might invade England and execute the sentence of deposition which the Pope had pronounced. The Catholic front seemed overwhelmingly strong, and the only allies which Cromwell could find abroad were minor German princelings. With these large issues in their keeping, Norfolk's faction vigilantly awaited their chance. It came, like so much of the action of this memorable reign, as a result of the conjugal affairs of the King.

As Henry refused to compromise with the continental Lutherans on matters of doctrine or modifications of the Church services, Cromwell could do no more than seek a political alliance with the Duchy of Cleves, which to some extent shared the King's attitude in religion, hating the Papacy,

Ruins of Bolton Abbey, in Yorkshire. Monasteries often owned rich sheep-farming lands, which added considerably to their value.

BREVIARIES OF HEALTH

The equivalent of our family health manuals, these extracts are taken from Andrew Boorde's Breviary of Helthe *which was written in the mid-sixteenth century.*

Sleeplessness

The cause. This impediment doth come through idleness or weakness of the brain, or else through sickness, anger or fasting, or else through solicitude or repletion, or extreme heat, or extreme cold in the feet or such like. A remedy. Take of the oil of violets an ounce, of opium half an ounce, incorporate this together with woman's milk and with a fine linen cloth lay it to the temples, or else use to eat of lettuce seeds, of white poppy seeds, or mandragora seeds . . . . Of each three drams, but above all things mirth is best to bedward.

Care of the eyes

Take the seeds of *oculi christi* (wild sage) and put into the eyes two, three or four seeds, or else take cold water and with a fine linen cloth wash the eyes divers times in a day . . . and change the water oft that it may be fresh and cold.

Treatment for baldness

Shave the head and beard and anoint the head with the grease of a fox. Or else wash the head with the juice of beets five or six times or else stamp garlic and rub the head with it and after that wash it with vinegar, do this five or six times. Or else make ashes of garlic and temper it with honey and anoint the head . . . Anoint the head with the oils of bitter almonds, or with the oil of wormwood, or with such like oils. The oil of myrtle is good, or the oil of galls or the oil of walnuts or the oil of maidenhair.

A physician visits a patient and examines the colour of the cordial he intends to prescribe. Sometimes powdered gold was added as it was believed to cure disease. An apothecary awaits instructions.

Holbein's famous portrait of Anne of Cleves. Within six months of her marriage to Henry VIII he divorced her and pensioned her off with a number of houses in England.

yet restricting Lutheranism. Then news arrived of a startling diplomatic development. Francis I had invited the Emperor Charles V, who was in his Spanish dominions, to pass through Paris on his way to put down a revolt at Ghent, and the Emperor had accepted.

The two sovereigns had resolved to forget old grudges and make common cause. An alliance with the princes of northern Germany against the two Catholic monarchs now seemed imperative, and negotiations for a marriage between Henry and Anne, the eldest Princess of Cleves, were hurried on. Anne's charms, Cromwell reported, were on everybody's lips. "Everyone," he announced, "praises her beauty both of face and body. One says she excels the Duchess of Milan as the golden sun does the silver moon." Holbein, the Court painter, and a masterly delineator of his age, had already been sent over to paint the portrait, which may now be seen in the Louvre. It does not flatter the Princess. "This," the English ambassador at Cleves warned the King, "is a very lively image." Anne, he added, spoke only German, spent her time chiefly in needlework, and could not sing or play any instrument. She was thirty years old, tall and thin, with an assured, resolute countenance, slightly pockmarked, but was said to possess wit and animation, and did not overindulge in beer.

Anne spent Christmas at Calais, waiting for storms to abate, and on the last day of the year 1539 arrived at Rochester. Henry had sailed down in his private barge, in disguise, bearing a fine sable fur among the presents. On New Year's Day he hurried to visit her. But on seeing her he was astonished and abashed. Embraces, presents, compliments, all carefully arranged on the voyage, were forgotten. He mumbled a few words and returned to the barge, where he remained silent for many minutes. At last he said very sadly and pensively, "I see nothing in this woman as men report of her, and I marvel that wise men should have made such report as they have done." Privately he dubbed her "the Flanders Mare".

The threat from abroad compelled the King to fulfil his contract, but the marriage was never consummated. Since he now knew as much about the

Anne of Cleves's house in Lewes, Sussex, as it exists today. The front part of the house dates from the early sixteenth century, while the back wing is Elizabethan.

Canon Law on marriage as anyone in Europe, he thus turned himself into the perfect legal example of a man whose marriage might be annulled. In fact Henry was merely waiting, watching the European situation, until it was safe to act.

Norfolk and Gardiner now saw their chance to break Cromwell, as Wolsey had been broken, with the help of a new lady. Yet another of Norfolk's nieces, Catherine Howard, was presented to Henry and captured his affections at first sight. The Norfolk faction soon felt strong enough to challenge Cromwell's power. In June 1540 the King was persuaded to get rid of Cromwell and Anne together. Cromwell was condemned, principally for heresy and "broadcasting" erroneous books and implicitly with treason. Anne agreed to have her marriage annulled, and Convocation pronounced it invalid. She lived on in England, pensioned and in retirement, for another seventeen years. A few days after Cromwell was executed on July 28 Henry was privately married to his fifth wife, Catherine Howard.

Catherine, about twenty-two, with auburn hair and hazel eyes, was the prettiest of Henry's wives. His Majesty's spirits revived, and he went down to Windsor to reduce weight. "The King," reported the French ambassador, "has taken a new rule of living, to rise between five and six, hear Mass at seven, and then ride till dinner-time, which is at ten in the morning."

But wild, tempestuous Catherine was not long content with a husband nearly thirty years older than herself. Her reckless love for her cousin, Thomas Culpeper, was discovered, and she was executed in February 1542 on the same spot as Anne Boleyn. The night before the execution she asked for the block so that she could practise laying her head upon it. As she mounted the scaffold she said, "I die a Queen, but would rather die the wife of Culpeper. God have mercy on my soul. Good people, I beg you to pray for me."

Henry's sixth wife, Catherine Parr, was a serious little widow from the Lake District, thirty-one years of age, learned, and interested in theological questions, who had had two husbands before the King. She married Henry at Hampton Court on July 12, 1543, and until his death three years later made him an admirable wife, nursing his ulcerated leg, which grew steadily worse and in the end killed him. She contrived to reconcile Henry with the future Queen Elizabeth; both Mary and Elizabeth grew fond of her, and she had the fortune to outlive her husband.

The brilliant young Renaissance prince had grown old and wrathful. The pain from his leg made him ill-tempered. Suspicion dominated his mind and ruthlessness marked his actions. At the time of his marriage with Catherine Parr he was engaged in preparing the last of his wars. Hostility between the Scots and English still smouldered. Reviving the obsolete claim to suzerainty, Henry denounced the Scots as rebels, and pressed them to relinquish their alliance with France. The Scots successfully defeated an English raid at Halidon Rig. Then in the autumn of 1542 an expedition under Norfolk had to turn back at Kelso, principally through the failure of the commissariat, which, besides its other shortcomings, left the English army without its beer. The Scots proceeded to carry the war into the enemy's country, but badly led and imperfectly organised, they lost more than half their army of ten thousand men at Solway Moss. The news of this second Flodden killed James V, who died leaving the kingdom to an infant of one week, Mary, the famous Queen of Scots.

Catherine Parr, Henry VIII's sixth wife, outlived her husband. She was very fond of her three stepchildren, Mary, Edward and Elizabeth.

At once the child became the focus of the struggle for Scotland. Henry claimed her for the bride of his own son and heir. But the Scots queen mother was a French princess, Mary of Guise, and the pro-French Catholic party, led by Cardinal Beaton, began negotiations for marrying Mary to a French prince. Such a marriage could never be accepted by England. Once again England and the Empire made common cause against the French. While Scotland was left to Edward Seymour, brother of Queen Jane, and now Earl of Hertford, the King himself prepared to cross the Channel and lead an army against Francis in cooperation with an Imperial force from the northeast.

The plan was excellent, but the execution failed. Henry and Charles distrusted each other. Wary of being drawn too deep into the Emperor's plans, Henry sat down to besiege Boulogne. The town fell on September 14, 1544, and Henry was able to congratulate himself on at least one tangible result from his campaign. Five days later the Emperor made his peace with Francis and refused to listen to Henry's complaints and exhortations. Meanwhile the English in Scotland, after burning Edinburgh and laying waste much country, ceased to make headway, and in February 1545 were defeated at Ancrum Moor.

Henry's position was extremely grave. Without a single ally, the nation faced the possibility of invasion from both France and Scotland. The crisis called for unexampled sacrifices from the English people; never had they been called upon to pay so many loans, subsidies, and benevolences. To set an example Henry melted down his own plate and mortgaged his estates. At Portsmouth he prepared for the threatened invasion in person. A French fleet penetrated the Solent and landed troops in the Isle of Wight; but they were soon driven off. Next year a peace treaty was signed, which left Boulogne in English hands for eight years, at the end of which time France was to buy it back at a heavy price. Meanwhile, the war in the north smouldered on, bursting into flame for a time at the assassination of Cardinal Beaton, but yielding no definite results. Henry completely failed in Scotland. He would make no generous settlement with his neighbours, yet he lacked the force to coerce them. For the next fifty years they were to tease and trouble the minds of his successors.

In 1546 Henry was as yet only fifty-five. In the autumn he made his usual progress to Windsor, and early in November he came up to London. He was never to leave his capital alive again. In these last few months one question dominated all minds: the heir to the kingdom was known, a child of nine, but who would be the power behind the throne? Norfolk or Hertford? The party of reaction or the party of reform?

A sudden and unexpected answer was given. On December 12, 1546, Norfolk and his son Surrey, the poet, were arrested for treason and sent to the Tower. Surrey's foolish conduct had made trouble inevitable. He talked wildly of the time when the King should be dead, and inconveniently remembering his descent from Edward I, he had quartered the royal arms with his own. The King's suspicions aroused, he acted swiftly; in mid-January Surrey was executed.

Parliament assembled to pass a Bill of Attainder against Norfolk. He was condemned to death on January 27. But that same evening the King himself was exhorted to prepare himself for death and took the grim news with fortitude. Shortly before midnight he sent for Cranmer, but when he came

TUDOR MAGNIFICENCE

Exploration across the oceans and a growing prosperity brought a new sense of national identity. This was an age of great houses and gracious living.

HAMPTON COURT PALACE, GREATER LONDON

HAMPTON COURT PALACE, GREATER LONDON, *was planned by Cardinal Wolsey to be the largest house in England. The gardens, (left) with their complex patterns, were designed to create a worthy setting for the rich clothes of the guests. Within the building there hangs "The Field of the Cloth of Gold", (below) in which the unknown artist captures Wolsey and Henry VIII arriving at the scene of Wolsey's most spectacular diplomatic coup, the summit meeting in 1520 of the kings of France and England. In 1525, in a vain attempt to stave off royal displeasure, Wolsey presented the house to his king. Hans Holbein's great portrait, "Henry VIII", Baron Thyssen Collection, (above) gives a revealing impression of Hampton Court's new owner, a clever and passionate man who was possessed by the love of power.*

HEVER CASTLE, KENT, (above) was the home of the Boleyn family, who converted it from a medieval castle into a Tudor mansion. At the end of the Long Gallery is the "Lover's Window" where, according to legend, Henry VIII and Anne Boleyn would sit together. After her execution, Henry confiscated the castle, and later gave it to his fourth wife Anne of Cleves.

HARDWICK HALL, DERBYSHIRE, is probably the most striking Elizabethan house in England. The Long Gallery, (above) an exceptional one hundred and sixty-six feet in length, contains portraits of its formidable founder, Bess of Hardwick, Countess of Shrewsbury, and of two of her four husbands. Many of the contents listed in Bess's 1601 inventory can still be seen today. The beautifully carved sea-dog (right) is from a sixteenth-century table in the Withdrawing Room.

ELIZABETHAN FURNITURE, as shown by this group (right) from the Victoria and Albert Museum, London, is typical of the flamboyant taste of Elizabethan England. Every available surface of their heavy furniture was carved with scrolls, rosettes, acanthus leaves or figures, to satisfy the customer that he was getting his money's worth.

BUCKLAND ABBEY, DEVON, *(right)* was converted into a country house by the Grenville family following the Dissolution of the Monasteries. Sir Richard Grenville, the adventurer, whose portrait *(above)* hangs in Montacute House, Somerset, was to command the Revenge, in its last fight in 1591. By then Buckland Abbey had been bought by Sir Francis Drake, and still contains many of his possessions, including his drum *(below)*.

THE MARY ROSE, *(right)* was Henry VIII's flagship. She was purpose-built to fire long-range broadsides. In 1545 she overturned in the Solent and was deeply buried in the mud. When salvaged in 1982, personal effects, *(below)* a wooden comb and leather case, a wooden pomander, bone manicure set and bronze purse mount, were found as the sailors left them. These and the remains of the ship can be seen at Portsmouth, Hampshire.

THE HILLIARD MINIATURE OF SIR FRANCIS DRAKE, now at the National Portrait Gallery, London, *(left)* shows him on his return from circumnavigating the world. It is said that he took his drum *(left)* on that voyage and aboard the Revenge during the Armada, and that it would beat of its own accord if England were ever again to face a threat from Spain.

"THE DEFEAT OF THE SPANISH ARMADA", *(above) records an event which brought feelings of immense relief and national pride that swept the country in 1588. Though much was due to Spanish incompetence and even more to the winds, this defeat rates as one of the world's decisive battles, in that it established England without question as a major force in a world increasingly concerned with discovery and conquest overseas.*

TUDOR MEDICAL EQUIPMENT, *from the* Mary Rose, *just as it would have been used at sea, can now be seen at Portsmouth, Hampshire. The barber-surgeon (he would have done both jobs) had left everything in order for use in battle. Shown here (left) are canisters, an apothecary's mortar, a chafing-dish base, drug-flask, bleeding bowl and syringe.*

COMPTON WYNYATES, WARWICKSHIRE, *(above)* *was built by the Compton family between 1480 and 1528. "Wynyates" is old English for "valley through which the wind blows". The house was one of the first to be designed for domestic rather than defence purposes. Tall moulded chimneys rose from warmth-giving fireplaces, and mullioned windows looked out on to decorative garden shrubs.*

"FETE AT BERMONDSEY", *(right)* *depicts a fete held in about 1569 in the village of Bermondsey, near London Bridge. Leaning against the tree in the foreground is the painter Hoefnagel, one of many foreign artists attracted to England at that time. The picture can now be seen at Hatfield House, Hertfordshire.*

STRATFORD-UPON-AVON, WARWICKSHIRE, *still has many buildings which remain largely unchanged from Shakespeare's day, including his birthplace (top). Of his own home, New Place, only the foundations of the house still exist, but there is (above) a reconstruction of an Elizabethan Knot Garden.*

ANNE HATHAWAY'S COTTAGE, SHOTTERY, WARWICKSHIRE, *(above) has changed little since Anne married William Shakespeare in 1582. She was then twenty-six and he was eighteen years old.*

BURGHLEY HOUSE, CAMBRIDGESHIRE, *the home of the Cecil family, is the largest surviving Elizabethan mansion. In the sixteenth century, its kitchens (right) would have catered for just two meals a day, but each might last two or three hours.*

THE BRADFORD TABLE CARPET, *(detail above) is typical of English embroidery of the sixteenth century, illustrating some of the country pursuits and pastimes of major landowners. It is now in the Victoria and Albert Museum, London.*

"A YOUNG MAN", *(above) from the Victoria and Albert Museum, London, is perhaps the best surviving work of Nicholas Hilliard. This miniaturist was a court painter to both Queen Elizabeth and James I. Hilliard was trained as a goldsmith, but as early as 1560 was painting miniatures which were probably worn as jewels.*

"THE RAINBOW PORTRAIT", *now in Hatfield House, Hertfordshire, is a superb exercise in artistic flattery. It was painted just before the Queen died but shows her earlier beauty. The Latin motto reads: "Without the sun there can be no rainbow". Elizabeth holds a rainbow in her right hand, the symbol of peace. The sun was the Queen herself.*

On his deathbed, Henry VIII appoints his son Edward, aged nine, to succeed him. Henry seems to have anticipated that his children would have no heirs: he named Mary, Elizabeth, and then the descendants of his younger sister, Mary, as future rulers.

Henry was too weak to speak; he could only stretch out his hand. In a few minutes the Supreme Head had ceased to breathe.

Henry's rule saw many advances in the growth and character of the English State, but it is a hideous blot upon his record that the reign should be widely remembered for its executions. Two Queens, two of the King's chief ministers, a saintly bishop, numerous abbots, monks, and many ordinary folk who dared to resist the royal will were done to death. Almost every member of the nobility in whom royal blood ran perished on the scaffold at Henry's command. Roman Catholic and Calvinist alike were burnt for heresy. The sufferings of devout men and women among the faggots, the use of torture, and the savage penalties imposed for even paltry crimes, stand in repellent contrast to the enlightened principles of humanism. Yet his subjects did not turn from Henry in loathing. He succeeded in maintaining order amid the turmoil of Europe without army or police, and he imposed on England a discipline which was not attained elsewhere. We must also credit Henry's reign with laying the basis of sea power, with a revival of parliamentary institutions, with giving the English Bible to the people, and above all with strengthening a popular monarchy under which succeeding generations worked together for the greatness of England while France and Germany were racked with internal strife.

CHAPTER 36

THE PROTESTANT STRUGGLE

THE ENGLISH REFORMATION UNDER HENRY VIII had received its guiding impulse from the King's passions and his desire for power. He still deemed himself a good Catholic. Monastery lands might be seized and the Bible printed in English, but Henry had restrained Cranmer's doctrinal innovations, and in the main upheld the whole Norfolk interest, represented in religion by Stephen Gardiner, Bishop of Winchester. Thus there was a working compromise. Henry wanted his own way on his throne

Portrait of Edward VI by Holbein. Edward was studious and religious, and showed great political ability during his short reign.

and in his choice of consort, but he saw no need to change the Faith or even the ritual to which his subjects had been born.

With the accession of Edward VI, a deeper and more powerful tide began to flow. The guardian and chief counsellor of the child-king was his uncle, Lord Hertford, now Duke of Somerset. He and Cranmer proceeded to transform the political reformation of Henry VIII into a religious revolution. Foreign scholars from Germany and Switzerland were given chairs in the Universities of Oxford and Cambridge to educate the new generation of clergy in the Reformed doctrines. The Book of Common Prayer, in shining English prose, was drawn up by Cranmer and accepted by Parliament in 1549. Then followed, after Somerset's fall, the Forty-two Articles of Religion. On paper at least, England became a Protestant State. Somerset and Cranmer were both men of sincerity; but the mass of the people neither knew nor cared about theological warfare, and there were many who actively opposed the imported foreign creeds.

Somerset himself was merely one of the Regents appointed under Henry's will, and his position as Protector, at once dazzling and dangerous, had little foundation in law or precedent. Rivals crowded jealously upon him. His brother, Thomas Seymour, Lord High Admiral, had his own ambitions. The pale child Edward VI, who was consumptive, might not live long. The next Protestant heir was Princess Elizabeth. She was living with Lady Catherine Parr, and Catherine Parr was now married to the Admiral. He thought fit to make advances to the young princess even before the death of his wife, and girlish romps took place in her bedroom that led to scandal. Proofs were discovered of Thomas Seymour's plots against his brother, and the Protector was forced in 1549 to dispose of him by the block on Tower Hill.

Far more serious than such personal threats were the distresses and discontents in the countryside. The life and economy of medieval England were fast dissolving. Landlords saw that vast fortunes could be made from wool, and the village communal strips barred their profits. Slowly and surely the rights of the village communities were infringed and removed. Common land was seized, enclosed, and turned to pasture for flocks. Dissolution of the monasteries removed the most powerful and conservative element in the old system, and gave fresh impetus to a process already underway. In some counties as much as one-third of the arable land was turned over to grass, and there was widespread distress and unemployment. The people looked in anger upon the new nobility, fat with sacrilegious spoil, but greedy still.

Somerset had thus to face one of the worst economic crises that England has endured. He himself sympathised with the peasantry, and appointed commissions to inquire into the enclosures. But this increased the discontent, and encouraged the oppressed to take matters into their own hands. Two rebellions broke out. The Catholics in the southwest rose against the Prayer Book, and the peasantry of the eastern counties against the enclosing landlords. This gave a fine handle to Somerset's enemies. In Germany in 1524-26 the Reformation had been followed by the bloody Peasants' War, in which the poorer classes rose against their noble oppressors. The same thing seemed about to happen in the England of 1549. Foreign mercenaries suppressed the western rebellion, but in Norfolk the trouble was more serious. A tannery owner named Robert Ket established his headquarters outside Norwich on Mousehold Hill, where about sixteen thousand peasants gathered in a camp of turf huts roofed with boughs. Under a large oak tree Ket, day after day, tried country gentlemen charged with robbing the poor. No blood was shed, but property acquired by enclosing common land was restored to the public, and the rebels lived upon the flocks and herds of the landowners. The local authorities were powerless. The disorders spread to Yorkshire, and presently reverberated in the Midlands.

John Dudley, Earl of Warwick, son of the man who had been Henry VII's agent, now seized his opportunity. He had proved an able soldier in the French campaigns of Henry VIII. He was a self-seeking, vigorous man, and the champion of wealth and property. Now he was given command of the troops to suppress the rising. The Government felt itself so militarily weak that the rebels were offered a free pardon. Ket was not unmoved. The herald came to his camp, but a small incident brought disaster. An urchin drew the attention of the herald's party "with words as unseemly as his gesture was filthy", and he was immediately shot with an arquebus. The murder enraged Ket's followers. Fighting began. Warwick's best troops were German mercenaries, whose precise fire-drill shattered the peasant array. Three thousand five hundred were killed. Ket was taken prisoner, and hanged at Norwich Castle. Warwick had by accident made his mark as a strong man.

Norwich Castle, now a museum. Ket's Rebellion took place near Norwich in 1549. It was caused by discontent over debasement of the coinage and by enclosures, which robbed the poor of their arable land.

Somerset's enemies claimed the credit for restoring order. They blamed the rising in the east on his enclosure commissions and his sympathy for the peasants, and the rebellion in the west on his religious reforms. Moreover his foreign policy had driven the Scots into alliance with France, and he had lost Henry's one conquest, Boulogne. Warwick became the leader of the Opposition. "The Lords in London", as Warwick's party were called, met to take measures against the Protector. No one moved to support him. They quietly took over the Government. In January 1552, splendidly garbed as for a state banquet, Somerset was executed on Tower Hill. This handsome, well-meaning man had failed completely to heal the dislocation of Henry's reign and fell a victim to the fierce interests he had offended. Nevertheless the people of England remembered him for years as "the Good Duke". The nominal King of England, Edward VI, cold and priggish, noted his uncle's death in his diary without a comment.

Somerset's successors were less scrupulous, and even less successful. The Government of Warwick, now become Duke of Northumberland, was held together by class resistance to social unrest. His three years of power displayed to the full the rapacity of the ruling classes. Doctrinal reformation was a pretence for confiscating yet more Church lands, and new bishops paid for their consecration with portions of the episcopal estates. The so-called grammar schools of Edward VI were but the beginning of spacious plans carried out in Elizabeth's reign for endowing education out of the confiscated lands of the monasteries. Thomas More's definition of government as "a conspiracy of rich men procuring their own commodities under the name and title of a commonwealth" fitted England very accurately during these years.

One gleam of enterprise distinguishes this period. It saw the opening of relations between England and a growing new power in eastern Europe, hitherto known as Muscovy, but soon to be called Russia. A small group of Englishmen conceived the idea of seeking a northeastern passage to Asia through Arctic waters. Upon the northern coasts of Asia there might be

The interior of Stratford Grammar School. Centuries of graffiti can be seen on the wooden desks. Many grammar schools, like this one, were founded in the reign of Edward VI, and several buildings have survived until today.

people who would buy cloth and other English products. In 1553 an expedition was financed by the Muscovy Company of Merchant Adventurers with the backing of the Government. Sebastian Cabot, a wise old seaman who some fifty years earlier had accompanied his father on his unsuccessful attempt to find a northwestern passage beyond the Atlantic to the east, was brought in as governor of the company. In May, three ships set sail under Hugh Willoughby and Richard Chancellor. Willoughby perished with his crew off Lapland, but Chancellor pushed overland to the Court of Ivan the Terrible at Moscow. The monopoly of the German Hansa towns, which had long blocked English merchants throughout northern Europe, was now outflanked and trade began with Russia. In a second voyage Chancellor was drowned in a storm. An associate of his, Anthony Jenkinson, paid three visits to Russia and became a trusted friend of the Tsar. In the course of his travels he got as far as Bokhara, in Turkestan, on the old silk road of Marco Polo; he crossed into Persia, and was the first man to fly the English flag on the Caspian Sea. But these adventures belong to a greater age than that of Edward VI and his successor.

Under the Succession Act of 1543 the next heir to the throne was Princess Mary, the Catholic daughter of Catherine of Aragon. King Edward was an invalid. Northumberland might well tremble for the future. For a moment he thought of substituting Elizabeth for her half-sister; but Elizabeth, now aged nineteen and wise for her years, had no intention of committing herself to such an arrangement. A desperate scheme was evolved. The younger daughter of Henry VII had married the Duke of Suffolk. The eldest grandchild in this Suffolk line was Lady Jane Grey, a girl of sixteen. Northumberland married this girl to his son, Guildford Dudley. Nothing remained but to effect a military coup when the young King died. But when Edward fell ill, Princess Mary, now aged thirty-six, took refuge on the estates of the Duke of Norfolk, ignoring a summons to appear at her brother's deathbed. On July 6, 1553, Edward VI expired, and Lady Jane Grey was proclaimed Queen in London. The only response to this announcement was gathering resistance: Northumberland was too much hated throughout the land. The common people flocked to Mary's support. The Privy Counsellors and the City authorities swam with the tide. Northumberland was left without an ally. In August Mary entered London with Elizabeth at her side. Lady Jane and her husband were consigned to the Tower. In vain Northumberland grovelled. Nothing could save him from an ignominious death. To one of his former associates he wrote, "An old proverb there is, and that most true—a living dog is better than a dead lion. Oh that it would please her good Grace to give me life—yea, the life of a dog." This may serve as his epitaph.

The woman who now became Queen was probably the most unhappy and unsuccessful of England's sovereigns. Mary Tudor, the only surviving child of Catherine of Aragon and Henry VIII, had been brought up in the early years of her father's reign with all the ceremony due to the heiress to the throne. She had been betrothed at different times to the heirs both of France and the Empire. She had then been declared illegitimate by Act of Parliament; she was pressed to forsake her religion, and endured bitter conflicts between her duty to her father and her conscience. She had clung to her confessors and her chapel throughout the reign of Edward VI, and was naturally feared by the ruling group of Protestant politicians in London. The Spanish blood in her was strong. Her accession portended a renewal of the Roman connection and a political alliance with the Empire.

Secure upon the throne, Mary proceeded to realise the wish of her life—the restoration of the Roman communion. In Stephen Gardiner, Bishop of Winchester, one of Norfolk's circle in the later years of Henry VIII, she found an able and ardent servant. The religious legislation of the Reformation Parliament was repealed, but one thing Mary could not do. She could not restore to the Church the lands parcelled out among the nobility. The Tudor magnates were willing to go to Mass, but not to lose their new property. Even so there was trouble. Mary never realised that the common people, particularly in London, coupled Catholicism with foreign influence. The English Bible and the English Prayer Book were in their hands, and there was a wide, if superficial, attachment to the Reformed Faith. There was rioting in the capital. A dead dog was flung through the window of the Queen's chamber, a halter round its neck, its ears cropped, and bearing a label saying that all the priests in England should be hanged.

The marriage of Mary, Queen of England, and Philip II of Spain. The two pet dogs symbolise fidelity. The marriage was unpopular with the people and it brought Mary little happiness. Her husband was often absent in Spain, and Mary suffered from a series of hysterical pregnancies. The picture is by Antonio Moro.

The most urgent question was whom Mary should marry. The Commons supported an English candidate, Edward Courtenay, Earl of Devon, a descendant of the House of York. But Mary's eyes were fixed overseas. She promised to wed the Emperor's son, the future Philip II of Spain. News of the Spanish betrothal filtered through the Court and reached the people. Ugly stories of the Inquisition and the coming of Spanish troops passed from mouth to mouth. The Commons came in deputation to beg the Queen not to violate the feelings of the nation. But Mary had all the obstinacy of the Tudors and none of their political sense. She was now on the threshold of her dreams—a Catholic England united in intimate alliance with the Catholic Empire of the Habsburgs.

All eyes turned to Princess Elizabeth, in watchful retirement at Hatfield, but Princess Elizabeth adroitly ordered Mass to be said in her household,

Lady Jane Grey was descended from Henry VIII's younger sister, Mary Rose. She was thus Edward VI's cousin and about the same age. She was reported by Roger Ascham to be a good scholar, but very much under the dominance of her parents. It is thought that they forced her to marry Lord Guildford Dudley as part of their plan to divert the succession from the Tudors to the Dudleys on the death of Edward VI. Lady Jane Grey died before reaching her eighteenth birthday.

and avoided communications with men under suspicion. The English succession was vital to the Courts of Europe. The French ambassador, Noailles, began to be active and Elizabeth was suspected of turning for advice to the Frenchman. It was suggested that she might marry Courtenay and in the west he precipitated a rising. Sir Thomas Wyatt raised his standard in Kent and marched slowly towards London, gathering men as he came. The capital was in alarm. The citizens went in fear of the sack of their houses. But Mary, bitter and disappointed with her people, and knowing she had failed to win their hearts, showed she was not afraid. In a stirring speech at Guildhall she summoned the Londoners to her defence. Straggled fighting took place in the streets, and the Queen's men cut up the intruders. Wyatt was executed. Courtenay's rising was a pitiable failure. This sealed the fate of Lady Jane Grey and her husband. In February 1554 the two walked calmly to their death on Tower Green.

Elizabeth's life was now in great danger. Though Wyatt had exonerated her she was the only rival claimant to the throne, and the Spaniards demanded her execution before their prince was committed to marrying the Queen. But Mary had shed blood enough and Renard, the Imperial ambassador, could not persuade her to sign away the life of her half-sister, now in the Tower, fearlessly and passionately denying all disloyal dealings with Courtenay or Wyatt. Perhaps Mary believed her. At any rate, after some months she was released and sent to Woodstock, where, in quiet and pious seclusion, she awaited the turn of fortune.

As summer came Philip sailed northward across the seas. With all the pomp of sixteenth-century royalty the marriage was solemnised in July 1554 according to the rites of the Catholic Church. Gardiner was now dead; but a successor was found in the English cardinal Reginald Pole. Pole had been in exile throughout the reign of Henry VIII, his family having been lopped and shorn in Henry's judicial murders. This grandson of "false, fleeting, perjured Clarence" was a jealous and austere Catholic, and now came as Legate to enforce the conversion of the whole land.

Mary has been forever odious in the minds of a Protestant nation as the Bloody Queen who martyred her noblest subjects. Their stories have become part of the common memory of the people—the pitiful recantation and final heroic end in March 1556 of the frail, aged Archbishop, Cranmer; Bishop Latimer's immortal words. "Be of good comfort, Master Ridley. Play the man. We shall this day light such a candle, by God's grace, in England as I trust shall never be put out." These martyrs saw in vision that their deaths were not in vain.

The Queen strove to join English interests to those of the Spanish State. She had married to make England safe for Catholicism, but hope of a child to secure the Catholic succession was unfulfilled. As the wife of the King of Spain, against the interests of her kingdom, and against the advice of prudent counsellors, she allowed herself to be dragged into war with France, and Calais, the last possession of the English upon the Continent, fell without resistance. This national disgrace, this loss of the symbol of the power and glory of medieval England, bit deep into the hearts of the people and into the conscience of the Queen.

Philip retired to the Netherlands and then to Spain, aloof and disappointed at the barrenness of the whole political scheme. Surrounded by disloyalty and discontent, Mary's health gave way. In November 1558 she died, and a few hours later, in Lambeth Palace, her coadjutor, Cardinal Pole, followed her. The tragic interlude of her reign was over. It had sealed the conversion of the English people to the Reformed Faith.

In its beginning the Protestant Reformation in Europe had been a revolt against the abuses of an organisation. But this motive was removed when the Catholic Church set its house in order. Now the entire apparatus of the Roman Church seemed to conflict with the forward movement of the human mind. Until the reign of Henry VIII there lay beneath the quarrels of the nobility, the conflicts between King and Church, between the ruling classes and the people, a certain broad unity of acceptance. The evils and sorrows of the medieval ages had lasted so long that they seemed to be the inseparable conditions of existence in a world of woe. No one had novel remedies or even consolations to propose. But, with the Reformation there came a new influence cutting to the very roots of English life, stirring the souls of all classes to action or resistance, and raising standards for which great and small alike were prepared to suffer or inflict the worst extremities. The old framework, which, in spite of its many jars, had held together for centuries, was now torn by a division in which all other antagonisms of class and interest were henceforward to be ranged and ruled.

Hitherto, amid their quarrels and tribulations, there had been one people and one system. Henceforward, for many generations to come, not only England but all the countries of Europe were to range themselves for or against the Protestant Reformation.

The violence of this convulsion can hardly be measured by us today, and it followed in England a less destructive course than in Germany or France. This was because the issue came to a head at a comparatively early stage, and under the strong government of the Tudors. Nevertheless the doctrinal revolution enforced by Cranmer under Edward VI, and the Counter-Revolution of Gardiner and Pole under Mary, exposed our agitated islanders

PUNISHMENTS TO FIT THE CRIME

William Harrison, writing his Description of England *(1587), gives some harsh details of contemporary justice.*

In cases of felony, manslaughter, robbery, murder, rape, piracy, and such capital crimes as are not reputed for treason or hurt of the estate, our sentence pronounced upon the offender is, to hang till he be dead. . . .

The greatest and most grievous punishment used in England for such as offend against the State is drawing from the prison to the place of execution upon a hurdle or sled, where they are hanged till they be half dead and then taken down and quartered alive. . . . And whensoever any of the nobility are convicted of high treason by their peers, that is to say, equals, this manner of their death is converted into the loss of their heads only, notwithstanding that their sentence do run after the former order. . . .

If a woman poison her husband, she is burned alive; if a servant kill his master, he is to be executed for petty treason; he that poisoneth a man is to be boiled to death in water or lead. . . . Perjury is punished by the pillory, burning in the forehead with the letter P. . . . Rogues are burned through the ears: carriers of sheep out of the land by the loss of their hands. . . .

Witches are hanged or sometimes burned; but thieves are hanged. . . . generally on the gibbet or gallows, saving in Halifax, where they are beheaded in a strange manner.

Rogues and vagabonds are often stocked and whipped; scolds are ducked upon ducking-stools in the water. . . .

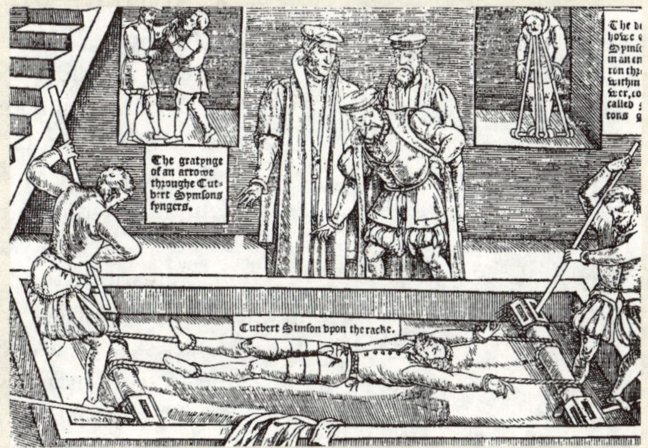

The rack was a particularly painful form of torture used against Protestants during the reign of Queen Mary, and against Roman Catholics during the reign of Queen Elizabeth.

Calais, retaken by France in 1558, was the last of England's possessions on the continent of Europe. Mary is said to have remarked that when she died the word Calais would be found engraved on her heart.

in one single decade to a frightful oscillation. Here were the citizens, the peasants, the whole mass of living beings who composed the nation, ordered in the name of King Edward VI to march along one path to salvation, and under Queen Mary to march back again in the opposite direction; and all who would not move on the first order or turn about on the second must prove their convictions, if necessary, at the gibbet or the stake. Thus was New England imposed on Old England; thus did Old England in terrible counterstroke resume a fleeting sway; and from all this agony there was to emerge under Queen Elizabeth a compromise between Old and New which, though it did not abate their warfare, so far confined its fury that it could not prove mortal to the unity and continuity of national society.

CHAPTER 37

GOOD QUEEN BESS

ELIZABETH WAS TWENTY-FIVE YEARS OLD when, untried in the affairs of State, she succeeded her half-sister on November 17, 1558. It was England's good fortune that the new Queen was endowed by inheritance and upbringing with a combination of very remarkable qualities. There could be no doubt who her father was. A commanding carriage, auburn hair, eloquence of speech and natural dignity proclaimed her King Henry's daughter. Other similarities were soon observed: high courage in moments of crisis, a fiery and imperious resolution when defied, and an almost inexhaustible fund of physical energy. She enjoyed many of the same pastimes and accomplishments as the King had done—a passion for the chase, skill in archery and hawking, and in dancing and music. She could speak six languages, and was well-read in Latin and Greek. As with her father, a restless vitality led her from mansion to mansion.

A difficult childhood and a perilous adolescence had been Elizabeth's portion. At one stage in her father's lifetime she had been declared illegitimate and banished from Court. During Mary's reign, when her life might have been forfeited by a false step, she had proved the value of caution and dissemblance. When to keep silence, how to bide her time and husband her resources, were the lessons she learnt from her youth. Many historians have accused her of vacillation and parsimony. Certainly these elements in her character were justly the despair of her advisers. The royal treasury however was never rich enough to finance all the adventurous projects urged upon her. Nor was it always unwise amid the turbulent currents of the age to put off making irrevocable decisions. The times demanded a politic, calculating, devious spirit at the head of the State, and this Elizabeth possessed. She had, too, a high gift for picking able men to do the country's work. It came naturally to her to take the credit for their successes, while blaming them for all that went wrong.

Portrait of Queen Elizabeth, aged thirteen. She was clearly very attractive when young, and stylishly elegant in old age. Her use of wigs and cosmetics disguised the scars left on her skin by an attack of smallpox.

In quickness of mind the Queen was surpassed by few of her contemporaries, and many envoys to her Court had good reason to acknowledge her liveliness of repartee. In temperament she was subject to fits of melancholy, which alternated with flamboyant merriment and convulsive rage. Always subtle of intellect, she was often brazen and even coarse in manners and expression. When angered she could box her Treasurer's ears and throw her slipper in her Secretary's face. Nevertheless she had a capacity for inspiring devotion that is perhaps unparalleled among British sovereigns. She gave to her country the love that she never entirely reposed in any one man, and her people responded with a loyalty that almost amounted to worship. It is not for nothing that she has come down to history as Good Queen Bess.

Few sovereigns ever succeeded to a more hazardous inheritance than she. Even before the death of Henry VIII England's finances had been growing desperate. The coinage, which had been debased yet further under Edward VI, was now chaotic. The old military danger, a Franco-Scottish alliance, again threatened. In the eyes of Catholic Europe, Mary, Queen of the Scots, and wife of the Dauphin of France, who became King Francis II in 1559, had a better claim to the English throne than Elizabeth, and with the power of France behind her she stood a good chance of gaining it. England's only official ally, Spain, suspected the new regime for religious reasons.

Elizabeth had been brought up a Protestant. Around her now gathered some of the ablest Protestant minds: Matthew Parker, who was to be her Archbishop of Canterbury; Nicholas Bacon, whom she appointed Lord Keeper of the Great Seal; Roger Ascham, the foremost scholar of the day; and, most important of all, William Cecil, the adaptable civil servant who had already held office as Secretary under Somerset and Northumberland. Of sixteenth-century English statesmen Cecil was undoubtedly the greatest. He possessed immense industry in the business of office and cautious good judgment marked all his actions. Elizabeth, with sure instinct, summoned him to her service. "This judgment I have of you," she charged him, "that you will not be corrupted by any manner of gifts, that you will be faithful to the State, and that, without respect to any private will, you will give me that counsel that you think best." It was a tremendous burden which the young Queen imposed upon her First Minister, then aged thirty-eight. Their close and daily collaboration was to last, in spite of shocks and jars, until Cecil's death, forty years later.

William Cecil, Lord Burghley, was Elizabeth's invaluable First Minister until his death in 1598. The Cecil family has a long tradition of service to the Crown: they have held office intermittently for nearly four centuries.

Religious peace at home and safety from Scotland were the foremost needs of the realm. England became Protestant by law, Queen Mary's

The Puritans were a sober and austere sect of Protestants who were disliked for their protests against drink and dancing. Shakespeare lampooned Puritans with his creation, in Twelfth Night, *of the censorious character, Malvolio.*

Catholic legislation was repealed, and the sovereign was declared supreme governor of the English Church. But this was not the end of Elizabeth's difficulties. New ideas were in debate, not only on religious doctrine and Church government, but on the very nature and foundations of political power. Ever since the days of Wyclif in the 1380s there had been, running in secret veins under the surface of society in England, a movement of resistance to the Church order. With the Reformation the notion that it might be a duty to disobey the established order on the grounds of private conviction became for the first time since the conversion to Christianity of the Roman Empire the belief of great numbers. But so closely were Church and State involved that disobedience to the one was a challenge to the other. The idea that a man should pick and choose for himself what doctrines he should adhere to was almost as alien to the mind of the age as the idea that he should select what laws he should obey. The most that could be allowed was that he should outwardly conform and think what he liked in silence. But in the great turmoil of Europe silence was impossible. Men talked: secretly to one another, openly in their writings, which were now printed in a thousand copies, kindling excitement and curiosity wherever they were carried.

It is at this point that the party known as the Puritans, who were to play so great a role in the next hundred years, first enter English history. Democratic in theory and organisation, intolerant in practice of all who differed from their views, the Puritans challenged the Queen's authority in Church and State, and although she sought for freedom of conscience and could maintain with sincerity that she "made no windows into men's souls", she dared not let them organise cells in the body religious or the body politic. She realised that unless the Government controlled the Church it would be too weak to survive the Counter-Reformation now gathering head in Catholic Europe. So Elizabeth had soon to confront not only the Catholic danger from abroad, but Puritan attack at home, led by fanatical exiles of Mary's reign who now streamed back from Geneva and from the Rhineland towns.

Nevertheless the Reformation in Europe took on a new aspect when it came to England. All the novel questions agitating the world—the relation of the national Church to Rome on one side and to the national sovereign on the other; its future organisation; its articles of religion; the disposal of its property, and the property of its monasteries—could only be determined in Parliament, where the Puritans soon formed a growing and outspoken Opposition. Parliament fell into two great divisions, those who thought things had gone far enough, and those who wanted to go a step farther. It was the future distinction of Cavalier and Puritan, Churchman and Dissenter, Tory and Whig. But for a long time it was subdued by common horror of a disputed succession and a civil war, and by the rule that only the Crown could initiate policy and public legislation.

The immediate threat lay north of the Border. French troops supported the French queen mother in Scotland. A powerful Puritan party among the Scottish nobility, abetted by the persecuted preachers, were in arms against them, while John Knox poured forth his denunciations of "the monstrous regiment of women". He meant of course that rule by women seemed to him unnatural. Elizabeth watched these doings with interest and anxiety. If the French party got control of Scotland their next move would be against her throne. Want of money forbade a major military effort, but the fleet was sent to blockade the Scottish ports and prevent reinforcements arriving from France. Arms and supplies were smuggled across the border to the Protestant party. At this moment Mary of Guise died. Elizabeth's efforts had been modest, but they prevailed. By the Treaty of Leith in 1560 the Protestant cause in Scotland was assured forever. Now Elizabeth could look squarely to the future.

The Edinburgh house of John Knox, leader of the Scottish Reformation. During Mary's reign, Knox fled to Geneva where he was influenced by Calvin. In 1599, he returned to Scotland but Queen Elizabeth, incensed by his book entitled The First Blast of the Trumpet Against the Monstrous Regiment of Women, *would have nothing to do with him.*

One thing seemed certain to all contemporaries. The security of the English State depended in the last resort on an assured succession. The delicate question of the Queen's marriage began to throw its shadow across the political scene, and it is in her attitude to this challenge that the strength and subtleties of Elizabeth's character are revealed. If she married an Englishman her authority might be weakened. The perils of such a course were borne in on her as she watched the reactions of her Court to her long and deep affection for the handsome, ambitious Robert Dudley, a younger son of Northumberland, whom she made Earl of Leicester. This was no way out. Marriage into one of the reigning houses of Europe (during the first months of her reign she had seriously to consider the claims of her brother-in-law, Philip II of Spain) would mean entangling herself in its European policy and facing the hostility of her husband's rivals. In vain the Houses of Parliament begged their Virgin Queen to marry and produce an heir. Elizabeth was angry. She would admit no discussion. Her policy was to use her potential value as a match to divide a European combination against her.

Meanwhile there was Mary Stuart, Queen of Scots. Her young husband, King Francis II, had died shortly after his succession. In December 1560 she returned to her own kingdom, and her mother-in-law, Catherine de Médicis, became Regent for the young King Charles IX. Thus in the last half of the sixteenth century women for a time controlled three countries—France, England and Scotland. But of the three only the grip of Elizabeth held firm.

Mary Stuart was a very different personality from Elizabeth, though in some ways her position was similar. She was a descendant of Henry VII; she held a throne; she lived in an age when it was a novelty for a woman to be the head of a State; and she was now unmarried. Her presence in Scotland disturbed the delicate balance which Elizabeth had achieved by the Treaty of Leith. The Catholic English nobility, particularly in the north, were not indifferent to Mary's claims. Some of them dreamt of winning her hand. But Elizabeth knew that Mary was incapable of separating her emotions from her politics. She had only been a few years in Scotland when she married her cousin, Henry Stuart, Lord Darnley, a weak, conceited youth. The result was disaster. Mary's power melted slowly and steadily away. Favourites brought from the cultured French Court to cheer her in this grim land were unpopular, and one of them, David Riccio, was seized in her chamber and stabbed to death. Her husband became a tool of her opponents. In desperation she connived at his murder, and in 1567 married his murderer, a warlike Border lord, James Hepburn, Earl of Bothwell, whose unruly sword might yet save her throne and her happiness. But defeat and imprisonment followed, and in 1568 she escaped into England and threw herself upon the mercy of the waiting Elizabeth.

Robert Dudley, Earl of Leicester, was the same age as Elizabeth and her favourite. He suffered from a scandal arising out of the death of his wife, Amy Robsart, who fell downstairs and broke her neck in 1560.

Mary in England proved even more dangerous than Mary in Scotland. She became the focus of conspiracies against Elizabeth's life. Secret emissaries of

PLAYS AND PLAYERS

LONDON WAS A CITY OF many shows and spectacles in later Tudor times. There were splendid weddings and funerals, and dramatic executions. At the Tower of London there was a menagerie containing lions (one was called Edward VI, after the King), a tiger, a wolf, an eagle and a porcupine. And, above all, there was the theatre, then at the height of its popularity. This was the London not only of Elizabeth I but of William Shakespeare.

Shakespeare came from the heart of England, Stratford-upon-Avon in Warwickshire. The theatre was as popular in the country as it was in London, and it was from the countryside that Shakespeare took many of his images and some of his plots. Indeed, in some of them he set the country against the city and against the Court.

Shakespeare's were not the only plays to be performed during Queen Elizabeth's reign. Before him had come Christopher Marlowe; after him came Ben Jonson. There was no author's copyright and plays were performed in several versions. The players were professionals. It was laid down by Acts of Parliament in 1532 and 1572 that outside the cities players had to have a licence, granted by a lord: for this reason players worked in companies under a lord's patronage. In London, and other cities, where plays and especially travelling players were often viewed with suspicion, they were regulated by irksome and restrictive rules. In 1581, however, London appointed a Master of Revels responsible for censorship, and players could now receive a government licence.

Shakespeare's Globe Theatre was situated in an ideally accessible position on the River Thames near London Bridge, which a French visitor described as "one of the most beautiful bridges in the world." The audience, which came from all levels of society, arrived by road or river.

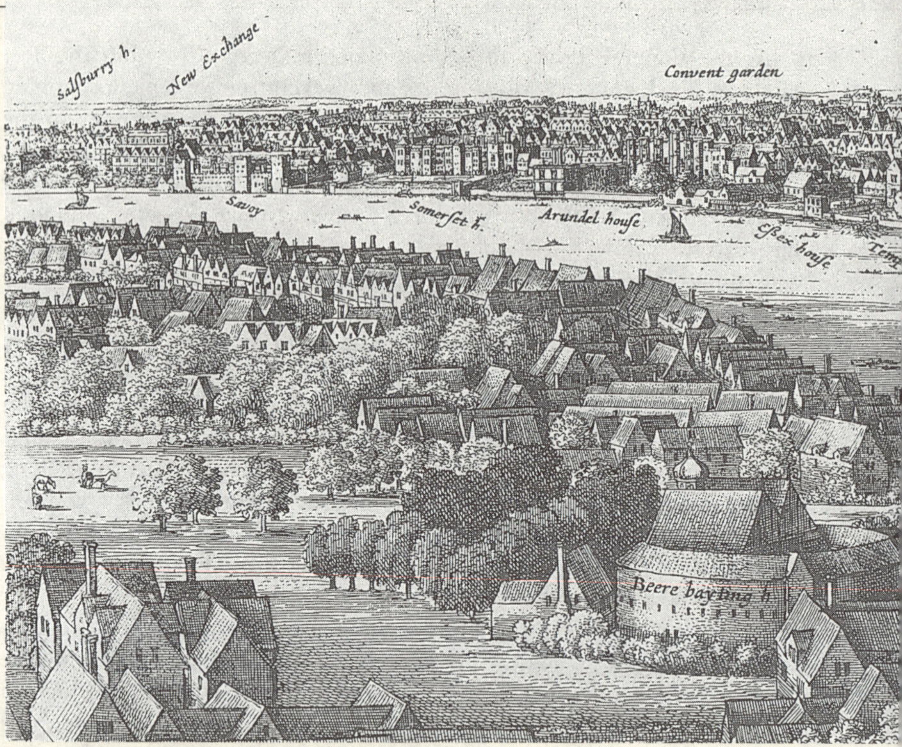

PLAYACTING AND BEAR-BAITING *were the most popular entertainments of the sixteenth century, and this panoramic view of London, looking across the Thames from the south, includes a bear garden and a theatre. The Globe Theatre is the circular building on the right of the picture near the river. It was erected in 1599 by the actor, Richard Burbage, who played leading roles in Shakespeare's tragedies. Originally, plays were acted in the market place or the yard of an inn, but in the second half of the sixteenth century rich men began to form their own companies of players and build theatres. There were no curtains in Elizabethan theatres and the wealthy often sat on the stage itself, which projected into the audience so that the "groundlings" who had standing room in the body of the theatre, milled around it. Audiences were not silent unless their attention was captured by events on the stage. There was a high incidence of fighting, intrigue and murder in the plays.*

A MEDIEVAL PERFORMING BEAR *(above) walks on its forepaws, urged on by a trainer with a big stick. Later, mastiffs were used to bait bears and bulls, and huge crowds gathered to watch both this and cockfighting. These events were so rowdy and disorderly that the term "bear garden" has come down to us to describe any riotous gathering.*

JESTERS *(above) were musicians and buffoons employed as far back as Saxon times to amuse the rich. They are shown here in the two-pronged caps which represented asses' ears. Originally they were tellers of traditional romances (gestes) but later they became clowns.*

MASTER DRAMATIST WILLIAM SHAKESPEARE *(above) wrote at least twenty-nine plays which form the backbone of the English theatre. Surprisingly little is known of his life except that he was the son of a glover in Stratford-upon-Avon. Born on St George's Day, 1564, he died on the same day in 1616. He was probably a schoolmaster before moving to London in 1594 to join The Lord Chamberlain's Men as occasional actor and assistant stage manager. He wrote a wide range of plays, including histories, comedies and tragedies.* Macbeth, King Lear, Othello *and* Hamlet, *his four great tragedies, all revolve round an important or royal figure who faces a crisis. His plays were "pirated" by copyists attending repeated performances.*

HENRY VIII'S JESTER, WILL SOMERS *(below) served him for twenty years. A witty fool could hold a privileged place in his master's affections and tell him the unpalatable truths that other servants shrank from divulging. Somers alerted Henry to the dishonesty of the auditors, surveyors and receivers of the exchequer by dubbing them "frauditors, conveyers and deceivers".*

The Tragicall Hiſtory of the Life and Death of Doctor FAVSTVS.

Written by *Ch. Mar.*

Printed at London for *Iohn Wright*, and are to be ſold at his ſhop without Newgate

MAGIC AND NECROMANCY *were subjects guaranteed to grip the audience and Christopher Marlowe's tragedy,* Dr Faustus, *was a box office triumph. The title page (above) shows Faustus bargaining with the Devil's agent, Mephistopheles, who appears in the form of a beast. Faustus sold his soul to the Devil in return for long life and the granting of all his wishes, which included a meeting with Helen of Troy.*

SHAKESPEARE'S RENOWNED CONTEMPORARIES *included Edward Alleyn, (above) who built the Fortune Theatre in Cripplegate with his partner, Philip Henslowe, in 1599. He played leading roles in Marlowe's plays, among them* Dr Faustus *and* Tamburlaine *and became wealthy enough to buy the manor of Dulwich where he founded Dulwich College. However, Marlowe himself died in a brawl before he reached the age of thirty.*

Holyrood Palace in Edinburgh was the home of Mary, Queen of Scots, from 1560 to 1568, when she abdicated the throne and fled to England. It was at Holyrood that her husband, Darnley, stabbed her Italian favourite to death before her eyes in a fit of jealousy.

Spain crept into the country to nourish rebellion and the whole force of the Counter-Reformation was unloosed against the one united Protestant country in Europe. If England were destroyed it seemed that Protestantism could be stamped out in every other land. But Elizabeth was well served. Francis Walsingham, Cecil's assistant and later his rival in the Government, tracked down Spanish agents and English traitors. This subtle intellectual and ardent Protestant, who had remained abroad throughout the reign of Mary Tudor, and whose knowledge of European politics surpassed that of anyone in Elizabeth's counsel, created the best secret service of any government of the time. But there was always a chance that someone would slip through; there was always a danger so long as Mary lived that public discontent or private ambition would use her and her claims to destroy Elizabeth. In 1569 the threat became a reality.

In the north of England society was much more primitive than in the fertile south. Proud, independent, semi-feudal nobles now felt themselves threatened not only by Elizabeth's authority but by a host of new gentry like the Cecils and the Bacons. Moreover the north remained dominantly Catholic. In the bleak, barren dales the monasteries had been the centre of communal life and charity. Their destruction had provoked the Pilgrimage of Grace and still incited a stubborn and passive resistance to the religious changes of Elizabeth. The idea was now advanced that Mary should marry the Duke of Norfolk, son of the executed Earl of Surrey, and his somewhat feeble head was turned at the prospect of gambling for a throne. He repented in time. But in 1569 the Earls of Northumberland and Westmorland led a rising in the north. Mary was confined at Tutbury in the care of Lord Hunsdon, Elizabeth's soldier cousin on the Boleyn side, a trustworthy servant throughout her reign, and one of her few relations. Before the rebels could seize Mary she was conveyed hurriedly southward. The rebels planned to hold the north of England and wait to be attacked. In the south the Catholic lords made no move. There seems to have been no common plan of action, and the rebel force scattered into small parties in the northern hills and across the Border to safety. The first act of the widespread Catholic conspiracy against Elizabeth was over. After twelve years of very patient rule she was unchallenged Queen of all England.

Rome was prompt to retaliate. In February 1570 Pope Pius V, a former Inquisitor-General, issued a Bull of excommunication against Elizabeth. From this moment Spain, as head of Catholic Europe, was supplied with a spiritual weapon should the need for attack arise. Elizabeth's position was weakened. Parliament became increasingly agitated at the spinsterhood of their Queen, and their constant petitioning irritated her into action. She entered into negotiations with Catherine de Médicis, and a political alliance was concluded at Blois in April 1572. Both women distrusted the Spanish power. For a short time events ran with Elizabeth. Spain's weakness centred in the Netherlands, where a robust population had long fretted under Philip's rule. The whole territory was on the edge of rebellion, and the treaty was hardly signed when the famous Dutch resisters of tyranny, who were known as the "Sea Beggars", seized the town of Brill, and the Low Countries blazed into revolt. Elizabeth now had a potential new ally on the Continent. She even thought of marrying one of Queen Catherine's younger sons, on condition that France did not take advantage of the turmoil to expand into the Netherlands. But a terrible event in Paris dashed such prospects. By a sudden massacre of the Huguenots on the eve of the feast of St Bartholomew, August 23, 1572, the Guises, pro-Spanish and ultra-Catholic, recaptured the political power they had lost ten years earlier. Feeling ran high in London. When the French ambassador came to explain away the event Elizabeth and her Court, clothed all in black, received him in silence.

Elizabeth was now driven to giving secret subsidies and support to the French Huguenots and the Dutch. Success depended on the most accurate timing, as her funds were very limited and she could seldom afford to help except when the rebels were on the edge of disaster. Walsingham, now Secretary of State, and second only to Cecil in the Queen's Council, was far from content. Exile in Mary's reign and service as ambassador in Paris had convinced him that Protestantism would only survive in Europe if England gave it unlimited encouragement and aid. Sooner or later war would come, and he urged that everything should be done to preserve and secure potential allies before the final clash.

Opposed to all this was Cecil, now Lord Burghley. Queen Mary's marriage with Philip had been widely unpopular in England; but in Burghley's view this was no time to go to the opposite extreme and intervene in the Netherlands on the side of Philip's rebels. When Burghley became Lord Treasurer in 1572 his attitude hardened. Aware of the slender resources of the State, deeply concerned for the loss of trade with Spain and the Netherlands, he maintained that Walsingham's policy would founder in bankruptcy and disaster.

Elizabeth was inclined to agree. She did not much like assisting other people's rebels—"you and your brethren in Christ", she once said mockingly to Walsingham. But Walsingham's case had been violently strengthened by the Massacre of St Bartholomew, and the Queen was compelled to move into a cold war in the Netherlands, and an undeclared war at sea, until she was confronted with the massive onslaught of an Armada.

These happenings had their effect on politics in England. Most of the

The signature of Elizabeth is probably the most famous example of the italic script in England. This portrait painted by an unknown artist shows Elizabeth I in her middle years and can be seen in the National Portrait Gallery.

Puritans had at first been willing to conform to Elizabeth's Church Settlement, which required church attendance but no statement of belief, in the hope of transforming it from within, but they now strove to drive the Government into an aggressive Protestant foreign policy, and at the same time secure their own freedom of religious organisation. Their position in the country was strong. They had allies like Walsingham at Court and Council, with whom the Queen's favourite, Leicester, was now closely associated. In the towns and counties of southeastern England they were vociferous. In defiance of the Church Settlement they began to form their own religious communities, with their own ministers and forms of worship. Their aim and object was nothing less than the establishment of a theocratic despotism. Like the Catholics they held that Church and State were separate and independent. Unlike them, they believed the seat of Church authority lay in the council of elders, the Presbytery, freely chosen by the flock, but, once chosen, ruling with unlimited scope and supplanting the secular power over a large area of human life.

To such men the Elizabethan Settlement, the Anglican Church, with its historic liturgy and ceremonial, its comprehensive articles and its episcopal government, were abhorrent because unscriptural, as Calvin interpreted Scripture. It had indeed some of the weaknesses of a compromise. Moreover, outside London, the universities, and a few great towns, the average parson in the early years of Elizabeth's reign was not an impressive figure. Sometimes he had kept his benefice by conforming under Edward VI, changing his creed under Mary, and finally accepting what a rural bench once described as "the religion set forth by Her Majesty" as the only way of earning a living. With barely enough Latin to read the old service books, and scarcely literate enough to deliver a decent sermon, he was no match for the disputants charged with enthusiasm and new ideas, who were stealing his flock from him, and implanting in them novel and alarming notions about the rights of congregations to worship in their own way, and to settle their own Church order. And why not, someday, their own political order? A crack was opening in the surface of English society, a crack which would widen into a gulf. The Lutheran Church fitted well enough with monarchy, but Calvinism, as it spread out over Europe, was a dissolving agency, and a violent interruption of historic continuity. Elizabeth knew that the Puritans were perhaps her most loyal subjects, but she feared that their violent impulse might not only provoke the European conflict she dreaded, but imperil the very unity of the realm. Neither she nor her Government dared yield a fraction of their authority.

Elizabeth's Council therefore struck back. The censorship of the press was entrusted to a body of ecclesiastical commissioners, known as the Court of High Commission, which had been constituted in 1559 to deal with offences against the Church Settlement. This combining of the functions of bishop and censor infuriated the Puritan party. They set up a secret, itinerant press which poured forth over the years a stream of virulent and anonymous pamphlets, culminating in 1588 with those issued under the name of "Martin Marprelate". Their invective shows a robust consciousness of the possibilities of English prose. The pamphlets are loaded with coarse, effective adjectives, though the sentences lumber along like the hay-cart in which the press itself was at one time concealed for months. In the end an accident precipitated the press out of the hay-cart in a village street and led to the arrest of the printers. The authors, however, were never traced.

The Catholic onslaught also gathered force. Throughout the 1570s numbers of Catholic priests were arriving in England from the English seminaries at Douai and St Omer, charged with the task of nourishing Catholic sentiment and maintaining connection between Rome and the English Catholics. Their presence at first aroused little apprehension in Government circles. Elizabeth was slow to believe that any of her Catholic subjects were traitors, and the failure of the 1569 rising had strengthened her confidence in their loyalty. But about the year 1579 missionaries of a new and formidable type began to slip into the country. These were the Jesuits, the heralds and missionaries of the Counter-Reformation. Their lives were dedicated to re-establishing the Catholic faith throughout Christendom. They were fanatics, indifferent to personal danger, and carefully chosen for their work. Foremost among them were Edmund Campion and Robert Parsons. A number of plots against Elizabeth's life were uncovered. The Government was forced to take more drastic measures. Queen Mary had burnt some three hundred Protestant martyrs in the last three years of her reign. In the last thirty years of Elizabeth's reign about the same number of Catholics were executed for treason.

ENGLISH INNS

In his Description of England (1587), *William Harrison applauds the standard of service to be found in English inns.*

Each comer is sure to lie in clean sheets, wherein no man hath been lodged since they came from the laundress or out of the water wherein they were last washed. If the traveller have an horse, his bed doth cost him nothing, but if he go on foot he is sure to pay a penny for the same: but whether he be horseman or footman if his chamber be once appointed he may carry the key with him, as of his own house, so long as he lodgeth there. If he lose ought whilst he abideth in the inn, the host is bound by a general custom to restore the damage, so that there is no greater security anywhere for travellers than in the greatest inns of England.

Their horses in like sort are walked, dressed and looked unto by certain hostlers or hired servants, appointed at the charges of the goodman of the house, who in hope of extraordinary reward will deal very diligently, after outward appearance, in this their function and calling.

In all our inns we have plenty of ale, beer and sundry kinds of wine, and such is the capacity of some of them that they are able to lodge two hundred or three hundred persons and their horses at ease, and thereto with a very short warning make such provision for their diet, as to him that is unacquainted withal may seem to be incredible. Howbeit of all in England there are no worse inns than in London, and yet many are there far better than the best that I have heard of in any foreign country, if all the circumstances be duly considered. . . . And it is a world to see how each owner of them contendeth with others for goodness of entertainment of their guests, as about fineness and change of linen, furniture of bedding, beauty of rooms, service at table, costliness of plate, strength of drink, variety of wines, or well using of horses. Finally there is not so much omitted among them as the gorgeousness of their very signs at their doors, wherein some do consume thirty or forty pounds, a mere vanity in mine opinion; but so vain will they needs be, and that not only to give some outward token of innkeeper's wealth, but also to procure good guests to the frequenting of their houses in hope there to be well used.

Many fine old Tudor inns, like this one at Ledbury, survive from the days when poor transport made innkeeping big business. Travellers rarely managed more than fifteen miles a day.

The conspiracies naturally focused upon the person of Mary Queen of Scots, long captive. She was the heir to the English throne in the event of Elizabeth's removal from the world. Elizabeth herself was reluctant to recognise the danger to her life, yet the plots sharpened the question of who should succeed to the English throne. The death of Mary would make her son James the heir to the Crown of England, and James was in safe Calvinist hands in Scotland. To avoid having another Catholic Queen it was only necessary to dispose of Mary before the Catholics, or their allies, disposed of Elizabeth. Walsingham and his party in the Council now concentrated their efforts on persuading the Queen that Mary must die. Plying her with evidence of Mary's complicity in the numerous conspiracies, they pressed hard on Elizabeth's conscience; but she shrank from the calculated shedding of royal blood.

Elizabeth would wait upon events. They were soon decisive. In the midsummer of 1584 William the Silent, leader of the Dutch Protestant revolt against Spain, was fatally wounded by a Spanish agent. English opinion reacted vehemently. At the same time Spanish feeling against England, already embittered by the raids, conducted with Elizabeth's connivance, of the English privateers, blazed into startling hostility. The Netherlands, once Spanish order had been restored, were to be a base for a final attack upon the island, and Elizabeth was compelled to send Leicester with an English army to Holland to prevent the complete destruction of the Dutch.

In 1586 evidence of a conspiracy by one Anthony Babington, an English Catholic, was laid before the Council by Walsingham. One of his agents had mingled with the conspirators for over a year. Mary's connivance was undeniable. Elizabeth was at last persuaded that her death was a political necessity. After a formal trial Mary was pronounced guilty of treason. Parliament petitioned for her execution, and Elizabeth at last signed the death warrant. Within twenty-four hours she regretted it and tried, too late, to stop the execution. Although she knew it was essential for the safety of her country, she had a horror of being responsible for the judicial murder of a fellow sovereign.

The scene of Mary's death has caught the imagination of history. In the early morning of February 8, 1587, she was summoned to the great hall of Fotheringay Castle. Accompanied by six of her attendants, Mary appeared soberly clad in black satin. In the quietness of the hall she walked with stately movements to the cloth-covered scaffold erected by the fireplace. The solemn formalities were smoothly completed. But the zealous Dean of Peterborough attempted to force upon the Queen a last-minute conversion. With splendid dignity she brushed aside his loud exhortations. "Mr Dean," she said, "I am a Catholic, and must die a Catholic. It is useless to attempt to move me, and your prayers will avail me but little."

Mary had arrayed herself superbly for the final scene. As she disrobed for the headsman's act, her garments of black satin, removed by the weeping handmaids, revealed a bodice and petticoat of crimson velvet. One of her ladies handed her a pair of crimson sleeves, which she put on. Thus the unhappy Queen halted, for one last moment, standing blood-red from head to foot against the black background of the scaffold. There was a deathly hush throughout the hall. She knelt, and at the second stroke the fatal blow was delivered. In death the majestic illusion was shattered. The head of an ageing woman with false hair was held aloft by the executioner. A dog crept from beneath the clothes of the bleeding trunk.

As the news reached London bonfires were lit in the streets. Elizabeth sat alone in her room, weeping more for the fate of a queen than a woman. The responsibility for this deed she shifted with an effort onto the shoulders of her masculine advisers.

CHAPTER 38

THE SPANISH ARMADA

War was now certain. The chances were heavily weighted in favour of Spain. From the mines of Mexico and Peru there came a stream of silver and gold which so fortified the material power of the Spanish Empire that King Philip could equip his forces beyond all known scales.

So long as Spain controlled the wealth of the New World she could launch and equip a multitude of Armadas; the treasure must therefore be arrested at its source or captured from the ships which conveyed it across the oceans. In the hope of strengthening her own finances and harassing the enemy's preparations against the Netherlands and ultimately against herself, Elizabeth had accordingly sanctioned a number of unofficial expeditions against the Spanish coasts and colonies in South America, where Spain was deliberately blocking the commercial enterprise of other nations. Gradually these expeditions had assumed an official character, and the Royal Navy was rebuilt and reorganised by John Hawkins, son of a Plymouth merchant. Hawkins had learnt his seamanship in slave-running on the West African coast. He had moreover educated an apt pupil, a young adventurer from Devon, Francis Drake.

This "Master Thief of the unknown world", as his Spanish contemporaries called Drake, became the terror of their ports and crews. His avowed object was to force England into open conflict with Spain, and his attacks

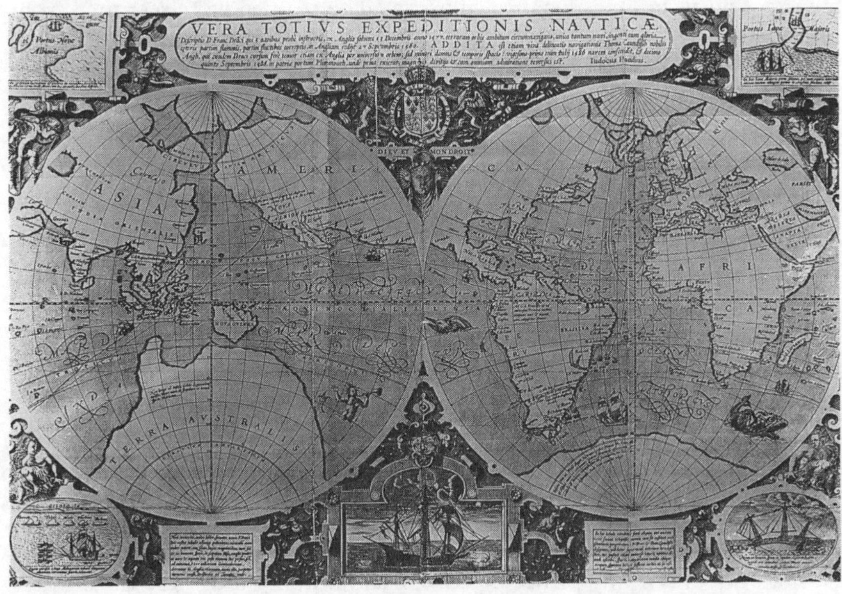

From 1577 to 1580 Drake sailed round the world, arriving home at Plymouth on September 26, 1580 with fifty-nine of his original crew of eighty in the Golden Hind. *This map was made in 1589 by a Flemish cartographer and traces his journey westward across the Atlantic, through the Magellan Straits and up the western seaboard of America. From there Drake sailed across the Pacific, through the East Indies and the Indian Ocean to the Cape of Good Hope and from thence, northward to Britain.*

For the Elizabethan gallant, fashion was important at all times, even on the battlefield. This design comes from an armourer's album in the Victoria and Albert Museum.

on the Spanish treasure ships, his plundering of Spanish possessions on the western coast of the South American continent on his voyage round the world in 1577, and raids on Spanish harbours in Europe, all played their part in driving Spain to war. From their experiences on the Spanish Main the English seamen knew that so long as reasonable equality was maintained they could fight and sink anything the Spaniards might send against them.

The Spaniards had long contemplated an enterprise against England. They realised that English intervention threatened their attempts to reconquer the Netherlands and that unless England was overwhelmed the turmoil might continue indefinitely. Troops were not the difficulty, but the building and assembly of a fleet was a more formidable undertaking. Most of the King of Spain's ships were built for use in the Mediterranean. They were unsuited to a voyage round the western coasts of Europe and up the Channel, while the galleons constructed for the trade routes to the Spanish colonies in South America were too unwieldy. But in the year 1580 Philip II had annexed Portugal, and the Portuguese naval constructors had experimented with classes of ships for action in the South Atlantic. Portuguese galleons therefore formed the basis of the fleet which was now concentrated in Lisbon. Every available vessel was summoned into western Spanish waters.

Preparations were delayed for a year by Drake's famous raid on Cadiz in 1587. In this "singeing of the King of Spain's beard" a large quantity of stores and ships was destroyed. Nevertheless in May 1588 the Armada was ready. A hundred and thirty ships were assembled, carrying 2,500 guns and more than 30,000 men, two-thirds of them soldiers. Twenty were galleons, forty-four were armed merchantmen, and eight were Mediterranean galleys. The rest were either small craft or unarmed transports. Their aim was to sail up the Channel, embark the expeditionary corps of 16,000 veterans from the Netherlands under Alexander of Parma, and land it on the south coast of England.

The command was entrusted to the Duke of Medina-Sidonia, who had no experience of war at sea. He also had many misgivings about the enterprise. His fleet was admirably equipped for carrying large numbers of men, but weak in long-distance culverins. The seamen were recruited from the dregs of the Spanish population and commanded by army officers of noble families who had no experience of naval warfare. Many of the vessels were in bad repair; the provisions were insufficient and rotten; the drinking water leaked from butts of unseasoned wood.

The English plan was to gather a fleet in one of the southwestern ports, intercept the enemy at the western entrance to the Channel, and concentrate troops in the southeast to meet Parma's army from the Flemish shore. An army was assembled at Tilbury which reached twenty thousand men, under the command of Lord Leicester. This, with the muster in the adjacent counties, constituted a force which should not be underrated. While the Armada was still off the coasts of England Queen Elizabeth reviewed the army at Tilbury and addressed them in these stirring words: "I am come amongst you, as you see, resolved, in the midst and heat of the battle, to live or die amongst you all, to lay down for my God, and for my kingdom, and for my people, my honour and my blood, even in the dust. I know I have the body of a weak and feeble woman, but I have the heart and stomach of a king, and of a king of England too, and think foul scorn that Parma or Spain or any prince of Europe should dare to invade the borders

English fireships caused havoc among the Spanish Armada. This eighteenth-century engraving shows how small vessels loaded with gunpowder blew up the clumsy Spanish galleons.

of my realm; to which, rather than any dishonour shall grow by me, I myself will take up arms, I myself will be your general, judge and rewarder of every one of your virtues in the field. I know already for your forwardness you have deserved rewards and crowns; and we do assure you, in the word of a prince, they shall be duly paid you."

Hawkins's work for the navy was now to be tested. He had begun over the years to revise the design of English ships from his experience in colonial waters. The castles which towered above the galleon decks had been cut down; keels were deepened, and design was concentrated on seaworthiness and speed. Most notable of all, heavier long-range guns were mounted. Cannon were traditionally deemed "an ignoble arm", fit only for an opening salvo to a grappling fight, but Hawkins, with ships built to weather any seas, advocated battering the enemy from a distance with the new guns. The English sea captains were eager to try these novel tactics against the huge overmasted enemy galleons, with their flat bottoms and a tendency to drift in a high wind. In spite of Hawkins's efforts only thirty-four of the Queen's ships, carrying six thousand men, could put to sea in 1588. As was the custom, however, all available privately owned vessels were hastily collected and armed for the service of the Government, and a total of a hundred and ninety-seven ships was mustered; but at least half of them were too small to be of much service.

Drake was for bold measures; he proposed sending the main body to attack a port on the Spanish coast, so as to force the Armada to sea in defence of the coastline. Thus, it was argued, there would be no danger of its slipping past them on a favourable wind into the Channel.

The Government preferred the much more perilous idea of stationing isolated squadrons at intervals along the south coast to meet all possible lines of attack. They insisted on concentrating a small squadron of the Queen's ships at the eastern end of the Channel to keep watch on Parma. Drake and his superior, Lord Howard of Effingham, the commander of the English fleet, were alarmed and impatient, and with the greatest difficulty

THE SEAFARERS

THE MOST EXCITING of the new Tudor horizons were distant horizons across the ocean. The English lagged several years behind other nations in crossing the Atlantic until John Cabot, an Italian living in England, got financial backing from Henry VII and sailed to Newfoundland in 1498. Twenty-four years later the Portuguese explorer, Ferdinand Magellan, successfully circumnavigated the globe.

In Elizabeth I's reign, however, English seafaring men established their reputation as bold adventurers. Henry VIII had developed the Royal Navy, and Elizabeth put John Hawkins in charge of it. He rebuilt many ships and built many new ones.

The great oceanic voyages were chronicled by Richard Hakluyt, who lectured in geography at Oxford and introduced the globe to English schools. He gave his support too to the idea of colonising North America. Humphrey Gilbert tried to found settlements in Newfoundland as did Sir Walter Raleigh in Virginia, but the days of colonisation were in the future. Sir Francis Drake, however, circled the world, crossing the Pacific "as a pelican alone in the wilderness". The *Golden Hind*, the sole survivor of a fleet of five ships which had set sail from England, arrived back in Plymouth in 1580 to a resounding welcome, after a voyage of thirty-three months. Drake became a national hero and was knighted by the Queen.

The late Tudor mapmakers excelled, whether they were charting the oceans or their own country. New companies were set up to exploit foreign trade. By 1555 the Muscovy Company had received a royal charter to trade with Russia, and the East India Company was launched on the last day of 1600. The administrative structure of the Company was later to become the basis for the entire Indian empire. The biggest profits for the companies came from their imports, including furs from Russia, wine from France, spices and silks from the East and tobacco from North America.

IMPROVED NAVIGATIONAL INSTRUMENTS made possible the huge expansion of seafaring in Elizabethan times. In the engraving by Johannes Stradanus (above), an astronomer scientist calculates a measurement of longitude by using the magnetic properties of the lodestone, which floats on a bowl of water in the foreground. Sailors' and mapmakers' instruments such as a globe, an hourglass and a sextant, fill the study. These were especially needed by sailors in northern latitudes, where cloudy skies often made it impossible to steer by the stars. Many schools, such as Gresham's College, were founded to teach sailors navigational skills. The mariner's compass shown below is one of the first of its kind and dates from about 1580. As in later models, its iron needle, magnetised by a lodestone to point to the north and mounted on a card that is marked with the principal directions, pivots on a central pin.

PIRACY AND PLUNDERING received royal approval if Spain was the target and the Queen had a share of the booty. Sir Francis Drake was the boldest adventurer of them all. The picture below shows a plan of his successful attack on the island of Santiago in the Cape Verde Islands in November, 1585.

NAVAL REFORMER, JOHN HAWKINS, *was Drake's kinsman. His first voyages were hugely profitable slave-trading expeditions to West Africa and the Caribbean. After being appointed Treasurer of the Navy in 1573 he overhauled each vessel and put the English fleet in superb condition. During its victory over the Spanish Armada, Hawkins acted as third-in-command. He streamlined the ships by increasing their length and lowering the huge platforms at bow and stern. He also introduced safety measures like the use of bowlines and boarding nettings, and a new method of striking topmasts. His portrait can be seen in the City Museum and Art Gallery, Plymouth.*

THE NORTHWEST PASSAGE *was the name of the quick sea route to Asia that Martin Frobisher hoped to find by sailing via North America. This was necessary because the Pope had granted Spain and Portugal virtual control of the eastern seaway. English traders were outraged that in addition to their treasure in the New World, the Spanish should have a monopoly of the spice and silk trade in the east. The picture (left) records Frobisher's friendly overtures being rebuffed in 1577 by the Eskimos of what was later known as Baffin Island. Frobisher's third expedition found, by accident, the opening that is Hudson Strait. Eventually, explorers abandoned the search for a northwest passage and directed their attention to the new continent for its own sake.*

THE ARK RALEIGH *(above) was built by Walter Raleigh as his own privateer, but he renamed it the Ark Royal and presented it to Queen Elizabeth. It was the flagship of the English commander, Lord Howard of Effingham, in the English victory over the Armada. The men who sailed in Tudor ships had a less than fifty per cent chance of survival: the bad diet caused scurvy, and overcrowding meant that any infection was speedily transmitted. But few sailors let their knowledge of the risk interfere with their sense of adventure.*

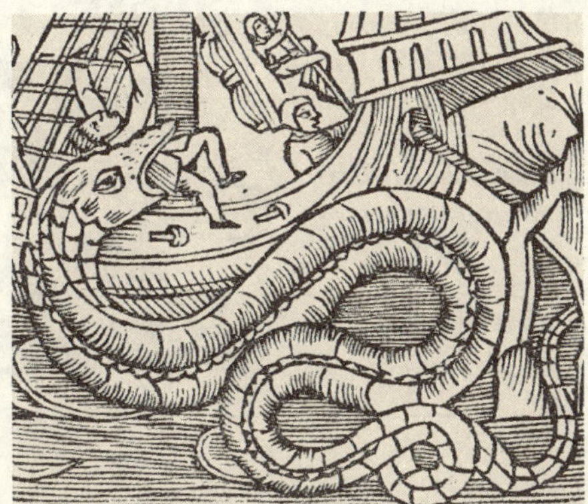

THE FASCINATION OF THE SEA *lay partly in travellers' tales propounded by medieval writers such as Sir John de Mandeville, who claimed to have spent thirty years exploring India and Asia. The woodcut by the cartographer, Olaus Magnus, (left) is a graphic illustration of a sailor's nightmare. Sea serpents, symbolising man's fear of the unknown, feature in many old maps.*

prevented a further dispersion of their forces. A southerly gale stopped their attacking the Spanish coast, and they were driven into Plymouth with their supplies exhausted and scurvy raging through the ships.

In the event they had plenty of time to consider their strategy. The Armada left the Tagus on May 20, but was smitten by the same storms which had repulsed Howard and Drake. Two of their one thousand-ton ships were dismasted. They put in to refit at Corunna, and did not set sail again until July 12. News of their approach off the Lizard was brought into Plymouth harbour on the evening of July 19. The English fleet had to put out of the Sound the same night against light adverse winds.

If Medina-Sidonia had attacked the English vessels to leeward of his ships as they struggled to clear the land there would have been a disaster. But his instructions bound him to sail up the Channel and unite with Parma. By difficult, patient, precarious tacking the English fleet got to windward of him, and hung upon the Armada as it ran before the westerly wind up the Channel, pounding away with their long-range guns at the lumbering galleons. On July 23 the wind sank and both fleets lay becalmed off Portland Bill. The Spaniards attempted a counterattack with Neapolitan galleys, rowed by hundreds of slaves, but Drake, followed by Howard, swept in

HEIGHTS OF FASHION

William Harrison, in his book Description of England (1587), *casts a critical eye on the more fanciful eccentricities of dress.*

Nothing is more constant in England than inconstancy of attire. Oh, how much cost is bestowed nowadays upon our bodies, and how little upon our souls! . . . How curious are a number of men and women, and how hardly can the tailor please them in making that attire fit for their bodies! How many times must it be sent back again to him that made it! What chafing, what fretting, what reproachful language doth the poor workman bear away! And many times when he doth nothing to it at all, yet when it is brought home again it is very fit and handsome.

Then must we put it on, then must the long seams of our hose be set by a plumb-line, then we puff, then we blow, and finally sweat till we drop, that our clothes may stand well upon us. I will say nothing of our heads, which sometimes are polled, sometimes curled, or suffered to grow at length like a woman's locks, many times cut off, above or under the ears, round as by a wooden dish.

Neither will I meddle with our variety of beards, of which some are shaven from the chin like those of Turks, not a few cut short like to the beard of Marquess Otto, some made round like a rubbing-brush, the barbers being grown to be so cunning in this behalf as the tailors. And therefore if a man have a lean and straight face, a Marquess Otto's cut will make it broad and large; if it be platterlike, a long slender beard will make it seem the narrower.

Some lusty courtiers also and gentlemen of courage do wear either rings of gold, stones, or pearls in their ears, whereby they imagine that the workmanship of God not to be a little amended.

In women also, it is most to be lamented, that they do now far exceed the lightness of our men . . . What should I say of the galligaskins (loose skirts) to bear out their bums and make their attire to fit plum round about them? Their farthingales (hooped petticoats) and diversely coloured nether stocks of silk, jersey, and such like, whereby their bodies are rather deformed than commended?

upon the main body, and, as Howard reported, "the Spaniards were forced to give way and flocked together like sheep".

A further engagement followed on July 25 off the Isle of Wight. It looked as if the Spaniards planned to seize the island as a base. But the English still lay to windward and drove them once more to sea in the direction of Calais, where Medina, ignorant of Parma's movements, hoped to collect news. The Channel passage was a torment to the Spaniards. The guns of the English ships raked the decks of the galleons, killing the crews and demoralising the soldiers. The English suffered hardly any loss.

Medina then made a fatal mistake. He anchored in Calais Roads. The Queen's ships which had been stationed in the eastern end of the Channel joined the main fleet in the straits, and the whole sea power of England was now combined. A council of war held in the English flagship during the evening of July 28 resolved to attack. The decisive engagement opened. After darkness had fallen eight ships from the eastern squadron which had been filled with explosives and prepared as fire-ships—the torpedoes of those days—were sent against the crowded Spanish fleet at anchor in the Roads. Lying on their decks, the Spanish crews must have seen unusual lights creeping along the decks of strange vessels moving towards them. Suddenly a series of explosions shook the air, and flaming hulks drifted towards the anchored Armada. The Spanish captains cut their cables and made for the open sea. Collisions without number followed. One of the largest galleys, the *San Lorenzo*, lost its rudder and drifted aground in Calais harbour, where the Governor interned the crew. The rest of the fleet, with a south-southwest wind behind it, made eastward to Gravelines.

The opulently attired Elizabeth stands on a map of the British Isles in this picture by the Flemish artist, Marcus Gheeraerts. It was painted in 1592, when England's prestige was high, and is now in the National Portrait Gallery.

Medina now sent messengers to Parma announcing his arrival, and by dawn on July 29 he was off the sandbanks of Gravelines expecting to find Parma's troops ready shipped in their transports. But there was no sail to be seen. The tides in Dunkirk harbour were at the neap. It was only possible to sail out with a favourable wind upon a spring tide. Neither condition was present. The Spaniards turned to face their pursuers. A long and desperate fight raged for eight hours, a confused conflict of ships engaging at close quarters. The official report sent to the English Government was brief: "Howard in fight spoiled a great number of the Spaniards, sank three and drove four or five on the banks." The English had completely exhausted their ammunition, and but for this hardly a Spanish ship would have got away. Yet Howard himself scarcely realised the magnitude of his victory. "Their force is wonderful great and strong," he wrote on the evening after the battle, "yet we pluck their feathers by little and little."

The tormented Armada now sailed northward out of the fight. Their one aim was to make for home. The horrors of the long voyage round the north of Scotland began. Not once did they turn upon the small, silent ships which followed them. Neither side had enough ammunition. The homeward voyage of the Armada proved the qualities of the Spanish seamen. Facing mountainous seas and racing tides, they escaped from their pursuers. The English ships, short of food and shot, were compelled to turn southward to the Channel ports. The weather helped the Spaniards. As Medina recorded, "We passed the isles at the north of Scotland, and we are now sailing towards Spain with the wind at northeast." Sailing southward they were forced to make for the western coast of Ireland to replenish their supplies of water. They were struck disastrously by the autumn gales and seventeen ships went ashore. The search for water cost more than five thousand Spanish lives. Nevertheless over sixty-five ships, about half the fleet that had put to sea, reached Spanish ports during the month of October.

The English had not lost a single ship, and scarcely a hundred men. But their captains were disappointed. Their ammunition had run short at a crucial moment. The gunnery of the merchant vessels had proved poor and half the enemy's fleet had got away. There were no boastings.

But to the English people as a whole the defeat of the Armada came as a miracle. For thirty years the shadow of Spanish power had darkened the political scene. A wave of religious emotion filled men's minds. One of the medals struck to commemorate the victory bears the inscription "*Afflavit Deus et dissipantur*"—"God blew and they are scattered."

Elizabeth and her seamen knew how true this was. The Armada had indeed been bruised in battle, but it was demoralised and set on the run by the weather. Yet the event was decisive. The English seamen might well have triumphed. The new tactics of Hawkins had brought success. The nation was transported with relief and pride. Shakespeare was writing *King John* a few years later. His words struck into the hearts of his audiences:

> Come the three corners of the world in arms,
> And we shall shock them. Nought shall make us rue
> If England to itself do rest but true.

CHAPTER 39

GLORIANA

Illustration of the Knight in the first edition of Edmund Spenser's long poem entitled The Faerie Queene. *This was the book which originally referred to Elizabeth I as "Gloriana".*

WITH 1588 THE CRISIS OF THE REIGN was past. England had emerged from the Armada year as a first-class power. The last years of Elizabeth's reign saw a welling up of national energy and enthusiasm focusing upon the person of the Queen. In the year following the Armada the first three books were published of Spenser's *Faerie Queene*, in which Elizabeth is hymned as Gloriana. Poets and courtiers paid homage to the sovereign who symbolised the great achievement.

The success of the seamen pointed the way to wide opportunities of winning wealth and fame in daring expeditions. In 1589 Richard Hakluyt published his magnificent book, *The Principal Navigations, Traffics and Discoveries of the English Nation.* Hakluyt speaks for the thrusting spirit of the age when he proclaims that the English nation, "in searching the most opposite corners and quarters of the world, and, to speak plainly, in compassing the vast globe of the earth more than once, have excelled all the nations and peoples of the earth". Before the reign came to a close another significant enterprise took its beginning. For years past Englishmen had been probing their way through to the east, round the Cape of Good Hope. Their ventures led to the founding of the East India Company. At the start it was a small and struggling affair, but dazzling dividends were to be won from this investment, for the British Empire in India owed its origins to the charter granted by Queen Elizabeth in the year 1600.

The young men who now rose to prominence in the Court of the ageing Queen plagued their mistress to allow them to try their hand in many enterprises. The coming years resound with attacks upon the forces and allies of Spain throughout the world—expeditions to Cadiz, to the Azores, into the Caribbean Sea, to the Low Countries, and, in support of the Huguenots, to the northern coasts of France. The policy of the English Government was to distract the enemy in every quarter of the world, and by subsidising the Protestant elements in the Low Countries and in France to prevent any concentration of force against themselves. The slow victory of the Dutch in Holland and the Huguenots in France brought its reward. The eventual triumph of Henry of Navarre, the Protestant heir to the French throne, was due as much to his acceptance of the Catholic faith as to victories in the field. Paris, as he is supposed to have said, was worth a Mass. His decision put an end to the French religious wars and removed the danger to England of a Spanish-backed monarch in Paris. The Dutch too were beginning to hold their own. The island was at last secure.

But there was no way of delivering a decisive stroke against Spain. The English Government had no money for further efforts. The total revenues of the Crown hardly exceeded £300,000 a year, including the fruits of taxation granted by Parliament. Out of this sum all expenses of Court and Government had to be met. The cost of defeating the Armada alone is reckoned to have amounted to £160,000. The lights of enthusiasm slowly faded out. However, in 1595 Walter Raleigh, who had already founded a short-lived colony in America, called Virginia after the Queen, again tried his hand, this time in search of Eldorado in Guiana. But his expedition brought no profits home. At the same time Drake and the veteran Hawkins, now in his sixties, set out on a last voyage. Hawkins fell ill, and as his fleet was anchoring off Puerto Rico he died in his cabin. Drake, cast down by the death of his old patron, sailed on to attack the rich city of Panama and swept into the bay of Nombre de Dios. But now Spanish government in the New World was well-equipped and well-armed. The raid was beaten off. The English fleet put out to sea, and in January 1596 Francis Drake, having assumed his armour to meet death like a soldier, expired in his ship.

An early map of Virginia depicts "the arrival of the Englishemen". Often, the first colonists were Puritans who sought freedom of worship abroad.

Tobacco was a highly profitable crop, for smoking was thought to be good for the health. It was used most commonly in clay pipes. There were no cigarettes before the nineteenth century.

It is well to remember the ordinary seamen who sailed in ships sometimes as small as twenty tons into the wastes of the North and South Atlantic, ill-fed and badly paid, on risky adventures backed by inadequate capital, facing death in many forms—death by disease, death by drowning, death from Spanish pikes and guns, death by starvation and cold on uninhabited coasts, death in the Spanish prisons. The Admiral of the English fleet, Lord Howard of Effingham, spoke their epitaph: "God send us to sea in such a company together again, when need is."

Victory over Spain was the most shining achievement of Elizabeth's reign, but by no means the only one. The repulse of the Armada had subdued religious dissension at home. Events which had swung England towards Puritanism while the Catholic danger was impending swung her back to the Anglican Settlement when the peril vanished in the smoke of the burning Armada at Gravelines. A few months later, in a sermon at St Paul's Cross, Richard Bancroft, who was later to be Archbishop of Canterbury, attacked the Puritan theme with the confidence of a man who was convinced that the Anglican Church was not a political contrivance, but a divine institution. He took the only line on which the defence of the Church could be sustained with an enthusiasm equal to that of its assailants: it was the Church of the Apostles still subsisting by virtue of the episcopal succession. But Bancroft saw also that to maintain the cause a better type of clergy was needed, men of "solid learning", and such he set himself to provide.

The Church Elizabeth had nursed to strength was a very different body from the half-hearted and distracted community of her early years: more confident, more learned, far less inclined to compromise; strong in the attachment of thousands to whom its liturgy had become dear by habit and who thought of it as the Church into which they had been baptised. Their devotion to the Church of England as a sacred institution was as profound and sincere as the attachment of the Calvinist to his presbytery or the Independent to his congregation. And, bitter as the coming divisions were to be, the whole of England united in prizing Elizabeth's service to her people and to religion.

By now the men who had governed England since the 1550s were passing from power and success to their graves. Leicester had died in 1588, Walsingham in 1590, and Burghley in 1598. The fifteen years which followed the Armada are dominated by other figures. War with Spain had set a premium on martial virtues. Young and eager men like Walter Raleigh and Robert Devereux, Earl of Essex, quarrelled for permission to lead enterprises against the Spaniards.

Essex was Leicester's stepson, and Leicester brought him into the circle of the Court. With Government in the hands of the cautious Cecils, he set out to create his own party in Court and Council. He was supported by the Bacon brothers, Anthony and Francis, sons of the Lord Keeper, Nicholas Bacon, who found Essex a convenient figurehead for thrusting a more forward policy upon the Queen. With their help Essex became an expert on foreign affairs and showed the Queen that he had ability as well as charm. In 1593 he was made a Privy Counsellor. Essex soon headed the war party in the Council; and in 1596 an expedition was sent against Cadiz under the joint command of Essex and Raleigh. In the sea fight for the harbour Raleigh was the outstanding leader. The Spanish fleet was burnt and the town lay open to the English crews. Essex was the hero of the

Robert Devereux, Earl of Essex, tried to seize power and establish the succession in the Queen's old age. Elizabeth saw the danger and ordered his execution in the year 1601.

shore fight. It was a brilliant combined operation, and Cadiz was held by the English for a fortnight. The fleet returned home triumphant, but, to Elizabeth's regret, little the richer. During its absence Robert Cecil had become Secretary of State.

Victory at Cadiz heightened the popularity of Essex among the younger members of the Court and throughout the country. The Queen received him graciously, but with secret misgiving. He was the incarnation of the spirit of this new generation, whose rash eagerness she feared. For the moment all went well. Essex was given command of an expedition to intercept a further Armada now gathering in the ports of western Spain. The English ships headed southwest and made for the Azores. There was no sign of the great fleet whose passage they were to bar, but the islands made a convenient base where they could await the treasure ships from the New World. Raleigh too was in the expedition. The English failed to take any of the island ports; the Spanish treasure fleet eluded them; the Armada put out into the Bay of Biscay with the seas clear of defending ships to the north. Once again the winds saved the island. The badly manned galleons tottered into a northern gale scattered and sinking. The disorganised fleet crept back into its ports. King Philip was kneeling in his chapel in the Escorial praying for his ships. Before the news of their return could reach him he was seized with a paralytic stroke, and the tale of their failure was brought to him on his deathbed.

Essex came home to find Elizabeth still vigorous and dominating. The muddle which had marred the expedition enraged her. She vowed never to send the fleet out of the Channel again, and this time she kept her word. Essex retired from Court, and thunderous days followed.

Troubles in Ireland, which now came to a head, seemed to offer Essex the chance of recovering both the Queen's goodwill and his own prestige.

AN ENCOUNTER WITH QUEEN ELIZABETH I

Paul Hentnzer, the tutor to a young German nobleman, recorded this vivid personal glimpse of the Queen in 1598, five years before her death.

Next came the Queen, in the sixty-fifth year of her age, as we were told, very majestic; her face oblong, fair, but wrinkled; her eyes small, yet black and pleasant; her nose a little hooked; her lips narrow, and her teeth black (a defect the English seem subject to, for their too great use of sugar); she had in her ears two pearls, with very rich drops; she wore false hair, and that red; upon her head she had a small crown, and she had on a necklace of exceeding fine jewels; her hands were small, her fingers long, and her stature neither tall nor low; her air was stately, her manner of speaking mild and obliging.

This portrait of Elizabeth as an old woman comes from an electrotype for use in making coins.

That day she was dressed in white silk, bordered with pearls of the size of beans, and over it a mantle of black silk, shot with silver threads; her train was very long, the end of it borne by a marchioness; instead of a chain, she had an oblong collar of gold and jewels. As she went along in all this state and magnificence, she spoke very graciously, first to one, then to another, whether foreign ministers, or those who attended for different reasons, in English, French and Italian; for, besides being well skilled in Greek, Latin, and the languages I have mentioned, she is mistress of Spanish, Scotch and Dutch.

The Ladies of the Court followed next to her, very handsome and well-shaped, and for the most part dressed in white; she was guarded on each side by the Gentlemen Pensioners, fifty in number, with gilt battleaxes. In the Antichapel next the Hall where we were, petitions were presented to her, and she received them most graciously, which occasioned the acclamation of, *Long Live Queen Elizabeth!* She answered it with, *I thank you, my good people!* In the Chapel was excellent music; as soon as it and the service was over, the Queen returned in the same state and order, and prepared to go to dinner.

Sir Walter Raleigh's room within the Tower of London. His wife and family lived there too, and one son was born in the Tower. Raleigh had angered Queen Elizabeth by marrying her maid of honour, Elizabeth Throgmorton, without permission, and by plotting against her in her old age.

Throughout the reign Ireland had presented an intractable problem. Henry VIII had assumed the title of King of Ireland, but this involved no real extension of his authority. Though Irish chiefs were given English titles, in the hope of converting them into magnates on the English pattern, they still clung to their ancient feuding clan life, and largely ignored the commands of the Lords Lieutenant in Dublin. The Counter-Reformation revived and reanimated opposition to Protestant England. For the Queen's Government in London this meant strategic anxieties, since any power hostile to England could readily take advantage of Irish discontents. In the first thirty years of Elizabeth's reign Ireland was shaken by three major rebellions. Now in the 1590s a fourth rising had erupted into a wearing and expensive war.

With Spanish backing, Hugh O'Neill, Earl of Tyrone, was threatening the whole English dominance of Ireland. In April 1599 Essex was allowed to go to Ireland, at the head of the largest army that England had ever sent there. He accomplished nothing and was on the verge of ruin. But he planned a dramatic stroke. Disobeying the express orders of the Queen, he deserted his command and rode in haste to London unannounced. Angry scenes followed between Essex and the Queen, and the Earl was confined to his house. Weeks dragged by, and a desperate plot was made by Essex and his younger companions, including Shakespeare's patron, the Earl of Southampton. There was to be a rising in the City, a concentration upon Whitehall, and a seizure of the Queen's person. To symbolise the result a new play, which culminated in a royal dethronement, was to be produced at Southwark—Shakespeare's *Richard II*. The scheme failed, and the end came in February 1601 with Essex's death within the Tower. Among the witnesses of the execution was Walter Raleigh. Silently Raleigh walked across to the door of the White Tower and climbed the stairway through the armoury, to look down upon the block, where he too, was to meet the same end. The young Earl of Southampton was spared.

Elizabeth well understood the issues at stake. Essex had been not simply a courtier soliciting, and even fighting for, the affections of his Queen. He was the leader of a bid for power. Acutely aware of the Queen's advancing years, he aimed to control the succession and to dominate the next sovereign.

This was not yet an age of party politics, but of patronage and clientage. No fundamental principle divided Essex from Cecil. The spoils of office, power, and influence were at stake, and victorious Essex would have dispensed appointments throughout England. But long years of statesmanship served Elizabeth better than the driving ambition of a courtier half her age. She struck back; and in destroying Essex she saved England from the consumption of civil war.

For the English cause in Ireland the flight of Essex proved a blessing. He was succeeded by Lord Mountjoy, a tenacious and energetic commander, who soon had the rebellion under control. When a Spanish force, some four thousand strong, landed at Kinsale in 1601 they were too late. Mountjoy routed their Irish allies and compelled the Spaniards to surrender. Even Tyrone finally made his submission. Ireland had at last, though only temporarily, been conquered by English arms.

If Essex challenged the political power of Elizabeth, more significant for the future was the challenge to her constitutional power in the Parliament of 1601. Throughout the reign the weight and authority of Parliament had been steadily growing. Now the issue turned on monopolies. For some time the Crown had eked out its slender income by various devices, including the granting of patents of monopolies to courtiers and others in return for payment. Some of these grants could be justified as protecting and encouraging inventions, but frequently they amounted merely to unjustified privileges, involving high prices that placed a burden upon every citizen. In 1601 grievances flared up. In the House of Commons an angry Member read out a list extending from a patent for iron manufacture to a patent for drying pilchards. If the Commons pushed their protests to a division the whole basis of the Queen's constitutional authority would be under fire. She acted swiftly. Some monopolies were abolished forthwith. All, she promised, would be investigated, and in a golden speech to a large gathering of her Commons summoned to her chamber she told them, "Though God hath raised me high, yet this I account the glory of my crown, that I have reigned with your loves." It was to be her last appearance in their midst.

The immense vitality displayed by the Queen throughout the troublous

A detail from a painting by William Camden of Elizabeth's funeral procession shows the ladies of the Court following the Queen's cortege on its way to Westminster Abbey. Elizabeth died early in the morning of March 24, 1603, at the Palace of Richmond, and her body was brought by river to Whitehall.

Sir Walter Raleigh and his elder son, Walter, who accompanied his father on one of his colonial ventures and died abroad. Raleigh lost his power and was executed by James I in 1617.

years of her rule in England ebbed slowly and relentlessly away. She lay for days upon a heap of cushions in her room. For hours the soundless agony was prolonged. The corridors without echoed with the hurrying of agitated feet.

At last Robert Cecil dared to speak. "Your Majesty, to content the people you must go to bed."

"Little man," came the answer, "is 'must' a word to use to princes?" The old Archbishop of Canterbury, Whitgift, her "little black husband", as she had once called him, knelt praying at her side. In the early hours of the morning of March 24, 1603, Queen Elizabeth died.

Thus ended the Tudor dynasty. For over a hundred years, with a handful of bodyguards, they had maintained their sovereignty, kept the peace, baffled the diplomacy and onslaughts of Europe, and guided the country through changes which might well have wrecked it. Parliament was becoming a solid affair based on a working harmony between Sovereign, Lords and Commons, and the traditions of English monarchical government had been restored and gloriously enhanced. But these achievements carried no guarantee of their perpetuation. The monarchy could only govern if it was popular. The Crown was now to pass to an alien Scottish line, hostile in political instincts to the class which administered England. The good understanding with Parliament which the Tudors had nourished now came to a fretful close. The new kings soon clashed with the forces of a growing nation, and out of this conflict came the Civil War, the Republican interlude, the Restoration, and the Revolution Settlement.